CW00505612

Acknowledgements
Once again I want to thank the
provided invaluable help in bringing this project together,
transcribing Hans and Jeans letters and translating Mutti
and Horst's German letters into English - Fiona Quinton, Brigitte Shade, Irmgard Gökova, Judith Usiskin, Helene Alder-
man, Thamara Freeman and Tom E Morrison.

Hans Klawitter
L.A.E.C. Hostel
Saltby
Melton Mowbray/
Leics
Oct 3<u>rd</u> 1948

My dearest darling Jean

Thank you for a very nice afternoon, sweetheart. Well, it came rather sudden about going to London, but, please, darling make it possible. I am sure your mother wouldn't object. If she asks just tell her the truth. Nothing to be worried about.

I arrived here at 10.15 and went down to Mr Chandler to bring the keys back. He was waiting with a nice cup of ~~tea~~ cocoa. I've got the rations ready for tomorrow and will go to bed now time 11.40. So good night and God bless. Pleasant dreams to you and thousand kisses.

Monday night Oct 4th 1948

Well, sweetheart I am so glad you've fixed everything up for going away. I bet we'll always think of those two days together in London. I've rung you tonight, but unfortunately you were out for the evening. So I better ring again tomorrow morning. It's awkward to get to Leicester on Wednesday morning but even if I've to go by bike to Melton. Don't worry

I'll be in Leicester in time.

Well, sweetheart, it's 10.15 and time to get the rations ready for tomorrow and afterwards to bed. I am still listening to that play 'The devil's general.' It's rather exciting, but a lot of nonsense.

So, goodnight for now and God bless, I am longing for Wednesday. All my love the kisses to you.

Tuesday Oct 5th 1948

Well, darling, here I am again. Only a few more hours till tomorrow morning. I'll call at 8.30 at your place and hope you'll be ready. You should've told your mother I am coming over to do the breakfast. Perhaps she'd have agreed to it. You don't know a chance, do you?

Well, sweetheart 5.30 tomorrow, leaving Saltby. Think of me, when you turn around for another few hours, will you?

So long, darling, I am sooo longing for the morning.

Goodnight and God bless you.

I'll be dreaming of you all night.

All my love and thousand kisses

Eternally yours

Hans.

R 7/10.48

Prenzlau, 27.9.48

Dear Hans!   6/10.48

I am sending you my Sunday greetings today. I am just having a quiet hour which I want to use to write to you. Otto has gone to a meeting. The girls went dancing and to the cinema. I have two big dogs living outside. They can bark as much as they like, I am not going out to attend to them. I also have a little dog in my room called Pilti, she is very sweet. I can talk to her. She gives me some happiness. If only the family would stop spoiling my few pleasures. We have managed to reach our target, but there is not much left over for us and by the time the cost for the seeds have been taken off, the granary is almost empty again. I am not worried about the future, I think our other animals will bring in some income, and also the breeding sow.

I went home this afternoon. It is a long way to walk but it's so nice to be at home. We now have another worry about mum, she is very unwell. It makes me so sad to see her like that. I shall be able to look after her tomorrow. Marga also worries us. She has hardly any money to buy much, not even for food. The little ones have got a problem with their lungs. They could get the medication in the Bizone* but she cannot afford to buy it. We are not allowed to send food parcels. Mum bought material to make a dress and swapped it for coat fabric. I gave her a pair of shoes. It helps to use the money for the bare necessities. The town is dead, totally in ruins, and there is more than enough work to be done. Next week we start harvesting the potatoes. It means we have to be on the fields every day. Perhaps you have received my letter in the meantime. Please write back soon. I am always happy to hear from you. It makes me want to read your letters for hours on end. I am asking so many questions. I would love to see you. Sometimes the longing makes me really homesick. But I have to be patient, I know. Being here is not easy for me. If you could see it all, I am sure you would sympathise. I have to pay for my deed and it takes time to heal. Inside I will never be happy. Health wise I am quite well at the moment. I am still worried about my operation.

Hansi, how are you? How are your mum and Horst? I often think of the lovely times the three of us spent together and how well we all got on together. I must not keep thinking of my faults, otherwise I reproach myself for what I have done again and again. Why did it have to be like that?

Have you still not traced your father? I wished I could take away all this uncertainty from you. Mum is sending her love. I told her that I would write to you today. Manfred is also sending his best wishes to you.

On the side:
I want to finish my letter and am sending you my very best wishes Hansi. Please write back very soon. Greetings (coming from the heart) Vera.

better known as THE WEST of Germany.

LAEC Hostel Saltby
Oct 7th 1948

My darling Jean,

I just can't thank you only with words for the two loveliest days I've ever spent. It was so nice of you to make it possible. I hope you've enjoyed these days as much as I have.

Well, my love I've been at Saltby at 10.00 o'clock. Don't be surprised, but really it would've killed me to walk another 2 miles. So I made up my mind when I got on the bus in Leicester to take a taxi from Melton. And I did. I hope you made it alright. I should've brought you home and make sure.

Well, I'll go to bed now. Goodnight and God bless you.

Lots of love and thousand kisses
Eternally yours
. Hans.

92 Wharf St
Oct 7th 1948

My dearest darling Hans

A letter as promised. I hope there will be one for me on Saturday if not I will know you have collapsed between Croxton and Saltby. You should be between Melton and Croxton, it is 9.15. I am thinking all the time of you. I am really sorry you have to walk all the way, but one day darling, if there is any walking to be done after we have been out we will do it together and I will carry the bags, and darling if you forget our 2 days together you won't forget the 2 mile walk to Saltby. I will never forget these last 2 days. They have been wonderful, I really did hate leaving you to go back to Saltby, but it is the only thing we can do at the moment. I don't think we will have to wait 20 years before we marry. I could not wait that long. I don't think we will have to either, everything has gone alright so far and things still keep going our way. We will be OK. My darling I hope we will be alone for a little while on Sunday, I will see if Betty will feed the dog and will you ring me this morning (Saturday)? Then I will tell you what time I am coming. So darling, thank you for 2 wonderful days.

All my love Jean

Monday Oct 8th 1948
This morning I received my papers from the office. Today is my last day with the A.E.C. I'll show you when you come on Sunday. You can take them back to the office. I heard Mr Ch. speaking to you, but he didn't give me a chance. Well, I'll hurry and give the letter to Mr Coy.

> So be good and think of me
> All my love and kisses
> Eternally yours Hans.

> Hans Klawitter
> ℅ R Maclean
> Pickwell nr
> Somerby/Leic's
> Oct 9th 1948

11.30pm.

My darling,

Thanks so very very much for the lovely afternoon. Sweetheart, I love you so much and it is awful to let you go. Our time will come soon.

I arrived here safe at 10.35 and it's 11.40 now, the time you'll be at home. Just be my best girl. God bless you. Thousand goodnight kisses, only yours Hans.

Sunday Oct 9th. 48, 10.00

Good morning, my love. How are you this morning? I am fine and I hope so from you. Well, I got up at 8.00, had my breakfast and started packing at once. I hope Mr Maclean gets all my things into his car. It is quite a lot. I shall see when he comes.

Did you get home alright last night? I really did feel rotten on my way back. I took two aspirins before I went to bed and felt lots better afterwards. I am quite alright now.

Well, I am only waiting for the dinner and then Mr Maclean to fetch me. Everything is packed except for the wireless. That'll be my last work here and the first job there. "There's no life without music".

I've asked Mr Chandler for a reference for the time I've been working with him. He's going to bring it over later on, but I hope before I leave. Did you ask Mr Edwards? Please don't forget. They'll come useful one day.

Well, my sweetheart, dinner is ready and I'll finish now. A few more lines from Pickwell. For now, all my love and kisses to you.

Pickwell

Well, my sweetheart, here I am at my new place. Don't ask me any questions!!!! Be sure I don't want to start grumbling after being here for one hour, but it's terrible. I've never seen anything like this before and believe me I'd only put pigs into this room. I've told you what the arrangements were when I was here last time. Anyway, nothing was done. It looks to me as if they just took any kind of animals out, put

7

3 beds and a table in. (Big enough for one man). There's nothing to put our cloth, nothing for food, just the beds. Dirt all over the place, the ceiling's broken down on a few places and still coming down on others.

To be honest, it took me a lot not to turn round straight away. I only thought of doing it for us. I can make a room comfortable and homely, but not this one. The boss came and asked me if there's anything he can do, I was speechless. I am waiting for the other two chaps to come and see their faces. I would be ashamed of myself if I was him to offer people such accommodation. Well, I was not living like this before, not even as a prisoner of war. You come next Sunday and have a look yourself.

I've made myself a cup of tea and it's a good thing I brought something along, otherwise I would've had to wait until tomorrow night.

We'll have to start work at 7.00 tomorrow morning.

Well, my dearest, I'll say cheerio now. Be good and think of me.

> All my love and kisses
>> Eternally yours
> Hans

> 92 Wharf St
> October 10th

My dearest darling Hans

By now, you should be at your new place. I hope you are settling down alright. What are the other two fellows like?

I arrived home safe last night, it was about 11.20 when I got home and everything was ok. I took Freddy out a little way, then I put the wireless on whilst I did my hair. It was quite good Jack Jackson playing records. I was hoping he may play "So Tired" but no he didn't. So I went to bed disgusted and it was a good job I was not going to Saltby. I did not wake until 8.45, then it was my cousin next door that woke me up. I had to leave the washing up until I had come back from taking

8

the dog to the vet. This is when I intended to clean through, but when I got back at 11.15 I washed up and just tidied then went round to Betty's for my dinner. The vet told me today he did not think Freddy would ever get right, the best thing would be to have him destroyed, so you can guess how I felt when I got back. I don't know what to do. I hate the idea of having to have him destroyed. I have been wondering if I should try something else to see if that would cure him, but the vet said he thought it was bred in him.

I have been to Bradgate Park with Betty, Susan and Cyril. It was beautiful there this afternoon. I would have liked it much better if you had been with me, but there would have been too many people about for us. I went back to Betty's for tea, after tea I made the excuse that I had better go and see how Freddy was, but the truth was that I wanted to come home and write to you.. I have "Variety Bandbox" on the radio.

Were you alright darling after I left you last night. I was worried about you and I hope you are ok now. I am very sorry for the way I treat you darling. I hope you understand. I want you just as much as you want me, but darling if I was to have to get married I would feel so ashamed as people in this country look on it as a terrible thing. I hope darling it won't be long before we can be married, then we can start everything the right way. If it were not for my mother I would marry you tomorrow. I don't want to have to live with relations when I am married and I want to be married, but I don't want to leave my mother on her own. I pray darling that everything will turn out alright for all of us.

Well darling I will say goodnight and God bless.

    All my love and kisses
    Forever yours
    Jean

    ___.
    Monday 4.0.
My darling

Thank you very much for your letter. It must have come by the 11.0 post, because it was not there when I came out at 9.0. I did manage to get up in time, but I did not have time to take Fred a walk. I went back home to fetch him this lunch time and take him to Betty's with me for dinner, that is when I got your letter. I read your letter before I went because I had to know how you had got on at Pickwell. I am sorry darling it is not very comfortable, but you do what you think is best, don't stay there if you are not happy. I don't want you to be unhappy. I know if you say it is terrible it must be, because you have never complained about the other places you have been and they have not been what you could call home. If you don't like it we will have to make other plans. I know we will be happy whatever they are.

So All my love and kisses

    Jean

    —.

Hans Klawitter
℅ R. Maclean
Pickwell, Melton
Mowbray
Leic's
Oct 11th 1948

My dearest, darling Jean,

How are you today, sweetheart? I hope you feel as fit as I do. Don't ask what my job is. I am going out the same time as the other two, 7o'clock, just get up earlier to have the breakfast ready in time. Well, I am working in department A, (poultry). This morning the poultry man took me out and showed me what to do. I'd to paint 11 chicken houses. He said to me "see you again at 1.00pm". I thought he wanted me to finish the work so I got cracking and finished 12.30. I met him again in the yard 12.45 and told him " work finished". At first I thought he got a shock, but of course I didn't ask any questions. This afternoon the two women came along and asked me how I got on in the morning. So I told them I finished the 11 houses. I thought they're going to lynch me. Then I asked what the matter was and they told me that 2 of them finished 7 houses a day. And I really didn't work hard.

Well, darling, the other two chaps are alright. We've had a good laugh all last night about this room. After having a word with the boss he agreed to give us a second room as kitchen-sitting room. He's also getting some paint and surely the place will look different in a fortnight's time. And now about Sunday. Please, take the 2.15 from Leicester to Somersby and you'll find me waiting at the bus stop.

Well, sweetheart it's 9.30 and time to go to bed. (Don't be surprised, but I've to get up at 5.30)

So just be good and think of me. Good night and God bless.

     All my love and kisses
      Eternally yours
     Hans.

     92 Wharf St
     Oct 13th 1948

My dearest Hans

How is life with you today? I am glad he (Mr Maclean) is going to make the place a bit more comfortable for you. I will see what the place is like on Sunday. I can't wait to see it. I inquired about the bus just to make sure and it does go at 2.15 from St Margarets bus Station and the last bus back is 8.44. I will call in at the Midland Red office for a timetable, it may come in useful. I have not been to the pictures this week. Yesterday Dora called me to ask me to go round if I was not doing anything. I wasn't so I took my needlework and I stayed there until 10.0. I started to write to you then but I was too tired. I hope you didn't mind. My aunty (the one I went away with) came into the office to see me this afternoon to see where I had been to. I have not been to see her for about 3 weeks. I will probably go Friday night to see her. I still have Freddy. I told my mother what the vet said, now we have decided to see what we can do ourselves. I took him a walk early this evening and I am going to take him a good walk every day. Then when I got home I rubbed him with some Caster oil. I have not put anything else on him because his skin is so dry. I give him Cod liver oil first thing to try to fatten him up a bit. I am going to see Alice tomorrow night. She asked me to go last week (this time last week we were just getting into Leicester).

Is there is anything you would like me to get in Leicester to bring Sunday?

I will say goodnight and God bless you, because I am going to see what I can do with my hair.

All my love and kisses
  Forever yours
    Jean

                                        Home Farm
                                        Pickwell,
                                        Oct 13th. 1948

My dearest, darling Jean,

I thank you very much for your nice letter that arrived here yesterday. Unfortunately the man used to work here got the letter and gave it to me this morning. He forgot about it yesterday.

Well, sweetheart, we've done the first 3 days work and I found it's not too bad. Our housing problem is getting better for Mr Maclean gave us the small kitchen today. We've changed the stove over and tonight the boss brought some paint we asked him for yesterday. Tomorrow night we'll paint the room so that it'll be ready for the weekend. That makes one of the rooms alright. The cleaning and painting has to be done in our spare time, and there isn't much.

I am so sorry Jack Jackson didn't play your favorite song, but be sure I'll tell him your request when I meet him. By the way they've played it twice last night.

I am getting used to lighting the fire only 3 times a day. We can't use so much coal now we're to pay for it ourselves. Look, darling, if the vet told you better to destroy the dog, do so. It might get worse and if it is really bred in him you won't cure him. Listen, darling, I'll be alright and I also understand you quite well. We can wait a bit longer. It won't be too long, anyway I know how difficult it is for you, but in spite of everything keep smiling and your fingers crossed.

Well, I'll say goodnight now and God bless. Just be good and pleasant dreams to you.

>   All my love and kisses.
>   Eternally yours
>   Hans.

>   Pickwell
>   Oct. 16th 1948

My dearest, darling Jean,

I thank you so very much for your letter I received at lunch time. The mail van came here into the yard and brought the letter right to the door. That's what I call proper service.

As I told you I am getting on alright. The first of the 52 weeks is over and I am still alive. You can form your own opinion about the place tomorrow. Our kitchen doesn't look too bad now, but there still is the whitewashing to do. We'll finish it next week. Please remind me to show you the reference I got from Mr Chandler.

If there's nothing important to do on Wednesday night next the 3 of us shall go to the pictures in Melton. It also depends on what we'll feel like.

Well, darling, if you think it's best to keep Freddy do so by all means. I hope you'll get him better again.

It's only 9.15 now, but I feel very tired. So I'll say good night now.

God bless you, darling and be thinking of me.

>   All my love and kisses
>   Eternally yours

Hans.
92 Wharf St
October 18th
My dearest darling Hans
We have had quite a lot of excitement today. Iris had a telegram from her husband on Saturday to say he had found a place and to go at once, but it will not be for a little while (about 4 weeks) because she wants to keep her nationality which I don't think she will be able to. I think at the end of this year she will be able to apply for her nationality back. She does not seem to want to go to France as an Italian, she says you don't know what might happen.

Well darling I am afraid I don't think much of your accommodation, it was worse than I expected. It is going to be very cold in that stable in the winter. I think you ought to get some more blankets and a pillow to make yourself a little more comfortable.

About that house darling you know I would love to take it. It is just the thing we want, but what do we put in it, and there is another thing darling that worries me very much and that is my mother. I don't know what she would do. If it was not for her I would not care what anyone thought. I would be at Pickwell tomorrow.

Do you think it would be better if I came Saturday afternoon? I could take the 2.15 and I could come home on the later bus, and then maybe those other 2 fellows would have gone out.

Well my love I will have to say goodnight it is getting late and I have to get up at the early hour of 8 o'clock. Good night and God bless
All my love and kisses
Jean.

Pickwell
Oct. 18 Th 1948

My dearest, darling Jean,

How are you today, darling? The alarm clock was the best thing this morning. Otherwise there wouldn't have been any breakfast again. What did you think of the thunderstorm this afternoon. I was out again with the horse and didn't know he couldn't stand thunder and lightning. With the first lightning he went up in the air and it took something to hold him. So what else was to do as waiting in the rain and keep him quiet. You should've seen me. I looked as if I'd had a bath with all my clothes on. In spite of everything my gun was ready when I came back and after all had some luck. I shot two rabbits tonight and was surprised how fat that little fellow was. Anyway that makes rabbits twice this week.

Listen, darling, don't you want to change your mind about Sunday? Mr Maclean offered us a chicken today so we shall have roasted chicken on Sunday. But as far as I know you won't change your mind.

Could you get a box of cartridges (12 bore no. 4) in Leicester? If possible, bring them on Sunday or shall I send a lorry for all that stuff I asked you for?

Well, darling, it's 10.15 and I'll get to bed.

Goodnight to you and God bless

      All my love and kisses

            Eternally yours

    Hans

Hans at Pickwell

92 Wharf St
October 20th
My dearest darling Hans
Thank you very much for your letter. I am sorry you got so
wet on Sunday night. If I had brought my mack you would
not have got so wet, I will bring it the next time it looks a bit
dull.
I don't think you need to send a lorry, ~~because~~ I think I will
be able to manage. I told you on Sunday my mother hadn't
any cups or soup plates. So I went back to work early and got
3 soup plates. I was only able to get 2 cups. I will try Friday to
get another one. I could not get any saucers. I also got some
material for a skirt. It is a very tiny pin head check in black
blue and orange. I like it very much but my mother wasn't
too thrilled with it, she did not say so, but I could tell, but
you know me that would not put me off.
I don't believe I told you Miss Scarlett was leaving (she's the
one that took Gwenn's job last year the same time that Iris
came) now it looks as though they are leaving together. She

leaves tomorrow night (Thursday). Lucy and I are now wondering what sort of a person will be in her place.

Darling, although I love chicken I have not changed my mind about Sunday. I am waiting to see what you think about me coming on Saturday.

Goodnight darling and God bless.

All my love Jean.

Pickwell

Oct. 20th 1948

My dearest, darling Jean,

Thanks very much for your nice letter. I hope you got my letter yesterday as I promised.

Well, darling, I really can't say anything to Iris affairs. Are you particular about keeping your nationality? I think it doesn't matter to a girl what nationality she is even if she doesn't know what might happen.

I could do with a few more blankets and a pillow, but everything in it's time. American Eiderdowns are 30.5 in Nottingham as Herbert told me. That's just what we need here. Perhaps a proper pillowcase. It'll get pretty cold in the winter, I am sure. Don't worry, maybe till then we'll be fixed up with something. About that house, nothing doing.

I asked Mr Maclean who it belongs to and if there would be a possibility to rent it. He said Captain Norman is looking for a groom to look after his horses and that's what he wants the house for. I told him I am looking for a house and want to get settled down. He asked me if I am leaving after getting married. Anyway he offered me work as long as I want it and would like me to stay on for good at his place. Time will show how things go.

If you better like to come on Saturday well, it suits me fine. I found out that I only have to work on Sunday not Saturday afternoon. So come on the 2.15 and take the 10.29 back. That gives us more time together. Well, darling I'll go to bed now. I can hardly keep my eyes open tonight. So Goodnight and God bless. Be a good girl and think of me. Don't forget the things on Saturday including cigarettes (if possible)

                    Loads of loves and thousand
                    kisses eternally yours
        Hans.

        92 Wharf St
        October 21st 1948
My dearest darling Hans
I am wondering if there will be a letter for me in the morning. I know you are very busy these days, but I couldn't help wondering what is the matter. I have only had one letter this week and it is so unlike you.
I had a letter from Bernhard this morning and at the moment he is very happy with life. He has a new member in his family, a boy and at the same time he was put in charge of his office. His wife is now moving to Kempen to be with him.
Dora has been tonight. She brought her knitting and I did a bit of mine, rather an exciting evening don't you think, but it wasn't too bad really. The only time I seem to do any knitting is when Dora comes.
Iris has put her notice in today, that means she will be leaving a week on Friday and she hopes to be on her way to Paris on Saturday. She is going to London one day next week to see about her passport. I doubt very much if it will do any good. Thank you for your letter. I will see you tomorrow (Saturday). I will catch the 2.15. I have 3 soup plates, 3 cups and a box of cartridges. Until tomorrow
 All my love and kisses
        Jean

        ___ ·

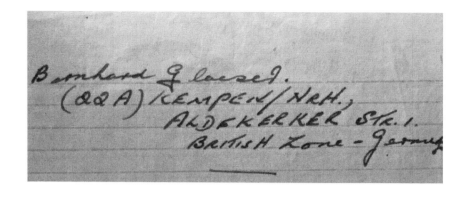

Bernhard Glaesed.
(22 A) KEMPEN/NRH.;
ALDEKERKER STR. 1.
British Zone - Germany

92 Wharf St
October 24th

My dearest Hans

I arrived home safe, it wasn't quite half past eleven. It only takes me 2 minutes now and I am home. I was going to take the dog a walk but I was too tired so I just took him in the yard, then to bed I went and I did not get up until 9.30 that is very late for me. This morning I went to see Aunt Miriam on my bicycle. She lives on the Peterborough Rd. Coming back I got into trouble with the police. I was going down a one way street. I thought you could do that on Sundays, but apparently you can't. The policeman told me to go back but there was an officer with him, he told me to carry on and go round the corner. For 2 pins I could have socked that policeman one. I am going to take Freddy a walk in a while that is about all I will do. I might write to Bernhard but at the moment I have not got the energy. There is only "Old mother Riley" on the radio and I can't stand that. Did you listen to "Over the garden wall" on Thursday? It is the same type of programme as "Old mother Riley" but it is very much better.

I will say cheeri'O then you will get this Monday morning. I wonder if I will be lucky.

All my love

Jean.

Beatrice(mother) Gertie and Miriam

Pickwell

Oct. 25<u>th</u> 1948.

My dearest, darling Jean,

I am so sorry you didn't receive a letter this morning, but when I came back from work yesterday afternoon, Helmut started talking about going to Melton. He wanted to see a picture ("Strange Affairs") and didn't like to go on his own. Anyway he talked me round and afterwards I was glad I went. Herberts girl came again and they sat here. You know I don't like to listen to other peoples conversations. Well, when we arrived at Melton we found a notice at the picture house "full". I had the funny idea to go to Great Dalby and see Mr Edwards. So off we went from Melton on the 6 o'clock bus. Mr Edwards was in and looked at me as if he'd thought I was 6 feet under the ground already. Anyway they were very pleased to see me again. We had a nice talk till 8.00 and then we took the bus home. Mrs Edwards asked me how you were and if I still see you. Well, she must have heard something about marriage and she almost got a shock when I said that's true. When I asked her why she was so surprised she didn't know what to do. During the course of the conversation he told me, he thought of getting me back to Goadby Harwood hostel as cook. Albert from Redmile is there now and he's got lots of complaints about the cooking. I informed him that as far as I know I can't go back on that job. He meant it might be possible that the Ministry changes his plan again one day. Well, wait and see.

I would've loved to see you when you're stopped by the police. Well, next week you better have some lessons about the highway code. Can I help you ma'am?

Today I really was fed up with the work. It was raining dogs, cats and pitch forks and I was told to go out with tractor and water tank to wash chicken houses. By 9.30 I was wet through in spite of my thick overcoat. I changed my suit and went out again until 1.00. In the afternoon I started painting hen-houses here in the yard and then the weather changed.

Well, sweetheart, it's 10 o'clock and I am very tired. I'll go to bed thinking of you. Good night and God bless.

All my love and kisses

    Eternally yours

      Hans.

                    Pickwell

                    Oct. 27th 1948

My dearest, darling Jean,

Today I've received 2 nice letters. One from Gertrude and one from Mr Chandler. Gertrude and her mother invited me to come over and spend my holidays with them so I've found a place at last.

Mr Chandler got my letter alright and I think he had a good laugh. He asked me to come over on Saturday, stay over the weekend at his bungalow and you to come on Sunday as well. It's very nice of him but I would like to ask you first. Do you mind coming over to Saltby? And please for the day. On

Saturday afternoon I have to go to Melton for a haircut and I also will have a look around for a greatcoat. Now I agree with you that I have to have one. It's getting pretty cold and still colder in Germany. I also have to buy a hat and another pair of shoes (brown) to the new suit. After that I'll save up. I hope there's a possibility to cash my american check in Germany. I am sure to get the check in £, but I would like to keep that one for when we go away. In Australia it's also sterling currency and £ better than dollar.

All day yesterday I was out with the tractor. It was pretty cold. It seldom happens that you see me working with the overcoat on, but yesterday I did it for the first time. Today I washed chicken houses and went feeding in the afternoon. By the way I've this weekend off, if it isn't clear to you what I said about going to Saltby.

Well, sweetheart I am very tired and go to bed, thinking and dreaming of you. Goodnight and God bless you. Be a good girl.

All my love and kisses

    Eternally yours, darling

      Hans.

     R   Aschersleben 3/10/48

   4/11.48   27/10.48

    My dear Hans

Today is Harvest Festival and I am sending you my best wishes. In the morning I went to church. We have not heard from you for over a fortnight and maybe you will have forgotten all about us by now. It is almost five years since we have seen each other, so we shall slowly get forgotten. During the week I am out every day digging potatoes, six hundredweight so far, another four hundredweight, and then we'll have enough. After that several times collecting wood and sugar beet, and then happily this difficult time is over. I had wanted to start working in the sugar beet factory, I had already applied, but Horst does not allow me to go, he feels that it will be too hard for me.

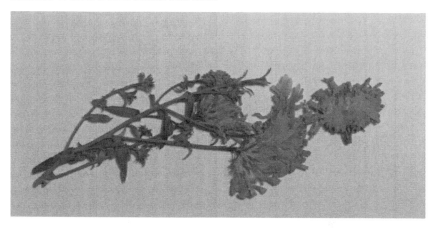

Pressed flower insert

Eight weeks today, on 28.11.48 it will be my 10th wedding anniversary, will Papa be with us? Otherwise it will be a very sad day for me. I hope Jean is with you. Please send her my best regards. Horstel has gone out for a bit, he is again in medical treatment, he has bronchial problems, he really cannot stand the air here. And he works too much. Hoping that health-wise you are feeling a lot better and you are almost certainly back in your old post and your exhausting job has finished. We do not receive much mail these days, have not heard much from the Streeses, they all become lazy about writing. Now my dear boy continue to stay well, lots of love and kisses from your always thinking of you mum and your brother Horst. Here's to a speedy Wiedersehen

R   Aschersleben 10/10/48
4/11/48   26/10/48

My dear Hans

It is now already three weeks that we have been without news from you. We are very worried – hopefully you are not ill? Or maybe the post is barely functioning. I am on my own today as Horst has gone to the hairdressing competition in Wernigerode, As usual, there are many participants, and Horst struggles with practising. He has a nice model, and I really wish him a lot of success. We have spent another week gleaning and digging, I have managed to bring in my 10 hundredweight, and I am delighted, but it is so exhausting. I shall carry on for another few days. It's always better to have a bit more than too little. The potato harvest has all but finished, and the farmers are already very busy with harvesting the beet. Generally we receive very little mail, everyone is so busy with their work that there is no time to write. Tonight I shall go to the movies with Mrs Ziemann, they are showing "Den Meineid Baüer"*. I've seen it once already, it is very good. Next week we shall have our kitchen renovated, it has become very dirty because of the use of all the raw coal, so when you have to sit in it all winter you are glad when it is all clean and bright. My dear Hans I shall finish my letter for today, let us hope that in the coming week we shall have good news from you. Stay well. This week we bought ourselves a bottle of oil, as we are sick and tired of eating a completely fat-less diet, but 100 Mark is of course a completely mad price. Many regards to Jean and all my love and kisses to you my son from your mum and your brother Horst.

*The perjured farmer

92 Wharf St
    October 28th
My dearest Hans.
Thank you for your letter, I received it on Wednesday lunch

24

time, it is a wonder you find the time to write being so busy. I think you should have found time to write when you got back on Sunday. You left Mr Edwards at 8.0 and it did not take you 2 hrs to get back. You would have had time to write even a page. You had used to make time when you were at Redmile. Is it because Herbert does not write to his girl-friend every night? Now I have that off my chest I will tell you what I have been doing. Monday night I went to see "Oliver Twist", it was very good. Tuesday I felt very fed up so I stayed in. I would have liked to have gone to the pictures but I had to go to collect some money on a bill. I had not been for a month so I had to make an effort, by the time I got back home it was too late.

My cousin and his girlfriend have just been, they are going to a dance and they have come to fetch the car. They came in to tell me not to say anything to my aunt, because if she knew she would soon be up in the air. My mother has gone out with my aunt and uncle. They went out about 8.0 they will be back about 10.0. I think they want a job to go out on a night like this, especially to sit in a pub. To get back to what I have been doing this week. Wednesday I went with my cousin Gertie (that is the one I went to Eastbourne with) to the tailors. She is having a costume made. That is what I would like, a new costume. If he makes hers alright I will probably get him to make mine, but at the moment my funds are not too good, and I really ought to have a coat to go to work in, my brown coat has about had it. And I don't like to wear my best coat for work.

I have bathed the dog, he seems to have lost a lot more hair but he is very bright. I have been doing a bit of my table cloth, by the time I have that cloth finished I will be old and grey. Iris left today and she sails to France tomorrow night. She took the day off yesterday and went to London to see about her passport and book her passage. She wanted to go on Saturday, but they told her that the earliest date they had to go to France was November 12th, but just as she was about to go someone cancelled their passage for Friday so she took that. She was unable to do anything about her nationality and she could not change her passport because she had to have her husband's passport. So she has to travel as a single person then change it when she gets to Paris. It is going to take Lucy and I weeks to get over the excitement. I wonder if I will get a letter before the weekend. I had better, otherwise I won't be there at Pickwell on Sunday. If I do hear from you I will be on the 2.15 bus on Sunday. Until then goodnight and God bless.

All my love and kisses

Jean.

> Home Farm,
> Pickwell
> Oct 28th 1948

My dearest, darling Jean,

Well, there was no letter for me today. Are you going to do the same I did last week, only two letters? I can't blame you, but you know how busy I am and so tired after my days work. It's only 8.10 now and I can hardly keep my eyes open. I've told you what my job is this week. Washing chicken houses and they are so small you can't stand up. Tonight I don't know if my back is still where it should be. Another two days and that job will be finished. You can't imagine how glad I am. Afterwards the houses have to be moved to another field. That's a better job anyway. A good thing houses are only to be washed once a year.

It would be very nice if you could come down to Melton on Saturday afternoon and come to Saltby Sunday morning. We could go to the pictures Saturday afternoon and I'll go on to Saltby after you've gone home. Or do you like to come along to Saltby on Saturday? I'll ring you up tomorrow night.

Well, my sweetheart, I'll go to bed now. Be a good girl and think of me. Goodnight and God bless you. Loads of love and thousand kisses, yours forever

Hans.

Aschersleben 17.10.48

30/10.48

My dear Hans

We thank you very much for your letter dated 8/10/48 and your postcard dated 7/10/48 from London, you have kept us waiting for a total of four weeks for mail. Well, so you have visited London! I can just imagine the difference between a metropolis and life in the country. But now, my dear Hans, to your decision. What I have gradually been expecting has now happened. Well, this is very hard for me, because when you had your big disappointment you wrote that you would not think about getting married for a long time, but you have clearly changed your mind. I had always hoped that one day we would all live together, and I have been really looking forward to it, but that is now water under the bridge. So, you are planning to get married!! Have you really thought about it carefully my boy? You know that getting married is a life-long step? I am sending you my very heartfelt blessings and wish you the best of luck. However it is bitter-sweet for me, as I had imagined everything to be so different. We have now been separated for five years, and the hope of living together again has vanished. I have raised both you children and a lot of the time it was difficult for me, and now I cannot even be at your wedding day. But how do you imagine your life in the future? You are planning to remain for another six months? And then what? What does Jean's mother say? Where you are, she is living a protected life in a safe environment, whereas being English you could not bring her here, she would not receive a permit to live here, so you would have to live in the West and find some means of living and as always the different zones are separating us. I have driven myself mad but have not found a way out. Everyone forges their own destiny. Now to your holiday plans. You know how much we have been looking forward to a Wiedersehen, you know you could go to Frieda's address, but it is impossible for us to go there, bearing in mind how little money we have, and 100 Mark of our money is only worth 20 Mark over there. Even having saved a few hundred Mark it is not in any way enough to pay for our travel costs. If only there was a place near the border – your cousin Horst Gogolin lives in Helmstedt, really near to the border, maybe it would be possible to stay there, or maybe he could find us a room, I will write to the Gogolins in Eisleben immediately, maybe one could cross the border easily? My head is spinning with all the worrying. Will you bring Jean? I cannot get hold of a birth certificate , but an affidavit from a lawyer will replace it. You have to present this, it is a legal document, but it involves a lot of running around. I do not understand why you have given up your good job, you seemed to be so content, we were very surprised. I would not have done it, just think about driving a tractor in winter, with your bad leg. But you are old enough and must know what you're doing. I don't know what it will be like when we meet there, it will be winter and nothing on our feet. We have bought sweetener several times, six Mark per packet, which we can ill afford. Now for today sending you love and kisses from your mum and your brother Horst. Best regards to Jean

Affidavit from lawyer regarding birth certificate for Hans

Home Farm,
Pickwell
Nov 1st 1948

My dearest, darling Jean,

Thank you so very much for your letter I received today instead of Saturday morning. You told me off nicely about not writing enough lately. Be sure, sweetheart, I love to write to you every night, but some days I am so tired that I go to bed straight away. It's only 8.30 now, but 9 o'clock will see me in bed. It was raining all day and there was nothing else to do for me as work outside. Of course I was wet through in no time. Anyway I stuck to it till 5.00. When I came "home" I changed everything. You should know it isn't because Herbert doesn't write every night. I am not doing the same anybody else does. Well, my love, I arrived here safe and sound at 10.50 and I hope you got home alright. I was in the first taxi that left the bus station. Bonzo is very comfortable. As soon as I went into the taxi he went on the back seat and lay down and kept quiet all the time. Now he's in front of the stove sleeping. I gave him a nice dinner tonight, fried potatoes and egg, and he liked it very much because he cleaned the plate as I've never seen it before.

Do you know the Berlin Philharmonic Orchestra is playing at the De Montfort Hall on Nov 9th. It's a shame because it's a Friday. I would like to go and take you along. But it starts at 7pm. That means I must finish work at 1.00 there's a bus at 4.44 to Leicester. We can talk it over on Saturday. By the way I've to work Sunday and have Saturday afternoon off. So we'll have more time for the last bus.

I thank you very much for the nice weekend. I hope you've enjoyed it as much as I have. Remember always that I love you very very much and I hope you'll always be happy.

Well, my love I'll go to bed now and dream of you. Just be good and think of me. Goodnight and God bless you.

Loads of love and kisses

Eternally yours, darling

Hans.

92 Wharf St

Nov 2nd 1948

My dearest darling Hans

I suppose you think, because you did not get a letter Wednesday, that I am doing the same as you did last week, but you are wrong. I was going to write this afternoon but I got in a mess with my knitting and if I had left it in the mess whilst I wrote to you my jumper would never have got finished. I have been doing it for a year now. Did you arrive at Pickwell alright with Bonzo? I saw you get a taxi o.k. I hope Bonzo is settling down. I was glad of Bonzo's company from Saltby to Croxton!!!

Mr Chandler came through to the Labour Dept today and he asked me if we saw anything of B-S on Sunday, because B.S. had told Mr Shilton, that on Sunday when he went to Saltby, he went into Mr Chandlers place and he thought the place was very untidy. Mr Chandler did not think he had been to the place as we would have seen him. Did you get very wet yesterday? I think that saying should be "it always rains on a Monday". I got soaked coming home at night, it threw it down once I was in. I stopped in. I thought about going to the pictures but I went tonight instead to see "The Bishops Wife", it was rather good. I rang Alice this afternoon and she is coming tomorrow night.

Well darling it is now 11.25 and I am very tired. Notice that it is late and I still found time to write even though it is only a few lines. Goodnight and God bless. All my love

Jean

                                        Pickwell
                                        Nov 2nd 1948

My dearest, darling Jean,

Well, sweetheart another day is over.

How are you today, my love? I hope fine. I've started cleaning chicken houses again that means started it the same I did before. My tractor is ready so I shall take it in the morning and go watercarting. Nobody tells me what to do. I asked the poultryman today and he gave me a rather funny answer. He said "you know yourself what work is to be done so just start where you think it's necessary". Well, I'll find something for myself.

Did you think of asking for the thermos flask permit?

Well, darling, I'll say goodnight now and God bless you. Just be good and think of me.

    All my love and kisses

      Eternally yours

Hans.

P.S.

Can you get a couple snaps developed. I put the negative in.
H.

> 92 Wharf St
> Nov 4th 1948

My dearest darling Hans

Thank you so very much for your letters.

About Saturday, couldn't we go to Oakham. I could catch the 2.15 from Leicester. Then you could get on it at Somerby. I have never been to Oakham and I would like to go. We could have a look around then go to the pictures. I am not getting on very well with this letter. At the rate I am going it will be time to go before I have finished it.

What happened to the snaps you wanted developed! ! !They were not in the envelope.

Alice came last night. I told you she was coming, but she did not come until 8.30. I was just getting interested in the play "Message for Margaret" when she and Bernie came. Bernie is an Irish girl who is living with them. She is a friend of Alice's brother in America. She went to stay with them for a few days when Alice's brother was home and Bernie has been there ever since.

I'm going to stay in tonight and wash my hair. It has not been washed for 3 weeks so I think it is about time it saw water.

I will say cheeri'O for now.

 All my love and kisses
Jean.

> Pickwell
> Nov 4th 1948

My dearest, darling Jean,

Thank you very much for your letter I received this morning. I was going to ring you tonight if I wouldn't have got one today. Well, I only waited 4 days. I was worried about you, and I am glad now to know everything is alright. Don't you think you better finish your jumper now after a year. What about one for me? Nothing doing I guess!!

Mr B.S. must have been at the bungalow just before us. Fancy gossiping to other people what it looked like there. Has he nothing else to do?

Now about the weekend. Well, darling, I would like you to come here. Herbert is going to Leicester for the afternoon and Helmut is going to Melton. So we'll be on our own. I get a chicken for Sunday and this time I want you to get a piece of it. I think I've told you already that I have the Saturday afternoon off and work on Sunday. You can take the last bus from Somerby at 10.29. I'll ring you tomorrow night. I have to write to my mother tonight.

Just be good and think of me. Goodnight and God bless you.

> Loads of love and Kisses
> > Eternally yours
> > > Hans.

> 92 Wharf St
> Nov 6th 1948

Sunday 2.30

My dearest darling Hans

Good afternoon, how are you today? Very wet I suppose after this morning. The rain has only just stopped here, it has been tipping it down all morning. How was Helmut (is that how you spell his name) when you got back, he hadn't smashed the happy home had he? I got into Leicester last night at 11.35 and it was about 12.20 when I went to bed. There was a good fire so I sat and read the paper and by the time I put my curlers in it was quite late, but I was not up very early, 9.30. I'm very sorry but I could not think of you getting up at 7.0. I was unconscious at the time. I will take your form tomorrow. I was going to take it this morning, but when it turned so wet I stayed in and cleaned out. I might take it after tea and take the dog with me, that will be when it is dark. I didn't care to take him when it is light, he looks such a mess. I am going to wash him tonight, he has not been done for about a week.

My mother is in today, it was too wet to go to Rothley. She has gone to bed at the moment, but I suppose she will be going out after tea with my aunt next door. I am going to write to your mother after I have finished this but heaven only knows what on earth I can write about. I also have a letter to write to Bernhard. This is the second I have to answer of his.

I have been doing some of my jumper today and I have nearly finished the sleeve. I have one more sleeve to do then (thank goodness) it is finished. I want to knit a cardigan to go with the jumper. I have the wool. When I have finished that I might (but I won't promise) knit you a-pullover ~~a short sleeved one~~ what I meant was one without sleeves.

What about your shoes have you had them mended yet? I have been meaning to ask you for ages. If you have not any-where to send them you had better give them to me to bring to Leicester.

What about next Saturday, do we go to Oakham or not? Let me know.

All my love and kisses
Jean

.

P.S.
I hope you have written to me today. Jean

Aschersleben 22.10.48

R 9/11.48   8/11/48

My dear Hans

Although I am very tired today I shall send you a few lines. I was speaking to Mrs Lehmann about your holidays and she said that we could use her sister's room and her sister could stay with her parents' They live in Weferlingen, very close to the border, meaning that our tricky financial situation would be helped a bit. That really sounds like a good idea, and I would be very happy. They are also refugees. We can buy food there. It would be great if you plan your holiday for the end of November or the beginning of December. Horst cannot take time off during the second half of December. In any event he has to take unpaid leave. What do you think about it all? Please let us know as soon as possible. On Tuesday evening Horst was so ill I had to call a doctor who diagnosed asthma. He needs a change of air and unless things change by spring we shall have to pick up our walking sticks and find ourselves a new abode, health is the most important issue. Now you can congratulate Horstel, at the hairdressing competition in Wernigerode he got fifth place amongst 50 participants in the masterclass, he was of course very pleased. Please forgive the bad handwriting, I am about to fall asleep? Please let us know immediately about the holiday. Lots of love and kisses from your mum and your brother Horst. Many cordial greetings to Jean

address of: Mrs Frida Fuchs

20b in Weferlingen / Krs Wolfsbuettel near Braunschweig

Pickwell
Nov 9th 1948

My dearest, darling Jean,
I thank you so much for your nice letter I received yesterday morning it was a real surprise because I didn't expect one on Monday. I hope you didn't mind not getting a letter today. I was very busy last night and only slept 3 ½ hours last night. After all we got the plasterboard for the ceiling yesterday

and decided to start straight away. We took all our things out of the room and pulled all that old stuff down. It was not half a mess. If you'd seen us you would've got a fit. Covered with cement dust all over. Our faces looked grey. Well we finished cleaning out at 10.00 and of course had to put the new ceiling on for we hardly could sleep in that room without anything over our heads. After 4 hours work we finished. It was 2.00 a.m. And at 5.30 I had to get up again. You can imagine I am dead tired now after the days work.

One of the next days my license should be here, they're pretty quick in sending the form back so I hope I'll get the license just as quick.

I haven't had my shoes mended yet. I think you'd better take them along when coming here the next time. I really don't know where to send them.

Now about the weekend. I have the Saturday afternoon off and as Herbert's girl probably comes I think we'd better go to Oakham. I'll be at the bus stop (postoffice) for the 3.16 bus. Please sit on the nearside of the road so I can see you. If you aren't on the first bus I'll wait for the second one. Maybe I can get those shoes in Oakham too. We'll have a look around and go to the pictures afterwards. Bonzo is sitting beside me. He sends his love. Well, my sweetheart it's 8.30 and I'll go to bed. Goodnight and God bless. Just be my best girl.

    All my love and kisses
      Eternally yours, darling
    Hans

                Pickwell
                Nov 11th 1948

My dearest, darling Jean,
Last night we're busy again. You remember those big holes in the wall. We cleaned up as much as we could. Herbert was cement mixer and I told him his mixture was not good. The cement fell down every time he put it on. So we had to throw it away and started afresh. After finishing the job the other

two went to bed and I had a good wash and shave. So I went to bed at 12.00

Tonight I feel so rotten and tired. I really worked hard today. In the morning we shifted chicken houses that means lifting them up on a carrier and that with only two of us. I know now how heavy those houses are. During the afternoon I was watercarting on my own. It usually takes 2 ½ hours when we go with two of us. Today I did it in 2 hours on my own. Of course almost running all the way. When I came back at 5.15 I had to start my nightly round and finished at 6.30 after all. I was almost sleeping whilst I had my dinner. My license came on Wednesday night alright.

Well, my darling, I can't write anymore for I can't keep my eyes open. So goodnight and God bless you. Be a good girl.

Loads of love and thousand kisses

Eternally yours

Hans.

Pickwell

Nov 12<u>th</u> 1948

My dearest, darling Jean,

Well now the work is finished for tonight I am able to write a few lines. Your chicken is ready, I only have to pack it tomorrow afternoon.

I thank you very much for that lovely conversation on the phone tonight. Anyway you're in rather a hurry. Going out? It was not at all like you and I was rather annoyed. Was somebody listening or what was the matter? Can't you find enough time even to speak to me on the phone? I am awfully sorry you didn't get my letter I wrote on Sunday, but it wasn't my fault. I most certainly shall see her about that tomorrow and tell her off. If she can't do something she promised she better should refuse to take any letters. Didn't you write just because you had to wait till Thursday? I hoped to get a letter and of course went over to Mrs Cooper twice a day and ask for mail. Tonight she looked at me rather funny because there was nothing all week. Always only the newspaper. Well I know now there won't be anything in the morning.

I am so glad there are only 5 hours to go tomorrow. This week I really got fed up with the work. Tonight I did my last round, shutting up. It got me down after the days work. It's not too bad for the women because they of course only do light work during the day.

Well, my love it's 10.15 now and I'll go to bed. Goodnight and God bless you. I shall see you tomorrow.

> All my love and thousand kisses
>> Eternally yours, darling
> Hans

Pickwell
Nov 14<u>th</u> 1948

My dearest, darling Jean,

Well, sweetheart, I am back at Pickwell and found the place still dark. Nobody at home. Why did you smile when getting on the bus. Was there anybody who knows you? I thank you very much, darling, for a very nice weekend. It was really lovely. Even the walk around town.

It's hot here now. I think I'd better go to bed. My leg does hurt a bit, but I hope it'll be better in the morning. If I'd to stop in bed here for a few days I certainly would die.

Now look, darling, about telling your mother. Do it as soon as possible and believe me it doesn't take much courage. Why should it be different after Christmas. You know that would be the best Xmas present, to settle everything. Don't you think your mother knows you want to get married one day sooner or later? Don't be afraid, my love, but don't say let time do it. That may mean years. Your aunty was right when she said you should make up your mind. You've made up your mind so everything is alright. I know you're longing for a happy family life and so am I. It, of course means hard work for a start, but I wouldn't mind because I know what I am working for. Well, sweetheart think it over.

There's another week to go till I see you again. I am soooo much longing for.

Well, my love, I'll say goodnight and God bless you. Be a good girl and think of me.

Loads of love and thousand kisses

    Eternally yours

    Hans.

                              Pickwell

                              Nov 15th 1948

My dearest, darling Jean,

It's only 5.45 and I think it's best to write a few lines now because I shan't have much time later on.

Last night we're busy plastering the ceiling and it does really look a lot better. Tonight we are going to finish the wall and start white washing. By the way, please don't forget to bring a few dog biscuits for Bonzo. I don't know if we can get some in Melton.

How are you today, sweetheart? I am fine and hope the same from you. We finished moving the chicken houses and I think the next job will be disinfecting. I only hope that other woman is coming back next week. Now you've to get cracking to get all the work done.

My leg was just nice when I got up this morning. Now after the days work it hurts again. Doesn't matter as long as I can walk alright. I went round to the pub last night for my fortnights cigarette ration and only got 20. Can you get more that 40?. If you can please bring more. As many as you are able to get. Will you please ask Mr Scott, Melton office, if he could let me have that snap he took of me in white cooks clothes? Please give him my address to post it on to me.

Well, my love I'll say cheerio now. The potatoes are almost done and that means dinner is ready. I hope it won't be too late tonight before I get to bed. So goodnight and God bless you. Be my best girl and think a tiny bit of me, if you can spare the time.

> Loads of love and kisses
> > Eternally yours
> Hans.

92 Wharf St
November 15th

My dearest darling Hans

Well, here I am again Monday morning, 11.30 and all is well. I arrived home at about 9.45. The two girls are Anna and Muriel, the one with glasses, Muriel, looked rather funny at first glance but she is really very nice. She works on the Leicester telephone exchange, she knew Iris and she asked me about 2 of the girls at Phoenix on 58147. She went to school with one of them. I told her I was at 65187. She said "oh, are you Jean" we were chatting all the way home the time went very quick. I have just had a visitor. Mr & Mrs Ward from the Market Harborough Hostel. I have spoken to Mr Ward everyday, but I have never seen him before. He gave me a ¼ pound block of nut milk chocolate. Am I not lucky.

I had a letter today from Iris. she said she felt as if she had lived in Paris for years.

I have not taken your shoes. I did not have time first thing then at lunch time I went out for my mother so she said she would take them, but forgot. She said she will take them tomorrow.

Lucy and I are going to the Opera House to see an "Ice Revue". It has been very full all last week and all the bookable seats are booked, but we hope to be able to get in at the very top of the house. That has been very full too, but Lucy leaves at 4.45 so she is going to queue, then I am going to join her at 5.15. We should get in, it doesn't begin until 6.45.

Is Helmut still in one piece? And did he need his knife? I am afraid I have not a very good opinion of anyone that carries knives about with them, not even for self defence, because a person that goes looking for trouble will find it. And if it was an Englishman that gave him the knife he must mix with some very funny people. So please don't you sink so low as carrying a knife and try to talk Helmut out of doing it. I would make a good preacher don't you think.

We have made arrangements about Saturday haven't we? I will meet you at Melton either at 3.15 or 4.20 whichever bus you are on. How are Micky and Minnie (the mice) have you seen any more of them? What about the stockings for Gertie you ought to send them on because the girl will be needing them. We can see about them on Saturday. By the way have you fetched your coupons yet. I am not waiting but I don't want you to miss the boat.

Well darling I will have to close now I am a very busy woman.

 All my love and kisses

    Jean

P.S.

I don't think I should have said kisses because I have been eating onions

    Jean

Pickwell

Nov 17th 1948

My dearest, darling Jean,

I thank you so very much for your letter I received this morning. Did you recieve my letter yesterday? How are you today, sweetheart? I hope fine. Well, half the week is gone and only 2 ½ more days to go. I saw you laugh when you got on the bus last Sunday night. So you had a good chat all the way. Who was the lucky one you're talking about?

Nobody comes to visit me and brings ¼ pound of Nut Milk

chocolate. Nobody except you. Tonight I miss you more than ever. I don't know what's the matter, but I feel very lonely. Well, my love I keep both my fingers crossed that everything will be alright and may our time come very soon.

If you don't get my shoes back for the weekend it wouldn't matter because I have waited rather a long time myself. Have you been writing the birthday letter to my mother? It's her birthday today, I just remembered.

So you're going to the "Ice Revue" and didn't even ask me if I wanted to go along with you knowing how much I would've liked to go.

Micky and Minnie are alright. When I came in tonight they're playing on the empty table and stayed till I was almost on the table. It would've been nice if you could've seen it. I bet it ~~would've~~ was worth taking a snap of it. We're going to leave the bosses cat in for a couple of days.

Do you think it's better to send the stockings on to Gertie or taking them along when I go. I just wonder when that'll be. Can't you find anything out for me. We'll see about the stockings and shoes for my mother on Saturday.

Tonight we're going to do some whitewashing. That'll make all the difference. By the way I was lucky yesterday. Mr Cooper went to Melton so I asked him to go to the food office and get the coupons for me. My old identity card was full so I got a new one as well.

You can send your kisses even if you've been eating onions. I myself like onions very much.

So goodnight and God bless you. Just be a good girl and think of me.

All my love and kisses

    Eternally yours

      Hans.

    92 Wharf St

    November 17th

My dearest darling Hans

I am writing this at work. I have only written these few lines and I am fed up with interruptions. One of your fellows has just been in. Iman is his name. He has been trying for ages to get his release from agriculture because of his health. He has had a letter from the Home Office today to say that he is released. Fortunately he did not stay very long, but usually when he comes he stays ages.

One of the photographs we had taken in London came today. They are not too bad, very clear, but neither of us are looking where we should. Lucy and I went to see the "Ice Revue" last night. It was good but not as good as the one we saw.. Mr Simpkin has been in. Have you written to him about the permit for the flask.

I will have to say cheeri'O and get on with my knitting

All my love and kisses

Jean

— .

92 Wharf St

November 18th

My dearest darling Hans

I thank you very much for your letter. I have had one everyday so far. No, you must have missed one day. I think it was Tuesday. I have just put my knitting down to write this. I have been knitting like mad all day long. I am sorry I did not tell you about the Ice show, but you would not have been able to go, it didn't finish until 9.0 and it began at 6.45. I have not been to the pictures this week yet. There is quite a good film on at The Savoy "Green Dolphin Street". I might go tomorrow night. I will have to find out what is on at Melton. I am very sorry but I have not written to your mother yet, but I promise to. I think it will take me a couple of days. I will also have to write to Horst again. I think I could write to Horst alright now, but it will be very hard writing to your mother. By the way, it was Freddy's birthday yesterday too, he was 1 yr and without any hair. Isn't it sad. I should've fetched your shoes back from the menders today, but I forgot. I'll go tomorrow, they are going to sole and heel them. I did not ask them to put steel tips on the toe, because I didn't want you to sound like a farm worker when you are out with me. I don't mind on your boots. Haven't I got a cheek?

Now, for the reason I wouldn't take my nail polish off when you ask me. Because I dye my hair, paint my face and paint my nails now and I have no intention of stopping when I am married. So you will have to take me as I am. I can't see why you don't like it. Anyway darling I think you had better find a hobby while I paint my nails, or better still you could do the scrubbing while I do it eh!!!

Well darling, I will have to say goodnight and God bless you. So I can get on with my knitting or else you will not get a pullover (short sleeves)

   All my love and kisses
   Jean

P.S. I have a lovely cold now. Jean
I thought I would tell you so you
Could feel sorry for me

Pickwell
Nov 19th 1948

My dearest, darling Jean,
I thank you so very much for your letter and I am very sorry I didn't write last night. I told you what I did and tonight Herbert is finishing the whitewashing. That's all then till the boss gets the blue distemper for us. I've told him about it and he promised to get some.

Your cold must be a real nice one. I could hardly understand what you said on the phone. Don't you also think it's better to ring you at the office? If only you wouldn't be interrupted so often, answering the phone. That fellow should be glad he's got the release from agriculture. Of course it takes some finding the right job now. If I could get the release I would try and go as bus driver. That's not a bad job.

Tonight I still have a lot to do. Helmut has gone out to have a look at the wires we put down for rabbits.

Well, darling, Helmut has just come back so we'll get cracking.

Goodnight for now and God bless you. Just be my best girl.

    Loads of love and kisses
      Eternally yours
      Hans

          Pickwell
          Sunday Nov 19th
          1948

My dearest, darling Jean,

Well, sweetheart I know I've spoilt what should've been a nice evening and agree with you there's no excuse for me. I was just fed up because I knew you were sitting here and I had to go again. The poultry man only told me this morning that he wanted to go away for the afternoon so I had to go shutting up. It almost drove me mad chasing the ducks and cockerels to get them into the houses. We moved the houses yesterday and they still keep going back to the old field.

After all I want you to know that I promise to behave myself better and not lose my temper again. I usually keep a promise.

I hope you get home well. Herbert went to the pub when we got here and Helmut isn't back yet. I'll go to bed as soon as I've taken Bonzo a walk and I know your home.

I can only always ask why do we have to part. You're going back home and I've to go back into my stables. It's really a good thing it looks a bit better now. If I could only get a house or a flat somewhere around here. I am sure it would make all the difference even in losing my temper. I am happy now, but I am very much longing for a happy family life. Being together with you all the time.

You once told me not to be sarcastic, but it was just the same when you said " you'd better nip around to the land army when I'm gone" you know well enough I don't even think of it. I love you too much to do anything like that.

What about the next weekend, love? As far as I know now Herbert is going to the registration office, to get his papers fixed. He's getting married on December 18th. So you had better come here, we can see then what we're going to do on Sunday. By the way, Mr Edwards apologised for not coming last Sunday and to fix something else.

Well, my sweetheart, I'll say goodnight and God bless you. Be my best girl and think a bit of me.

Loads of love and thousand kisses

Eternally yours ,darling

  Hans.

92 Wharf St
November 21st

My dearest Hans

It is getting rather late, but I will write a few lines just to let you know I am not quite so annoyed as I was last night. I may as well tell you I couldn't stand you being like that very often, in fact I don't think I would. So if you want to marry me you had better make up your mind to change your temper. You made me feel as though I hadn't ought to have gone to Pickwell. You never even help Herbert get the tea ready. If I remember rightly, I did not want to go. I told you on Saturday, but you said " oh please come". I came and I only wished I hadn't. Another thing, I did not like what you said when I said I would like to get Bernhards baby something. If it had

46

not been for the other two being there I would have told you something, but notice I managed to control my temper and believe me I was very annoyed.

I arrived home safe, the bus was about 5 minutes late which wasn't bad considering that it was very foggy. You would have laughed if you had seen Fred, my mother had taken a cushion out of the chair and put it on the table and blow me if he wasn't asleep on it on the table.

I will have to say goodnight it is getting late and it takes me all my time to get up in the morning.

     Love

               Jean

.

               Pickwell
               Nov 22nd 1948

My dearest, darling Jean,

Thank you so very much for the letter you brought on Saturday.

Did you get home alright last night? I don't know what the matter was with me today. I hardly got any work done and couldn't get off my mind what you said last night when we're waiting for the bus. It's 9.00 now and 9.30 will see me in bed. I don't feel well. I was sweating like anything in the afternoon with colds running down my spine. I only hope it isn't malaria again. Last night I felt a bit funny already. Good thing you didn't notice.

Well, darling now to something you said in the letter about painting nails and dying hair. You know I like to accept every little wish of yours. For instance you haven't dyed your hair lately and now it looks really nice. Please, wear it as you did yesterday and I would like it very much if you would leave the nail polish off. Of course, please yourself and do as you think it best. You needn't care about my wishes, sweetheart. It was only a suggestion.

It really was a shame I came back so late from shutting last night. Tonight the poultry man went and asked me to give him a hand. When we came out there everything was in order, the ducks and cockerels in already. They must have stayed out on purpose yesterday.

I've written to my mother again tonight, though I haven't had any letters from her for about a fortnight now.

I've just remembered that I've to get my washings ready tonight in case anybody goes to Melton tomorrow. That'll take me another half an hour.

So I'll say goodnight and God bless you always. Just be my lovely girl and remember how much I love you.

    Loads of love and kisses

        Eternally yours, sweetheart

        Hans.

P.S.

I think the date I put on yesterdays letter was wrong. Please excuse it.

        Hans.

        92 Wharf St

        November 23rd

My dearest darling Hans

I am glad to hear the ducks are getting trained where to go at night. That is another thing I may as well tell you about. Why were you annoyed because Mr Maclean asked if you needed any help when you had finished. You must remember that he owns the farm and that he need not have asked. It was really very nice of him to offer to help. You will never get anywhere by losing your temper. I bet it didn't have any effect on the ducks. Why don't you try to take life as it comes a bit more. What is to be will be without losing your temper. You had better let me know before Saturday if you are suffering from malaria. Then there won't be any need for me to come.

I am very sorry, but I have been painting my nails for years. So you see I will still have to do it, but you need not worry, someone was talking on the wireless or I read it, I can't remember, it was something to do with cleanliness in the kitchen, saying that painted nails were quite alright and nail polish wouldn't hurt anyone and I am sure you would not mind having bits of nail polish in your dinner.

We have a new girl (about 30 if you can call her a girl), she is very nice so far. She has come from one of the other depts, but we did not know her, she has taken Miss Scarlett's place. We never called Miss Scarlett by her christian name and that always bothered Lucy, so when this new girl started Lucy said to her my name is Lucy what would you like me to call you. To that she could not say any other than call me Margery.

Well darling I will have to say goodnight and God bless you I will come over to Pickwell on Saturday if you want me to

    All my love

    Jean

      .

Pickwell

Nov 24th 1948

My dearest, darling Jean,

I thank you so very much for your letter I received this morning and I am very glad to hear you're not so annoyed now. You're quite right to tell me off about it. It was my fault and as you said there's no excuse. Believe me, darling, I didn't like it myself when thinking about it afterwards, but then it was too late. Listen, I promised you something and please if you notice any signs remind me of my promise. I don't think I shall forget it. You know how much I like to be with you and that's why I asked you to come on Sunday. I also know I shouldn't have said anything about sending something for

Bernhards baby. If you don't like writing to my mother, just leave it, but as far as I know her I bet she was waiting for a letter from you. And now why I didn't help with setting the table. I watched him all the time and he kept looking at his girl as if he was just showing how to do it. So I thought if he wants to do it, let him. I really don't like messing about.

Wasn't it cold the last two days. Unfortunately I had to go out with the tractor watercarting today. For one hour I had to thaw the tank up and then took my battle dress jacket and my top coat and went out. Believe me I looked like a ball, but kept warm. Feeding this afternoon and shutting up finished the days work. That woman with the glasses took the afternoon off as usually and I shut up for her. Next week (Sunday) it's my turn, she does it on Sunday for me.

Last night I had a good long chat with Mr Pickering. I rung up to find out if Michel was still there. Unfortunately he left yesterday afternoon. Mrs Cooper asked me if I could recommend one of our fellows for the farm next door. So I thought of Micheal. Bill told me that the men had permission from the Home Office to stay if they could find a farm. Mr Barker-Swain however, refused to keep them. Isn't that nice. I only hope the boys are taking action now and hope B.S. would get told off from the Home Office.

Well, sweetheart, till Saturday and try to ring you again Friday at 5.00pm.

So goodnight for now and God bless. Be a good girl and forget the dreadful Sunday evening. I'll be thinking of you all the time.

All my love and thousand kisses
     Eternally yours, my love
     Hans.

P.S.
Could you bring some more biscuits for Bonzo. He likes them.

Love Hans

Pickwell

Nov 25$\underline{^{th}}$ 1948

My dearest, darling Jean,

It's getting late tonight, but I'll write a few lines so you shall get a letter on Saturday morning. Only another day and a half to go till I see you again. You don't know how much I am longing for it.

Well, today I was in Leicester and didn't even have a chance to ring you. We went to a mill and fetched a lorry load of stuff for the hen houses. Till 9.45 I finished distempering the other room, but it didn't turn out as I thought it would.

By the way, sweetheart, could you get a pair of working gloves for me (as cheap as possible). Herbert is going to Melton (Registry Office) on Saturday morning and goes to Leicester afterwards. So there's nobody here.

Tomorrow night I shall probably go to Saltby with our lorry and fetch the stove I asked Mr Chandler for. I'll ring him tomorrow dinner time.

Well, sweetheart, I'll get my things ready for the morning and then go to bed. Just be a good girl and think of me.

Loads of love and thousand kisses

Eternally yours

Hans

R 26/11.48

Prenzlau, 14.11.48

26/11.48

Dear Hans

It seems a long time ago since your lovely letter reached me. I have been waiting with anticipation I was very surprised to read in your letter that you have changed jobs again. Did you have to leave or did you prefer to get another job?

Hans, why don't you not come? You want to stay there for another year. I am not clear about your plans. Do you not want to let me know them? Do you want to become a foreigner forever? Or does Jean, as she will then be your wife, want to come to Germany? You are coming in December and are only allowed to get as far as the Bizone. Are you coming alone? Where do you want to go to from the Bizone? I am sure that you want to see your relatives. You know Marga's address: Gross-Rhüden, Schlackenstrasse 179. It is situated between Hildesheim and Seesen, 20 km away from Goslar. It wold be nice if your relatives could go there to meet up with you. Aschersleben is not that far away. There is just one little hitch. You would have to come a bit later because Marga and her children are staying with us over Christmas. She let us know the happy news that she has managed to get an Inter-Zone passport and wants to get on her journey on 15 December. Well Hansi, please think it over. Marga will be staying with us until mid-January because her pass is valid for 4 weeks. I would like to help you, your lovely mum and also Horstel. I shall ask Marga to do her bit. It will be very painful for me if I cannot see you then. Hans, I wish you only the best and would not want you to have the life I am having. It is cruel but deserved. I am not kidding myself anymore and I am not looking forward to the long winter evenings. My little dog Pilti has been run over during the week. Although it was only a dog, I am missing her a lot. Manfred has a little girl now. She is sweet little Dagmar, a tender little thing needing a lot of care. He nearly lost his wife and child within one night. I want to give them as much support as possible because they are very happy together. Mum has recovered now. Her current husband care's for her a lot. He does everything for her and she has everything she needs. Little by little I have come to the conclusion that mum has done the right thing. It is always so lovely when I spend time at home. I did miss your congratulations on my birthday but I refuse to believe that you are not thinking of me anymore on my big day. Otherwise I am getting on alright and hope you are too. I am sending you my best wishes. Vera.

Pickwell
Sunday Nov 28th 1948, 9.10
My dearest, darling Jean,

I thank you very much for a nice weekend, especially for coming today even if it was for such a short time. I love you so very much that I fight for every minute I can be with you. So please excuse if I always try to keep you here till the last bus. I think you can imagine how it is to be out here in the wilds and just longing to see you at the weekend and I'll say it again how much I am longing to be with you forever. Let's cross our fingers that it will be very soon. How did you get the idea I wanted you to take me home if I would've come along tonight. Well, sweetheart, to be honest, I would like it very much if you would do so, but that's one thing I leave to you. If you think it's not time yet I'll have to wait. You couldn't make me a better Christmas present. I would love to talk to your mother. Perhaps even Cyril would change his mind a bit.

I hope you got home alright and in time to look after Susan. It's not foggy now when I left Great Dalby. Mr and Mrs Edwards were pleased to see me again, in fact, they're waiting with tea for me. Well we've had a good chat and they, of course, asked how you are. When I left Mrs Edwards gave me a small parcel but didn't say what it contained. I bet you would've had a look on the bus. I could even wait till I got <u>home</u>!!! Shall I keep you waiting a bit longer? Well, it contained 6 home made sausages and home made butter. They killed the pig last week and she wants me to taste her sausage. Be sure we'll enjoy tomorrow's breakfast.

It was cold in here when I arrived back, because we also forgot to close the window. What else could I do as to start the fire again. I am listening to "Variety Bandbox". Are you? How wonderful it would be if I could sit beside you in front of the fireplace. They're just playing "Robin Hood"

Well, my love, Just be my best girl and think of me. Goodnight and God bless you.

> Loads of love and kisses
>> Eternally yours
> Hans.

92 Wharf St
November 29th

My dearest darling Hans

I have brought a pen can't you tell. It is a Rollball but I can't make up my mind whether or not I like writing with it. I brought it from a man at work for 12/6. I don't know whether that is cheaper than you can get in the shops. Is the one you have a Rollball? He is going to get me a refill, they are supposed to last a year. Did you go to see Mr Edwards after you left me. I had to wait until 6.35 for the bus. It started back straight the way and I arrived home about 7.30 in plenty of time. They, my sister and mother, didn't go out until 8.0. I did my knitting and went to bed about 10.30. I keep promising myself an early night in bed because I don't get up in the morning and my mother gets so annoyed. The 8.45 from Somerby did run. I spoke to the girl that goes to Knossington she said it was only 10 minutes late getting into Leicester. Werner from Billesdon (the fellow that knows Miss Redmile) came into the office to say goodbye. He is rather hard to make out. I don't know why. I never know whether to believe what he tells me. Anyway he is going to write or at least so he says. I have just been listening to a play. It was a spy story. I wonder if you listened, I have washed my hair tonight and I have not cut it, if I do decide to cut it it will be about Thursday. Then I will also get the bottle to it.

Well darling it is getting late. So goodnight and God Bless you.

All my love
Jean

Tuesday

I have been speaking to Kath this afternoon and she said "Sitting Pretty" was on at Melton, but only until Wednesday.

Connie Goodman came in this afternoon, she stayed quite a while. I will write probably tonight.

    Love Jean

      ——·

             Pickwell
             Nov 29th 1948

My dearest darling Jean

How are you today sweetheart? Did your bus arrive in Melton in time? When Helmut came home he said that the bus from Leicester to Melton was ¾ hour late. I only hope you got home in time to keep your promise.

First thing in the morning I attended a funeral, burying a few dead hens and then went out disinfecting till dinner time. In the afternoon, of course, my routine work – cleaning out – I've got a good fire going and still I am cold. I want to listen to that boxing match tonight and hope it's something decent.

Well, my love, now something. This time I give you one week to think it over. Next Saturday I shall ask the question, "anything particular you would like for Christmas." And don't you come and answer 'nothing' or I shall be very annoyed.

 I'll say goodnight and God bless you. I also want to write to my mother tonight.

So just be my best girl and remember how much I love you.

          Loads of love and kisses
            Eternally yours
              Hans.

             Pickwell
             Wednesday Dec 1st 1948

My dearest darling Jean

I thank you very much for the letter I received today. On the address I saw already that you wrote with a rollball pen,

12/6 is rather cheap because I paid 20/- for mine and – lost it. I didn't say anything I lost it when we're in London. That's the reason why I bought this one. Anyway it's cheaper than in the shops. The small one I've got costs only 5/-. I am glad to hear you got home in time so nobody could say anything. I didn't listen to that particular play and certainly would've done if I had known.

Please, darling, don't cut your hair short and please don't use the bottle. You really look lovely as you do it now and I like it very much. Can't you change your mind once? Just for me.

I was going to Saltby tonight, but unfortunately the driver that was coming along didn't turn up. It's 8.30 now and too late.

So Connie came in to see you. Did you give her my regards and tell her not to cross my way again? If I could only get hold of her sometime. There's a bill to make up.

I wonder what's the matter at home. I haven't had any letters for almost 3 weeks now. Hope it's nothing serious. Another 23 days and it's Christmas. Remember my question!!

Now about Saturday. Herbert is going to Leicester so we could meet in Melton and after we've finished shopping, go to Pickwell. I would like to go to the barber again. I'll see you at the bus station at 3.15. Don't you think that's the best? I also could ask if that shop has got the shoes I wanted. Well, my love I'll say goodnight and God bless you.

Loads of love and thousand kisses
Eternally yours my darling
Hans.

92 Wharf St
December 1st
My dearest darling Hans
I thank you for both your letters. I know you did not get one from me on Monday. I'm very sorry but I am trying to get my knitting done so I can start a pullover (short sleeves) for you.

What is your chest measurement, and what colour do you want? I thought a brown one then if I get on with that alright I will knit you another, but that I won't promise.

I have just about murdered the dog, he went and had a good drink of water then came back and tiddled on the mat. You ought to see him now he is looking at me so sad. My mother will say poor thing, he couldn't help it. She has gone out with my aunt and uncle. I have been knitting and listening to the play 'Lady from Edinburgh.' I don't suppose you heard it, it was quite good.

Look darling, I know you would like to come home with me, but my mother never says anything to me about you, and I have no idea what she thinks. If she wanted me to bring you home she should say so. It does not bother me whether you come or not, but it does worry me when you say you want to come because I don't think I have enough courage to ask you. I wish we could find some way, I want to get married and have something to live and work for. I have thought it all out. If we found a place I could go out to work but we would have to live on your money and either save or spend on our home from what I earned because one never knows what may happen. Then I remember what would my mother do? It may sound a bit mean but I have got to be on my own. I have enough faith to believe what is to be will be so if we are meant to marry soon we will. I wish I could explain myself better but you know I am very mixed up myself.

Another thing that is worrying me now is Christmas. I was hoping you would be going to Germany for your Christmas holiday, but it does not look as though you will, so I'll have to bother about that. While I am on about Christmas what would you like for Xmas and don't you say nothing. I have also got you 10 cigarettes extra. I didn't take that money into Lloyds Bank until today. I hope they have not fetched the wireless back.

What shall we do on Saturday? If you ring me Friday let me know then. Don't you think it is about time you had an extra blanket on your bed, it is getting cold, getting isn't the word, it is cold. If I come on the bus you got on at Somerby then we can go to Oakham and if there isn't anything on the pictures we could catch the bus back to Pickwell. Then you could see if they had any shoes and a blanket.

Well darling I will have to say cheeri'O, it is 11.15.

All my love and kisses

Jean

P.S

I think the best thing would be for me to marry you tomorrow because then I would not have to write. Love and kisses

Jean

——.

Thursday

I will go to Melton, I will not see you Sunday so if you want to make another arrangement you will have time.

Jean

Aschersleben 18/11/48

My dear Hans

At last after five weeks we finally received your dear letter dated 4.11.48 – you have kept us waiting for so long. I thank you very much for your birthday wishes, which arrived on time, which made me really happy. Well, now I am a year older, and that's all. Horst really has done everything imaginable to make me enjoy myself. Now I have to tell you something really exciting, last week a postcard arrived from Mrs Halling, to my old address at Pfeilergraben, she didn't know my new address saying a letter had arrived for me. Sender Bruno Klein. You can imagine how shaken we were, and I immediately requested a copy of the letter to be sent by telegraph. It arrived after eight days, you can imagine the pleasure it gave me for my birthday. I immediately sent a telegram to Aunty Lina with Bruno's address and another one to Bruno with Aunt Lina's address. I am sure the joy has been amazing on both sides. If only we were to receive such a wonderful message about our dear papa!! Bruno is in the lower Rhine area, in the English zone, he is well, he had already tried everything to find us, and then he found our address in his old clothes from 1945, when we were in Prenzlau, fleeing. How strange god's ways are. It was through the Hallings that we located you, and now Bruno. Mrs Halling sends her best wishes, she asked if you were already married, she wishes you the best. Manfred got married in July, 20 years old, and he now has a daughter. Marga's husband died on July 13th, Vera does not have any children as yet, she works from morning to evening, and does not really know why, as the business does not belong to her husband. I had already told you about the hairdressing competition. Until now your letters have not been censored. These last weeks have been such a rush from one job to the next, I was so exhausted that I nearly fell over my own legs. On Sunday and Monday I have made syrup from seven hundredweight of beet, and in December another five hundredweight. At least we'll have something to spread onto our bread. But please do not ask about how much work was involved. I have lost another nine pounds. The prisoners of war are supposed to be released by the end of 1948. Let's hope so. I was never aware that on the birth certificate it said Joachim. I hope that does not cause any problems, otherwise you would have to send it again, with the alteration. How good that you have been given four weeks of holiday, at least first visit the Streeses. There's no point going to see Horst Gogolin, he is unwell and in Goettingen most of the time, but I had sent you the address in Weferlingen of Mrs Lehmann's sister. I am really sorry, but Christmas will not be possible for us, because Horst cannot get time off work. But maybe just after Christmas? Once you are at the Streeses you will have to send us a telegram to let us know when we should come. Now my dear

Hans, lots of love and kisses from your mum and your brother Horst. Best regards to Jean. Here's to a healthy Wiedersehen.

Aschersleben 21.11.48

My dear Hans

We thank you for your dear letter dated 9.11.48. Today is the Day of the Dead and I went to the cemetery with Mrs Ziemann and Mrs Rueckbrecht we have just come back. Many people were there visiting the graves of their loved-ones. If only we could decorate grandma's grave – there it lies so lonely and abandoned, the thought of it is so painful to me. For Aunty Lina The day of the Dead will not be so sad because she knows that Bruno is alive, I think of her all the time. What ishouls I do with the wool I have here for your jumper, I wanted to wait before starting to knit it until you were here, but all of that is now no longer relevant. Horstel is not doing too badly health-wise, but he cannot get rid of the cold, he's had it since we came here. If only we knew where to go, back home would be best. But who knows when this will become true? I still cannot understand why you have given up your job, especially now in winter. But you must know what you're doing. I am curious as to what is going to happen with your holiday, you will have to let us know from Gertrud's via a telegram. Might you be able to bring some spices? (cinnamon, cloves, nutmeg and pepper) Please do remain really well, and we shall soon see each other again, let us hope it all works out. I have written today to Mr Albinus, the road maintenance manager in Pyritz, he lives right near the border. He wanted to be helpful to us. Now my dear boy, lots of love and kisses from your mum and your brother Horst. Best wishes to Jean. Here's to a healthy Wiedersehen

Pickwell
Dec 2nd 1948

My dearest darling Jean

How are you today, sweetheart? I am fine and hope so from you, too. Today I received two letters from my mother. After being missing in Russia for 4 years my cousin turned up. My mother got a postcard from him coming from the British zone. He arrived there a year ago and since then tried to find relatives. 3 weeks ago he found between old papers my mother's old address and she got his card in spite of having moved to another town. My auntie will be glad to know her son is still alive. She lost her husband and two sons during the war. He's the only one that's left. She'll be happy now. My cousin told my mother that all the POWs from Russia will be released by the end of 1948. So she's hoping again. Well, I also hope for the best for her sake.

I think I have to buy a new lead and collar for Bonzo on Saturday. Today he came twice knocking at the door so I had to put him on a chain. I hope the nail will be strong enough to hold him.

Is everything alright for Saturday? I'll ring you 5.00pm tomorrow and find out. Well, my love I'll say goodnight and God bless you. Just be my good, girl and think of me if you can spare the time.

Loads of love and thousand kisses.

Eternally yours my darling

Hans.

PS My mother sends her greetings to you.

Love Hans

Pickwell

Dec 3rd 1948

My dearest darling Jean

I thank you so very, very much for the lovely letter I received this morning. Well, I can't tell you my chest measurements, you better have a look yourself tomorrow. Don't you think a light brown colour with white stripes will be the best? We can talk about it tomorrow.

Can you also get mad with your dog? It seems as if I am not

the only one. Never mind, you'll get used to. I can only say that poor little dog.

Well, darling, now to our big problem. Didn't I tell you that your mother won't ask you to bring me home because she doesn't know how we stand. Please sweetheart, don't get worried when I ask you, but you're the one who has to tell your mother. I can only think and guess what my mother would do. She certainly would wait till I would tell her and I am very sure your mother is waiting for you. She would've told you if she doesn't like it.

Don't tell me you haven't the courage to ask me. Look, darling, if there's no one else you think you can speak to I want you to know that I am always there. Let nothing be between us and I am sure we shall be very happy all our life. A perfect understanding is the fundament of our future life. I am always thinking how it would be. Just the two of us, happy and satisfied with everything. If you would tell me that we'll get married as soon as I've found a place, believe me I would try hard. Of course we would've to live on my money, that's what I also think. I'll work hard so we could save some of it and get our home nice and comfortable as I like it. If you want to continue work for some time, alright. You know I don't like it very much, but agree that it'll give us a bit of a start.

And I also know we'll get cracking because it's for us and our family. Then one day we will be able to say we did it ourselves! It was a bit hard but we did it! So be brave and show that you have plenty of courage.

And now about Christmas. It looks as if there's nothing about going home and I don't want you to bother about me. I'll have to be alright and spend Xmas here in one of our stables. Herbert will be away, but Helmut will probably be here. If he should go away I'll just be on my own, that's all. So don't worry about me.

We can see about those shoes tomorrow. I hope they've got some in at the shop. Do you really think it's necessary to have an extra blanket. It's not very cold yet but, in fact, it is very nice of you to think of it.

Well, my love it's getting late. I was listening to the film play, 'Call Northside 777.' It was very nice. Did you listen to it?

Now it's time to go to bed. Just be my best girl and think of me. I am longing for tomorrow to see you.

Goodnight and God bless you always.

Loads of love and kisses

Forever yours, Hans

PS Marry me tomorrow and you don't have to write any more.

Love Hans

Aschersleben 28.11.48

My dear Hans

I am sending you many dear Sunday greetings, it is our 10th wedding anniversary and secretly I still hoped that papa would be with us, but unfortunately just as before, we are still alone! How very different I had imagined our life to be 10 years ago. The last years have been so full of sadness and worries, if only everything could turn out well in the end. Where might our dear papa spend this day? We had a letter from Gertrud, she said you confirmed that you would spend the holiday with them. She has now invited both of us cordially to spend the holiday with you. We are so pleased about it but we can hardly expect them to put up with us, as we cannot bring much food, It will take another few weeks, for us to save, because it will cost 400 Mark, and we haven't got that amount together, and some of it has to cover our stay there as well. Pity you can't bring Jean along, we would have so liked to meet her. Next Sunday I will be making syrup, not here at home, but at the butchers near us. Five hundredweight of beet makes one hundredweight of syrup, we have to pay 25 Mark for the use of the venue and the equipment, plus hand over five pounds of syrup, but it means I don't have all the stress with it. For some time now we have had more trouble with our landlord, his envy drives me mad. But I have given him a piece of his mind. For a few days my heart has been giving me trouble, as well as rheumatism. We should be going to collect more wood, but I cannot manage it. Now my dear Hans please stay well, and here's to a speedy Wiedersehen. Lots of love and kisses from your mum and your brother Horst

Papa and Mutti

Pickwell
Dec 4$^{\underline{th}}$ 1948

My darling

66

How are you this morning sweetheart? Still tired? I hope your mother wasn't annoyed with you on a lovely Sunday morning like today for I bet you didn't get up early today. My alarm was set for 6.45, but I, of course, didn't hear a sound. At 7.15 somebody knocked at the door, shouting for me. It was Margarete and she'd been waiting already for 10 minutes. I went to bed rather late last night, 12.15 it was. Helmut came back in a taxi from Lester at 11.30 and told me he's missed the last bus: Herbert didn't turn up at all. I think he stayed at Jean's place. I've just peeled potatoes, finished our chicken soup and put the hen in the oven, A smashing dinner for the two of us. It would be nice if you're here now and help me eating the chicken. Well, we'll see about that after Christmas. Be sure I'll find a place for us. We'll be happy and I want to tell you that I love you very much, much more than anybody else.

Did you get home alright last night? Helmut told me when he came back that on the way from Leicester to Melton was densest fog and two buses lay in the ditch. Then I was so glad we didn't stay in Melton and you took the bus from Somerby. Darling, I don't know what I would do if anything would happen to you. I daren't think of it. Be always careful wherever you go.

It was pretty cold when we did our round this morning and now it's lovely. The sun is shining and it really is a shame I have to work and you aren't coming. It's the ideal weather for a nice walk. I am not going anywhere tonight. It'll be 5.00 when I have finished shutting up and I don't think then I'll feel like going away. Helmut is gone out to see if he can shoot a rabbit. I hope he's lucky and brings something.

Well, honey, I'll finish for now. The potatoes are boiling, that means dinner is almost ready. I'll write a few more lines when I have finished work tonight. All my love and kisses to you.

8.45pm

Well, my love here I am again. You should've been here just

now. A really lovely picture. A tiny little mouse came from underneath the stove, sat in front of it and looked at me as if it was asking for something to eat. I moved and off it went. I would've love to see you jumping at it.

I hope you're back from your tea party by now, otherwise I've had it for Wednesday morning. Anyway I keep my fingers crossed. Did you have a nice time. I bet much more comfortable than here and the tea not tasting like coffee.

The fire was almost out when I came back so I've started it again and it gets a bit warm now. Don't get home too late and remember all the early nights you promised yourself!!! Except Saturdays!!

Helmut went away this afternoon and I bet he's coming back tight. I am glad I haven't got that habit.

Are you also listening to 'Variety Bandbox' It's nothing decent up to now.

Well, my sweetheart, I'll say goodnight and God bless you. Just be good and think of me.

Loads of love and thousand kisses

Eternally yours

Hans.

92 Wharf St

December 6th

My darling

Darling you will never guess what, I have lost that piece of black cotton you measured yourself with. I took it out of the powder puff and put it in a safe place, but you know what my memory is. So could you please do it again not over your mac, and jersey. I don't want to knit it too big. I told you that I had a pattern for a pullover in 4 ply wool. I went to 2 or 3 shops this dinner and I could not get any, there was some, but it was awful stuff. I will see what I can do tomorrow, then if I can't get any I will have to get 3 ply, but as you may know 4 ply knits up quicker.

Well darling you were right I didn't get up very early Sunday morning. It was about 9.45 I was going to wash my woolly dress, because it was such a nice day, but I thought I had better put my bicycle away before it goes rusty, I will probably need it a lot next year eh!!! I put Vaseline on it, I don't think it will hurt it.

I did not go to a tea party, I went out to tea. There is a difference between a party and going out to tea. Violet and I had quite a lot to talk about, we were very good friends before she married. She has two children one 3 1/2 and the other 3 so you can guess what a time she has. Her sister Iris lives with her and her husband and little girl 2. Both Iris and Violet kept telling 'you stay single, I wish I was.'

Then her other sister came with her 2 boys, the eldest, he's a tough one, fighting with all the other kids, you should have heard them. I didn't get home till gone 10.00, so I didn't listen to Variety Bandbox.

I have changed pens as you can tell and I find this one much easier to write with than the Rollball.

What was your chicken like? I hope you enjoyed it, I wish I had been there, but wait until we are married then you can cook one for me.

What do you do these evenings now you have finished the room. You ought to find yourself a hobby like making me a lamp stand, out of what I don't know.

Well, darling I will have to say goodnight and God Bless you.

All my love and kisses
Jean

Tuesday

I went to see if I could get another pattern, one with cable in it, but I shall have to have your chest measurements. If you are about 38" I can get a nice pattern, so please don't do it with your overcoat on.

Pickwell

Dec 6th 1948

My dearest darling Jean

How are you today, sweetheart? Fine I hope. I can't complain myself. Well, another day is over and the week began alright. This morning I started with egg packing, afterwards finished disinfectioning. In the afternoon I did some real farmwork. Muckcarting from the place where our horse - we use for feeding – lays. Tonight we have a lot of visitors. All eight Irishmen are here to listen to the boxing match. Can you imagine how crowded it is. They are sitting on buckets and it really looks lovely. I wonder who will win that fight.

I don't know yet if I shall be able to ring you on Friday night for I've to do the shutting up this week. It's impossible to get back before 5.15. Anyway I know that I am off this weekend. Will you come down here on Saturday afternoon?

I'll see if Helmut goes to Melton to take the watch, otherwise I shall have to go myself and meet you there. Anyway I'll let you know in good time.

Well, my love I'll say goodnight and God bless you. It's 8.55. Just be good and think of me.

All my love and kisses

Eternally yours, Hans.

92 Wharf St

8/12/48

My darling

I wasn't going to write while I was at work, but here I go. I thought I had better write now as I am going round to Dora's for tea so I would not be writing until Thursday night.

I asked Dora to come home with me last week, but yesterday she rang me up and asked me to go home with her as she was going to do her mother's hair with a home perm, I will take my knitting with me I have almost finished my cardigan. I am doing the band round the neck. I finished the jumper last night, all but the buttons.

I got a pair of stockings for Gertie this dinner time I will bring them on Saturday. Are you going to send them to her, I think you had better. About Saturday, I think you had better take your watch yourself. Ask Helmut where he took it. I could come like I did last week then go back to Pickwell. Then please may I catch the 8.40 from Pickwell?

I was going to get some nuts this lunchtime but I'll get them tomorrow. I thought I would get some now for Christmas, I will bring them on Saturday. Then you can keep them. Do you think it is possible? You need not bother to ring on Friday save your sixpence. If you think we will go to Melton first. I will see you there.

All my love

Jean

PS I had a letter from Bernhard yesterday. He is still OK

Pickwell

Dec 8th 1948

My dearest darling Jean

Thank you so very much for the letter. Just bad luck I didn't get one Tuesday morning. You're the lucky one again, getting one on Monday already. That's what I call proper service.

It's rather late tonight. I was feeding this afternoon so I was able to start shutting up as soon as we finished it. I was back here at 5.10 and Helmut and I decided to go to the pictures. 'The Bishops Wife' was on, but as you said, it wasn't too good, we went to the other one, called 'Cheyanne.' A cowboy picture. Lots of shooting. It wasn't to bad. On the way back I met Vera from Melton office. We had a good chat on the way. She was going home to Thorpe Satchville.

Have you finished your cardigan already, being in such a

hurry about the pullover (short sleeves)? I would've never guessed the thing you lost, because I remember you saying when you put it into the powder box 'I won't lose it.' Well I've put another piece of string in and I am really sorry to say we haven't got a ruler to measure the length. Please do it yourself. Don't tell me anything about 3 or 4 ply wool, because I've no idea what it means. You'd better keep your bike nicely. We'll do a lot of riding next year, just the two of us. I think it nice when one can stop for a picnic wherever he likes. You also like it, don't you?

If you happen to see Violet or Iris again tell them I am going to wring their necks. Fancy telling you to stay single. I am sure it's just talking in fact, they are surely glad they got married.

Our chicken was lovely. Alright it's a date. I'll cook the chicken for you when we're married with the greatest of pleasure. I am sorry I didn't write last night but I was too tired, I went to bed – don't be surprised – at 8.30. And so did Helmut.

Do you think I've really got no hobby? Well, these evenings I am writing to you – that's my best hobby – otherwise I am going to fresh my shorthand up again. Perhaps I can use it again one day. One never knows. You'd better pinch a typewriter at your place and bring it along so I can fresh typing up as well.

Now about Saturday. Will you please come down to Melton on the 2.00 bus and I'll meet you at the station. I have to have a haircut in spite of it being cold. Then I have to bring my watch down and buy a collar for Bonzo and a belt for myself. Well, my sweetheart it's 11 o'clock. I'll say goodnight and God bless you. Just be good and dream of our time.

Loads of love and kisses

Eternally yours, darling

Hans.

Pickwell
Dec 9th 1948

My dearest darling Jean

I was very disappointed this morning. No letter. Well, I shall have to wait till midday tomorrow. Wasn't it an awful day? And being out cleaning chicken houses gave me the rest. I really stuck to it till lunchtime. In the afternoon I stayed in and did some mending, And one good thing only another day shutting up. After the rain it was so slippy one does one step forward and two backward. I was glad to get back. Bonzo has had a good run. He likes to come along.

How are you today, sweetheart? Fine I hope. By now you'll have received my measure and I hope it's not more than 38 so you'll be able to get the pattern. I shall see on Saturday. Listen, darling, can you get a writing pad with small, narrow lines to do some shorthand?

Today, I got a letter from my mother. She said Gertrud invited her and Horst to come over to their place so we can spend the holidays together. She accepted, but hopes it'll be in a month to have enough to get the railway ticket. She also said it is a shame I am not bringing you along. My mother would like to meet you. She sends her kindest regards to you.

Well, darling, I'll say goodnight and God bless you. Just be good and think a bit of me, if you can spare the time.

Loads of love and kisses
Eternally yours, darling
Hans.

PS See you Saturday, 2.45 pm.

Love Hans

My darling

Thank you so very much for a lovely weekend. You may believe me or not, I certainly enjoyed the evening today. Both of us sitting in front of the fire and working. Now afterwards I am really glad I've got three socks done.

The clock just struck 9.00 when I arrived back at the stables. In time to listen to 'Variety Bandbox' It wasn't bad at all tonight.

You remember those two Christmas cards with something on about the silver Tea? They just came right for my mother and Gertie. I've got them ready tonight so they'll be there in time.

The two fellows aren't back yet. The water is boiling so Helmut will be able to have 'another' drink straight away.

As you advised, I'll bath my eye now and then go to bed. It'll be early tomorrow morning and another week of hard work ahead.

There's one more thing I want to tell you before I close. I love you very, very much, darling, much more than anyone else and be sure I always will do.

Goodnight now and God bless you.

Just be good and think of me.

Loads of love and thousand kisses

Eternally yours, my sweetheart

Hans.

92 Wharf St

December 10th

My darling

I thank you very much for your lovely letter I got just when I was going back to work after lunch.

I too had a lovely weekend, you made everything so nice for tea, I am sure it always will be like that. You will have to find some more socks to darn so I can get on with your pullover. I have done quite a lot tonight. So you will have it at Xmas if all goes well. Darling, wouldn't you rather have a shirt to go with your brown suit for Christmas than the pyjamas, but please yourself I don't mind, only I thought you needed a shirt to your brown suit.

I was going to write to your mother tonight. I have been so busy knitting I have left it too late. I also have to write to Muriel. I also have to get her a Christmas present. The dog has been trying all night to get on my knee and he has only just made it. I couldn't stand him crying while I was trying to write, he has made himself very comfortable and has gone to sleep.

We are having a Christmas party on Wednesday, but I am not going, at least I am not up to now. Lucy and I were going but Lucy will not be able to get back to Birstall and I don't particularly want to go. So Lucy and I are going to have our tea out then go to the pictures. Now darling about Christmas. I wish we could spend it together, but it isn't my house and I don't really know yet what my mother and I are doing. For the past years we have gone to my uncle next door. Betty wanted us to go round to her place, but I don't think my mother wants to go unless next door go. I would rather go round to Betty's, it is very dull next door, but darling I really would rather spend it with you in the stable.

Well darling it is now 11.30 and you know what trouble I have getting up in the morning. So cheeri-bye and I love you very much.

 All my love and kisses

        Jean

PS Miggy asked me where and when (time) Herbert was getting married. So could you find out and I will let her know.
Tuesday
Could you possibly be able to get me a chicken this weekend,

but don't worry if you can't. I have had a good idea. You know the feathers you get off the fowls, save them and then we could make a pillow. What do you think of that?

Tuesday afternoon

I am very annoyed. I have just been speaking to Vera at Melton and I think it is too bad of you to tell her you are to be married. It is now all over Melton office. It isn't the first time. So please don't.

Pickwell

Dec 14th 1948

My dearest, darling Jean,

I am very sorry for not writing last night, but I was so tired that I went to bed without listening to the boxing match and that surely means something. The work was not heavy, but tiring. All day long on the tractor carting stones for the gateway. Yesterday morning I got wet through, came back and changed, but unfortunately the same happened again just before midday. I really was surprised about myself not getting fed up with it, in fact I was in a very good mood. Am I improving?

Well, sweetheart, how are you today? Wasn't it a lovely conversation on the phone? Why are you so annoyed when anybody asks you about getting married? I think I understand you. There's nothing else than gossip at Melton office. Don't worry, darling, one day it will be real. It always makes me laugh when I ask you about meeting you at the office.

You know, honey, I am just joking to hear what you say. I don't know yet how I shall go on for Christmas. If you don't invite me home I shall be very lonely here 'being on my own!' After all Helmut is also going away to his friends in Leicester. Herbert of course will be with his wife – and I? Poor fellow has to sit here in our stables, his sweetheart miles away. Well, my love, think it over.

Wasn't it a lovely day today? I thought everything was

swimming along. When it stopped raining after breakfast I went out ditching. It didn't look too bad for a start, but when I found that the place, where I had to build the new ditch was an old gateway, I almost got a shock. Only stones for about 3 feet. Well I got it done after all but I feel my back. I'll sleep like never before.

About the weekend. Please come on the 2.15 and go straight in when you arrive here. You know where everything is, so please get the tea ready. Can you bring some cake from Leicester like we've had last Saturday? Just a few pieces for us two. I keep the fire going and hope the water will be boiling by the time you arrive. You know I'll hurry up as much as I can. The key is always in the door. By the way, if you like bottle coffee with milk, there's a bottle on the top shelf, the milk in the milk can. I would love some.

Tomorrow night Helmut and I are going to see 'You are made for me' I hope it's something decent.

Well, my darling, I'll follow the other two chaps now. It's only 9 o'clock. So just be my best, girl and think of me.

Goodnight and God bless you always.

   All my love and kisses

      Eternally yours, sweetheart

        Hans.

        Pickwell

        Dec 15th 1948

My dearest, darling Jean,

I am glad to hear you also enjoyed the weekend. Be sure I wouldn't miss the Saturday afternoons for anything in the world. It's so nice to see you happy and you are right, it'll always be like that.

By the way I've asked the foreman about a chicken for you and he said it will be alright. So don't be 'annoyed' if I have something to do when I come back from work Saturday afternoon. I'll get the chicken ready for you to take home. Sorry, but I haven't any more socks to darn.

I am also glad my pullover is making good progress. You are a dear trying to get it ready for Xmas. Do I deserve it? How small will my present look!!! Can't you think of anything else besides the powder box?

Well, now about pyjamas or shirt. I have thought it over and came to the conclusion that it had better be a shirt to go with the new suit. That's if you don't mind.

I wonder if you went to the xmas party after all or preferred a good picture. I guess it was the last one. It's getting late tonight. 11 O'clock. We (Helmut and I) went to the pictures and saw 'Night has a thousand eyes' with Edward G Robinson. It wasn't bad but I hope I am not dreaming about it tonight.

Well, my sweetheart, I'll say goodnight and God bless you. I shall see you tomorrow afternoon at 5.15. Just be good and think of me.

Loads of love and thousands of kisses,
Eternally yours
Hans

PS The chicken will be a 4lbs one to boil. He hasn't got a young one this week to roast

Love Hans

.

Pickwell
Dec 19th1948

My darling

Well, sweetheart, here I am back at home. It's just 9.00 gone. I bet you you're only got half of what I told you on the way, So here I go again. These are the last instructions for the next fortnight. One thing is clear. I'll be waiting for your call Friday night at 8.00. The number is Somerby 38.

Please, see what you can get this week. I don't think it's wise to leave everything till last week. If you can get an aluminium suitcase it, would be alright, because it certainly gets thrown about on the way, but remember the fairly big size. Make sure, to get the suitcase till Sunday. There are the shoes for my mother and my brother and also the stockings. 3 to 4 pairs.

Now about Christmas. I would like it much more to stay the night at your place than at the other one. I'll bring my ration book along on Sunday and when I go to Billesdon the following Friday I'll come and call at your place to collect it. After all I just wonder what's left in it. If Mrs Cooper takes more points than she ought to she's had it.

Can you suggest anything I could take along for Gertie's mother? I suppose I can't let her go without anything. I mean we are staying at her place.

On Saturday, Jan 1st. I shall have to go to Melton to the police station to have my registration card signed. Don't you think it's the best to finish work on Thursday night, 30th of December? I don't want to get to Billesdon too late in the day for I think most of the chaps will go on the last day.

Please, enquire if I've to Pay the £1 at Leicester Office or Billesdon Hostel. Also see about the form for the check. My military number is A 572859. You forgot the note yesterday. I thank you so much for coming again today. It finished the Sunday off nice.

'Variety Bandbox' was very nice tonight. There was a 12 year old girl playing a trumpet just lovely. I've never heard it better. Also the comedians were very good. I don't know if that word is right, but I hope you know what I mean.

You looked so excited when you sat down beside Miggy. What did she tell you? Anyway I hope the time passed away quicker. You'll be home by now. It's 10.10. None of the chaps is back yet. I'll have a bit to eat and go to bed.

Well, my darling, I'll say goodnight and God bless you. Remember I love you very much. Much more than anybody else in the world. So just be good and think of me.

Loads of love and thousand kisses

Eternally yours, sweetheart

Hans.

My dearest, darling Jean,

Well, the phone call was dead on time. Thank you very much for all the bother you've had.

We promised each other always to tell the truth so I'll be honest this time. It took quite a bit saying I don't mind you going to that funny place tomorrow night. Well, by the time you get this letter you'll be back. Can I help it being just a bit jealous? Thinking of somebody else holding you in his arms!! I love you so very much darling that even the thought of it hurts. Be a good girl and for heaven's sake take care of yourself. I shall count every minute till you ring me again to know you got home safe and sound. I was going to say something on the phone about last Saturday, but I didn't want to annoy you.

Thank you so very much for arranging for staying at your place. Could it be our big chance of getting things straightened out? Let's see how everything goes. I'll be in Leicester by 1.45 and at your place at 2 o'clock. I hope you'll be at home by then.

That suitcase for £2-16-0 will be alright. It has to be strong because it might get thrown about. Well, let's make it a cardigan for my mother and Gertie's mother and a blouse for Gertie. I just thought of something. I can't buy socks on Friday for you've got the coupons. Well the old ones will have to do.

It's 9.30 now and time for me to say goodnight. Once again be careful tomorrow. God bless you always. Be good and keep thinking of me.

Loads of love and kisses

Eternally yours, sweetheart

Hans.

Aschersleben 12.12.48

My dear Hans!

We thank you very much from your letter dated 22.11.48 - we have also not had any mail from you for three weeks. So you still do not know anything more about your holiday? Let us hope everything works out with our trip. At the moment everything is looking very difficult for our journey, but by then things might get better. Yesterday I made our last lot of syrup. Thank God this job is finished, it is not the most pleasant of jobs, but at least we have provided enough to put on our bread, even though it is a huge amount of work. I shall be helping Mrs Ziemann make syrup the following week, but then I shall be glad that there is a bit of peace. Being a cook, you will surely have had it easier. Horst has gone to an exhibition, he has submitted two entries, now before the holidays he is particularly busy. There are only 12 days before Christmas, and I really don't feel very much like it, if only we could have been together, but unfortunately we have had to do without so much for so long. Well, you are shooting rabbits, so we can come to lunch at yours? You have even got a dog? Will you be going to Jean's for Christmas? You won't have to work? Now my dear Hans, we are sending you and your Jean a very merry Christmas and all the best. Yesterday it was Thea's wedding, of course she cannot remain alone forever, it is six years since her husband died, and she is only 26 years old. Please let us have your news soon. Sending you our love and kisses - mum and your brother Horst. Regards to Jean

Pickwell
Dec 27th 1948

My dearest darling Jean

Well, my sweetheart, I can't tell you how thankful I am to you for the last two days you gave me. It was the best Christmas I ever spend. Wasn't it lovely coming down in the morning finding you there and being together with you all day. I can't think of anything nicer. Please, my love, let our dream become true very soon. As soon as I am back I'll get decent living accommodation for us and we'll start our own family life. Aren't you longing for it? Do you have enough courage now to tell your mother? Please, do so.

Will you please, thank your mother again for her hospitality. Everything was so nice and comfortable.

I arrived here at 7.25 just right to listen to "Pantomania". It was very good. What are you doing now? Doing a bit of your tablecloth? To be honest darling, I didn't want to go back tonight. Staying at your place spoilt me. Especially your bed.

Well, my love, I'll say goodnight and God bless you. Just be thinking of me when you go to bed and be good.

All my love and thousand kisses

Hans.

92 Wharf St

28.12.48

My dearest darling Hans

Well darling how has work gone down today. I have been very busy. I helped my mother with the washing this morning and ironed it tonight, I wrote to Iris this afternoon. That is one good job done.

I will ask for Friday off but I don't think I will come to Pickwell in the morning because I can get some of the things done. Then I'll come in the afternoon, or I could go to Melton and meet you there.

Did Helmut get my card, ask him, he probably would not like to say anything to you. I know they have some funny ideas in Germany about women eh!!! I meant to ask you if you would let me go to the dance without you after we are married but I can assure you never need be worried about me. I know what I am doing.

Well darling I do hope you have had a very happy Xmas even if you did have to work Christmas day.

I have to close now honey. I have to get some shut eye.

All my love

Jean

P.S. It seems ages since I wrote to you

Aschersleben 20.12.48

My dear Hans

Thank you very much for your dear letter dated 2.12.48, which we received the day before yesterday. So, our holiday in December is no longer on? We were hoping to be able to spend the end of the year together, let us hope it won't be too cold. Mr Albinius from Pyritz is expecting us, and as soon as I have more details from you I will let him know, we would be so happy if everything went according to our wishes. Horstel is out at work, he is hoping to earn as much money as possible, so we shall have enough money for our trip. Healthwise I am a little better. So you have postponed your wedding, wasn't it meant to be at the end of the year? We have not been getting on with our landlord for some weeks now, the arguments are terrible, as soon as he sees our stash of wood it is like a red rag to a bull to him. You work so very hard and then it is…. Life is tough enough and then you have some fool who can't keep the peace, I have put a lot of pressure on him, but eventually it gets on one's nerves. He lent us an old clock, so that we would at least know what the time is, but then he took it away from us again. If only we could buy an alarm clock, but there is nothing to buy here. With regards to your jumper I shall see what can be done. So that's why you changed your job. This afternoon we are invited to the Ziemann's birthday, but of course Horst cannot come be-

83

cause he is working. Now my dear Hans I wish you and Jean a very happy new year and all the best for you. I am sending you lots of love and kisses from your always thinking of you mum and your brother Horst. Here's to a speedy and healthy Wiedersehen

Aschersleben   Christmas   Eve

1948

My dear Hans

Thank you very much for your dear letter dated 9.12.48. Today is Christmas Eve, although we are not in a festive mood, as from one year to the next we have been hoping to be together for the next Christmas, but no luck, the two of us have to carry on wandering alone. At Christmas it feels particularly hard. Presumably you will spend Christmas at Jean's? If you get married I have a request which no doubt you can fulfil – please send us your wedding photo. Even there the cost of the photographs cannot be that expensive, as even here people are able to pay for it. Now my dear Hans I am sending you Horst's shoe size, it is between 43 and 44, depending on how they come. If it's a big 43 it will be enough. Horst would be so happy. Bruno has not replied, the letter I received five weeks ago was written on 30.8.48. I do not know if he is still there. I shall today write to the registration office, maybe he has moved? Aunt Lina is really waiting for mail from him. When will your holiday finally happen? We are very much looking forward to having that coffee. Such a pity that Jean cannot join us. Is it not possible to organise it? Now my dear Hans I shall end my letter.Stay well and many greetings to Jean from your mum, and lots of love and kisses to you from your ever thinking of you mum and your brother Horst. Here's to a speedy Wiedersehen.

Pickwell
Jan. 3rd 1949

My darling,

It's 8.30, only half an hour to go. I've got everything ready, just put my coat on and go. The headache is gone but still a funny feeling around the stomach.

Did you get home alright last night? I had a good wash when I came back and afterwards went to bed. I didn't hear Helmut coming home, it must have been late.

So, of course, I had to tell him off when he got up this morning. It looked to me as if he didn't take it too serious. I am very sorry I couldn't give the money back to you yesterday.

Well, darling, remember I shall be thinking of you every minute and be longing to get back to you. Don't say I am soft, but I love you so very much. Life is nothing without you. Please tell your mother whilst I am away.

I shall ring you from Melton. Cheerio, sweetheart and be good. Keep thinking of me

All my love and thousand kisses

Yours forever, darling

Hans.

Pickwell
Jan. 4th 1949

My dearest, darling Jean

As promised, here's the letter from Harwich. I have little time so it'll only be a short one.

The train was half an hour late in Melton and we arrived here at 7.45. Lorries transported us to the camp (3 miles from the station) where a warm "meal" was waiting for us. Army cooks are cooking, but if the soldiers here get the same food I feel sorry for them. I am not complaining because it's only for a day. Be sure if I had cooked stuff like that, they would've given me the sack straight away.

Well, after I've had my dinner last night, I went to bed straight away. (Headache). Breakfast this morning was from 6.30-7.30. At 8.30 we start going on the ship. It's leaving at 1.00 pm. The next letter will be from Germany. It's 8.10 now and I've to get myself ready. So I'll finish now.

Cheerio and be good. Take care of yourself and think of me.

All my love and thousand kisses

Forever yours, sweetheart

Hans,

P.S.

The hat I bought in Melton is smashing.

Love
Hans.

92 Wharf St

3.1.49.

My dearest darling Hans

This is the first letter I have written to you this year, in fact I think it is the first for sometime at least it seems ages. I suppose you're in bed or talking, it is now 10.30. I don't suppose the place where you are staying the night is much of a place. I hope tomorrow will be a warmer day otherwise you will be frozen. It is very cold tonight. I have been to the pictures to see "Life with father". It was very funny. I wish you could have seen it but still maybe you will be able to see it in Melton or Oakham, we'll have to go there one Saturday, to the pictures.

I am sitting on the mat in front of the fire and Freddy has curled up on my knee, it will be such a pity to disturb him, but I am afraid I will not be able to stay down here all night. Any minute now I am expecting my mother to call down to see what I am staying up for.

I picked Miggy up (what I mean by picked up, I wanted a number through the exchange), we had quite a good chin wagg. I think the fellow gave up hope of ever getting his call.

She's probably coming into the office about Otto's money sometime this week. She may also bring my toeless and heel less shoes with her. I hope she does although I know I will not be able to wear them until the summer.

Please darling don't worry about the money, even if Helmut never pays you back. There are a lot more things in the world to worry about than money or to fall out with someone about it, so long as you never get in debt it does not matter. And another thing darling, please <u>do not</u> carry a knife about with you with the intent to protect yourself. I think that is a very low thing for anyone to do. Above all keep out of trouble.

Tomorrow night I have promised to go to Dora's and (it is about time) take her Christmas present. I bought her some Yardley's hand lotion, but someone bought me a spray gloss for hair. I would prefer the hand lotion so I have decided to give Dora the spray gloss. I'm sure she would prefer that.

I have not made the parcel up yet. I intended to do that to-night but I will have to do it tomorrow. Someone told me that it took about 6 weeks to get there, in that case brother you have had it, but still after you have stayed the month they will need it.

Well my darling I must close now or I will not be able to get up in the morning.

Good night God Bless

<u>Thursday</u> 9.0

Well darling you should have arrived at your destination. I received your letter posted at Harwich Wednesday lunch time. I was very pleased with it until I got to the P.S. my only comment on that is don't you dare bring it back to England. I hope Mr Sanders did not see you in it. You have had it if you ever come out with me in it.

I will tell you what I have been doing so far. Tuesday night I went round to see Dora and took her a Christmas present (the spray gloss) she had washed her hair, so by taking her that I was just in time.

Wednesday night I was a bit browned off so I went to the pictures again. This time to see "A Foreign Affair" it was very funny. I really enjoyed it. I don't suppose I will go to the pictures again this week, there isn't anything else on worth seeing.

I have just cut myself a ham sandwich. It reminds me of Stathern. I haven't had any ham since then. Freddy has just come to see what I am eating. I have given him a bit but he hasn't eaten it. It has mustard on. Poor little thing.

I have had my office painted. I should say distempered. It looks very much better and cleaner. I took some polish and polished the switchboard, it didn't look like the same place when I had finished. I am getting used to the new girl Sheila. When I knew she was coming to be relief I was very pleased. I know all her domestic affairs. So far this week her husband hasn't hit her.

I was speaking to Miggy today and she was telling me they (her and Otto) have a chance of a cottage at Knossington 5/- per week. 2 rooms up and 2 down. She is going over on Saturday to see it. She won't be able to have it until April. I was talking to her again this afternoon and I think the supervisor caught her because another operator took the call.

Mary came in yesterday, that is the girl that had the accident on the motorcycle. She had heard from Iris and the thing she missed the most was a cup of tea. She was looking for a job in Paris. I think she will find that very difficult as she wants a clerical job.

While you are away I can catch up with my bits and bobs. And have a really good time looking after my face, hair and hands. So by the time you get back I should be beautiful. I have washed my hair tonight. I think next week I will go to the hairdressers to have it cut. Talking of cutting hair don't forget to have yours cut the English style please. I think it is much smarter and more manly.

I sent your parcel off yesterday and the man at the G.P.O said there wasn't any Express to Germany and that customs hold the parcels up for a fortnight before they are sent, because they have such a lot now. So it looks as though you have had it, this is what is in it. 2 tins of milk, 1 tin of luncheon meat, 3 bars of chocolate, 1 jelly and some toffees.

Well darling I think I have written enough otherwise it will cost me more than 3d to send it.

All my love and kisses

(have a good time) I would

Jean

View from the "Empire"

Aboard the "Empire"
<u>2500</u> tons
2.30 p.m.

Jan 4<u>th</u> 1949

My dearest, darling Jean

Here I am again. Excuse the handwriting, but there were gale warnings for all sea areas this morning and we are right in it. I've just been on deck for an hour because I couldn't see my fellows die. The sea is rolling heavy and so is our little ship. I am quite alright, good those trips to America. You would've a good laugh seeing all the corpses laying about. The fish got plenty to eat today. Heinz and Herbert went downstairs when we went aboard because it was warm there. I stayed on middle deck for the air is better here. When I came in I had a look down the staircase and it looks a mess. Later on I'll go down and see how they are. We should be in Hook of Holland at 8.00. That makes another 5 hours.

Well, sweetheart, one day we'll go together and see if it affects you. Cheerio for now. I'll try and get some sleep now and write a few more lines later on.

Thursday, Jan. 6th 1949.

Hello, sweety here I am at my temporary home. Do you mind me not writing before? We made it til 8 o'clock to Hook of Holland, got something to eat when we arrived and left by train at 1.30 a.m. for Münster. There we arrived at 8.00 a.m. got our release papers and our bonus checks cashed. A good thing I didn't send my check away. Otherwise I would've to wait now. We left Münster again at 3.00 in the afternoon on a fast train to Hamburg where we arrived at 8.30 and left 9.30 for Lübeck. In Lübeck I had to wait from 11.30 to 5.10 a.m. so after all I arrived here at 6.40 this morning, dead tired. Everybody was still sleeping, of course, but I found the described house and started shouting. You should've seen their faces. They didn't expect me so early.

I had something to eat first and then went to bed. Believe it or not but I didn't wake up till 4.00.

Please, darling don't forget to send the parcel by express because otherwise it takes 4 weeks. Quickest are 1 lbs parcels. They only take 3-4 days.

Well, my love, how are you today? I hope fine. Last night my ankles began to swell for I've had my shoes on almost all the time.

I just made it from the station down here. One of my fellows gave me a hand in getting my suitcases and myself to the train in Lübeck. I can walk alright now, but it's still swollen. Tomorrow I shall have to go to get my ration book and cash the American check. One can buy quite a few good things in the shops, but people haven't got enough money to afford it. We look like millionaires with hundreds of marks in the pocket. I'll give the rest of my money to my mother before I leave on Feb. 4<u>th</u>. She wrote today saying she'll probably be here next Sunday. Believe me I wouldn't have taken all the bother if there was no chance to see my mother. I really got fed up sitting in trains for days. I shall be glad when I get back and be with you again. I'll be thinking of you all the time.

Well, my sweetheart, I'll say cheerio now. God bless you. Please, give my kindest regards to your mother. Look after yourself well.

All my love and kisses

 Eternally yours, darling

Hans.

<u>P.S.</u> If you want me to get your letters quick send them by airmail. It only takes one day then.

Love Hans.

91

Frau Stresse and her daughter Gertrud at Woltersmühlen Jan '49

Hans Klawitter
Woltersmühlen
Post Pönitz/Ostholstein
Germany, British Zone
Jan. 8th 1949

My dearest, darling Jean

By now you'll have received my last two letters I hope. I've settled down, in fact, was shopping already today in the next town, just as big as Melton. After I've had a good look round I can only say prices are impossible. I cashed my American check also today and now really feel like a millionaire with all those 100 Mark-notes in my pocket. In all, I've got 600 Mark in cash. And you can imagine how much that is when I tell you that Gertrud and her mother only get 24 Mark a week. And that just keeps them going. They, of course, can't afford anything else besides their rations. When I went to town I saw some tinned fruit and fresh fruit and took some along. They didn't believe their eyes when I unpacked. You know I also like a bit of a change in food.

I also found out there's a possibility to get cloth, like frocks, skirts and blouses, in the shops. Also cotton, wool, thread. If my mother wants anything I'll be able to buy her a few things. Then after the four weeks are over I shall see how much money there's left. There'll be something for you anyway.

It's 5.30 p.m. here, 4.30 at your place. As usually we would sit in Pickwell now, having tea together. Well, darling I am so much longing for you. Everything would be perfect if you're with me. Won't you come over? You know where to find me. Ask for the "spiv" and everybody will tell you. One thing will probably satisfy you to hear. Gertrud liked my white scarf very much so as you didn't, I'll leave it here when I go. I bet that does suit you very much.

Tomorrow is Sunday, and I hope my mother and my brother will arrive. I am really longing to see them. I shall be looking out for every train that comes in.

Well, my love it's almost time for dinner so I have to clear the table. I'll write again tomorrow.

Just be good and remember how much I love you. God bless you and your mother. Please give her my kindest regards.

> All my love and kisses
> Eternally yours, sweetheart
> Hans.

The Stresse's house Woltersmühlen

Woltersmühlen

Germany

British Zone

Jan. 10th 1949

My dearest, darling Jean,

I've just posted a letter for you this afternoon and as there's some time to spare, I'll write a few more lines.

You'll know by now, that my mother and brother have arrived here safe last night at 7.30. We're just having our tea when I heard the well known voices in front of the house and a few minutes later they came up here. You should've seen our faces! Both have changed very much. My brother stands up 6 feet 6 inches in his shoes. That means I've to look up to him. Anyway he's quite the gentleman. Of course, my mother wanted to have a look at your photos and the first thing she asked me for was the one I had in the frame. Do you mind if I let her have it. She said I shall have you back shortly and she at least wants a nice photo. So I gave it to her.

You can imagine how much there is to talk about. I hope we'll get everything talked over during the time she's here. This afternoon we went for a good walk round for a couple of hours and after all were glad to get back into the warm room for it was rather cold later on. We made it just in time before dropping dead.

I looked out for the postman today but nothing for me. Please, sweetheart send the letters by airmail. It only takes 1 to 2 days then.

How is life treating you, darling? I hope not too bad. I am alright here but believe me I am longing to see you again. The time almost flies and a good thing it does. Life is rather dull here. No wireless here and you can imagine what that means to me.

There's a lovely sea quite near. Isn't it a shame it isn't summer now. I would've had a nice swim and you could come and join me. On Thursday or Saturday, Gertrud, her boyfriend and I are going to see the "Faust" in Lübeck. I'll certainly enjoy that.

Well, my darling, it's time now to go to bed. Perhaps you are asleep by now. So goodnight and God bless you. Give my kindest regards to your dear mother.

> All my love and kisses
> Eternally yours
> Hans.

P.S. Many greetings from my mother and Horst

> 92 Wharf St
> 11.1.49

My dearest darling Hans

I received your first letter today (Tuesday) It took 5 days to get here which I don't think is bad going. You too should have had one today. I posted it Friday so maybe it will be tomorrow.

Well darling what have you been doing with yourself while you have been there. Last weekend seemed a very long one but there are only 3 more to go. I stayed in Saturday evening. I went into the town in the afternoon and I bought a coat, a pale blue one. I think it is very nice. By the way it is the new look.

Since last Saturday I have not felt too well. I think I must have eaten something that didn't agree with me because I have been feeling sick after everything I have eaten, but this evening I have almost recovered. I will feel much better still after this weekend, at least I will be relieved.

Last Sunday I went with Alice and Bernie (that is the Irish girl I went with to the R.A.F. dance) to see Oscar Robin and his band. It wasn't bad but it could have been better. I don't care for Jazz dance bands very much, but last Friday I rang Alice to ask her to come to tea but she said they (her and Bernie) were going to see this band and would I like to go to her home for tea then go to with them. I could not do any other but go. Her brother had sent some books from America. You should have seen one called "the American Home" there were some beautiful things in it, just what I would like and you would have to like, if I ever have the chance to get them.

Wednesday.

I am writing this at the office, only I am not on the switchboard so until the new girl gets in a mess I can write a few lines to you. I didn't tell what I have been doing since Sunday did I. Well, Monday I did not go anywhere, I was in bed at 8.30, but it didn't make any difference to me getting to work on time, it has been 9.8 every morning. I made a new year resolution not to be late in the new year, but the first morning I broke it and I did not seem to be able to be any earlier or later than 9.8. Tuesday I went to see "The fallen Idol", it was very good. I had to wait ¾ of an hour before I got in. I was getting fed up with waiting but I kept waiting. I did not like to come out the queue in case they went in the minute I moved so I kept on waiting half frozen.

Thursday

Another day gone and I have not posted this one yet anyway I'll post it today if this is all I write. Well you will not have this posted today I was finishing it at work, but I had to put it away because I was expecting Mr Hafeldine to come down to tell me off for being late this morning. I got caught, Mr Hafeldine wanted a call and I did not arrive until 9.10 but he never said anything. Then this afternoon I was 10 minutes late again and Mr Fleming was calling. He reported me to Mr Bembridge but I got away with that. I now hope that Mr Fleming and Mr Hafeldine do not get together and find out that I have been 20 minutes late in one day. I will have to be early tomorrow even if I have to go to work in my nighty and curlers.

Wednesday
evening

I went to see my aunty at Birstall. I have not been for a few weeks. I did not intend to go last night. I rang my cousin to say I could not go but before I could get it out she told me they were expecting me. So I could not do other than go.

I saw Mr Maclean one day this week. I think it was Tuesday. I was just going upstairs to fill the kettle and he was looking for the Supplies Dept.

How has the weather been with you? Here it has been beautiful cold but dry. I have been wishing I was in Switzerland. There have been some photographs of people on holiday there in the papers and it makes me really envious. I would love to go there. not this month maybe but I will go sometime, so brother you had better get yourself a good job (like laying eggs) then we can go.

I have invited Alice and Bernie to come to tea this Sunday so I shall have a busy day. I will not have time to be lonely.

You did not tell me in your letter what sort of a place

Woltersmuhlen was like. I do not mean how many people there are. Have you been swimming or has it been too cold for you.

Your mother would have arrived by now so give her my regards and to your brother, wish them a very happy new year from me please, and to Gertie and her mother. Please darling be thoughtful in the house and help them as much as you can. I know you would but I just wanted to remind you. I was going to tell you off for waking them up at 6.0 in the morning, but being as you had not been to bed for 2 nights I forgave you but please don't wake me at 6.0 ! ! !

Well darling I will close now so goodnight God bless
All my love and kisses
Jean

P.S.
The Major asked me to go to a Saltby dance, don't worry, I'm not going. I told Mr Chandler to tell him it would be too late when I arrived home. I really hate having to tell him that because I feel so very sorry for the Major.

> Woltersmühlen
> Germany, British
> Zone
> Jan. 11th 1949

My dearest, darling Jean,

I thank you so very much for your lovely long letter I received this morning. You're right, sweety, it seems ages since you wrote last.

Don't be surprised, when you wrote your letter on Monday, Jan. 3rd I was in bed already. In fact I was the first in our hut that went to bed. It wasn't much of a place. No fire and the night was cold. Well, I didn't mind at all.

Have you got your nice shoes yet? I mean the toe and heelless ones?

Well, sweetheart, you know what I think about the money I

lend to Helmut. I've told him before I left to save it up whilst I am away. He promised to and I shall see when I get back. Heaven help him to have it ready when I come.

Don't worry about me carrying a knife about with me. Remember what I promised you and you also know I shall keep it. I've got a big knife here but only for the purpose of cutting bread.

If parcels really take 6 weeks well, then I've had it and with me my mother and my brother. I only wanted them to have some of the sweets. Still, it can't be helped. I shall get sweets when I come back, shan't I?

What was the matter with the P.S. in my first letter? The remarks about my hat? Don't you worry, love, everything will be alright when I come back. The hat looks really smashing. My brother is really crazy about it and everybody tells me it suits me best.

My mother thanks you ever so much for choosing those shoes. She likes them very much and they fit nicely. My brother, however, wants two sizes bigger. I'll try to change them here.

See, Miggy and Otto were ~~looky~~ lucky in getting a cottage. I hope we'll be able to get one after my return.

Well, ducky, look after your face, hair and hands whilst I am away and be a beauty when I come back. You know how I like you best. Just as you are. One day this week all of us shall go to see the "Faust". We've changed our mind for we want to do some shopping as well.

Well, sweetheart, it's time to go to bed now. So just be good and think of me. I am with you all the time. Take care of yourself, darling. Give my kindest regards to your dear mother.

> All my love and kisses
> Forever yours, sweety
> Hans.

Woltersmühlen
Germany, British
Zone
Jan. 13th 1949

My dearest darling Jean,

What's the matter sweetheart. You aren't ill I hope. No letters yesterday and today! Well, I am so far away and nothing else to do than waiting. Please, darling, don't let me wait too long. Send the letters by airmail.

Every day is the same. Today we went to the next village to look for smoked fish, but couldn't get any. It makes quite a change in our meals because we get only 2 ounces of meat for ten days. We've tried a few times to get my brother's shoes changed, but up to now we couldn't find anything near to it. If you could only see the shoes one can get in the shops. Terrible prices and the material is awful. I don't think the soles would stand a fortnight's English weather. A cup of coffee we had on the train, for instance, costs 5 times as much as during the war. I almost got a shock. One gets used to the prices as long as there are lots of money.

Yesterday, my mother and I went to Eutin, that's a small town 10 miles away and did some shopping. I bought her so-called rubber overshoes and a lot of small things. I also got a lovely present. I'll show you when I come back. The first thing my mother did, she congratulated me to our engagement. She seemed very pleased with everything.

One of the next days we shall go to the photographer, all three of us. It'll be a nice souvenir after these long years. The only thing my mother was annoyed about, is that we haven't sent her a photo of us yet. That's the reason she took your photo out of the frame for. After all I had to promise to send her one as soon as possible.

Please, give my kindest regards to your dear mother.

Be good, my love and think of me. My thoughts are with you

all the time and believe me I am so much longing for you. I love you very, very much.

All my love and kisses

Forever and only yours

Hans.

Horst, Hans and Mutti in Woltersmülhen

92 Wharf St

16.1.49

My dearest darling Hans

I thank you so much for your letter No. 3. I have not had No. 2 yet, unless the post card was No 2. This is my 3rd letter to you, maybe you have not had as many letters from me but at least I have been sending 6 pages not 1 ½ like you.

I have not got comfortable yet at the moment. I am lying on the floor on my tummy. I want to be near the fire. Poor little Freddy is keeping me company.

Now for what I have been doing. I believe I told you I went to Birstall last Wednesday, I am going out on Sunday. Then my auntie, cousin and I are going to have a Xmas party, they have been away all Christmas and have not cut their cake so they said 'we'll have a party on our own.'

Thursday I stayed in and I did not do anything. By the way you have had your socks for the time being, I have offered to knit something for Betty. I am not very thrilled with the idea, but she has not started to knit anything herself yet and she expects the baby next month. So I hadn't really any choice but to offer. I want to have a go at some toys. I have been thinking maybe I could do the socks at work. I can't very well sit knitting baby's things in the office. What would Lucy say?

Friday night I went to the pictures to see "The Miracle of the Bells", it wasn't very good. I have not heard anymore about being late. Friday morning I was on time but Sheila wasn't, it does not matter as long as one of us is on time. That will have to be me because Sheila has her baby to look after. The reason she has to come out to work is that they are in furnished rooms and are paying £3 a week, she has tried to get somewhere cheaper but that seems impossible.

Saturday, when I came home at dinner time, I did not go out

again. I wrote a letter to that Harry Johns and started one to Bernhard. I have to finish that sometime. Then I did one flower on the tablecloth I am working on. When I have written this I will get it out again.

Alice and Bernie are coming to tea. I had to nip round to Betty's this lunchtime. I was annoyed. I was down on my hands and knees when someone rang up asking us to tell Betty not to go to Mrs Searle's (that is Cyril's mother). I did not stay long, it gave Fred a walk. You should see him now. He is asleep on my knee. I was thinking about having him put to sleep for good last week but think it is as far as I get. His hair does not seem to be growing at all, I'll wait a little longer to see. I really don't think it will grow but I hate having to part with him. When I have another dog it will still be a dachshund. I am going to breed dogs one day. I hope you like the idea. You can look after the kids and I'll look after the dogs eh!!!

Well my darling are you having a good time. You have not said much about what you have been doing, what is a matter daren't you tell me, don't you think I would understand?

Was the picture on the postcard near where you are? If not send me one of where you are.

Well darling I will close now. I don't mind you being away so long as I know you still love me.

All my love and kisses

Jean

Woltersmühlen
Germany, British
Zone
Jan 16th 1949

My dearest darling Jean,

I am really disappointed, sweetheart. Only one letter within the last ten days. Are you so busy?

I am getting bored with sitting here and believe me, darling, it's you I am missing. If I could only be with you. You may remember what I told you the last few days before I left. I shall be longing to get back to you. Nothing else can interest me. Shall I tell you again that I love you very, very much? You know it, don't you?

Well, darling, how are you today? Fine, I hope. Another Sunday is over another day. There was nothing decent the last two weekends. A dance at the pub of the next village, but you know that's nothing for me. So, of course, everybody went and I sat here reading a good book and believe me I enjoyed myself too. I can't think of anything better than sitting in front of the fireplace – with you – next week, my mother, my brother and I shall go to Lübeck and do a bit of shopping. They are leaving here next Sunday. Horst has to start work again on the 24th.

You would have a good laugh seeing everybody looking at the letter trying to read it. It looks as if I shall never finish the letter.

This afternoon Gertude's boyfriend asked me to visit him. I enjoyed it because he's got a wireless and I was able to listen to the BBC 'Ituna' was on.

If we are together here another few weeks I shall come back without any photos. My mother and my brother would like to take them all.

Please give my kindest regards to your dear mother. My mother and brother also send their regards.

Goodnight and God bless you always.

All my love and kisses

Forever yours, darling

Hans.

Hans with Gertrude Stresse

Woltersmühlen
Germany, British
Zone
Jan 17th 1949

My dearest darling Jean,

I thank you so very, very much for your lovely long letter I received today. I really was longing for it.

There is nothing much I could do with myself. Every day is the same. I get up at 9.30 in the morning by that time you're working already for <u>20</u> minutes. I am a lazy fellow, am I not? Today was wash day so there was something to do for me. I had to get the dinner ready for the five of us. After all, everybody was satisfied and nothing left. Believe me, darling, the last two weekends were just as lonely for me as they were for you. By now only 2 more to go and I am glad.

So you bought a new coat. Pale blue should look very nice thinking of your blue costume. Don't worry, I'll also like it. Even if it is the new look. If it is too long, I'll take a pair of scissors and cut a bit off. Don't you think that's the best?

I am sorry to hear you weren't well. Take my advice, don't eat anything that doesn't agree with you. It looks as if you miss our nice tea on Saturday afternoons. I do, anyway.

So you've decided to furnish our home in 'American style.' Well, we'll have to see about that. I know one can get beautiful things there and also rather expensive ones.

If you happen to ask me to come to tea, be sure, sister, I won't refuse and stay away.

You are a good girl, aren't you? Going to bed at 8.30 I mean.

It takes me a bit longer to finish our evening conversation. There are lots to talk about as you can imagine.

What did you say? You're late every morning? I am surprised. How can that happen to you? Well, I think I'll get you out of bed in time to catch a bus or get to the office in time. Your new years resolution was unsuccessful, wasn't it? Poor girl, waiting for ¾ of an hour to get into the picture house. Waiting would've been much more comfortable if I'd been with you.

The weather here hasn't been nice at all. I only hope it'll be better tomorrow for we are going to the photographer.

Now about you being envious about other people in Switzerland. Look, sweetheart, one day we'll be off well enough to spend our holidays in nice places. Then let other people be envious. I am really sorry, but I don't know how to lay eggs and I don't think I'll ever learn it.

Now, what sort of a place is Woltersmühlen. I told you that Gertie wrote in her last letter how to get to her place. Well, it was dark when I arrived here. I asked at the railway station for the way to the village. I had to cross a farmyard, then 10 minutes walk as I was told. It took me twice the time, however I found a few houses. I really expected a big village, but there are only 6 houses altogether. The trains go by, but don't stop, because the place is too small. We usually say 50 people ~~leaving~~ living here, 49 of them are thieves. Can you guess who the good one is?

I haven't been swimming yet, it really is too cold, though there's a lake right in front of the village. I've given ~~you~~ your regards to all of them and they all send their regards to you. Look, sweetheart, it's very good of you to remind me of being helpful in the house. Be sure I do everything I can.

Alright, tell me off for waking them up at 6.00am. It'll be just the same when I come back. 2 nights without sleep in the least. And you wouldn't open the door when I knock so early? Don't be so rude with me. What if I arrive in Leicester early in the morning? Shall I wait till 8 o'clock, till you get up? Well, sweety, I don't know yet when I am arriving.

A good thing you didn't go to the dance in Saltby. I know you can take care of yourself, but it's a strange lot there.

Well, my love, I'll say goodnight and God bless you. Think, it is only 2 more weekends to go till I see you again. Cross your fingers and time will fly.

Please, give my best regards to your dear mother. Be good and take care of yourself. I'll do it for you when I come back.

All my love and kisses

Forever yours, darling

Hans.

P.S. The parcel hasn't arrived yet. My brother doesn't want to go before it arrives. He likes chocolate very much.

Love Hans.

92 Wharf St

18.1.49

My dearest darling Hans

I thank you so very much for your letters, I will send this one airmail if I have enough money. I am nearly stoney. Well not actually, you see I have started a new ~~thing~~ system this year, I have a book and put down everything I spend, I start the week with so much, it is only ~~Wednesday~~ Tuesday and I have spent more than I allowed myself, but I will have to borrow off next week to buy an air mail stamp. I do this so I can get into the habit so I will know where I am when I'm married.

I have brought some shoes today, wait till you see them, as I stand about 6 foot in them, I think they are lovely navy blue. They make my legs look oh! You will have to have a pair of stilts to keep up with me.

I have just got myself some bread and cheese and put my milk on to heat, when I have had that I'm ready for bed.

I got the dog licence today, about time isn't it? The post office put on yours, Johannas Klavitter. I did not know whether the Johannas is right, but I spelt the Klawitter out to her and she has still put it wrong, but that will not matter.

I saw Helmut yesterday when he was passing by the showroom. He had been to Billesdon to get his release papers. I asked about Bonzo and he's fine, I think he said he lets him run loose now, anyway he hasn't been in any trouble yet.

You know how I hate people that belong to me coming into the office. I always look at it this way, if I owned a place and had people working for me, I would not want them to have visitors in and out, so I do the same thing. It is different when people come in to see me that talk to me on the phone, they are nothing to do with me. So please do not keep asking to come in like you did before, when you used to come into Leicester.

I have got Fred a licence so you know I have changed my mind. I have started to try and keep him away from the fire and give him some tablets. I went up the street to get some shoe cleaner (for Boots), I took Fred with me. A man came in and he told me what to get to cure him. I will see how the tablets go on and if that isn't any good I'll try what he says.

I'm having 26th and the 27th January off, I sent my leave form in today. I don't think I will go anywhere, we've quite a bit of washing to do so that is what will happen Wednesday morning, and sometime I will have a good look round the shops.

Well darling I will say cheeri'O. Be good

All my love and kisses

Jean

.

PS Give my kind regards to your mother and brother and the rest of the household.

92 Wharf St

19.1.49

My dearest darling Hans

Well, darling, how is your holiday going? If the weather has been as good as it is here you will be O.K. (sorry, alright).

Connie Goodman came yesterday to see me. They moved to Saxelby about a fortnight ago. The living accommodation is very much better than at Enderley but they are miles from anywhere. It takes Connie 1 ½ hours to go and come back when she takes Roger to school. She has asked me to go over to see them. I still don't think she's told Leslie Green what Mr Saunders said she did. She may be bossy but I doubt whether she would do anybody any harm. When I get the chance I will ask her.

I believe I told you Sheila was in rooms paying £3 a week. The landlady gave her notice and they have to be out by the 29th January and at the moment it seems hopeless. She is worried to death because she doesn't know what on earth they are going to do. She has rung places but as soon as they know there is a baby, they've had it. If she does get somewhere and has to pay £3 she will still have to continue working and now when she leaves this place she won't have anyone to mind the baby, the landlady has been looking after it so far. This housing situation has got me down today, what with Lucy as well trying to find a place, then if that wasn't enough there is a girl in another office trying to get a house and she has been down with us all afternoon.

While I think of it, why do you always say 'I almost got a shock' either you had a shock or you did not, you can't almost have one.

Anyway I had a shock on Tuesday. Someone rang up and said 'Is that Jean, this is Iris' I replied 'Iris who?' I only knew one Iris and she wasn't in England, or so I thought. Iris had been back in England about a week. Don her husband has gone on tour. It would have cost too much for her to go too. She could have stayed in Paris and got a job, but she thought she may just as well come home and get a job here until he comes back to Paris. She is coming in to see me so I will have all the gen then.

The doctor came to examine Betty yesterday and she has got to go to the infirmary next Monday to have an x ray. The baby has not turned. My mother is very worried and will be glad when it is all over because she hasn't been well.

Well darling, goodnight and God Bless you.
All my love and kisses
Jean
PS I will send this AIR MAIL it is only 4 1/2d

Woltersmühlen
Germany, British
Zone
Jan 20th 1949

My dearest darling Jean,

I thank you so very much for your nice long letter I received yesterday morning. Please, forgive me for not answering at once. As I told you in my last letter we're going to see Goethe's 'Faust.' We left here at 10.30am rather early for me, because my mother was going to do some shopping and also visit a few people from our hometown who are living here now (Lübeck), Horst, Gertrud and I went to a friend of hers where we had our tea and afterwards got ourselves ready. It started at 8.00 and you know how it is with getting ready. It was just as if we were going to catch a bus. We came just, but not just in time. Now about the play. I don't know if you've ever read it. It was marvellous and I've never seen an actor playing his part better. I was only annoyed because we had to leave before it finished. Our train was at 11.00 and the play finished at 11.45. There was no possibility to stay in Lubeck otherwise I would have done so.

Do you remember I told you about one of my fellows from Saltby camp now living in Lübeck? Well, I went to look him up, but couldn't find him. Of course I knew his address but something is wrong somewhere. It really doesn't matter because I shall go again before I leave. Can you guess why I go again? I found something you'll love, but prices are going down in a week's time and the shopkeeper will keep it for me till I come again. Please, don't ask me what it is. I shan't tell you this time. So let it be a surprise. I only hope I'll get it through the customs alright. Doesn't matter if I have to pay tax for it. I have to get it through because I also love it. My brother liked my hat very much so I gave it to him and – bought another one yesterday. I also gave him my white shirt. Do you want me to get rid of my silk square? I thought of it because you didn't like it.

The food is not as good as it is over there. For breakfast there's only bread and syrup, I don't mind because people here have to live on the same. The shops are full of goods, but you should see the prices. People here, even if they work, can't afford buying them. A frock, for instance, costs £14.

Did you enjoy your Xmas party and nice cake? It was a bit late, but still the cake has to be eaten. It is a shame I wasn't there. I would love a piece now. Can't you save one for me?

A good idea to start knitting baby things. You'll have some practice for later. You know quite well I don't mind waiting for the socks.

Look, sweetheart, don't you think it really is the best to have Freddy put to sleep for good? You still have the possibility to buy another one. You can't take him out as he is now. OK you breed dogs one day and I look after the kids! Wouldn't it be nice when I come home from work at night and ask you 'any baby things to wash?'

Now something else. You know darling that I tell you every-thing I do. Why did you say, 'daren't you tell me?' Was there ever anything I didn't tell you? No! Most of the time I am here at home. You know I don't like it very much going out, except seeing you. I told you about my shopping with my mother. Yesterday we went to Lübeck and last Tuesday we went to the photographer. That's all I've done up to now. Horst usually goes shopping in the morning whilst I help with the dinner. In the afternoon I read a book, write to you or talk with my mother. Maybe you can imagine how much we have to talk about. So goes on day after the other. Fortnight tomorrow is my day for leaving here. I have to be in Munster on Feb 4th 16.00 hrs. Half the time is gone. My mother and brother are leaving next Monday. I'll be lonely then. Won't you come over?

Well, sweety, I'll say goodnight and God bless you always. Please, give my regards to your dear mother. And you be a good girl and think of me if you've got the time to spare.

My thoughts are always with and remember I love you very, very much.

So to you,
All my love and kisses
Forever yours, my darling
Hans.

Woltersmühlen
Germany, British
Zone
Jan 21st 1949

My dearest darling Jean,

Thanks very much for the letter I received this morning. My mother said,' look, he's got a letter again.

Believe me, sweety, I am surprised to hear you're broke. It's a very good idea to put down everything you spend and make the money last the week through. Don't worry, my love, we'll be alright. I know how to handle money and you, too, know I don't spend it for anything not necessary or worth it. When we put our money together we'll have enough to live on and save some to spend on our home. I also like it to be comfortable. When we sit down after a day's work we want to enjoy ourselves and be comfortable don't we? As I told you before, one day we'll look back and are able to say 'we've done it all on our own!' Don't you think that'll be very nice? A fortnight today I shall be in Münster again on my way to you. It'll be lots better for if I start here first thing in the morning (5.30) I shall make it in time. I've to be in Münster at 4.00pm. Not later otherwise I shall miss the transport and have no possibility to come back. So I thought of starting here on Thursday evening already. I don't want to miss the chance. Doesn't matter if I have to wait 2 days in Münster, but I would be very unhappy if I took the last train and missed the transport then.

Now about your shoes. How do you know I shan't like them? Let me see first and I don't think I shall say anything. Don't make yourself too big. Think what it looks like, you so tall and I am so small. It'll look smashing, don't you think? Well, I'll see it later on.

I don't think it'll make any difference on the dog licence as long as I have a licence at all. It's nice if Helmut let Bonzo run loose. He'll be alright then when I come back.

Look, sweetheart, I've told you before I understand quite well why you don't want me to come into your office. I was only joking when I said I'll come and see for myself what it looks like now. You needn't tell me off.

Well, my pullover is almost finished, my mother is putting the pieces together now. Only the collar is to be done. The pattern are almost the same as those you've knitted into the sleeveless one. It looks quite nice. She's also brought a sleeveless pullover for me, the only piece she's saved from our house. Our town is destroyed, not a single house left over. She told me everything that happened on her way and then we've had a good laugh. Horst, for instance, must have been a good actor. Every time the Russians came he started limping and pretended to be a cripple. He was lucky except once, when they took him away to work. He escaped after a few days and walked about 50 miles to find my mother. He showed me how he walked as a cripple and believe me I couldn't help laughing. Well, darling, it's too dark now to write. I'll write a few more lines after tea.

Here I am again, sweetheart. Writing whilst my brother does my fingernails. You'll be surprised seeing my nails when I come back. I've told him to come along and look after you. He's done my mother's and Mrs Streese's hair and I really was surprised. He knows his job. Tomorrow week I'll go and fetch our photos and bring a few along.

We have just finished our manicure. It didn't take long, only 2 hours.

Today I killed someone with a knife. Don't worry, it was only a rabbit. A lovely one and it's going to be the last dinner here for my mother and brother.

I don't think we'll get the parcel before I leave. Somebody living here in the house told me that she got a parcel from London and it only took 8 weeks. Well, it doesn't matter as long as it arrives at all. I still can send one to my mother when it is allowed again.

Well, my love, please give my kindest regards to your dear mother. My mother, brother and the rest of the household also send their regards to you.

Goodnight and God bless you. Be good, darling and think of me. I love you so very much.

All my love and kisses

Forever yours, sweetheart

Hans.

Woltersmühlen
Germany, British
Zone
Jan 23rd 1949

My dearest darling Jean,

How are you today darling? I hope you aren't as lonely as I am. Well, it doesn't matter, only one more weekend to go. That is 2 more, but the second one I'll be on my way, perhaps with you already. Is everything alright with your mother when I leave the train in Leicester and stay the night at your place? It would be very nice because then I could go to Billesdon straight away and collect my papers and do everything in Melton on my way back to Pickwell. So please, let me know. According to the time it took me on the trip over here I should arrive there on Sunday or Monday, Feb 7th 1949. And I hope you don't mind even if I come at 6 o'clock in the morning. I shan't disturb you in case I arrive during the night. Then I shall stay at the station till it gets light.

Yesterday all of a sudden my cousin came. You know the one I told you about. The one that was in Russia, got released and was working in the British zone. Last Monday my mother got a letter posted on from her place, saying that my cousin was still working at the same place. The day after a letter from himself came, telling us that he was coming here, even if it only was for a few hours. So last night when the train passed by my mother said 'he's coming on this one.' And she was right. He's leaving early tomorrow morning with my mother and brother. The train leaves at 5.20 am, and they'll cross the border on Tuesday morning. It is better than at night for they can see where to go. After all, my brother did not get his shoes changed. On the way home, he'll have time to try in Hamburg. If he doesn't get them changed there, he'll try to take them over into the Russian zone. I keep my fingers crossed that everything goes alright.

I didn't go anywhere yesterday, because there were lots to do for me. I baked two cakes for today's tea and now they won't let me go. Anyway, I've told them you are also waiting. So everybody agreed that I'd better go back to you. Well, darling, <u>nobody</u> is keeping me back here. I know where I belong. Only to you, sweety, only another 10 days.

Well, my love I'll say goodnight and God bless you. Tomorrow morning I'll get up early and see my mother off at the station.

My mother and brother send their kindest regards to you and please, give my kind regards to your dear mother.

So be good, darling, and think of me. My thoughts are always with you and remember I love you more than anything else in the world.

All my love and kisses
Forever yours, darling
Hans.

Woltersmühlen
Germany, British
Zone
Jan 24th 1949

My dearest darling Jean

I thank you so very much for your letter, dated 19.1.49 which I received this morning. It was almost like Saltby for I was still in bed as the postman came. He also told me that your parcel has arrived. I have to collect it at the Post Office in the next village, half an hour away from here. It really is a shame, for my mother has left early this morning and a few hours later the parcel arrives. Well, it can't be helped. As soon as we are allowed to send them into the Russian zone again I'll do so. Horst was looking for the postman every day and now he's had it. They are hoping to cross the border to-morrow morning if all goes well. I hope for the best.

After all I bought my mother a few more things she needed so there was quite a lot to carry.

We got up at 5.00am the train was leaving 6.20. I saw my mother, brother and cousin off, came back and had a few more hours in bed. To be honest I didn't like to go to the station because I know my mother. The farewell is always the worst. She kept weeping all the way, but told me it is for the best to stay with you. It is the place where I belong now. If I came back here, I wouldn't even get a job. Thousands of people are unemployed. And believe me I also know where I belong because there's no living for me without you, darling. It is rather quiet now, 3 people less means a lot.

Don't be too sure about Connie Goodman. Remember what she told you at your office about Redmile. That means enough to me.

As I told you, sweetheart, I think it is a shame giving Sheila the notice because she has the baby. I hope she'll get accommodations before the day she has to leave.

Thanks for giving me an English lesson. I'll see what I can do about having a shock! Didn't I ask you to correct me if anything is wrong? Please, carry on with doing so.

I hope everything will go alright with Betty's baby. I understand what your mother feels like. Well, my love, it is time now to get ready to go to the Post Office. My mother and brother send their kindest regards to your dear mother.

Be good, darling and look after yourself well. It shan't be long now till I come back and be with you.

All my love and kisses

Eternally yours, sweetheart

Hans.

<u>7 o'clock</u>

I am very sorry darling but I forgot to post the letter. As I told you I was going to collect the parcel this afternoon. I did some shopping first and went round afterwards. I asked for the parcel and was told to come into the office. The mailbag was opened before my eyes and there I found it.

On arrival in Hamburg the parcel was open and the man in the office wanted to know if everything was alright. A good thing I took your letter along. The weight was 3lbs 14oz and the chocolate and toffees were missing. Only one toffee was left for me to taste. Anyway 14 ounces less than it was put on the wrapping paper. You didn't say anything about a tin of egg powder in the letter, but there was one. The meat, milk and jelly were the contents.

Anyway I thank you very, very much for sending those lovely things and be sure we'll enjoy them. Tonight the tea tasted much better with the milk. We'll be able to have some sort of pudding tomorrow, the first time since I am here.

My brother asked me for your address so don't be surprised if you get a letter from him one day.

Well, darling, I'll say goodnight and God bless you. Be good and think of me.

All my love and kisses

Only yours, sweetheart
Hans.

P.S.

I am going to write to Helmut now.
Love Hans.

92 Wharf St

24.1.49

My dearest darling Hans

I do hope you are still missing me. I have been really very busy doing the washing so I need not bother on Wednesday when I have my day off. Saturday afternoon I looked after the shop (my mother went to have a rest) and washed my dirty underclothes and my green check skirt. Then I fetched the rations. I also scrubbed the floor and cleaned out before my Ma got up. I did not do much in the evening, only worked my tablecloth. Sunday I was up bright and early. Washed 4 sheets, I also washed the jacket that goes with my check skirt. I hadn't been able to wear it for years but since I have got thinner it now fits. In the afternoon I did my cloth then Mamma, Freddy and I went to Betty's for tea. I came home at 8.0 intending to write to you, but I couldn't resist pressing my jacket to see how it would look. It doesn't look too bad but it will want pressing again.

Freddy has just made himself comfortable on my knee. You would have laughed on Saturday. We were having our tea, when Susan knocked on the shop door I put my cup of tea on the stool went to see what she was knocking for (she wanted the gate at the back opening). Freddy is excited and flies back straight into the stool where my cup of tea was, knocked it all over the floor, it was a mess. Fortunately for Fred I saw the funny side of it.

Well darling you haven't said what day you will be coming or are you definitely starting back on 4th Feb. Look, darling I know you are not going to like this, but I think it would be better if you went back to Melton then rang me, because you don't know what time you will arrive and it may not be possible for you to stop here. Susan is here tonight and will be here while Betty is away. So I think it would be best and we will know where we are.

Betty went to the City General (that the place you went to in the lorry) this morning and has to go tomorrow they will probably keep her for a day or 2. So I have already told you Susan is staying here tonight. She hasn't school today, because she has come out in spots. I am sleeping with her so if you hear I have the measles don't be surprised ,but darling if I have to have them I will see if I can manage German measles just to please you.

Well darling I will have to close. Goodnight and God Bless.

All my love
Jean.

92 Wharf St

26.1.49

My dearest darling Hans

Thank you very much for your nice long letters. I had one yesterday, one this morning and another at lunchtime.

I took my mother to the pictures last night. It is the first time she has been for ages. She isn't a picture fan but last night when I came home she said she would very much like to see 'The Winslow Boy' so we left the washing up and went, it was very good.

I am glad you like Faust. I always thought Faust was an opera not a play. Don't they open late there. Here everywhere is closed at 10.30 most of the theatres by 9.30. I have never read Faust as you may have gathered.

I have not spoken to Miggy for over a week. She is at the Anstey exchange now, but yesterday I had to get an Anstey number so I asked for her, I had a few words with her. She is coming into the office on Thursday evening. She has to come in to see what Otto can do about his money. Then I will see her and we can have a good chinwag (talk).

I was speaking to Mr Chandler on Tuesday afternoon for quite a while, Sheila, his daughter, has had her baby. I think it was a little boy. She is coming down to Saltby next week for a few weeks. Mr Chandler said you would have to go over for the weekend, after his family has gone back. I also have an invitation to go over. He also said I could go while you were away, he said you wouldn't mind.

So darling you would have had my last letter telling you to go to Pickwell. If you come early Sunday morning that is before 10.30 you can come on to Leicester but after that time you had better go to Melton, because if you come to dinner after my mother has got ours ready it would put her in a flat spin, and as you know darling I hate to put anyone to a lot of trouble, I would not mind if it were myself, but it is not, and as I have already told you Susan might be coming to stay here anytime. So if you do have to go on to Melton ring me and I will come over to Pickwell.

I shouldn't worry too much about me being taller than you. Look at Mr and Mrs Churchill and a few more famous people. Do you think we might look like Mr and Mrs Chandler?

Fancy you wasting your money on a hat. I was glad you let your brother have the other one, but why on earth do you have to buy another one. I hope you haven't had your hair set too. You will look a real spiv if you have.

If you do miss that train you had better pick a nice spot for a house and start building right away. Make it big then we could open it up as a hotel and café with a notice outside ENGLISH SPOKEN HERE. I think we would do a good trade. Lucy had a letter from a friend in Belfast. This friend had brought a business last March for £600 and sold it before Christmas for £3000.

Well darling I have to powder my nose now, my auntie will wonder what has happened to me.

All my love and kisses

Jean

Woltersmühlen
Germany, British
Zone
Jan 27th 1949

My dearest darling Jean

What! No letters for three days! Well I am surprised!!

Well, I'll tell you now what I was doing with myself lately. On Tuesday I was sitting here all day waiting for my mother's telegram to arrive. As I told you they're crossing the border Tuesday morning. Anyway, nothing happened that day. Yesterday I went to Lübeck for the last time to do some shopping. I took the 7.00 train and stayed away all day. I can tell you now what I was going to buy for you. A wonderful table lamp. It was a big crystal bowl on the bottom and had a lovely shade. I know you would have liked it. When I went into the shop and asked for that particular lamp I found that the bowl was broken on one side and there wasn't another one in the shop. So, I went round town all day long, looked for a similar lamp in every shop I could find, but still, was unsuccessful. After all the running around I was so annoyed but found something else you'll like. It'll match nicely with your new blue coat. Guess what it is? Wait and see!!!

Later in the evening I went round again and after all found my fellow. He was surprised to see me and said he's never had a thought of seeing me again. I stayed at his home for a short time and then we went to the pictures 'Adam and Eve.' It was very nice, Kurt brought me to the station at 8.00pm and at 9.00 I was back here again.

Here I found my mother's telegram waiting for me, saying that she and Horst crossed the border safely in 12 hours. I don't know yet if they got caught on the way or were hiding somewhere, for crossing the border it only took them 5 hours the last time. I hope to learn more about it before I leave.

I can hardly wait till Saturday to see how our photos turned out. Then there's only another trip to do before I leave. I have to go to the next small town to get something unrationed to put on my sandwiches, but you should see the prices and what it tastes like. Horrible stuff, called sausage with flour and vegetable in it.

Well, sweetheart, I'll finish for the present because I can't see any longer. We have to save electricity and wait till 6.30 to switch the light on. I'll write a few more lines after dinner.

I've enjoyed my dinner and feel strong enough to finish the letter. There's another thing I have to do before I leave. The customs want a list of everything that's going to be taken back to England signed by the police. We are allowed 46lbs only. Less than on the way over here. I shan't have so much anyway.

By the way how is Leicester going on? What does your hair, face and fingers look like ..

Well, my darling, I'll close now. My mother, brother, Gertrude and her mother send their regards and please give my regards to your dear mother.

Cheerio for now and be a good girl. Think of me and that I love you sooo much.

> All my love and kisses
> Forever yours, my love

Hans.

> (24) Woltersmühlen
> Germany, British Zone
> Jan 28th 1949

My dearest darling Jean

To start with: I am still missing you very much and I also say the third weekend is gone and only one or maybe two more to go. Anyway I thank you very much for your letter from

24.1.49 which arrived this morning. Now about the day I am coming back. Up to now the date is still the 4th. I believe I told you in one of the first letters that we have to listen to the 18.45 news on Febr 3rd to know if there are any changes. Well, after all I have decided to leave here on Febr 3rd to get to Münster in time. So I shan't be able to listen to the news. My train leaves here 19.04 and I have to walk about 15 minutes.

I'll send a note to my friend in Lübeck and ask him to hear the news and then come to the station and tell me about it and see me off. That would be the best way I think.

Well, another problem. How do you know I don't like the idea of leaving the train at Melton. If I can't stay at your place I'll have to. Anyway I hope to oblige you in stopping in Melton, ringing you from there. If there is a possibility of staying in Leicester for the night I still can take the next bus and come over. In case we arrive later in the afternoon I'll ring you at home. So please, stay in Sunday and Monday night, if you don't mind. The trouble is that I can't do any-thing in Melton before I've been to Billesdon. I just thought of something. When I arrive at Melton late I shan't be able to get a bus to Pickwell and I don't know if I shall have enough money to take a taxi. Think of me staying in Melton all night. That'll be the third one without sleep. Well, we'll see how it goes.

Please, be careful and don't get measles. Not even German ones. You can't please me with that.

Well, sweetheart, I'll say cheerio now. Please, give my kind regards to your dear mother. Be good and look after yourself.

All my love and kisses

Forever yours, my love

Hans.

Woltersmühlen
Germany, British Zone
Jan 30th 1949

My dearest darling Jean

To begin with, sweetheart, I am very lonely and glad to say it's the last weekend here. Only 4 more days to go. Days are getting boring. The four weeks here have also been a good test and I found that there isn't anything in the world I would exchange for the time which lies ahead – with you. These four weeks have been a long, long time for me, it seemed a year.

I know now how it'll be when we're married. I'll be longing for you every day, longing for the moment to get home and find you there. And it is going to be, what it should be – the time of our life. But there's only one question. Will it be soon? Please, my darling, make it possible. It's up to you.

How are you today darling? As lonely as I am? I wonder what you're doing now. Also at home? You at least are able to listen to a radio. There's nothing like that here. Well, it doesn't matter for these few days.

I was busy yesterday afternoon, making a cake. The one I made a fortnight was very nice so I was asked to have another go. As filling pudding and self made marzipan. That's one of the first things I am going to do when I come back. The only things I need are a cake tin and some almond oil. That'll be something for our Sunday tea. And there are also a few more kinds of cake my mother told me about. I've put it all down on paper so I won't forget them. Everything has to be tried.

How's Freddy going on? Still bald? I hope your new idea will help him.

My mother told me that she has a few certificates about my profession and was going to post those onto me as soon as she's got home. Perhaps tomorrow or the day after if I am lucky. One never knows if one can use them one day. You know I don't like to be a farmworker forever. Not if I get anything on my own, like a chicken farm or breeding dogs!?! Looking after kids eh!!!

Well, my love, it's getting late. Gertrud is gone away to see her boyfriend and Mrs Streese is reading.

Please, give my kind regards to your dear mother. So be good, think of me and remember I love you more than anything else in the world.

Goodnight and God bless you,

All my love and kisses

Forever and only yours, sweety

Hans.

Woltersmühlen

Germany, British Zone

Febr 1ˢᵗ 1949

My dearest darling Jean

I thank you so very much for your nice letter I received today. It took 6 days in spite of being send by air mail. Still I am glad the letter arrived at all. I am well, knowing that the day of my departure isn't far away. Day after tomorrow I shall be on my way.

I've had a shock, reading that you went to have your hair cut. Well, I shall see what it looks like. Anyway I know your taste so it should be alright.

I've just finished the list of my property and shall go tomorrow morning to have it signed. There's the picture 'Cornwall Rhapsody' on at the picture house in Eutin (the nearest bigger village, 10 miles from here). I think I shall have enough time to see it in the afternoon. It'll be the last picture here in Germany.

'Faust' in its original style as it was written by Goethe is a play and not an opera. I'll take the chance of seeing it again if there ever is a possibility. Of course, as it started late, they had to open late. Pictures houses usually close at 10.30 except times when they have special late performances at 10 o'clock.

How does Mr Chandler know that I don't mind you going over on your own whilst I am away? Did you go after all?

Anyway I don't think it is advisable to go as you told the Major it was getting too late for you coming home.

In the meantime you would have had my letter about the problem of staying at your place. It really isn't a 'problem' is it? I don't think I shall arrive before 10.30 on Sunday morning so I go to Melton and ring you from there. I'll have to make that round trip then on Monday. So please, keep Monday night free, if you don't mind. We might be able to go to the pictures.

Anyway, I'll ring you at once after I have arrived.

Look, sweety, don't tell me anything about Mr and Mrs Churchill or Mr and Mrs Chandler. The only thing that matters are you and I. If you put your high heeled shoes on I'll have to get a pair as well. That's alright with you isn't it?

Problem: hat. Nothing I can say to excuse myself. I just fulfilled my mother's wish.

Not a bad idea; your house with the notice 'English spoken here.' Come and pick a nice spot yourself. Don't forget to powder your nose.

Well, sweetheart this will be the last letter from here. Otherwise I shall be there before the letter arrives. I'll deliver the next one myself. Don't be annoyed, when I come at six o'clock in the morning. Wouldn't that be nice?

Well, my darling, I'll finish now. Mrs Streese and Gertrud send their kind regards and please, give my regards to your dear mother. Be a good girl and think of me. Remember I love you very, very much.

> All my love and kisses
> Forever yours, sweety
> Hans.

> Pickwell
> Great Britain
> Feb 3rd 49

My dearest darling Jean

This is going to be the letter which I shall deliver myself. The time is 2.30pm another 5 hours and I shall be on my way. In an hour's time we'll have our tea and then it's only a matter of waiting. All my things are packed, ready to go. Well, sweetheart, as I told you before I am glad to come back. There's nothing that can keep me here.

Mrs Streese and Gertrud went early this morning to collect their money, 15 miles away from here. So I got the dinner ready. You should've seen their faces when they opened the door and found the dinner ready and the table set. The cake I made yesterday is also ready.

I went to the butcher yesterday for some meat. It is only 12 miles away. So you guess what this village looks like.

Well, sweety, I'll close for now and write more in the train tonight. Mrs Streese wants to get my sandwiches done and I'll give her a hand. Be good.

11.20pm

Well, sweety, here I am again. I'll never make a bus conductor, writing in a train, I've just changed the train in Hamburg and this is a non-stop to Münster. Till now everything went alright. I left Woltersmühlen station at 7 o'clock and had to wait only ¾ of an hour in Lübeck. As arranged my fellow was waiting for me at the station to tell me there was nothing about changes on the wireless. So I was happy to be able to continue my journey. In Hamburg I only had to wait 25 minutes and I shall arrive at Münster Station at 4.03am tomorrow. That means plenty of time to write if only the train wouldn't do as if it was drunk. There was a farewell party this afternoon but no whisky. And you know I don't drink any. I hope we don't stop in Münster too long. My mother told me in her last letter that she met a lady on her way home. She'd also visited her son on leave from England. Her son has had to be in Münster like us on Friday afternoon and left for Holland on Saturday 6pm. I wish we would leave straight away. I shall see you earlier then. Well, darling, that's all for now, I'll try and get some sleep. Goodnight and God bless you. Be a good girl.

Friday 11.15am

Hello, sweetheart. More than a day is gone since I wrote last. Well, I'll tell you now how things went till now. I arrived in Münster at 4 o'clock yesterday morning. When I left the station I found a bus waiting already. I was going to stay in the town till later on, but decided to go on that bus. Well, I arrived here quarter of an hour later and went to bed for a couple of hours. At 8 o'clock was breakfast, then at 10.00 I went to the pictures (here in the camp) and also at 18.00 and 20.00 hrs again. We have to get rid of the money and I don't like to drink beer or whisky. I went to bed at 23.30 and had a nice rest till 7.00 this morning, thinking of you. At 8.00 after a 'smashing breakfast' the customs examination started. Well, sweety, I am glad to say I was lucky. Nothing taken away. I'll try everything to get your present through. Another examination is to be undergone at Harwich. This one here was not too bad. There's nothing more to do this afternoon. Only another examination of the things we keep with us. Then at 6.00 the train is leaving for Holland. Anyway I am sure now I shan't make it before 10.30 Sunday morning. Sometime in the afternoon I think and that still depends how long we'll stop at Harwich. Best thing would be from the ship straight on the train but there we'll get our £1 back.

Well, my darling, you'll hear more on the train or ship. So long, and be a good girl.

Sunday 5.00pm

Well, my darling, here I am again. I am in rage. We left Hook of Holland at 5 o'clock this morning and had a lovely crossing. No wind at all, the sea looked like a mirror. Well, I was able to get a so called bed, went to sleep and woke up one hour before we arrived here at Harwich. Now we have to wait till our train goes at 6.35 tomorrow morning. The nice Sunday is spoiled. We arrived here early enough to make it to Leicester till 5 o'clock this afternoon, but it is a special train and doesn't leave before tomorrow. I'll get to Leicester at 11.40 and ring you at once. Wouldn't it have been nice to be together for at least a couple of hours? If I am lucky tomorrow you might tell me I can stay the night at your place. We'll see about that tomorrow oh! Jeany it was a job to get your present through the customs. I told the officer a tale about being my wedding present and so on. Well I got it back after all and believe me I was so glad.

The other fellows lost a lot. Especially cameras. Everything that was new had to be paid for. We only had one £ so where should we get the money from?

Well, my love I shall see you tomorrow. It's time now for tea. I am longing to be with you again and counting the hours till I see you. I love you so very, very much. Will you be thinking of me?

Tuesday 8.2.49

'My darling' good morning sweetheart are you feeling better? I hope so. I was sorry when I came yesterday and you had to get out of bed, but then I rung the office and Sheila told me you're ill, I rushed off because the bus was just leaving. That's how I got there so quick. I couldn't wait any longer when I hear you're ill. So, please, forgive me. Anyway I was so glad when I saw you.

You should see our 'kitchen'. It looks filthy. I don't think Helmut cleaned it since I left. My iron was broken so I fixed it again last night. Everything as I expected. No money safed So one has to straighten things out.

It's 8 o'clock now. I am going down on the 8.15 to the food office and come back as soon as possible to do a bit of ironing. The boss has been here already and is glad I have come back after all. Nothing said about the day off.

Well, my love, I'll say cheerio and write again tonight. Be good and I hope you'll be well again soon. I love you soooo much.

All my love and kisses

Forever yours Hans.

Pickwell

Jan. 8t<u>h</u> 1949

My dearest, darling Jean,

How do you feel, my love? Better I hope or have you been to work today? Well it's about 4 o'clock and things look a bit better now I took the 8.20 this morning and went round the police station and food office. I was ready to go back at 9.30 but unfortunately there was no bus til 11.20. Whilst walking around I met Mr & Mrs Chandler and her daughter. They were going to Leicester. Mr Chandler has asked us to come over, but I told him it shan't be for the next few weeks.

Well, I came back here on the 11.20 and without having any lunch I started scrubbing. The stove was rusty all over. You know how I got it shiny, don't you? Oil also does it. Anyway I like it much better now.

I've just had enough money to pay to Melton and back and get some writing paper and envelopes. Only 2d left till friday. It has to be enough.

I think I told you about changing the grocer before I went home. It really took me a lot not to say anything to the foreman's wife when I asked for Helmut's ration book. I told her we would like to change to the grocer at Somerby so we're able to get things whenever we need them and don't have to wait til the co-op van comes Tuesdays. All she said was "if you aren't satisfied with me getting everything for you, you'd better get the bread and meat also yourself. And another thing now I want my milkcan back and you can buy one yourself" However as she said that I got a bit hot. I told her to keep her can and went to fetch something else. What does she think she is!! The only thing she was angry about was loosing the bonds from the co-op. I'll go to Somerby now and see the shop manager. I can collect the things then when I meet you on the bus Saturday afternoon. The butcher and baker also live in Somerby.

Something else, sweety. Have you got any cake tins in your shop. Round ones (big) and small one in the shape of the bread. If you have any please bring one each on Saturday. Then we can make a nice cake for our Sunday tea. And also three teaspoons. Don't worry we'll have some money to pay you!!! Even if I have to confess I am broken at the moment. When I get back from Somerby I'll go and see if I can get a rabbit.

Just be good and think of me and remember I love you very, very much.

> All my love and kisses
>> Forever yours, sweetheart
> Hans.

Pickwell
Feb. 9TH 1949

My dearest, darling Jean,
The first day is over. I didn't think it would be so difficult after four weeks holiday. And it was a lovely start, wasn't it. It was pouring at 7 o'clock and I had to go watercarting. Of course I was wet through when I got to the tractor which was somewhere in the fields. It broke down there and was left outside because they couldn't get it started. The boss asked me if I think I could bring it in, a rather funny question after it broke down. I've had an idea what the matter was and he was surprised when I came back after being away for only an hour, driving it. When I finished at lunchtime the water was running down my overcoat. I had to change. This afternoon I took my old horse and went cleaning chicken houses.

How are you today, my love? I hope not as tired as I am. It's only 8.00 but it won't be long before I go to bed. We have to change our beds into the other room. It's cooler there. I'll tell the old man tomorrow that we have to have a stove in that other room. My boots which I left there look awful. It's too wet.

I am listening to a play "Frieda". I don't remember if you've seen the picture. The play is very nice. I missed the picture myself.

Herbert has just come back. As I told you last night he was going to see and ask at the labour exchange about another job. Well, he was told that he can look for any other jobs he wants. He'll get it from the Labour Exchange. That is when he's married. There's no need to get permission from the Home Office. So he'll leave here as soon as he gets anything. Shall I do the same? Up to you, darling

Well, my sweetheart, I'll say good night now. I am sorry, the letter is only a short one, but my eyes. I can hardly keep them open. I'll write more tomorrow.

Be good, darling and God bless you. I am longing for Saturday and I love you so very very much.

All my love and kisses

    Forever yours, my love

      Hans.

From this point on Mutti resumes her writing in the Suerterllin Script, this was taught in German schools up until 1941

Written top corner, page 1, upside down

I had to put your exercise book into a safe place and will send it to you tomorrow, when I have found it.

Aschersleben, 26.1.49

My dear Hans, dear Marta and Gertrud

Last night we arrived here at 23.30, after an awful struggle. We are happy but totally exhausted. We hope you received our telegram, which we sent off yesterday afternoon at 3pm, as soon as we arrived in Neuhaldensleben. I am now going to tell you what our journey was like. When we arrived in Lübeck, we got on an express train at 08.12 to Hamburg . It only operates on a Monday and does not stop at every station. It meant we got there three quarters of an hour early. Horst immediately went to the information desk but to no avail. At 10.25, our train was due to depart and Bruno's train left at 11.21. It was so crowded, that we had to stand all the way from Hamburg to Hanover. It was no fun. We met up with a woman who had also been to see her son who also came from England during his leave. He had to go back to England on 17 January. At 3.30, we arrived in Münster and in the evening, everyone went to the cinema. On the next day, our train left Münster at 6pm. We finally reached Helmsted (the border) at 8.30pm. There were lots of fellow sufferers and we had to find the right people first. There were two women, one aged 63 and one aged 56, who were also going the same way as we were. At 10 o'clock, everybody who wanted to go the East, had to clear the waiting room, so we went to the railway commission, where we were able to have a little rest. At 1.15 in the night, we went on our journey. Unfortunately, we went in the wrong direction because the woman who guided us, had made a mistake and we finished up at the Police Station. They were very kind and gave one woman a drink. We were told to get nice and warm before setting off again, but decided to go sooner rather than later, because we now had to go all the way back again before we could continue with our journey. We met people on the way who said that it had been practically impossible all day to get over the border and the border police were capturing people by the hundreds. But when one is on one's way, one has to keep on moving. We also met some people on their bikes, who did get across. We had to make big detours. It was just awful, via uncountable meadows and fields and we often fell down, stretched out on the mud. Luckily, it was not too cold, but as we had some snow, the ground was very slippery. The passage seemed to have no end and we came across some strange looking people. One of them asked how many people there are in our group, but it looked like he did not have the courage to say or do anything further. He had quite a lot of luggage on him and I don't think they were his own, because he wore ladies' gloves. He wanted a cigarette from Horst but I had looked right through him. He started to tell us some stories about having lost his wallet etc. We did not want to have anything to do with him and did not enter into a conversation, and just walked on. One woman had a very bad heart, so Horst carried her heavy rucksack for seven hours as well as our bag. He could hardly walk and my bags got heavier and heavier. When we arrived in Hörsingen at 9 o'clock, we were totally exhausted and filthy like pigs and – there was no train. What were we to do? As we were in constant fear of being caught, we decided to walk a further 19 kilometres to Neuhaldensleben. It was almost an impossible task, but one we had to undertake. Then came a woman who loaded our bags onto her wooden cart and walked with us a further nine kilometres. There were two more women who joined us and we all had to pay 10 Marks for this service. It was outrageous, don't you think? Just before Haldensleben someone gave us a lift in a car. Otherwise we would have had to be left unconscious on the road! At 18.30 we managed to catch a train from Neuhaldensleben to Magdeburg. It was very cold on the train and our teeth started to chatter. We were so glad to be back at home. But, for the moment, we are well fed up and have had enough! When we got to the station there was a police raid, but I did not get caught.

Aschersleben, 27.1.49

My dear Hans

After a long search, I finally found your papers. I thought I was going mad! That's what you get when you put something in a safe place. It is 7 o'clock in the morning here. I decided to get up but am still very tired. Horst wants to get up in a minute. He has his first day in his new job behind him. His clients and also his new lady boss were all very pleased to see him in the shop.

Dear Hans, Horst is apologising to you again for having been a bit grumpy at times. He says he was miserable because he missed his work – nothing else. Now he is back in his element again. I shall have to have your work book weighed, because a letter must not exceed the limit of 100g. The book has to be sent separately.

Lots of love to you all, your mum and Horst

Dear Marta, I am returning to you the bread ration coupon because we did not have an opportunity to buy anything for it.

I am sending you, again, my heartfelt greetings,

Hedwig

Aschersleben, 29.1.49

My dear Hans

Six days have passed since we had to say 'good-bye' to you and, who knows, for how many years. Thank you very much again for everything you have done for us. You cannot imagine how hard our parting was for me. How we would have loved to stay with you longer, but I had the feeling that the Streeses were quite glad to see us go. I am sending this letter to England so that you do not have to wait too long for post from us. I cannot find my peace since I have been back. I was sick in the first few days with a swollen face and swollen feet. It was all too exhausting for me, and Horst looks awful too. I am feeling very homesick. Up until now one was always looking forward to a reunion, and now even that has been taken away from us!! Life is very hard. Three weeks ago today we were travelling to you. Mrs. Lehmann visited her parents too. She was asking why we did not come and stay with them. We would have lived well there, everything is cheaper and you could have saved a lot of money. They pay 75 pence for 10 white bread rolls, 1 pound of meat costs 3 Marks and Butter 6 Marks. Horst would have had a lot of work and things would have been better food wise. Most of all, we would have had a lot of milk. Well, it's over now but should we be in this situation again, we would know exactly how to deal with it. Mrs. Lehmann is going back again in a week's time. Her parents are going to have one of their animals slaughtered again. She found a different route which means she does not have to walk such a long way. The fare is not very expensive – and it is not too far from Helmstedt. Had we stayed with them, we would also have been able to wait there until you had to leave. What have you been starting on in the meantime? I suppose you collected the photos today. We hope they will get here very soon. Did you receive the papers/documents and my letter? Horst has not been able to exchange his shoes yet, because they did not have his size. He doesn't like it here anymore, mainly because of the food. If only it would get better! My lovely shoes suffered a lot during the journey. The leather has warped. I have put something into the shoes to stretch and reshape the leather. The trip was too long. Horst went to a masked ball tonight, just to watch. I am thinking that you may never come back here again and we will be separated forever!! It doesn't bear thinking about!! Oh, if only Papa were here!! When will my wish be fulfilled? I hope you were able to buy Jean a nice souvenir from Germany. I was really sorry – I felt you were being taken advantage of. Gertrud had a long wish list. Horst was very disappointed in Gertrud. She treated him like a schoolboy at times, which he found very annoying. He was very happy about your presents. All his lady customers were very pleased that he is back again. He said to me tonight over a meal 'if only Hans could be with us'! If the journey were not so complicated, one would not think twice about it. As it is he has his job to go to every day, so he would not be able to come with me. But not to Holstein! It's not really what we want. We had post from Auntie Else, she is anxiously waiting to hear from Heinz. We hope he gets home alright with all his things! Frau Lehmann might also move to live with her parents. She has already applied to the mayor for permission. It will probably take a while. Uncle Erich and Auntie Grete visited Lina last week. In a week's time you will be on your return journey, I hope you have a pleasant trip. I shall be thinking about you. Now, my dear boy, I want to close my letter for today. It is almost time to go to bed! Give our love to Jean and also to your mother-in-law. We are sending you our special love and kisses, from your mum who is always thinking about you, and your brother Horst. Mrs. Lehmann and Mrs Ziemann are sending their best wishes to you. I hope the photos don't take that long to get here

Aschersleben, 4.2.49

My dear Hans

We received your lovely letter dated 29.1. and thank you for it from the bottom of our hearts. We were very happy to receive the photos. The one with Horst standing over you is really wonderful. The three of us look very natural. You and Horst also look very good on the other two photos, only I don't look good – I look like Mariechen. I hope very much that you have one of the nice ones for yourself too. Horst would also love to have one of them. I shall write to the Streeses and ask if they can get us another two. Frau Lehmann is going to see her parents on Sunday, she can take the letter with her and put the money in. Today, you will be on your way and leave your homeland again, how much longer – I wonder? Did you not feel, my dear boy, how my thoughts were with you every step of the way? Again and again, I was thinking 'now he should be leaving', 'now he is on the train', 'what will he be doing now?' I hope you did not find the wait in Münster too long! Jean will be waiting for you already and when you get there, you will be very welcomed. I am sure it was a long wait for her too until she sees you again. I hope you have a good crossing! How nice it was for you to have found your pal in Lübeck. Horst has not been able to exchange his shoes yet because they still have not got his size. I hope they will soon get a new delivery. I hope Jean likes her new handbag. It should go really well with her blue coat. I can well believe that you will be glad when you have reached your destination. What a good job you received the three letters and papers before your departure. At least you were able to take everything back with you. I take it the parcel did not arrive while you were there. What a pity! If we had known, you could have sent it to Mrs. Lehmann's parents. She would have been only too pleased to bring it back to me when next she is here. It's only a few train stops away from the border. I exchanged the pound of coffee today. I would have loved to drink it myself, but we badly need the fat. We need it for cooking, and there is no fat on the meat either. One litre of oil and a good pork joint weighing several pounds were very much appreciated. You will have noticed how poorly Horst looked. After this trip he was so exhausted. Everyone noticed that he looked as though he was about to collapse. It will take quite a while before he builds up his strength again – especially with the type of 'fodder' we are getting here. Well, dear Hans, how quickly has our reunion come and gone, the good times always seem to go quicker! I can only hope that our next reunion will not be that long away! The years just fly by. We must treasure every hour and not waste any time in which we can be together. Have you received my letter dated 29.1. in the meantime? It was meant to reach you around the time of your return back to England. I did not want you to have to wait too long for post from us. Now, my dear Hans, I am going to finish my letter for today. It's time to go to bed. Horst invited me to the theatre on Tuesday. He wants me to stop dwelling and think of other things. It was lovely. The film is called "A season in Salzbrunn". Give my love to Jean and also your mother-in-law. To you, my dear Hans, we are sending all our love and kisses, your mum, who is always thinking about you, and your brother Horst.

Please write again soon!

Pickwell

Feb. 10th 1949

My dearest, darling Jean,

I am so sorry, darling, but you shan't get a letter tomorrow and Saturday. I haven't even got 2 ½d for a stamp to post the letter. Perhaps you've noticed the 3d stamps on the last two letters. I know I wouldn't like waiting so long, but please, forgive me. As you know I don't like to borrow any money. By the way, I was surprised when there was no letter this morning. I hope you aren't ill in bed again. I shall find out when ringing you tomorrow night.

Well, sweetheart, another day is over and only day and half to go till Saturday. I wish time would pass a bit quicker. 6 weeks are all awfull long time. For me, anyway.

You would've had a good laugh seeing me just before lunchtime. The following happened: It was 12.15 when I finished cleaning and took the last load (cart) to the muck heap. I got a shock when I saw the heap spread all over the field. Of course, I always tried to keep it neat, but the fellow who did my job in the meantime dipped it just somewhere. I tried to get the horse and cart on top of the muckheap, though it was too soft. The horse wouldn't do as I did, went down and what else could happen. The cart turned right over sideways and the horse had to do the same. A good thing I wasn't on top of the load otherwise I wouldn't write to you now. Believe me I was sweating for ½ hour, taking the harness to pieces to get the horse out. Well, after all I succeeded. The horse got up after I gave him one with the line. It looked to me as if he liked laying down better than standing up. Now, how to get the cart turned over again. A chain on the cart and the horse pulled it over. I was really glad when I finished because it was a few minutes before 1o'clock, but I was back in time and glad the horse was alright. A good thing nobody was watching me.

Well, my love, it's 10.00 and I'd better go to bed. The other two have gone already at 9.00. Everybody is tired today.

Goodnight and God bless you always. Do you love me? Be good.

All my love and kisses
Forever yours, sweety
Hans.

92 Wharf St
13.2.49

My dearest darling Hans,

I hope you did not mind not seeing me today. I couldn't write this before ~~because~~ so you would get it in the morning, but Cyril and Susan were here all afternoon and I can't write letters when anyone is about.

I have just put Susan to bed, I have just been up again, she hadn't got a handkerchief, this sort of thing goes on for about an hour, so don't be a bit surprised if at the end of the next fortnight I say I never want to see another child.

Betty had a little girl at 6.0 this morning. She did not go into the home until 1.30 after all, my mother and Cyril have gone this evening to see her. I don't know what she is going to call her. If it had been a boy it would have been Robert Ian. So I think she must have wanted a boy, but no one on our side of the family has had a boy. So it looks as though you will have to put up with 5 girls in our family. Do you think you could stand that? That is if I have not changed my mind at the end of 2 weeks.

Did you arrive back safe and sound? I hope Bonzo had not finished off your cake. I got into Leicester at 11.30. Late isn't it. I was so tired I didn't bother to do my hair. I had a warm

milk, then went to bed. I have not done anything today only cleaned up and did my tablecloth this afternoon. I am going to bring it with me to Pickwell and I am going to do it. Do you think you could possibly find yourself something to do? Well darling I will close now I want to have a good wash
All my love Jean

Pickwell
Feb. 15th 1949

My dearest, darling Jean,
Thank you very much for your nice letter I received today. What a funny question, of course, I always mind not seeing you. Life begins for me when my only wish is fulfilled. Do you know what wish I mean? Shall I say again, let it be soon, darling.
I also don't like writing very much when anyone is about. Still, nobody can disturb me.
Look, sweetheart, even if Susan takes lots of your time, never say you don't want to see another child. Don't you think it would be different if it was your own child? And another thing, children aren't always the same. There's one day when you'll be proud of your kiddies. And that's lovely. So one has to put up with everything till the kiddies are grown up.
If you go and see Betty, please give her my regards and all the best for her and her little daughter.
Well, darling, even if there was no son on your side of the family, our first baby is going to be a boy. I don't like to say I know it, but on my side of the family the first one always was a boy and it'll be in my family, if you don't mind. Don't you think I could stand 5 girls? They take some looking after, but that doesn't matter. One always lovely as the other one. Just as lovely as their mother is.
Well, I told you what I did on Sunday. Bonzo didn't finish the cake off, but something else happened on Sunday morning.

You'll be very pleased to hear it. He was left in and got hold of my nice hat. So I've had it. You know what teeth he's got. He also must have liked my hat very much or he listened to your talk on Saturday when you said you don't like it.

Now about the weekend. I am not sure yet, but I shall probably have to work. So, please come over Saturday and have the tea ready for me when I come home. Then we can take a walk together if the weather keeps fine. I have to go shutting up afterwards, you may do the tablecloth and be sure I'll find something to do for myself. There are always socks to be darned. Or perhaps a letter to write.

I was going to make potato pancakes for us tonight. When I went and asked Mrs Cooper for a grater she said she had none. Could you possibly bring one on Saturday? I hope you know what I mean. A thing to grate potatoes, but not a small one for nutmeg. And please, don't forget that cake tin. See, there's something to do for me. Make a cake again. But something different this week.

Well, my love, I'll say goodnight, being very tired. Just be good and think of our 5 baby daughters.

God bless you always

     All my love and kisses

       Forever yours, my sweetheart

    Hans.

    92 Wharf St

    6-2-49

My dearest darling Hans

It is now 8.15 and I have only just sat down. My mother has gone to see Betty, she went about 6.0. The tea was ready, but I had to get Cyril's because he does not come until after 6.15. We had egg and toast. I burnt the toast, but that was alright. I soon scraped the burnt bit off. Egg wasn't done enough, it was all runny, so Cyril boiled it up again. I put the bottles in the bed then gave Susan a good wash. And put her hair in curlers.

I am just eating one of the peppermints you gave to me, they are very nice.

I thank you very much for your letter. It is a good service, don't you think? It was here at lunch time. i

What is the bit that it is a boy first? And another thing. I think you had better carry on working hard so we can have a maid, I would then probably be able to cope with the situation. As you can see it takes me all my time to help look after Susan.

Remind me to kiss Bonzo when I come. I think it is the best thing he has ever done.

I don't know what you mean by a potato grater. Doesn't a fork do just as well. And the cake tin I think you mean a sandwich tin. I will bring 2, because that is what we use, we put a little bit in each tin then one is the top and the other is the bottom with jam in between or something.

What are you doing about getting your things from Somerby? You had better let me know if there is anything I can bring for tea.

I have not seen anything of Iris since she came back. I told Lucy that it was funny she hadn't been in. I was beginning to think she had left Don and she did not like to come into the office. I still think she may have left him. Mary is now back at work and she said Don was still in Paris and had not left to go on tour yet. Since Iris has been back she finds she is going to have a baby. I do know she will not be going back to Paris until things improve because she said ~~she did not~~ before she went from Leicester, to go to France, that she did not think things there in Paris were right to bring up children

Well darling I will say good night and God bless

    All my love

    Jean

    ——.

P.S.

Don't ring me Friday I am leaving early to have my hair set

Jean

Jean with Bonzo

Pickwell

Feb. 17th 1949

My dearest, darling Jean,

How are you today, darling? Fine, I hope. And how is your sister? How long does she stay at the home? Is Susan still taking most of your time?

What do you think about Saturday? Would you like to come around with me shutting up? It really is a nice walk if the weather is fine. Today it was like midsummer and I really enjoyed the afternoon out, working in just the shirt with the sleeves rolled up. Wouldn't you like to start here with me on poultry, working in the sunshine all day long? That's the only reason why I like work on a farm.

Last night when I came back at 6.15 Helmut asked me if I would like to go to the pictures with him. So I hurried up and we took the 7 o'clock bus. Arriving at Melton we just threw a short glance at the poster, saw something like "When we are married" and thought that wouldn't be too bad. I went to the booking office and asked for a ⅔. Of course I was surprised when I was told it's only 2/-. I didn't think of it. However, as we went into the picture house the big surprise was waiting for us. It was a play by the Melton Players. Well, after a conference of 15 minutes we decided to stay. It wasn't too bad although those players are only local ones. After all we enjoyed it. As much as we were able to understand, sitting upstairs. Anyway the next time I shall have a better look.

My leg hurts terribly today, but I don't want to stay in bed, remembering that it got lots better last time when I kept walking around. And when I lay down I can't get up for the next couple of weeks.

Well, my love, I'll close now. I am so very tired. Be good, darling and sleep well. Are you thinking of me? Goodnight and God bless you. Please, give my regards to your dear mother. Remember how much I love you.

> All my love and kisses
>> Forever yours, my sweety.
> Hans

> Pickwell,
> Febr 18th 1949

144

My dearest, darling Jean,

Hello, sweety, how are you today? Well, only another day to go till I see you again, though it's a full working day. In one way I am glad the day is over and the situation much clearer. Herbert and I have had a row again at lunch time. I've told him straight away what there was to be said and he's changed a bit tonight. It all started because of the shopping. As you know I have to go shutting up this week so I really didn't know how to manage to get to the shops before they close. There was only one way of doing it. Either one of them had to go shopping or shutting up for me. Of course I asked both, but Helmut didn't say anything, Herbert, however started. He said: 'It was your idea of doing the shopping, so you do it yourself. Doesn't matter how much time you have.' That made me see clear. He also said he wouldn't work another minute after 5.00. I made the suggestion if he doesn't want to help, to take his ration book to buy his things himself and get his meals also somewhere else. His reply made me jump. He said: 'You've started here under the condition to cook for us.' I would've liked to give him a few in his grinning face.

As he said that, Helmut went outside. He knew what was near to happen. Well, I kept my temper and asked him who is getting up at 5.30 every morning whilst he's still sleeping and who's keeping the rooms clean. Also who's doing the washing up. If I don't start dirty dishes would stay on the table for days. He hardly touches anything. If Helmut is coming a few minutes later at night he's sitting reading the paper instead of making the fire. Well, I am not his servant. I don't mind getting up early, but with 3 of us everybody can give a hand and make things easier. For the last half an hour we sat here quietly. Tonight, however, the first thing when he came in, he went for wood and started the fire, whilst I went to Somerby and fetched the rations. When I came back he's set the table nicely and as I washed up and was going to dry as well, he asked to do it to give a hand. That's improved anyway. I don't see why I always should stay up for hours to keep things clean whilst he laughs at us.

Remind me to tell you what the boss said about accommodation. I've had a talk with him.

Well, my darling, sleep well and pleasant dreams. Be good.

Goodnight and God bless and all my love and kisses to you,

Yours forever, Hans

Pickwell,
Saturday Febr 19th
1949

My dearest, darling Jean,

You are gone again and I shan't see you for another week. Well, my love, now what we're talking about when the bus came. I am not so sure you understood what I meant. See, if we go somewhere together, for instance, to Skegness and take a bungalow we can only stay together if we are married. Don't you think it will be possible to get married soon? I know you have to think of your mother. It's much easier for me to ask you. Look, my love, if we could get this place here then you tell me you can't get to Leicester every day. It's right, but I would like you to stop work then. I have thought it over last week. I earn £4-10-0 clear every week and as we live now, the three of us, I know how much money we had to spend on food. If we spend £2 a week we'll live decent. That's about half the wages. Believe me I would make as much overtime as I could work every weekend if necessary so we could save some money up for our house. There's the furniture to think about. That's the only thing that worries me, too. You should let me talk to your mother and I bet she certainly could give us an advice. Of course, such things have to be talked over. And I am sure we would find a way. Nothing is impossible and I am not afraid of doing what's in my power to make it come true very soon. Please, my darling, let's get cracking on that big problem. Do you know that I am only waiting for your word to start? As soon as we could fix everything and have it talked over with your mother so I could say we're getting married on that day, even the boss would take a bit more interest in getting accommodation for me. He's too much afraid of me leaving. As I was speaking to him night before last he said everything might be easier if I was married already. He asked me when I was going to be married and I could only say soon. He then meant lots of people just say so, but only the fact of being married could help.

I'll leave everything about our holidays to you, so please let me know during the week. Think it over and tell me what you have in mind. I would like to make arrangements. I mean to book places if we know where we want to go. Do you mind if we would go somewhere being on our own and not a place with thousands of people about. If your mother also wants to go, alright, let's go, the three of us. Once I have been talking to your mother these things are much easier to arrange.

Well, my darling, don't forget to answer this letter at once. Tell me everything that's on your mind. Perhaps it's also easier for you to write about it.

Be a good girl and give my regards to your mother. Goodnight and God bless you always. I shall be thinking of you all day tomorrow. And you? Remember I love you more than my own life.

All my love and kisses
Forever yours, my sweety
Hans.

Aschersleben, 13.2.49
13/3
My dear Hans

Today I want to send you my loving Sunday greetings again. You have now been home eight days. We have not yet received your post, but we hope something will come during the week. Five weeks ago today we were able to celebrate our reunion, and we have almost been back home three weeks to the day. Time flies unbelievably quickly. We are having beautiful weather at the moment, it feels like spring. It is quite unreal, because we are still waiting for winter to come. The saying goes that 'if we don't get a winter, then it usually follows that we won't have a real summer'. Are you still enjoying your work after your holiday period? I am sure Jean was very pleased to have you back again. Please give her my best wishes and also remember me to your mother-in-law. I sent a letter to the Streeses this week asking if Gertrud could have two more photos of the good ones developed for us. When Mrs. Lehmann goes back to see her parents, she will take the 4 Marks and post it over there. I do not want to put it in a letter from here, it is too risky. Horst has still not been able to exchange his shoes because they have not yet had any more sizes delivered to the shop. They only have small sizes. He is getting quite depressed about it. Mrs. Lehmann's parents are having a pig slaughtered. She wants to bring a lot of meat back. I would love to be able to do that. I am planning on going to Berlin on Tuesday to collect the bed from from Aunt Emilie. Otherwise, I will never come to a proper bed. I am not looking forward to this journey, but needs must. Now, my dear boy, stay healthy. I shall write more next time.We are sending you our love and kisses, your mum and brother Horst.

92 Wharf St
20.2.49
My dearest darling Hans
I have just sat down, 7.30. I nearly came to see you this afternoon then come back early, go to Melton and come back on the 7.0. I would have been in time for my Mother to go out, Cyril had gone up to see if his mother would like to go and see Betty, but when he came back at lunchtime he said she

wouldn't be going so my mother said she would, without asking me. I was annoyed. I stayed in Wednesday, Thursday and Friday so she would be able to go out but I think she would not have gone if I had told her I was going to Pickwell. I wanted to go and give you a surprise.

Cyril was going to take Susan out today but this morning when she got up she had a rash all over her. Almost like scarlet fever but she hadn't a sore throat (I have that at the moment). Cyril is either going to take her to the doctor or send for him. She cried because she couldn't go out so I told her when it is nice I would take her to Pickwell. I hope you don't mind. I wish Fred would grow his hair, then I would bring him to Pickwell.

So you may have gathered I arrived home safe and sound, the bus was in Leicester at 11.15. It was a good job we hurried a bit. I think the conductor had been on the beer, I gave him 2/6 and he gave me 1/6 change. I was 5d better off.

So you don't like my hair short. I don't think you have very good taste so I will never take any notice of what you say. But you had better let me choose the things for you. There is a lot of truth in the saying clothes (and hair cut) make the man.

Now about our holiday. I have not thought about it. I only think I would very much like to go abroad somewhere. My mother has said she would like to go away but I have never said anything to her.

I will have to say goodnight and God bless you. I am very tired and couldn't think.

All my love and x

Jean

.

Aschersleben, 20.2.49

My dear Hans

Thank you very much for your lovely letter dated 6.2.49, it seems you had a very good trip and we are so glad you are now back in situ again. My trip to Berlin is also behind me now. I left early in the morning on Tuesday and returned on Thursday afternoon. Aunt Emilie is sending her best wishes to you, also Hilde, Jürgen and Klaus. But I have caught a terrible cold. Aunt Emilie does not heat the room, even though she could afford to. She prefers to keep the firewood in the cellar. I would like to know why she is saving her money and for whom? She is 83 years old and her behaviour shows signs of stinginess. This is how people get when they are older! She is so different from grandmother. She gave me the worst bedcover she could find instead of something more decent which is still usable. I shall have to have it dry cleaned and have to buy more feathers before one can call it a bedcover. One pound of feathers costs 18.50 Marks. I gave her 30 Marks for the bedcover and three pounds of flour, three pounds of syrup, peas, beans, pearl barley, two loaves of bread etc. In my opinion I paid her quite well. It would not have been quite so bad if she had given me a cover for the feather bed as well. We don't want anything for nothing from her, but she cannot part with anything. Horst is looking after his clients again today. He is very restless, always wants to do something. He is participating in another Hair and Beauty Competition in Halle! Yesterday, he arranged the veil of a bride. He is always very pleased when he has done a good job. He was very annoyed last week when he discovered that he lost 25 Marks out of his coat pocket, after he had worked for it so hard. You can imagine how furious he was. It is a real cheek. He works non-stop and loses his money in such a way. It must have been stolen by one of his lady colleagues. It looks like the parcel service from England is restored, although the parcel service to the West is still taking longer. Overall, parcels are coming in again. I think the Streeses must have been quite annoyed because of their parcel. I heard that more parcels from the West to us are being stolen than parcels from here to the West .My dear Hans, I am sending you lots of love and kisses for today, your mum and your brother Horst.

Love to Jean.

92 Wharf St
21.2.49
My dearest darling Hans
You asked me to answer it straight the way I will try to do that now, but Susan kept shouting to me to go to bed.
Well darling I want to get married very much, I want a place of my own and a very happy family. I know you are the only person that could possibly make that come true, but when I think of it being in a week or month it seems rather quick, I want to put it off for a bit longer that would give us time to save. I know it is awful for you living in that place but it could be a lot worse. You could be living in on the farm and you would have to pay more and you wouldn't have as much freedom. I can tell you it would not be any good asking my mother for advice. I have heard her say to people 'let them please themselves what they do then they can't blame you' so I know she would not say anything. Even if she didn't like the idea. You say we could manage, I suppose we could there are hundreds of others that have to manage some with very large families. And I really like the idea of living in the country, but I would rather wait a little longer. I have some money saved but I would not put that all into the home because if I was to have a baby I would hate to be penniless and have to depend on help from other people. You know that when I have a baby I want everything nice and you know I like expensive things for myself so I would want them for my child too. That goes for my home too. I would rather have only a few things in a house than a lot of cheap stuff. That's

one thing I do know what I want, whether or not I get it remains to be seen.

Well my darling I hope you are not too annoyed with me but will try to understand I will have to say cheeri'O and God bless you

All my love and kisses

Jean

·

Pickwell,

Febr 21st 1949

My dearest, darling Jean,

Hello darling, how are you today? Well the first day of this week has gone, that means only 5 more days to go till Saturday. Did you get home well last Saturday night? I bet you didn't bother about the curlers and went straight to bed. I hope you got my letter this morning, the one I wrote on Saturday after you had left.

Yesterday work went like Saturday. On our way in Margaret asked me if I was shutting up those houses near the road and also the cockerels. I really didn't know because the foreman hadn't told me. We are only 2 on that side of the poultry lot so we have to do it between us. M. went the far way and I do the others. Didn't I say I was glad I had finished shutting up? Well, I have had it. Next week I shall do the big lot again, starting on Sunday. When I finished yesterday I decided to go to Melton to see a picture. You'll have noticed that on the stamp. I took the 6.30 and posted the letter. When I went round the picture house there was a notice put up 'Full' I went back to the bus station, caught my bus and was here again at 7.30. I at least posted your letter.

When I came in at lunchtime today I could've strangled Bonzo. He's had a look at my snaps, but a good thing he hasn't torn any up. It took me quarter of an hour to sort the letters, stamps and snaps out again.

Well, sweetheart there's something else I found out today. I told you about those council houses at Knossington, didn't I? There are 14 of them, but only 7 allocated. So there might be a chance to get one of those. Please, sweety, think that over how it would suit you. I am getting cracking now. To-night I shall get the address where to write to about those houses. Is Miggy going to Knossington?

Another thing I am not quite sure about. Can't we get furniture and pay in weekly or monthly rates? I think I saw something about it in shop windows in Leicester. Please, have a look how much the weekly rates are. We'll fix everything, darling, don't despair. As I told you in my last letter I am only waiting for you to say the word and I'll arrange things.

Well, my love, I'll say goodnight now and God bless you. Be a good girl and remember I love you so very much. Please give my regards to your mother.

All my love and kisses to you

Forever yours, my love

Hans.

Pickwell,

Febr 22nd 1949

My dearest, darling Jean,

I thank you so very much for your lovely letter I received this morning. Well, how are you today, sweetheart? Wasn't it a rough day? In the afternoon the wind was awful. When I got on the top of the hill, the wind almost blew me out of the float. I even had to take my nice hat off. I put it on the first time on Sunday. On Monday morning the boss was in the yard when one of the men shouted across 'You look like a gentleman' and I shouted back for the boss to hear, 'I've seen gentleman farmers, why shouldn't I be a gentleman farm worker,' He looked a bit funny, but didn't say anything. Today he asked me if I had thought about that house on top of the hill and if it would suit me. My answer was 'no, for I want decent quarters.' Anyway I wouldn't like you to have to live up there.

How is your throat darling? Better I hope for I expect you on Saturday. I'll ring you on Friday night at 5.00 before I go to Somerby shopping.

Of course, I don't mind you bringing Susan along. But only when the weather is fine. It looks as if she catches a cold easily. Fred is also welcome. Then Bonzo has someone to play with.

I think I shall be working again this weekend. For a special reason I'll tell you when you come. So you would rather like to work on the land. What about having a go on poultry. Work with me and I'll do your work besides mine.

Now about not having a good taste. To be honest, darling, with the hair cut short as it is now, you look lovely. I think it suits you, still I haven't seen you wearing long hair. I also know the saying, clothes make the man, but remember there's another one saying 'Tailors make the clothes.' You may choose things for me but I hope you don't mind me saying a word to it.

About the holiday. We'll go abroad, darling, if you wish. Where, for instance, would you like to go. Or did you mean, you rather go on your own? We'll talk about it on Saturday afternoon.

Well, my love, I'll say goodnight and God bless you. Be my best girl and think of me.

Please, give my regards to your mother and Betty if you see her.

All my love and kisses

Forever yours, my love,

Hans.

Aschersleben, 23.2.49

My dear Hans

We thank you from the bottom of our hearts for your letter dated 12.2.49. We have been longing for several days to hear from you. Horst has been asking me constantly if Hans has written. I am on my own today. This evening, Horst went to a neighbouring town, together with the Fashion Committee. They were invited to demonstarte some hairstyles. He is coming back home again tomorrow morning and I want to take advantage of the time to write my letters. I am finding it hard at the moment, because my rheumatism is giving me a lot of trouble again. Both my ribs and back are so painful. We have a lot of people here who are suffering from the flu. The schools were closed a fortnight ago. I hope we are not catching anything. I have just made myself a nice cup of coffee to stop me from falling asleep. You know, dear Hans, I was not impressed at all by Gertrud. I did not say anything, but got quite upset. It was certainly too much for her when two loaves of bread were finished in a day. But what are two loaves for five people? We eat more bread at home than we had there, and you really paid them well. I am sure you also gave her money again before we left. They would have had more from us than they actually spent. Gertrud should give her mother more money from her unemployment benefit, and spend less on herself and her Hans. If I had a daughter, I would never allow her to spend every evening with this rascal. It is not appropriate. I would be very unhappy if you had such a girl as your bride. You paid 25 Marks for a handbag for Jean! The main thing is she was pleased with it. We hope Jean is better now. We hope you will bring her with you the next time you come here. We are looking forward to meeting her! You had better both start with your language lessons, so that we can all talk. She would not like to be here at the moment! If the Streeses had told us we should stay a little longer, we would not have left, but it would have cost us our last pennies. You heard it too, saying that one needs at least 300 Marks for five people's food in four weeks. Well, I could have managed with 300 Marks for twice as long. We were not five, but only three people. I got on extremely well with Mrs. Streese and felt very much at home with her. Gertrud has always been known for her moods, she smoked like a chimney! No, we don't want to move to Holstein and it would not be very good for Horst to live out in the country. He wants to better himself.

It looks like you went back to work quite quickly. We had a letter from Elsbeth today. I am still quite upset that we did not have her correct address at the time. I would have loved to have seen Uncle Hermann again. They are all sending their love to you. I also received a letter today from grandma. She wants to go and live with Werner. I don't think things work out very well there with Erwin. Well, people are different now to what they used to be. But grandma must not think that going over the border is easy. I really don't want to go do this journey again and take her. I am still suffering from our last trip. Grandma is sending her love to you too. Now, my dear Hans, I want to finish my letter for today. Stay healthy. We are sending you our love and kisses, your mum and your brother Horst. Much love to Jean. Don't worry, I know how to pronounce her name. Practice makes perfect!

        92 Wharf St
        Feb 24th
My dearest darling Hans
I hope you don't mind if this is a small letter, but darling at the moment I don't feel too good, my throat has been sore today, it has been sore, for the first time I have felt bad. I think I will recover in the morning to go to work. I wasn't going to write then I thought you may ring tomorrow, after the letter I sent last.
I went to the pictures Tuesday to see 'Summer Holiday'. I thought it would be good but it was terrible. The other one wasn't too bad ,at least I had a laugh. Laurel and Hardy in

"Swiss Miss".

Last night I went to see Alice and did not get home until 11.15. Was I late? You know I hate coming home late, but when you sit talking the time flies.

I will be on the 2.15 bus, would you like me to get the tea ready? Just like I did last week!!! I will try this week.

Well darling I'm going to bed now I'm ready to drop. Goodnight and God bless.

All my love and kisses

Jean

.

I am just waiting for you to ring me but just in case you don't I may not be on the 2.15, if not I will come Melton way because I may have to fetch Betty as Cyril is at work. I may probably be there before you get back.

Love

Jean

.

Pickwell,

Febr 24th 1949

My dearest, darling Jean,

Please, excuse my writing with pencil, but there's something wrong with my fountain pen. It has to be cleaned.

Well, I thank you so very much for your letter I received in the morning. Anyway, you've told me a few things straight. Please. sweety, don't think I am annoyed. You should know me by now. Such problems have to be talked over more than only once.

I also thank you for saying that I am the only person who could make you happy. Believe me, darling, I will. Life is worth living again with you. Don't you think it's only because you're used to the idea of getting married, that makes you feel a bit funny when you think of it? What do you mean by putting it off a bit longer? Months or years? You're quite right it would give us time to save some money but look sweetheart, there still is something else I thought of. When I, for instance, should be able to get a council house then we would know where we stand with accommodation. I can't see the housing situation improving. I am getting so fed up with sitting here, living in these stables, thinking of my own home. I also know it could be worse.

Well, if you don't think it worth asking your mother's advice we'll leave it and do everything ourselves. We are old enough anyway.

I have reckoned it over again and again and found that we could manage with only my wages. See, if I work overtime as I did last week I get about £6 clear. That's alright isn't it? Or what about a job where I can earn £20 a week. Don't you know one? I wouldn't mind the work because it's only for you.

It's a good thing you like living in the country. I don't mind where our home is as long as I am with you and both of us – happy. You shall be comfortable, not only if you were to have a baby, but always of course, our furniture has to be nice. That'll all come in time.

Well, my sweetheart, I'll say goodnight and God bless you. We'll talk about everything on Saturday, only two days to go. Be my best girl and think of me.

Please, give my kindest regards to your mother.

All my love and kisses

Forever and only yours, sweety

Hans.

PS Can you bring some dog biscuits for Bonzo?
Love Hans

Pickwell,
Febr 26 th 1949

"My darling"
You're gone again, sweetheart and I shall have to wait till to-

morrow afternoon to see you. This situation makes me feel so unhappy. I don't know what it is, but think it's because of you asking me to put it off. Do you remember the early part of last year when we agreed to wait another year? And now it'll be just the same. I said I am getting fed up with living here, but life for me is really nothing else than that of a gipsy who can't call anything his own except his own mind. When you said you have to take criticism I felt what I really am – nothing else than a foreigner. I know how difficult everything is. Wouldn't it be much easier if I could say I have got the money to give us a start. Unfortunately I haven't. And even if I save up, work harder, it'll take some time. To be honest – years. Still I don't give up because I love you so very much, darling. There's one thing that seems to be different to our country. If I get married I take the responsibility for my family, not my wife. Everybody has his plans, but it looks as if I will have to wait a long time till my only wish becomes true.

When you wrote about the holiday abroad I thought of my part of the money and so last week I told the poultry foreman I am going to work every weekend as long as possible to save up for our marriage and holiday.

Believe me, for the last few months I daren't say anything about getting married, because I was afraid of the answer that was coming.

I just got that idea of having my own home into my head and when I see other fellows getting married and make it possible I can't understand why I can't.

Well, my love, I feel so tired and think I better go to bed. Be good and at least think of me. Good night and God bless you

       All my love ~~to~~ and kisses

       Forever and only yours

          Hans.

                Tuesday March 1st 49,
                8.30pm

Hello sweetheart, here I am again back at my 'home.' You would've been surprised if I had rung you from Humberstone Gate wouldn't you? Just after you had left a bus came in. I got on and it was just ready to go as I found out it was the Humberstone bus. The 6 o'clock bus had left already and so I had to wait until 6.20. Still I got the 7.00 from Melton and arrived here at 7.20.

We didn't have much time did we? Well I hope you like the writing case. I am not coming to Leicester very often so please, don't say I shouldn't have bought it. I remember that a long time ago you said you would like a writing case like mine. Well it isn't like mine, but very nice too.

Believe me I feel so uncomfortable with my hair cut. Another thing it's cold and I don't want to have my hair catching a cold. Anyway I hope you are satisfied now.

Well, sweetheart, I'll say goodnight and God bless you always. Be good and think of me. Please give my regards to your mother.

> All my love and kisses
> Yours forever, darling
> Hans.

92 Wharf St
2.3.49

My dearest darling Hans

I hope you did not mind not going home with me yesterday, but with Betty and the family being there it makes rather a lot to look after. I don't think my mother would have minded but I don't think it is fair to take anyone in without warning. I would have if the family had not been there.

This baby is just like Cyril but it looks as if the poor little thing is to have our nose. She is quite funny to look at but still most babies are until they're about 3 months old.

I did think I had got over the shock of sitting on a glass I have recovered now but it is very painful to sit down. I have to do it gently, it is quite a joke now.

I had a letter from Muriel, it wasn't her turn to write but she had some news for me. She is going to have a baby in July. She wants a girl. I never thought she would have any because she has been married 4 years and would be about 34 years old.

I thank you very much for the writing case, I think it's beautiful but you really shouldn't have. May I ask why you bought it, I really don't deserve it. The reason my writing is so haywire is because I am writing on top of the dog poor thing must be very uncomfortable, he won't move.

I will have to close now I am still tired.

All my love
Jean

P.S. Your hair looks so much better, don't take any notice of what the other 2 say.

Pickwell,
Mar 5th 1949

My dearest, darling Jean,

I thank you so very much for the letter I received today. It wasn't a very long one, was it? I don't mind as long as you write a few lines at all.

How are you today darling? Wasn't it an awful day? I went out feeding at 7.00am and came back soaked to the skin. So of course I had to change but as it kept raining finished work until 2 o'clock. There was nothing else to do than cleaning out and that didn't suit me. My health is more to me than a nasty cold.

Of course I understand that you couldn't ask me home on Tuesday with the house full of people. It really doesn't matter.

Funny what babies look like isn't it? We'll see for ourselves one day. I hate when other people look at a baby and say. It has got her eyes, his nose, grandma's mouth and so on.

Listen, sweetheart, I should know if you deserve a nice present or not. And I know you always do. Didn't I tell you not to say 'you shouldn't have?' So you want to know why I brought it? You once mentioned the wish to have a writing case, didn't you. Well, I don't forget so easily and if I can fulfil your wishes I certainly will – always.

I am pleased with the haircut myself and the other two haven't said anything. It doesn't concern anybody else than myself.

Well, my love, it's time to go to bed. Goodnight and God bless you. Be a good girl and think of me. Remember that I love you so very, very much.

All my love and kisses

Forever yours, my darling

Hans.

Aschersleben, 6.3.49

My dear Hans

Today is Sunday again. Unfortunately, I cannot answer any post from you, because we have not had any news for quite a long time. You are not going to get too lazy to write to us, are you? Would you believe, winter has returned to us again, in March, but surely it cannot go on for much longer. We were both suffering from a cold, but are getting better now. We fought tooth and nail not to go to bed during the day and we are happy to say that we are now completely back to normal. Lots of people around us are ill with the flu. It is now 8 weeks ago when we were on our way to meet you. It is very sad that the lovely time we had with you has passed!! We have not heard anything at all from Gertrud. I wrote to her when we got back home and asked if she would be so kind to re-order two more photos for us. Perhaps she is frightened that we won't pay her. Well, she can calm herself: whatever I order, I pay for. On Thursday I went to Stassfurt to have the featherbed dry-cleaned, and I also bought three pounds of feathers to go in it. I paid a total of 64 Marks. Adding this to the money I already paid to Emilie, the total comes to 124 Marks. This does not include the food I gave them. It can't be helped, because Horst is in need of a featherbed. When Mrs. Lehmann moves away one day, she will have to take her featherbed with her. I now have to look for some lining for Horst's coat. We cannot get this sort of thing at all, only in a free shop, where one meter costs 48 Marks. I need two and a half meters for the jacket plus special pocket lining. Then, the labour is 90 Marks. It is really quite unmanageable. The material for the suit cost 42.70 Marks. Horst works hit butt off and we are still not getting anywhere!

Uncle Erich and Auntie Grete want to come and see us. We are not sure whether they will be able to. He wrote that their work ox has been ill for a long time and he cannot leave him on his own. Heinz is already home. I have not heard anything from Auntie Else, but I received a letter from Uncle Erich, in which he said that Uncle Gustav, Auntie Else and Heinz all came to see them. I was in a lot of pain with my ribs and back for a fortnight. Horst nagged me until I went to see the doctor. My lungs are alright but the doctor said that I have very bad rheumatism, which is a very serious disease and affects the heart. I don't think it can be cured. The doctor prescribed short wave treatment and I also have to take a powder. In the summer I am starting saline bath treatments. And what will become of my trips to collect the firewood in the forest? We cannot live without it. If we had to buy the wood, it costs 80 Mark a meter. Where shall we get all this money from?? Now, my dear Hans, give my very best wishes to Jean, and I am sending you all my love and kisses, your mum and brother Horst. Uncle Erich is sending his love to you as well.

> 92 Wharf St
> 7.3.49

My dearest Hans

Well darling, I thought I could settle down and write to you without Freddy bothering me but no, he was asleep on the chair but as soon as I sat down up he got. I have to let him get on my knee or else he barks until I do.

I am ready for bed. I have had a good wash and stuck my plaster on. I have only to put my curlers in. I ought to have put them in before I started this, now they only might get put in. My mother is in bed, she went at 8.30. Betty and family went about 6.45 that isn't soon enough for me. I said to Betty 'if you don't go mad I'll be surprised'. Cyril is nattering at Susan trying to make her do as she is told (he only does that when he is in a bad mood) the baby was crying so you can imagine the entertainment we have.

When I got on the bus Miggy was on it. She said Herbert was on the bus going down, and he did nothing but talk all the way, she had to do the listening because Otto wouldn't bother, she said Walter (the other fellow at Knossington) saw Herbert on the bus and got on the other one. He told Miggy that he is trying to get his old job back or to do what he did in Germany. She could not quite make it out but thought it was something to do with the police. He also told her that we were going to get married in June. I told her he knew more than I did.

Look darling I don't want you to work 7 days a week day and night. Please darling if you find that it is too much working all those hours stop doing it, it isn't any use working yourself to death. I don't want to marry anyone half dead.

Do you mind when I don't get the tea ready and only get it half done. Just think how exciting life will be when we are married. You won't know whether tea will be ready when you home from work, it would be boring to come home every night and find your tea waiting, where as if it was ready once in a while, it would be a nice surprise.

Well darling I have to go to bed now without putting my hair in curlers.

All my love

Jean

Pickwell,
Mar 7th 1949

My dearest, darling Jean,

This is the first letter, but not the 'only' one. How are you today darling? I hope you got home alright on Sunday night. I was back here in time for Variety Bandbox and didn't even have to go alone. Don't be alarmed!! No Land Army. The fellow who got off the bus when you got on was the foreman of the Irishman. That's the one who has got a council house at Knossington. We're talking about it on the way because sometime ago I asked him to which address the application has to be sent. He said I would stand a far better chance if I was married already. The houses will be ready in about 2 months time. Wouldn't you like to go to Knossington? When Otto and Miggy get the house there it'll be alright having somebody to talk to. Excuse my writing but my hands are still stiff. It's 9.15 and I have just finished egg washing. That room is awful cold. We started at 6.30 and have only done half the lot. That means tomorrow night again for a couple of hours. I don't think it'll take me long to get the £50 together. Of course it would be a job to catch up with your savings. One day I will. Today I have started with my old job again. Cleaning out. There's at least one good thing. I am inside most of the time and don't have to go out when it rains as on feeding.

Is it snowing at your place? It's awful here. It started late in the afternoon.

I overslept this morning. One can notice that the week has seven working days for you. It tires me out, but just a bit, 12 hours work a day.

Please, sweetheart, don't forget to look for those small screwdrivers and try to get some dog biscuits for Bonzo. He's sending his love sitting by my side.

Well, my darling I hope you don't mind this short letter. I am really very tired.

So goodnight and God bless you always. Please give my regards to your mother. Be a good girl.

I love you so much so take

All my love and kisses

Forever yours sweetheart

Hans.

Pickwell,

March 9<u>th</u> 1949

My dearest darling Jean

Believe me I was surprised finding your letter when I came back at dinnertime. I thank you so very much for it. I really didn't expect one today as you told me on Sunday you're going out Monday and Tuesday.

It looks as if Freddy likes to read your letters. It's a good thing I haven't Bonzo taught to sit on my knee. It would look a bit funny.

Oh, darling I am tired tonight. I'll go to bed after I have finished this letter. I was going to write one to my mother but I shan't bother. One needs a few hours sleep at least. I'll tell you what I did yesterday and today.

Yesterday morning the poultry foreman asked me when I wanted my afternoon off. I told him I don't want any time off this week. He said the boss wants me to take the afternoon every week because I am working quite a lot already. Perhaps he thinks I overwork myself. That, however, takes quite a bit more. So there was nothing else to do than talking yesterday afternoon. I went to Melton on the 1.10 and came back on the 2.00 from Melton and just did a bit of shopping. I bought an army shirt and battle dress jacket, also a raincoat for 30/-. It is not bad at all. Ex W.L.A. so I have at least something in common with them. Now I really don't know which of two raincoats to take for work for the new one is quite nice. You can see for yourself on Saturday. I only have to make buttonholes on the right side. So there's definitely something to do for me on Saturday and I would like you to bring some kaki thread, strong and as thick as you can get it. I know how to do the holes properly.

I sure was fed up today. A real working day. First thing this morning the tractor wouldn't start. Somebody else used it whilst I was away yesterday and generally I have had it if anyone else messes about with it. Anyway it made me an hour and a half late with my job. At 12.00 I managed to catch the trailer on one of the houses and it came off the stone posts. For half an hour my watch stopped whilst I tried to get the trailer free off the house. I got that done and then on the way to the muck heap I got stuck twice. After all I unloaded the trailer and when I passed the church it was 1.45. I just had one sandwich and went out again at 2.00 doing the egg collecting all on my own because Margarete was off today. I arrived back at 4.50 then did our dinner and the shutting up soon afterwards. Then a 10 minute sit down and the egg washing started. 9.15 was the finish for me. Now I am ready for bed, believe me. And as long as I know why I do hard work everything is alright. It certainly takes a lot to die.

Your idea of having the tea half ready or even not at all is smashing. I am sure we'll have quite a bit of fun at that. I shall think all day if the tea is ready or not when I come home from work. I'll leave the hunger on the farm.

Well, my darling, I'll say goodnight now and God bless you always. Be a good girl and see if you can spare some time to think of me, loving you so very much. Please give my regards to your mother.

    All my love and kisses
        Forever yours, sweetheart
    Hans.

Did you get the screwdrivers?

Hans Klawitter
Home Farm, Pickwell,
Melton Mowbray/Leics
March 10th 1949

My dearest darling Jean

Hello, sweety, how are you today? Fine, I hope. I myself have had quite a bit of fun. It was watercarting this morning so I took my old tractor and went out. It was alright for the first hour but when the sun came through I had had it. During the following half an hour I got stuck about a dozen times. Good thing I took 2 chains along so I managed to get free. At about 11 o'clock I got stuck again and that finished the job. I went back to the yard and fetched a caterpillar to do the rest and left my tractor standing in the field. At 3.30 the boss came and told me to bring the tractor in. There was something wrong with the engine and I went out to have a go at it. I got it fixed alright but somehow the engine kept speeding up. You should've seen me on it down the big hill.

Margarete just came back from feeding and held the gate open for me. When I came into the yard I thought I was going to hit the wall. Anyway the boss didn't say anything instead was glad I brought it back.

Could you possibly get a zip for me? About 5 inches. It's for the pullover my mother knitted. The one that's in now broke when I put it on last Tuesday.

How are things going at your place? Is Betty still there? I only hope you don't get mad before they go home. It must be quite a change for you coming here where it is rather quiet.

Well, my darling, that's all for today.
Goodnight now and God bless you. Be good.

All my love and thousand kisses
Forever yours, sweetheart
Hans.

Aschersleben, 13.3.49

My dear Hans

Thank goodness, after three weeks, we finally received your news. Thank you for your lovely letter dated 2 March. You have kept us waiting for a very long time. You know how much we love to hear from you. We have another ten days of winter behind us, with very little snow. It is now much milder. The shrubs are already showing some green leaves and the flowers are coming up as well. Easter is upon us in four weeks' time. I can quite believe you that your first day back at work was not easy, but I am sure you are now settled back into your routine. So, you want to wait with the wedding a little while? Well, you will have to buy certain things and it takes a while before you find what you want. There is a lot to be sorted and time goes so quickly. Where are you going for your Honeymoon? Dear Hans, I am sure our trip to Berlin is not quite what you think. I went from one sector to another and nobody stopped me, and the other travel companions did not have any problems either. I already told you all about my trip three weeks ago. Are you still getting more holiday in the summer now that you have already had four weeks off? Or does your last leave not get deducted? We received our first mail from Schmiedenfelde since January. I am enclosing their letter. I was surprised to hear about Edith's wedding on 11 January. She asked me to send you the announcement, as she does not have your address. Every other day I have to get radiation treatment for my rheumatism. Now my dear boy, please stay healthy, give our love to your Jean and your mother-in-law, and we are sending you our love and kisses.

Yours

Mum and your brother Horst.

Aschersleben, 16.2.49

Dear Hedwig, dear Horst

Thank you very much for your lovely letter and card. We are very happy for you that all went well with your big journey. We can well believe you that it was an extremely stressful journey and hope that you have both recovered by now.

Aschersleben, 2.3.49

Dear Auntie Hedwig, dear Horst

Mum started this letter 14 days ago, and I want to now continue with the writing. We have just returned from our Honeymoon. You must be quite surprised, that everything happened so quickly in the end. After I had sent the necessary documents to Siegfried (which I had obtained from the Mayor, Police and Local Authority), he was able to collect the interzonal pass * and he arrived here on 28.1. We had a lot of complications just before the wedding on 11.2. As the centrifuge was only set up 8 days before our wedding, we had not collected sufficient coupons to get our rations of butter - it would have been nice if we could have offered some butter to our guests. At the same time, Heinz wrote from the Quarantine Camp in Eisenach that he can arrive home on 14.2. We sent him a telegram immediately, upon which he was allowed to start his journey a few days earlier and subsequently arrived two days before the wedding. Thus, we were able to celebrate the wedding and also our reunion. It would have been very nice if all our relatives could have been here for the reunion, but we have neither the space nor the facilities. Our Honeymoon period after the wedding was also very short, because Siegfried had to leave again on 22.2. I would have loved to have gone with him, but leaving from up here without a permit, is meant to be very difficult. I want to wait until I receive the travel and relocation permit from Siegfried. If these take too long to come I might go over the illegal way. How did you two get over? Was it very difficult or not as difficult as one assumes?

How are you now? I hope you have recovered from your ordeal. Now to your letter, Auntie Hedwig. It reached us in the best of health, thank you very much. Before I forget, I want to give you Lotte's address: 57 Lehrter Strasse! Everyone here seems to have a bad cold. Herta and mother have been in bed for several days. Otherwise, nothing much has changed. Don't worry about the spinning wheel, Auntie Hedwig. it is not necessary because we have no sheep yet.

Please can you post one of the (wedding) announcements to Hänschen as I do not have his address. Remember me to him, and we are sending you our love, yours Edith, parents, siblings and Ingrid!

*required to get from one zone to another in Germany after WW2

Pickwell,
March 14$\underline{th}$ 1949

My dearest, darling Jean,
How are you today sweetheart? You didn't mind the rain did you? Till midday I also didn't mind because I was egg washing after lunch. In the afternoon I should go out with the tractor. It wasn't running very well so I drove it into the workshop for the mechanic to have a look. The boss was also there so they started fixing it and – broke it. I really couldn't help laughing. One always knew it better than the other. Well, they have messed it up now. I hope it finishes

the tractor for good so he has to get a better one for me. He wanted me to give the mechanic a hand. That's what I did till 3.30. It was lovely then, raining and windy. The poultry foreman sent me shifting hen houses in that rain. Well, I went and now something you like to hear I took the ex W.L.A mac. It got dirty so I shan't wear it again when I go out. Are you satisfied now? You know I always like to oblige you.

Did you get home well, last night? I was back here in time for 'Variety Bandbox.' It was very nice.

Well, darling, you certainly were a dear last night doing the shutting up on your own. This morning I could hardly wait to get on top of the hill to see if all the hens were in. And they were, however, I forgot to tell you one thing. The shutter on the last house on the big field doesn't shut properly. I was only 3 houses away when it opened and all the hens came out. Good thing I was near enough to count them.

I've had a look at your watch and found that the mainspring is broken and so is the balance axel. When I get to Melton I'll try to get spare parts to fix it.

Well, my darling, I'll say goodnight now. God bless you always. Be a good girl and think of the 16.7.49 What a grand day it'll be. I love you more than my own life.

All my love and kisses

Forever yours, my love

Hans.

Aschersleben, 16.3.49

My dear Hans

Although we have not received any mail from you, I want to write to you today anyway. I am afraid I have no good news to bring to you. I had to go back to the doctor's yesterday because I had excruciating pains in my right side. He gave me a thorough check-up and sent me straight to the hospital yesterday afternoon, to see a specialist. The result is that I have to have an operation because I have a tumour as large as a child's head. You can imagine how I feel. I was awake most of the night and all sorts of things went through my mind! It looks like I am spared nothing!! I have experienced such torment in my life and what will become of my usual potato picking this year, not to mention gathering the fire wood? I always wanted to make sure we had enough to eat and some money left! The specialist told me immediately that I should not worry, because he can give me a 100% guarantee, that the tumour is not malicious. However, the operation has to be carried out. We hope everything will go smoothly. I have to go into hospital immediately after Easter, in four weeks from now. Horst was so shocked, he felt like he had received a big blow to his head. I am sure you can imagine it. He wants to work even harder so that we can afford to buy more for us. But, I won't let him because he has hardly any spare time now. Dear Hans, please don't worry about me. I am sure everything will be alright in the end. When I think about it, it is very unfortunate to become ill in these miserable times. I heard that the hospital food is not very good. I was so happy that I have recovered fairly well and now I am starting all over again. Now, my dear boy, please stay healthy and give my love to Jean and your mother-in-law.We are sending you all our love and kisses, from your mum, who is always thinking about you, and your brother Horst.

We are hoping for a healthy reunion.

The operation does not cost me anything, because I am insured through Horst's work.

What luck!

Pickwell,
March 17th 1949

My dearest darling Jean
I hope you don't mind getting only two letters this week. Nothing much happened so there wasn't anything to write about as you usually say. I was going to write last night, but

as we (Helmut and I) decided to go to Melton. We saw "A Foreign Affair" You have also seen it haven't you? Well, we went on the 7 o'clock and came back at 10.20 had our dinner and went to bed at 12.00. You can imagine how tired I was. Of course I overslept this morning.

I know your hair looked a mess on Sunday. I noticed you were very tired and would've liked to stop here. It would have been nice if we were at our home, wouldn't it? You said so yourself, but still keep joking about the <u>16.7.49</u>. Remember that date.

I told you in the other letter that I'd taken out my mac (the new one) and I hope I have pleased you with doing so. Anyway I shan't wear it at weekends for it got dirty.

I hope you don't mind if I close now. I am really very tired. So till Saturday be good. Goodnight and God bless you.

All my love
Hans.

92 Wharf St

My dearest darling Hans.

I arrived back in Leicester quite safe at 9.45. I felt very tired but I managed to put my hair in curlers. My mother asked if I was going to curl it because it looked a -mess. I had been working quite hard in the morning, we had been washing, I had cleaned the room out and I had to give the mats a good brush and I'd scrubbed the floor. I also chopped an orange box up, so before I started out to Pickwell I was tired.

My mother did not feel well tonight and has gone to bed, she went about 6.45, it is only 7.30 now and I am ready for bed, but I am not going just yet. I had a wash and I thought I may as well put my night kit on. I had cleaned my boots, it took me ages and I have not got them properly clean.

I did have a rush this morning. I started to clean my boots and decided that it would take too long and they were much too dirty to wear, so I had to find myself a pair of shoes, I had put them away and also find a pair of stockings because the ones I wear with my boots are too thick to go with my shoes. This is at 8.50. I am not dressed. I told you my suspender had broken so I had to go and find my other corset. I got to work at 9.6, that was not bad.

Did you wear your mac today (the new one). I wondered if you had it on when it was pouring. I think that is more suitable for work than the other one, it will stand the weather better. Don't you think so? I hope you do.

Well darling I will close now goodnight and God bless.

All my love

Jean.

Thank you so much for your letter. I have changed the zip and have got an 8" one if that isn't big enough you can sew the hole up a bit. What half day are you having? What about the 16.7.49, I have forgotten already!!!

92 Wharf ST
MARCH 21st

My dearest darling Hans

I have just noticed that it is the first day of spring and it has been a beautiful day. Different from last night when I arrived in Leicester it was pouring, I walked with Miggy to Wharf Street so that took longer and I got wetter than I would have if I had been on my own. It is nice to have someone to talk to, it passes the time away but last night I felt awfully sick while on the bus I was glad to get in the air. Miggy told me all her troubles, she had been in the canteen too long (23 minutes) and had to write a report out of what she had been doing. The head supervisor has threatened to take the matter further.

The new girl turned up this morning. So far she seems quite nice. She hasn't been out to work since last April. She had been working on a farm at Somerby. You know the church, it is the farm at the side, down the lane. She goes out with June's brother (the girl that works in the Melton office and lives almost facing the bus stop) but from what I gather from today she doesn't like his family very much.

I saw a cookery book today and I am wondering whether or not to buy it. I saw this one advertised a few months ago and it costs 42/-. It should be very good for that but I don't know whether to wait until I need one or get it while I have the money. When I need one I probably won't have the money. What would you do chump?

It is near my bedtime 9.50 so I will have to close. Goodnight and God bless

All my love
Jean

.

Pickwell,
March 21st 1949

"My darling"

Did you get home well last night? I noticed Miggy wasn't on the bus you got on. The other one was behind. It was pouring with rain when I was on the way back. As usually I listened to "Variety Bandbox" and it was very good. Especially Franky Howart! He was on for 20 minutes. Just after 10.00 I went to bed and had a nice long rest. When I woke up this morning I would've loved to have another couple of hours. Nobody told me to so I had to get up. I thought of you turning round again.

Wasn't it a grand day today? When I went feeding in the morning I took my jacket off and rolled the sleeves up and really didn't feel like work. I hope it's the same again tomorrow.

Well darling it looks as if I shan't get a rabbit. Herbert didn't bring any cartridges and also the Irishmen haven't got any left. I hope I don't forget to buy some next Saturday. Will you remind me?

And now about the 16.7.49. I still hope you, the one that means everything to me, won't disappoint me. You can't even give a reason why you think it's too soon. Please darling think it over again and say 'yes' on Saturday. Is it so difficult to get used to the idea. Anyway it shows me that you're not really longing for a family life and a place of your own.

Herbert got told that they're going to get him out of agriculture. It might take some time.

Till then he wants to go to a place nearer to Leicester. I myself don't believe it but he said he's giving his notice this week. Well, we'll see.

I hope you don't mind this short letter. I am so tired. I just have to cut a bit of wood for the morning and then I shall go to bed, my thoughts being with you.

Be a good girl and think of our great day (16.7), goodnight and God bless you. Please give my regards to your mother.

All my love and kisses to you
my sweetheart,
Yours forever Hans.

Pickwell,
March, 22ⁿᵈ.1949

My dearest, darling Jean,

Quick few lines to you sweetheart because I shan't be able to write tomorrow night. I found that 'No orchids for Miss Blandish' is on at Melton and we've decided to go and I really wonder what it'll be like.

How are you today, sweety? I hope you aren't as tired as I am. Can't you tell me why I am always so tired? Believe me I was browned off at dinnertime today. The foreman wanted me to go watercarting and put all the water tins outside. So I finished putting the tins outside at 1.15 and went watercarting at 2.00. It was 5.30 when I got back here. My feet are aching. It's 9.00 now and I will be going to bed in a few minutes. Only you could stop me from doing so.

I took Bonzo out again with me and he behaved alright. There were quite a few sheep about but he didn't chase any. He seems to be tired for he's sleeping already since 5.30.

This morning I asked the foreman for a hen and he said it would be alright. So I'll bring it on Saturday.

Well, my love, I'll say goodnight and God bless you. Be a good girl and think of me. Please, give my regards to your mother.

To you All my love and kisses

Forever yours, sweetheart

Hans.

Pickwell,
March 24th 1949

My dearest darling Jean

I thank you so very much for your letter (Monday's) only another day and a half to go and I shall be with you again. I shall be coming on the same bus than last week. 2.10 at Leicester. That'll give me plenty of time to go to the barber. I've told the poultry foreman about a hen and he said I should pick out myself what I think is right. So, of course, I'll take the best one I can find. I've set my eye on one for a long time.

We have had good news today. Guess what it is? Our fellow is giving his week's notice tomorrow, changing to a farm five miles from Leicester. Can you imagine how glad we are? I am sorry but I had to tell him off again today. He's had funny ideas about the things we all have paid for. Do you remember the prices of those plates and cups you brought along? I am going to reckon up every penny. He'll be surprised when he gets the bill.

You'd better get that cookery book now whilst there's time. You'll start your cooking on July 17th 1949. I don't like the idea of getting poisoned. Just do it exactly as they say in the book, that is if you've got everything.

How are you today, darling? I shall ring you tomorrow night about the Grand National. To make sure I'll put the horses down again on the back of this sheet. Please put on a shilling each way for each horse.

Well, sweetheart it's bedtime. I'll say goodnight and God bless you always. Be a good girl and think of me.

Please give my regards to your mother.

> To you all my love and kisses
> Forever yours, my love
> Hans.

1/- Cromwell   E.W.) (means
1/- Cloncarrig   E.W.) each way)
1/- Happy Home E.W.)

Aschersleben, 24.3.49

My dear Hans

We were very happy to receive your airmail letter today dated 17.3.49. I am sure you will have, in the meantime, also received my letter dated 16.3.49, in which I told you that I need to go into hospital for an operation. I wish everything was behind me already and that I would be happily back at home again. Now to your letter, which I want to answer immediately, as you have asked me to. You want to know about the parcel. Well, first of all, we would be very happy if you could manage it! It would be such a help to us. Please have it sent to Berlin. It would definitely be worth it for us go and collect it there. The fare would cost around 30 Mark. We would only be able to purchase half a pound of butter here, but the parcel would have such a lot of lovely things for us. Now to your second question. Whether 10 pound of sugar or fat, meat, cheese etc., we would choose the fat, meat, cheese etc. instead of the sugar. Do you have to pay a lot of money for all this? Will you be able to manage it? You would make us very, very happy. With good food, I would make a much quicker recovery after the operation, because the food in the hospital leaves a lot to be desired. Well, it cannot be helped, I have to have the operation – it is a non-malignant tumour. It is the size of a child's head and is growing. This is due to the lack of fat and protein in my body, and also the physical strain I have had to endure. All I ever wanted was to be able to keep our heads above water, to look after ourselves and have some food on the table. I bought a hundredweight of firewood today. It is ridiculous to have to pay 90 Marks for it. I had intended to go back to the Harz Mountains before Easter to get some firewood, but it is not possible. Horst will not let me go. He is worried that I will get worse. But I am thinking with these high prices, what's going to happen, how are we going to manage? It is just impossible. I realize now how much work I did do, now that I cannot do it any-more. Who would have thought all this when we said 'good-bye' to each other not so long ago? I wonder what else I have to go through. I am hoping that they don't take me into the hospital too long before the operation, but if it is really ne-cessary, then I would rather go earlier than later. Horst has been invited to take his meals in his friend's house. Mrs. Zie-mann has offered to do the washing and the cleaning every Saturday. I shall be in hospital for at least four weeks. Horst worries a lot. He wants me to be home again on his birthday. Well, we can only hope for the best. His working hours are changing from today: from 08.00 to 12.00 and 14.00 to 18.00. That's a lot better. It gives him more time to have his lunch. He is leaving in a minute to see to his private clients, whose hair he used to do in the mornings. He does not in-dulge himself in a lot of spare time. He will not be able to visit me in the hospital during visiting hours. I shall have to get a letter from the doctor so that he can come in the evenings to see me. We are having the most beautiful spring weather at the moment. I want to go for a little walk as soon as I have finished my letter. I can imagine you will be extra busy with the spring orders. Please take some time off to have a rest, you need it, it will be good for your leg. Give my love to Jean and your mother-in-law. I have to go for my radiation treatment every other day. We are sending you all our love and kisses. From your mum, who is always thinking about you, and your brother Horst. We are hoping for a healthy reunion. I am sure we will manage somehow to collect the parcel from Berlin.

Pickwell,
March 28<u>th</u> 1949

My dearest, darling Jean,

How are you today, sweetheart? Did you get home well last night? Miggy was on the second bus, but I think Otto was with her. I've only had a quick glance when the bus went by. On the way back I had company. Margarete came back from Oakham. Still I was here in time for "Variety Bandbox". It was very nice.

My mother told me in her letter I received today that she's to have an operation week after Easter. Her thigh was swollen so she went to see a doctor. He told her it's nothing serious but there's something wrong inside and it has to be cut away. She has arranged with the hospital already and also told me not to worry. They've got something similar to the National Health Scheme so she doesn't have to pay for it herself. She told me to give you her love and kindest regards to your mother.

So to say today was a pleasant day, full of surprises. When I went out feeding this morning I saw a strange face in the yard. Female. After breakfast I was introduced to my new workmate. She is 19 years old and a member of the W.L.A. Somerby. Face and figure not bad at all. Looks just like a doll.

Perhaps the boss thought I need a complete change. I think I shall be alright, shan't I? You know I don't like the W.L.A. very much, but working together changes the situation. We'll get on well together I hope!! But still there's only one I love and that's you. They could send a thousand girls and it won't make any difference to me.

Look, darling, you should occupy your mind a tiny bit more with our holidays. Time is getting on and nothing done. Don't let it get too late because I have to make arrangements here. We can't all go at the same time. And also get use to the idea of getting married on 16.7.49. Please let me know about the weekend. Especially Saturday afternoon.

Well, that's about all I had to say tonight. I am going to have another go at your watch and see if, after all, I can't the get balance out of my watch into yours.

So I'll say goodnight and God bless you. Be a good girl and try to think of me. Please, give my regards to your mother.

All my love and kisses

Forever and only yours

Hans.

92 Wharf St

28.3.49

My dearest darling Hans

I arrived home safe and sound. Miggy was on the bus I didn't mind because my head ached a bit. The week before I felt sick. I just had to sit and listen and I kept wishing I was on my own. The old bus I got on was the duplicate, it did not go through South Croxton or keep to the timetable, I was at home listening to "Variety Bandbox" at 9.35.

Did I say how nice the chicken was, I have just had a piece of skin off it, delicious. I am just drinking some Ovaltine as I have got to keep my strength for when I marry you later on.

I do write my letter funny, it is Tuesday afternoon and I am writing this at work. I was too tired to think last night I went to the "Odeon" to see 'You Gotta stay Happy.' It was very funny. What are you going to do about getting a sports jacket? Are you going to get one in Leicester, Melton Oakham etc. I hope you don't mind me telling you what to get but I have better taste than you. I know you have to wear it. ~~But~~ I don't want my friends and relations to see you looking like a D.P. or a spiv. I try to make you look English and in temper. When I am finished who knows you might become Lord Klawitter with Maclean as farm labour!!! What a hope.

You had better come to Leicester on Saturday. There is quite a good picture on at the Savoy, I don't know if it is good but it looks OK, it is in colour. You had better let me know what else you want to do.

I will have to say cherri'O. It is my turn to mash the tea and if I don't get cracking Arthur will be getting on to me.

All my love

Jean

92 Wharf S
30.3.49
My dearest darling Hans

I don't think it would have been Otto with Miggy. She told me the other week that a friend of Otto's was going over, she thought it would be Saturday he was going but she hoped it would be Sunday. Did you know Otto hurt his foot last Saturday playing football? He has got to go to the Melton Infirmary to have an xray. I have not been able to ask Miggy how he got on because she has to be careful at the moment.

I am sorry your mother has to have an operation. When you write, give her my kind regards and I hope she will soon be well.

It didn't take you long to find out your new working companion's (sounds better than work mate) ages. You also might have told me a few more things about her as well, You had better start interrogating her so you have all the answers when I see you.

Look darling I could think about our holidays but you want to get married then go and you know at the moment I don't want to get married just yet. If it was just a matter of going on our holidays we could fix up somewhere.

About getting married in July. I know it is hard for you to understand. I want to marry you very much but I somehow feel that I don't want to get married just yet. We are not old and you're married an awful long time, at least I hope we are, but there is one thing I would never stand, that is being shouted out and I don't like anyone to lose their temper with me. I have been thoroughly spoilt, besides being spoilt, a gipsy told me I had a wicked eye. She did not say which one!!

Today we found out (Lucy and I) that Nancy's (the new girl) boyfriend must have been a conscientious objector. I think Lucy dislikes those more than the Germans, she is always carrying on about them.

I almost forgot the most important bit of news. I have a shocking cold. I have done nothing but sniff all day. I am just going to have some milk and then off to bed. There is another thing I ought to warn you about. The bed clothes in the morning are one side of the bed and the thing with feathers in is on the other side (I can't spell it) I don't know how I managed it.

Well darling I will say goodnight and God Bless you

All my love

Jean

.

Pickwell,

March, 31<u>st</u> 1949

My dearest, darling Jean,

I am glad to hear you liked the chicken. We haven't had one for quite a while. What does Ovaltine taste like? I'd better get some myself to keep my strength for when I get married to "<u>you</u>". Was it necessary to put those two strokes underneath 'later on'? Well July does mean later on to me.

Helmut and I went to Melton last night. We saw 'Fury at Furnace Creek' it was about Soldiers, Cowboys and Indians. Just the sort of pictures he likes. In fact, it wasn't bad at all. I read in the papers about 'You gotta stay happy' It should be nice.

So, you would like to know what I am going to do about the sports jacket. Well, I shan't buy one yet so we'll have something to argue about. I don't mind you telling me what you like best. Still I have to wear it and you don't want me to look funny do you? Of course I don't like looking like a D.P. because I ain't one, but looking like a spiv would be too bad. Well, I'll come to Leicester on Saturday afternoon, same time as usually. We could go to the pictures. I want to buy a small lampshade after all and also a 60w bulb. A few lbs of biscuits for Bonzo. That's all I can think of.

How are you today darling? Fine, I hope. I was cleaning out today and got fed up with it. Only another day and a half to go till Saturday. Margarete said this morning she's fed up with the sight of chicken and eggs. It drives me mad when the hens make such a noise.

Well, sweetheart, I'll say goodnight now. I am so very tired. Be good and think of me. I'll see you on Saturday.

God bless you always. Please give my regards to your dear mother.

> All my love and kisses to you my darling, yours forever.
>
> Hans.

Aschersleben 1.4.49

My dear Hans

Today I shall write you a few lines, waiting as always for mail from you. It has been eight days yesterday since I have replied to your letter, and in the evening as a total surprise grandma visited us, she had received my letter saying that I had to go to hospital, so she could not remain calm. We were pleased that someone visited us. The coming week she will return, she cannot stay anywhere for long. She does not want to go and meet Werner, what's the point, he is out of work and does not have his own room, so there's no point in going, bearing in mind she has no access permit, nothing is easy. We now have wonderful spring weather here, and what is ahead of me. I so wish that it was all over and done with. Maybe I will go into the clinic, at the hospital it is so overcrowded and the care is supposed to be a lot better at the clinic. Next week I shall have to go for another examination. Yesterday and today I had terrible pain, it will have grown again, as my skirt is becoming tighter. The surgery will definitely stop me from going digging, why did it have to happen now? I must not dwell on it. At this time so many transports arrive, bringing returnees back, if only our papa were amongst them!!! I would wish it with all my soul. Before Easter I had to do an enormous amount of washing so that everything is okay whilst I am away, and afterwards it will take some time before I can work again. Why on earth are the Streeses not writing? I had written regarding the pictures. Now my dear Hans we are sending you and your Jean a happy and healthy Easter, and please remain well. Many greetings for today, and sending you love and kisses from your always thinking of you mum and from your brother Horst. Grandma sends her love. Here's to a healthy Wiedersehen

   92 Wharf St
   April 5th 1949

Dear Hans,
So you expected to get a letter today, did you. Well you will be lucky if you can call this a letter. I am writing it at work again. I hope you don't mind the heading, but when anyone

comes in they look to see what I am doing and I feel so daft if anyone reads my dearest darling.

I went to the pictures last night to see "The Paradine case" it was quite good. I thought we could go to the Savoy on Saturday to see "Cass Timberlane" I would like to see that.

I have made an appointment to have my hair set on Easter Saturday April 16th at 12.0. We have Good Friday, Saturday and Monday off. What about your hair will you get it cut this Saturday or wait until Easter Saturday. You would need one then.

I have bought myself a jumper this lunch time a grey one. Quite plain.

I am only sending the one ration book just in case it did get lost. Don't forget to bring it one Saturday, we have not fetch the ration yet.

I don't know whether or not to come this Sunday because you have to rush so to get the birds shut up. I could also wash my hair and blond it a bit. I want to do it before I go to the hairdresser and I will have to wash it twice.

I was speaking to Mr Chandler this morning his daughter Sheila has come to live with him at Saltby. She was unable to find a job at Southsea so she has come to see if she can get one either at Melton or Grantham.

I have not heard Miggy for about a week I have been trying to pick her up. I will ask one of the girls if she is still there.

Well, my darling I will close and if I feel like it I will write again sometime this week

    All my love

    Jean

    ——.

                      Pickwell

                      April 6th 1949

My dearest, darling Jean,

Thank you so very much for your letter I received this morning, that means the ration book got here safely. Well, the heading in your letter was rather short and simple, but I take your explanation for it. Do you know what I do with people who look over my shoulder whilst I am writing? They get one on their nose so they certainly won't do it again. Coloured noses usually look smashing.

I have to tell you quite a lot today. At 4.30 p.m. yesterday the poultryman told me to go out and dig a hole to bury the dead hens today. It was pouring with rain so I said I will if it doesn't rain. It kept raining hard so I did something else instead. This morning he asked me if I had done the hole. My reply was "no" so he said rather sarcastic, you'll find out that you have to work even when it rains hard. Don't worry, I didn't loose my temper, but I wasn't far away from it. I just said " I certainly will work when it rains, but no blinking unnecessary jobs that can be done any other time" he looked at me rather surprised and as he didn't say anything I went away. He told the boss, but he didn't say anything to me.

Tonight, Helmut asked me if he could borrow my raincoat for he'd to go unloading a load of lime at 6.00. I told him not to mess the coat up and you should have seen him when he came back-the coat full of lime and wet. One has to be careful because wet lime burns everything. I could have smacked his face. I hope rinsing the coat will help to prevent the worst.

He went to the pictures tonight. I didn't bother, but went over to Somersby to fetch the tin of salmon for you. I got it alright, but there were only 24 points in your book so I had to give 4 out of mine. I'll have to be very careful with my points now. You know what temptation is? I can see the tin from here!!!

About Sunday we'll have a word when I come over. Perhaps you are right. I hope you'll wear your new jumper on Saturday when I take you out. Let me have a look at it.

Well, my darling, I'll close now. It's bedtime. Please give my regards to your mother. Be good and think of ~~you~~ me. Remember how much I love you.

All my love and kisses to you
Forever and only yours,
Hans.

92 Wharf St
April 6th 1949

My dearest darling Hans

It is only 9.0 and I am in bed. Wouldn't it be nice if I could cuddle up to you and to get nice and cosy. My mother hasn't gone out this evening it was too wet. I intended to listen to the play on the radio "The Paying Guest" but it was not until 8.30 I remembered about it. It had been on half an hour then, so I boiled some milk and brought it to bed.

Nancy went to Somersby for the weekend I brought the village scandal back. You are certainly living in a bright part. During the last fortnight 3 men have gone off with other women. The first is a builder in Somerby, he has gone to live at Loughboro' with a girl from Little Dalby. The second went with a land girl to live in Luton. A few months ago he asked his wife to have the savings transferred, now he has taken the lot and the furniture except for a few things. To make things a bit more spicy the land girl is going to have a baby. The third fellow had ordered the furniture removers to fetch the furniture. The removers call round to see how much furniture there was and his wife was in. So that put paid to his little game. I said you can't blame the men when you have seen some of the women at Somerby. That is not all the scandal I have this bit was more interesting to me a little bit about Pickwell. Mr Hastie, he works at the War Ag. you know lives at the house as you just come into Pickwell. He has been going out for ages with a Mrs Moon or Noon (she lives in Pickwell too). Find out who it is. Someone sent Mrs Hastie an anonymous letter, she went about it in a big way went to see a solicitor. He sent Mrs Moon a letter. I think that is the end of that. I do hope it isn't catching or you never know what might happen. You might be going off with the new land girl. I have cleaned the window out, my mother and I did it last night, it looks much better. I seem as if I have no end to do I have to give my bedroom a good clean, it's terrible at the moment. I also want to spring clean down stairs and dozen of other things. I'll have to get cracking before Easter. I may go to Alice tomorrow night. I rung her on Monday it was her birthday.

Well darling I will get some sleep Goodnight and God bless

Friday

I was going to post this letter yesterday, but when I received your letter at lunchtime (thank you very much) I thought I would write a few more lines after I had washed my hair but I did not wash my hair. I was going to Hiltone it. I thought I had some left but when I had a look it had all gone, so that put paid to washing my hair. So I went up to Alice's and did not get home until 11.30 then it was too late to start writing.

It is very low to go around punching anyone on the nose. It is not done in the best circles, I think the best thing would be to say "wait until I have finished then you may read" that would make them feel worse than ~~hitting~~ punching.

You cannot blame Helmut for your mac getting covered with lime. When you lent it to him you knew what the weather was and what he was going to do.

>I will see you tomorrow so till then cheeri'O
>All my love
>Jean.

>Pickwell
>April 10th 1949

My dearest, darling Jean,

I thank you very much for your letter and a lovely Saturday afternoon. I certainly enjoyed the picture, the best one I've seen for a long time. My bus arrived in time and the time went very quick. It's much better if one has got the chance to talk to somebody. Miggy has been talking to him about you and I, but he didn't know I was Hans. He told me they are definitely getting married in June or July. So what about a double wedding? He also said Walter is going to be married in July. Why are we waiting?

Miggy has had a very bad cold and german measles and stayed away from work since a fortnight. Well, that settles all. That's why you didn't hear from her.

I finished egg-collecting at 4.30, started early, because on the back of my mind I had a secret hope. I really hoped you might have changed your mind and come over after all. Just a little surprise for me. As I turned into the yard I couldn't see light here so I knew you hadn't come. It's 6.00p.m. now. Radio Luxembourg is just playing "So Tired". It's very nice. You'll be able to listen to "Variety Bandbox" tonight. I shall miss it because I have to go shutting up at 7.30, just when it starts. It's a shame for it really is the only program I am waiting for all week.

I'll put some ~~money~~ hours in this week to have a bit more when we go away. I haven't had a chance yet to talk to the foreman about Easter but I will do tomorrow and let you know at once. Don't you have to book seats for Skegness?

Wouldn't it be nice to go to bed at night and cuddle up to each other to be comfortable and cosy?

Well, you now know what I think about village scandal around here. I don't take any interest in village life and you also know how I think about other peoples private affairs. Let them do whatever they like because I'll do just the same. Even if it was catching you needn't be afraid of me going off with someone else I rather shoot myself. I know what a girl or better angel I have got hold of.

By the way, have you still got the paying-in-book? Next week it's time for paying again.

What have you been doing this afternoon, sweety? Or is "honey" better? Been busy? I forgot to have a look at the shop window to see what it looks like now. I certainly will when I come the next time.

Bonzo is waiting already for his run. I took him out this morning, but left him in this afternoon because lambs are on the field. I haven't had time to watch him.

Well, sweetheart, I'll say cheerio now. Get myself a drink and go shutting up. Be a good girl and think of me if you've some time to spare. Please, give my regards to your mother. I love you so very much.

All my love and kisses

    Forever yours, darling

     Hans.

    92 Wharf St

    April 10th

My dearest darling Hans

It is now 2.30 and all is well. Will you be able to ring before Thursday, because we may have the afternoon off, we have not heard anything official, but we had it last year. I know I will ring you Tuesday night about 7.30, is it Somersby 38. You will have this letter tomorrow (Monday) you can answer it Monday night and you can let me know what time suits you so let me know if that is the correct number.

Do you have to work Sunday morning, because if you don't you could come on Saturday. I have to go to the hairdressers Saturday 12.0. I forgot about that when I said I would come over to Pickwell Saturday. I may have time, on the other hand I may not have time to get the Oakham bus. You also will want a hair cut, but it looked alright yesterday.let me know what you have to do.

I think it is going to be a wet Easter, because the new moon came in wet so I hardly think it would be worth going out for the day to the sea. We could probably go at Whitsun tide. What do you think ?

Can you get a chicken for next weekend? Not forgetting to pluck it! ! !.

Well darling I will have a wash (I have not had one yet) and take this up to the G.P.O. Don't forget I will ring you 7.30 Tuesday.

All my love

Jean

.

Aschersleben 10.4.49

My dear Hans

Many thanks for your dear letter dated 29.3.49. It has been 14 days since we heard from you. We have had horrible weather here, storms, rain, and snow. If your boss has pulled out the snow plough, snow was clearly something unexpected. At home we were used to different things! My dear Hans, how could you take such a risk and take most of your clothes off during your work. You are writing that you were working in your shirt sleeves, well, lucky you still have shirt sleeves! But I know from Woltersmüehlen how little you have to wear. Have you forgotten that spring is the easiest time to catch something? Please do not be careless, please do not 'ask' for pneumonia. Please do not be so careless again, it worries me terribly. You seem to be doing a lot of overtime, probably saving for your wedding. I shall order good weather for you. Well, it is quite a move forward if, for you everything is available without coupons, at least they will be good materials. I have run around everywhere trying to find lining material for Horst's suit, but impossible, he would have loved to have a suit made, but there is no stiffened linen. The material is dark brown, but no comparison to yours. You have to hand over two points for a small roll of strong thread, which is outrageous. Horst has not been able to change the shoes, they are all only available in small sizes. New ones are vital as his other ones are literally falling off his feet, the shoemaker cannot do anything more, they were completely worn out when crossing the border. If only in the independent shops it wasn't so expensive, a pair of shoes costs 290 Mark. Where should the money come from? I absolutely have to buy three and a half meters of curtain material. As I can no longer wash the old ones, but that is also not available. Yesterday Mrs Brandt received a parcel from her brother in England, it took only four and a half weeks to arrive, a dress for each of the girls, as well as a suit and shoes, the shoes are new, the other clothes are second-hand, but it all arrived undamaged. Today is confirmation day, so Horst has even more work than usual, he looks so worn out and I have told him off several times not to overwork himself. Last Sunday he did 30 women's hair. On Thursday we received an invitation to Leyerhof, to Martin's confirmation – it was planned to take place at Whitsun but it is now going to happen today. Grete wrote: Come, we are serving Fricassee. Well, that is certainly something one would like to eat again one day, but firstly, Horst cannot leave work, and we cannot shake 150 Mark out of our sleeves and I cannot consider undertaking such a long journey as I am always in unbearable pain. On Tuesday I had another medical examination, they did not have a bed available in the week just after Easter, but I will be admitted on the 27th. Presumably the operation will then take place on the 28th. I am not going into hospital now, it is always so overcrowded, but going into a clinic that has been recommended to me – there's a very old doctor, 72 years old, and a brilliant specialist. Above all it is very quiet there, there are only six patients to one room. If you can pay five Mark per day, you can book second class, meaning that there will be only two patients or three per room, but I do not want Horst to struggle to pay for this. Grandma left again on Thursday, she was here for a fortnight, but she became restless, although she liked staying with us. Dear Hans you are asking how I managed to get consumption, all of this is as a result of the fatless and proteinless diet plus the incredible strain I've been under, a woman's body cannot cope with that forever. It would be wonderful if you could cook for Horst, he is always amazed that his big brother has calmed down and has become a real man. Yes, he has changed a lot, and you would be surprised to see how much work he has. On May 23rd he will be taking part in the hairdressing competition in Halle. Now my dear Hans, please send our best regards to Jean and your mother-in-law. Sending you lots of love and kisses from your mum and your brother Horst.

Pickwell
April, 11$\underline{th}$1949

My dearest, darling Jean,

I was so very much surprised to get a letter this morning. Well, I know you're a good girl. I am only sorry to say that you won't get one before Tuesday morning. So I can only thank you very very much. Time is 9.00 and I have just finished my day's work and shall have something to eat after I have finished this letter. I won't bother with potatoes, just a slice of bread and an egg will do. Helmut is gone away to Little Dalby and will have something to eat there. I am so very tired today. It won't be long before I go to bed. If I could only cuddle up to you then and be cosy?!! Daydreams in spite of it being dark.

Tonight I finished at 7.00 without a break and went shutting up at 7.30. I could hardly walk for I am so tired.

Well, darling, 7.30 will be a bit too late. Make it dead 7.00. I don't want to leave too late for shutting up. The number is right. Somersby 38.

Now about Easter. I am sorry, darling, but I won't be able to come Saturday afternoon. Look, if I can arrange with Margaret that I take Friday and Saturday all day, she could take Sunday and Monday. I would be able to come over Sunday midday and stay till Sunday night. That young fellow would do the feeding on Monday morning. Then, of course, you would have to come over on Saturday and fetch the chicken. I have got one already here in the yard. I'll keep feeding it till Friday and get it ready for you on Friday night.

Don't worry about my haircut. I can't go anyway and you'll have to take me as I am or send me back again.

I leave everything about going away or not, to you. Please yourself sweety. Don't mind me.

I hope you don't mind if I close now, but I am really ready for bed. So just be good and my best girl.

Please give my regards to your dear mother. I love you so very much.

> All my love and kisses
> > Forever and only yours
> Hans.

Aschersleben, Easter 1949

My dear Hans

Today I want to write to you again. Unfortunately, we have not received an Easter Greeting from you. I would think it will be arriving a little late. We are having the most wonderful Easter weather and intend to go for an Easter Walk. Last week, we were very lucky. One of his clients let us have one and a half meters of hardwood. It cost 60 Marks. Normally, one meter already costs 60 Marks. I immediately got someone to cut and chop it for us, which cost another 15 Marks. I am so glad that this is done now and at least the wood fire problem has been resolved for this year, and is out of the way. I can now relax a little and need not worry anymore where the wood will come from. I went about stacking all the wood and when I went down the step ladder I slipped slightly. In order not to fall, I jumped down a little and must have sprained my muscles. I woke up with terrible pain in the night and on Good Friday I was still in excruciating pain.

Had it not been a Bank Holiday, I would have gone to the clinic. Thank goodness, it is a little better now. On Wednesday week I shall have to go for my operation. If only it were behind me! Finally, Horst has been able to exchange his shoes. He got a lovely pair of brown shoes for the ones he exchanged, and he is very happy with them. I wish we could get some lining for his suit now. The suit he wore at the time in Woltersmühlen is very warm in the summer. I am sure you will be spending Easter at Jean's. Maybe you are undertaking a nice Easter Walk at the moment. The Easter Bunny brought me two nice collectible cups and saucers, Antique Lavender (scent) and two writing sets (paper and envelopes). Horst got 24 eggs, 100g wool, a pair of stockings etc. and some very generous tips with a large plate of cake. But in the long run, it will be too much work for him.

Mrs. Lehmann left today to stay with her parents. I hope she has a good journey, it is always very difficult. Dear Hans, if you could get some more of the soap which you gave us when we met in Woltersmuühlen, you know it was a large green piece with the picture of a baby on the wrapper, please would you send us some more? It is wonderful soap, but only send it if it is not too expensive. Finally, we had a letter from Mrs. Streese during the week. Apparently, she thought that Gertrud had answered our letter. When she asked her, Gertrud said that she had not written, Mrs. Streese told her off. Gertrud wants to wait with the photos until after Easter because she bought herself a pair of shoes and she has to save more money now. Now my dear Hans, give my love to Jean and your mother-in-law.

Please stay healthy. We are sending you our love and kisses from your mum and from your brother Horst. We are hoping to have a healthy reunion.

Pickwell
April, 18th 1949

My darling,

I want to thank you and your mother for a lovely Easter I was able to spend at your place. And so I am thankful to you for making it possible and all you have done for me. You are the loveliest girl in the world and I love you more than anything else on earth. Everything would be perfect if you could only fulfil my wish. All I can say is: please. Take your courage and think it's only once in a lifetime you have to go through with all this and don't you really think it is worth it? I am so really lonely now you have gone. We were just in time, but only just. The buses were 14 minutes too early and I can't understand how that happens. Even the last bus from Leicester waits at the stops when he's earlier. One should complain to the Midland Red.

Well, my darling, I just wanted to write a few lines tonight and continue tomorrow night. It's only 9.25, but I'll go to bed and think of you. You are almost in Leicester by now.

So be good and think of me. My thoughts are only and always with you. Goodnight and God bless you.

Loads of love and kisses

Forever and only yours, darling

Hans.

92 Wharf Street

19.4.49

My dearest darling Hans,

I arrived home safe and sound. It was a good job we went to the bus early, it must have been 8.0 from Oakham. It was the last bus from Twyford too. They pack them in the bus like sardines in tin. You would have laughed if you'd been there when we arrived at Queniborough a very fat lady came right from the back of the bus to get off. I did not see Miggy until I got off the bus at Leicester then I almost missed her. I stood talking to her for a while she is still away from work at the moment she hasn't any teeth. She said she had been to Knossington for the day and had been for a picnic by a lake near

Knossington. We will have to try to find it one Sunday and have a picnic when it is a nice day. Miggy also mentioned that she did not think they would be able to be married in June as Otto had been away from work a few weeks and have put them behind with their saving.

I suppose now I had better finish off where we left off yesterday. Today I want to get married, but other days I want to wait a bit longer until we have something saved. I have about £120 in the bank and I think I have about £26 in saving certificates, but I don't want to put that all into our home as I would hate to feel that I was penniless and was completely depending on you if there was anything I ever wanted. Or at least if I ever got thrown out I would have something!!! Anyway it will turn out alright in the end. Don't worry so much. Look darling I will try and explain about the river!!! you say that I am alright (I had better be) I know it is hard for you to understand why I kept you off, but for something that would only last a couple of minutes I know it would not be worth the worry I would have. I don't think it is right it is something that belongs to being married. I have pride and self respect and I don't want to lose that, because if you lose that, you may as well be in the river. I want my children to grow up in a very happy home with a good mother and father in every way. Not to find out they had to get married. They might think they can do the same, remember it is breeding that counts. I hope I have made myself clear.

My mother has washed your shirt and towel. You know if you ever want a bath there is a public bath at the top of Wharf Street. I never thought of it until today. By the way don't think because I have said it that I think you are dirty. I would hate you to misunderstand me. I will see you Saturday.

> All my love
>   Kisses,
> Jean

>   ——.

Pickwell
April 21st 1949

My dearest, darling Jean

I thank you so very much for your lovely letter that explains everything so nice. This morning at 7.00 the boss came and held a little speech. He said he wants me to be in charge of the laying hens and do everything as I think it best and also meant I showed quite a bit of interest on the job so he thinks I know enough to manage the lot myself. Well, I will. I have kept my eyes and ears open since I started on the job. There's no cleaning out and watercarting anymore for me. I just go feeding, collect the eggs and wash them. That young chap has come back on poultry and has to do the other work.

I've had a good laugh when the boss told me about the egg washing . I remembered what a fuss he made telling Doris how to use the washing machine so I asked him to give me instructions. He looked bewildered and said "you should know how to work it without getting told" so I had a go and it went alright. He also told me I am getting very useful on the job so he naturally tries everything to keep me and will see what he can do finding a cottage. Well, I'll leave that to him.

I was getting ready for doing the shopping tonight and was just leaving when I remembered the shops are closed Thursdays. Anyway I'll fix something for tonight and it's fish and chips tomorrow

Last night I felt terrible. When I came back from shutting up I couldn't stand on my feet any longer and went to bed straight away. Time was 8.30. I didn't sleep all night. It's better today. For a start I wasn't getting up but then thought of the money I would lose and decided to get up.

I didn't know there's a lake near Knossington. Of course we'll have a look one Sunday. By the way, we have changed weekends work again. One week I shall be on Saturday and Wednesday afternoon off, the following week have Saturday off and work Sunday. It'll be Saturday off this week. So I'll be over as arranged.

This weeks wages came up to £7-10-10. That's not bad, is it? Of course at least 10/- income tax.

Now about us. I can understand that you feel like getting married one day and change your mind the next. I only want a sports suit now and will be able to save up then. Even if you had to spend all your money it wouldn't matter. You are definitely wrong in thinking I could throw you out. I love you far too much to do such a thing, because my life wouldn't mean a thing to me without you, darling. I have told you before that when I get married I feel responsible for the family and you know I want you to be happy, comfortable and satisfied in every way.

Please, darling, don't ever mention water again. It makes me feel so selfish and I don't want you to be worried. You are right it isn't worth for something that lasts a couple of minutes. I am very proud of you telling me about pride and self respect. That's what one should have, now I really understand you and be sure you'll find me changed. And I do mean it. Sometimes it is hard for me, but I am only human and love you so very much. In future I know what to do.

Thanks for telling me about the public bath. I'll go one day. I'll ring you tomorrow night at 5.00.

Well, sweetheart, I'll close now and get myself something to eat. Believe me I am hungry.

Be good, darling and think of me. God bless you always. Please give my regards to your mother.

All my love and kisses

    Forever yours

      Hans.

Pickwell

April 25th 1949

My dearest, darling Jean,

How are you, darling? Did you get home alright? When I

walked along the hill I saw your bus coming down the road. So you have had plenty of time to get there. I was back here at 9.15, had something to eat and went to bed at 10.00. I know you're at home by that time. Do you mind if this is only going to be a short letter. I want to go out and get a rabbit for you. Helmut is also going out tonight so it's a chance to go early.

I have had a letter from my mother today saying that she'll be going to the hospital on April 27 th and probably have the operation the following day. That would be in three days time. Please, remind me of a letter on Wednesday. I have to post it Wednesday.

Please, darling, don't forget the money for the wireless.

That'll be all for now. Just be good and keep thinking of me. I love you so very much. Please, give my regards to your mother.

> All my love and kisses to you
>> Forever and only yours
>> Hans.

Aschersleben 27.4.49

My dear Hans

Today, just before I take the difficult step to enter the clinic I will send you my greetings. It is 5am, I will be going at 10am, but before that I have a lot of work to do – as you know, when one leaves home for a few weeks there is a lot to do. Let us hope that everything will go well. The operation will take place tomorrow morning, hopefully it will all go well. Horstel will keep you informed about how I am. We thank you very much for your dear letter dated 15.4 which we received yesterday, after not having received any mail for three weeks. The post we send to you also seems to be taking a terribly long time. We would be so pleased if the parcels would finally arrive. You thought that when your letters reached me everything would be already done. Yesterday we had a massive thunderstorm, here it is very autumnal too, so I am really sad to be in bed for a few more weeks. I can very well believe that you have lots of work with the spring orders, I imagine it will carry on like that non stop. Dear Hans, so you have to slave away for a whole week for the parcels. You are thinking that I will be home for Horstel's birthday, but I have to lie down for three weeks. I thank you very much for Jean's and your mother in law's good wishes, please return my best wishes to them. Now my dear boy stay really well, as soon as I can I will write to you again. I hope it will all turn out well, but if not please never forget that you are brothers. Now farewell and here's to a healthy Wiedersehen. Lots of love and kisses from your mum and your brother Horst.

Pickwell
April, 28th 1949

My dearest, darling Jean,

How are you, darling? Fine, I hope, in spite of the rain. Of course it has to start now my shutting up time comes. Wasn't the "cheerio" a bit hasty last night. I didn't even know if I had lipstick on my cheek. Nobody looked at me in particular so everything must have been in order.

By the way, darling, I still forgot something. Do you remember that piece I borrowed from the workshop for the cooker? Get me one of those please. I think Woolworth is the best place. I have put the new spiral in and it's going lovely.

I shan't be able to get a rabbit for Betty tonight. It is raining and they won't be out. I'll try tomorrow night and when we go together on Saturday. I shall be lucky then with a lovely girl by my side.

Can you get anything nice for Saturday tea? I leave it to you. "Housewife's choice". By the way, don't forget to inquire about that "Danish Smoked Dinner Sausage"!! I just fancy something like that.

There's no meat on the menu tonight but we are having that lovely cauliflower. Made in the german way. A smashing dish.

I just remembered. I haven't had a letter yet from you. What do you think about that. Awful isn't it?

Well, darling, that's all for now. Be a good girl and please give my regards to your mother.

All my love and kisses to you

    Forever yours

        Hans.

<u>P.S.</u>

Can you get me some writing paper and envelopes? Hans.

Aschersleben 28/4/49

Horst Klawitter

    My dear Hans

I am sending you a few lines. Today was the most difficult day for our dear mum. I called the hospital at 9am to be told that the operation was not yet finished. I called again at 10am and by then the operation had been concluded. I went up to see mum at 15.45 but she had not yet woken up, since 7.00 in the morning. I stayed with her until 17.00. It was absolutely heart-breaking, the horrendous pain mum had to endure. I could'nt bear it and cannot find peace. I am meant to write to you, Jean and everybody else. I spoke to the OR nurse and she said it was a difficult operation and already very big. Mum nearly died of thirst, but she will only be given something to drink tonight – if only the first three days were over, then everything would not be too bad. I have also received presents from my clients in order to cheer her up and get better. It's great that I am on leave so that I can visit mum regularly. The amount of suffering mum has to endure is terrible. Hopefully we will hear from our dear papa, it would stop mum's greatest worry. Dear Hans, I shall carry on with this letter once I have seen mum this morning. Now my dear Hans I shall continue this letter. I was with mum today from half past two, She is feeling better today, but still in terrible pain. I feel so very sorry for her and I am so worried. Someone is missing. Today I have brought mum some tulips and some hydrangeas to give her a bit of pleasure. They are giving her an enema tomorrow, so hopefully things will improve. I spoke yesterday with the doctor and she said it was a complicated operation, and high time and the growth was bigger than a childs' head. Our dear mum sends you many greetings. I went back at 8.45, and from lying on her back she had bad back pain, and I've been running around all over to find her an air cushion, which I finally found, and I was happy to have been able to help mum. Please my dear Hans do not worry, whatever I can do for our mum I will do. Mum is waiting for mail from you. Today is May 1st and before we know it the summer will be over. The main thing is that our mum will be happy and healthy again, otherwise I would not know how to carry on. How is Jean? Now I shall finish. Mum sends her best wishes. Best wishes to you dear Hans and Jean, Horst and mum Here's to a speedy Wiedersehen

92 Wharf St
May 2nd
My dearest Hans
Well darling did you arrive back safe. I got home about 9.40 about the same time you would get to Pickwell. I felt very happy yesterday. There is one thing we shall be able to look back on our courting days, as being different from everyone else. We have covered some ground Saltby, Stathern, Redmile and Pickwell. I wonder where we will end up?
Well darling, it looks as though I am going crazy. I went with Lucy and her husband to see Leicester City come in. We left off at 5.45 and had a 15 minute wait until 6.30. You should

have seen it. I have never seen so many crowds for ages we had a good laugh.

Well darling I will go to bed otherwise I won't get up in the morning. Goodnight and God bless you

> All my love and
> Kisses
> Jean

—.

Pickwell
May 2nd 1949

My dearest, darling Jean,

How are you today, sweetheart? Did you get home well last night? I arrived here at 9.20. It was just the right time for you to get on the bus. Even on the relief quite a few people had to stand up. Some were left behind. My bus was full up, but I was in time to get a seat. I really was sooo worn out!!

When I arrived back here I had some supper and went to bed. It's still the best place, except that place in Leicester. And that dear little wife of mine!! (16.7.49). Oh, darling, we'll have a lovely time. I am always thinking about it. Plan everything.

I was just listening to "Fanfare" a comedian told a nice story. At a railway station he saw a fellow drinking out of a saucer. So, of course, he thought of good manners and asked the fellow where he comes from. The answer was: from Leicester. He had to drink out of the saucer because Wolves got the cup. Hope you've been listening to "Spot the Lady"? It was not too bad.

I have cracked all the nuts tonight and have almost finished eating them. Awful, ain't I? Don't you ever leave any nuts, sweets or cake about. I'll finish those off easily.

Now I am listening to Boxing. Smashing. I would love to have a go. "How common"!

That'll be all for now. Be good, darling and remember I love you much more than anything in the world. Good night and God bless you. Please give my regards to your mother.

All my love and kisses
    Forever yours
Hans.

My dear boy

Today is the first short hello from me, the first day when the fever has diminished a little. Out of 30 women I am the worst off as far as my temperature is concerned, and my doctor wagged her finger at me, telling me it was a very difficult operation and about time. I knew it well in advance. I have not closed my eyes for the last five nights, and last night I nearly passed out with pain. Horst always worries so much about me. If only I had an appetite, Horst always has to eat my supper, as I cannot eat anything, only drink. Now I cannot write anymore.

Lots of love and kisses from your loving mum and your brother Horst

    Here's to a healthy Wiedersehen

    92 Wharf St
    May 9th

My dearest darling Hans
I have not much time as it is late, but I have been to the pictures.
Miggy was on the other bus. When we arrived at Twyford she came and asked me to go on the other bus. I don't know

why she could not have come on the bus I was on. I did not think of that until I was off. When the bus was ready to go, the conductress missed me and stopped the bus, fortunately I was in the front seat and she saw me. Miggy told me all the news, she looked really well after her holiday. She is really very glad that Otto is leaving and I still don't think he wears the pants. You can tell Helmut that if he wants to marry a woman he can boss, not to marry an English girl, for the only girls here that you can boss are either daft or dead. You need not worry I'm daft ~~??~~!!

Otto has the idea that if he comes to Maclean he will be working until 9.0 overtime. They are not getting married until Sept, because they have been put behind with their saving. Otto broke his ankle and she's been on holiday, else it was to have been June..

You said something about you would not like to live in the same house with another jerry and an English wife because of comparing the two. Do you mean the Jerry's will compare the wives or the wives the husband?

Do you do that with me now? Do you think I might think the other fellow better than you?

Well darling I must go to bed. God bless you darling. All my love

Jean

P.T.O.

P.S. <u>warning</u>

Miggy is coming over to Pickwell with Otto Wednesday evening so you had better tidy up.

Will I have to starve this week or do we get a rabbit

      Love and kisses

       Jean.

P.S.

It doesn't matter if you can't get a rabbit. You could probably have given it to Miggy and I could have met her off the bus but it is too late unless I get her on the phone.

Pickwell
May, 9th 1949

My dearest, darling Jean,

How are you today, sweetheart? Feeling well? I hope so. I got back here at 9.00, had something to eat, and went to bed. Thank you so very much for a lovely weekend. Everything was so real. I think we are married already. It'll be lovely darling, our time to come. Shall I say again, please, let it be 16.7.49. We'll never regret it, I am sure. Believe me I am so fed up with living at this place with the chance of having a home of my own. You've seen for yourself yesterday what the place looks like, when my mate is about. You should know by now that I am not used to anything like that. What's the use if I try to keep things a bit clean when he's messing about. Can't you imagine how I can get fed up with living here. Of course when he came back last night we had a row. I told him something about being clean and asked him if he wanted a lesson. He kept quiet because he knew I was right. Anyway, a good thing he didn't say anything. I was in the right mood.

Well, my darling, my washing is boiling so I have to get cracking. Goodnight and God bless you. Be my good girl.

Please give my regards to your mother.

All my love and kisses to you,

Forever yours, darling

Hans.

Pickwell
May 5th 1949

My dearest, darling Jean,

Two days to go and I shall see you again. How are you today, sweetheart? I arrived at Melton 9.20 last night. The bus was late so no chance for me to catch the 9 o'clock. The 10.00 bus got here 10.25 and after having something to eat went to bed. Helmut was sleeping already. It was late again ~~tonight~~ this morning. 20 to 7. Still we had something to eat before starting work. I wanted to go shooting crows tonight, we have to have some meat. Helmut has just left to see if he can get a rabbit. By the way, did you keep both rabbits for yourself or did you give one to Betty? We could get another one on Saturday. That sausage is not bad at all. I'll save some to have it with the potato salad. I hope you'll like it.

About the motorbike. I have told the fellow tonight that I've changed my mind. Look, sweetheart, I don't want it only for myself if you don't like going on it. So we'll have a car instead, one day. Of course it takes some saving up, but I am sure one day we can afford it. Let's get settled down first. I think you didn't quite get me when I said I don't like it very much what you said about having to pay yourself for the wedding. I told you sometime ago that I am going to save up now I have got the suit and believe me I will. There's one thing I would like you to do. Every weekend you come over you can take my money with you and keep it for me. Put it into a bank or do whatever you like. I know I could save it myself, but I want you to see that I mean what I say. I don't agree with wife's saying "where's the money" on Friday night, but still if we want to get somewhere and let our children have a good education, it's the best way to do it. For instance, if we throw our money together on Fridays, we can put so much away for the case of emergency and spend the rest on our home. We'll do it alright! Let's make it July.

About where to get married, please yourself darling. Let's do as you think it's best. To be honest I would love to see you getting married in white. One shouldn't upset the aunties, you know!! I am sure we'll find a way to please everybody.

I always feel so happy coming over to Leicester. It's just as if I am home. Don't you also think it was much nicer than going to the pictures last night. And you have your tea at teatime not 9.00.

Bonzo is on my knee or rather his front legs. He wants me to give you his love. Shall I let him write a line?

Well, my love, the potatoes are done so I'll finish the dinner and write a letter to my mother afterwards. Be good. Good night and God bless you always. Please give my regards to your mother.

> All my love and kisses to you
> Forever yours
> Hans.

Pickwell
May 11th 1949

My dearest, darling Jean,

I thank you so very much for your most interesting letter. That means I also got your call for help. You know, sweetheart, I shan't let you starve. So I have got something ready for you and I hope you'll enjoy it. I was in a rush shot the rabbit whilst I was collecting eggs this afternoon and got the other thing half an hour ago. Please clean the inside out a bit. I had to hurry because I expect Otto and Miggy any minute now.

So just be a good girl and think of me. Please give my regards to your mother. See you Saturday.

Good night and God bless you always.

> All my love and kisses
> Forever and only yours,
> Hans.

Pickwell
May 12th 1949

My dearest, darling Jean,

Well, sweetheart here I am again. How are you today? Fine I hope. Another nice day's gone. Cross your fingers for weather like this when we go for our honeymoon in July. some far away places!!!

Well, it was a rush last night. Still I was so glad I met Miggy.

I was waiting here until 8.15 and nobody turned up. I knew there was the 8.51 bus from Somerby to Leicester. Thinking and racing over was one thing. The bus, of course, was 15 minutes late, but I was lucky. Miggy was on alright and believe me I was glad. She was going to ring you this morning and let you know she's got the parcel for you. Did you get it in time? I am sorry, darling I didn't skin the rabbit, but I haven't had time. I was back from shutting up at 10.20 and ready for bed.

I have told Helmut about marrying a daft girl and he said "with pleasure". What did Otto think about working overtime till 9.00. Mac doesn't throw his money away if it isn't necessary. And there wouldn't be anything to do for Otto to work later than 5.00.

I am surprised to hear ~~Helmut~~ Herbert has a girl. Well, I have told you what our first one is going to be!!!

Don't be afraid that I'll ever fall into Helmuts habits. I feel really sorry for him for he doesn't seem to be able to look after himself properly. And when I see this mess here it makes me fed up with everything- except you! His affairs are definitely his own concern and be sure I shan't give him a hand or encourage him in any way. Still I always try to keep him back from doing anything stupid. Everybody has his faults.

Only 1 ½ day to go till Saturday. I have had a look on that clock. The main spring is broken. I'll bring it along on Saturday and try to get a new one. I can fix it up alright when I get the spring.

Well, sweetheart, I'll close now.

Be good and look after yourself well.

Please, give my regards to your mother.

Remember I love you so very much.

    All my love and kisses

      Forever yours, darling

    Hans.

Aschersleben, 15.5.45 *

My dear Hans

It is now three weeks ago since I last heard from you. Every night, when Horst gets home from work, he is very sad when I tell him that there is still no post from you.

Today is day number 18 since my operation and I am still in bed, but it is the first day I can say that those dreadful pains have reduced a little. I am only a shadow of what I was when you saw me in January. It is hard to believe how one can so easily forget, and in addition to all this there is my high temperature. They tried everything possible to get my temperature down, to no avail. It seems that today it is working. I was sweating so much during the night, it was awful. At 3 o'clock this morning, I had to ask to change my night clothes. I was soaked through. The last two nights though, I managed to sleep without waking up, thank goodness, and I have regained a little bit of an appetite! I doubt whether I will be back on my feet completely by this summer. They made me get up on the 11th day after the operation. The moment I was up, I had horrific pains in my calf muscles and I was ordered to go back to bed and stay there. The high temperature continued and they said it was a kind of thrombosis. However, it did get better after the treatment. I hope I will soon be able to get out of bed again. I am supposed to have some radiotherapy when I can get out of bed. Oh, how I long to be back home for Horstel's birthday! He does everything for me and I want to pay him back with my love by being there on his birthday! My cut on the surface has healed well but the enormous internal wounds are not quite healed yet.

Now, my dear Hans, I want to finish my letter. I am absolutely exhausted.

Give my regards to your Jean and mother-in-law.

To you, I am sending you all my love and kisses,
Your mum and your brother Horst

*The date is clearly wrong. It should read 16.5.**49** or possibly
15.5.**49**, 18 days after the operation

Pickwell
May, 17th 1949

My dearest, darling Jean,
Sandy has just been playing "Jeanny with the light brown
hair". It is nice, but still I like the girl herself much better. How are you today, sweetheart? Fine, I hope. You know
Monday is my washing day and that meant my towel was
due. It took me an hour to get it clean, but it looks white
now. It was 9.30 when I finished and afterwards I wrote and
replied to my mothers letters. She'll be waiting every day
now she's in bed. I've written quite a few times lately. What
about you sending her a few lines.
Wasn't it lovely this afternoon. Fortunate enough I took my
raincoat along. So I just put it on and kept going. The lightning must have struck a tree in the spinney. For a moment
I couldn't see anything. I held the horse by the bridle and
so went up with him in the air. When I came down I first
thought I had broke a few ribs getting one of those shafts in
the side. It pains a bit but it is alright. At least he didn't get
the chance of going off with the eggs in the float.
I spoke to the new girl today when I was collecting. She's
going to paint the chicken houses after finishing paraffining.
She knew that I did 12 houses the first morning I started
here. I bet she and Doris have pulled us to pieces already. But
one still can't beat it!!!
Helmut is gone to Little Dalby again so I didn't bother to
cook. I just fried an egg for myself and had a glass of milk to
keep me going till the morning and I am not really hungry
tonight. You should've seen Bonzo when it thundered the
first time. He was off and later on I found him underneath the

chicken house. I couldn't help laughing.

It'll be alright for a hen. I've asked the foreman and he's getting me one for Friday night. I'll get it ready for you, of course.

Well, darling, I'll see you tomorrow afternoon. I only have to get a birthday card for Horst and dog biscuits.

Be good, darling and give my regards to your mother. Good night and God bless you. I love you so very much.

> All my love and kisses
>> Forever yours, darling
> Hans

> Pickwell
> May 19th 1949

My dearest, darling Jean,

How are you today darling? I arrived back safe at 10.20 after waiting ¾ hour at Melton. A good thing it wasn't raining very much. I went round and had some chips and met Helmut. He's been to the pictures and saw "The Jolson Story ". He said it was really nice. Something about the singer Jolson. Believe me I really enjoyed that picture yesterday. For a long time I haven't seen such a funny one. If I get the chance to see it again I'll certainly go.

Well, my darling, it's 1.55. Get ready to start again. I'll write a few more lines tonight. So long, babe.

Here I am again. Time 7.15. Potatoes are boiling and the sauce is ready. At first I didn't know what to cook because no meat left. Helmut has gone out shooting but it'll be too late to wait for him. I don't know if you know boiled eggs and mustard sauce, but I rather like it. Shall we try it one day?

It's 7.45 now and Helmut hasn't come back yet. I am still waiting with the dinner, it'll be late and I am getting hungry. By the way, darling, have you got a milkcan in the shop. About 3 pints (not less, otherwise Mrs Cooper puts less in) but it has to have a lid on. Last night Helmut forgot again to fetch the milk so from now on (when you bring the can). I'll take it over at midday and Mrs Cooper is going to leave it filled outside her door. She also does it with the other people's milk.

I am just listening to "Opportunity Knocks" isn't there anything I could do? Perhaps the B.B.C would take me on.

Isn't it nice, I've got nothing else to do tonight as listening to the wireless. A real quiet evening, but it would be perfect with you being here. Still I have to wait until Saturday. What a shame it can't be before then. Please, darling, bring us a box of cartridges 12 bore No. 4.

Well, darling, I'll say goodnight for now, and God bless you. Please, give my regards to your mother. And remember, I love you more than anything else in the world.

     All my love and kisses
       Forever yours
     Hans

                        Pickwell
                        May, 23rd 1949

My dearest, darling Jean,

How are you darling? Did you get home well last night? After all I saw somebody last night at the bus station. Did you get me what I meant? I still have to laugh when I remember your face. And you like joking, don't you? Well, please leave it, darling, and don't ever mention it again. Can't you understand, darling. I have finished with everything years ago and I don't like to be reminded of it. It once was the blackest day of my life and I was really disappointed. Now, however, I am glad and thankful for as it happened I met you and I love you more than anything else. You are and always will be the only one. I know I behaved foolishly and perhaps spoilt your birthday afternoon, but you'll forgive me if you understand what I mean. Anyway I thought it the best when I said "no". I've promised to tell you everything. A perfect understanding means everything when we're married. And we'll always remember it, won't we?

I thank you so very much for the nice afternoon. Everything was so real. Please, sweetheart, let it be soon. I have given up hope for July, so you won that round. But let's make it this year. It would make me so happy.

I arrived here at 9.20 last night and as I told you Helmut had finished the cake up except for a tiny piece he left for me. When our bus left the station I saw Helmut standing at the timetable. At first I thought he's had one over the eight and didn't see the bus, but when I asked him this morning he told me he was waiting for the girl and came back in a taxi. He's playing the big man again and wonders where his money goes. He wants me to get a shirt for him an Saturday for about 40/-s. Shall you get yourself ready so we can have a look around before going to the pictures. And please, don't forget to fetch the spring for the clock. I'll take it along on Saturday and fix it. That gives us more time.

Well, darling, I'll say cheerio now. God bless you and be good. Please give my regards to your dear mother. I love you so very much so

All my love and kisses

Forever and only yours

Hans.

92 Wharf St

May 23rd

My dearest darling,

Did you get on the bus alright? You waited rather a long time before you went to get on the bus. I did not see Helmut didn't he go into Melton. I nearly went and got on the other bus when I saw Vera's double. I could have done a bit of studying but I still think the conductress is better looking although Vera has the nicest eyes. Now about the photograph. It wasn't because you had them. I really did not mind and I wish you had not destroyed them. I feel awful about that. It was because I want you always to tell the truth. I know you thought it best I did not know, but I think the truth is always best no matter what it is. There may be a day when ~~you will~~ it will be important that you may want to be believed and unless you tell the truth the whole of the time. Anyway we may as well forget about it, we can't get the photographs back unless we send for some more.

I have just finished my "Ovaltine" and I'm ready for bed (are you coming) so I will have to say cheeri'O and God Bless you.

All my love
Jean

——.

92 Wharf St
May 23rd
My dearest darling Hans,
I thank you so very much ~~about~~ for your letter, by now you should have had one from me. I am very sorry you can't bear to be reminded of Vera. In future I will try never to mention her again, but I can't help it if I do, because I will admit I am jealous of her, more so since you don't like to be reminded.

I can't understand this bit "anyway I thought it best when I said 'no'". "No" to what?

I have written to Muriel tonight 5 pages. I always have a lot of news for her. Did I tell you she is expecting a baby in July. She is hoping it is a girl. I started a little coat this afternoon to send to her, but I have not got on very well with it, I had done a few inches and had to undo it.

Gwen rang me this afternoon and was talking to me for an hour and a half. She has her little girl living with her now. I don't know whether they intend to have any children. Sep (that is Gwenn husband) is more attached to the child than Gwenn, she goes everywhere with him. I wonder if he ever thinks about the Yank!!! I should be thankful I have not that to remind me.

One of the girls at work Joyce Marshall is hoping to be married in September that is if her divorce goes through July alright. Her boyfriend has bought a house today at Ashby Nr Market Harborough for £2000 and it hasn't even got water laid on. They have to get it from a pump. I think it is quite a big house.

What is a matter with Helmut is he too shy to go and get his own shirt, not that I mind, don't say he works every Saturday.

I have not been to pay the wireless fee but I will go tomorrow.

I had better ring Gertie tomorrow to see if she will be in. I have not been for a little while.

I will have to close I have put some water on to have a wash with. I am going to put my feet in some hot water just to make sure.

I will say cheeri'O be good. By the way, what did you think to my letter I wrote to your mother. I know there isn't much in it, but it was very difficult.

> Goodnight and
> God Bless
> All my love
>   Jean

——.

Home Farm,
May 25th 1949

My dearest, darling Jean,

I thank you so very much for your nice letter I received this morning. I was hoping to get one and was fortunate. Are you going to save the money you spend on stamps or why don't you write as much these days? Nothing much to say really after seeing each other twice a week, is there?

I told you Helmut was in Melton, didn't I? He was waiting for the girl and came back in a taxi. I would have laughed you getting on that second bus, but you would have been disappointed. I was looking out for "her", (not the double) and couldn't see her anymore. On the other bus was a conductor. Perhaps she was on the Grantham bus. She's better looking, but still you're lovelier than both of them put together. Look, darling, I myself am really glad I burned those pictures. So it's done with once and forever. You might feel awful, but I am glad. Well, you're right let's forget all about it, but then I shan't write for more photographs, I am sure.

I got a letter from my mother today dated 15.5.49. She's better but still has to stay in bed for a few weeks. She said the wound is healing up alright. The fever was still high a fortnight after the operation. She has lost a few stones on weight. Anyway she hasn't been back for my brothers birthday. I'll write to her tonight and put your letter in, too.

How are you today, darling? Fine I hope.

Well, Wednesday is over and now it shan't be long till Saturday. I'll be there at the usual time. Shall we go and see "April Showers". I think it is nice. Still, I leave the entertaining to you- entirely. By the way. My mother sends her kindest regards to you and my "mother-in-law"

Well, darling, my coffee water is boiling so I'll just have a few sandwiches instead of a warm dinner. Helmut is gone to Melton again. A good thing for I don't really know what to cook tonight. A sandwich or cornflakes with milk will do me.

Please, give my regards to your mother. Be a good girl and think of me, if you can spare the time.

> All my love and kisses
> > Forever yours, sweetheart
> Hans.

Aschersleben 25.5.49

My dear Hans

Finally after four weeks we have had post from you, and thank you for your letter dated 8.5.49 Did you really not write during that time. I have been at death's door and have waited for a few lines from you every day. Horst came every day looking down cast, saying he had nothing from you. Do you really have so little time for your mum? This is not meant to be a reproach but..

I have been home since Saturday, Horstel's birthday, but I am so weak that I had to promise the lady doctor that I shall rest. I get up for an hour each day, then I go back to bed. The doctor said that I always look so terrifyingly pale when I am up. I lost 13lbs whilst in the clinic, and have lost some more since I have been home. I cannot eat. What I would like to eat is not available, and they have taken away the margarine and the sugar until the end of this decade. I had pinned my only hope on the parcels from you, but I have given up on this. You never mentioned anything about these in your last letter. It might have become too expensive for you, or maybe you sent the coupons and they did not arrive? Horst is so happy that I am home. On Sunday he bought half a pound of butter for 25 Marks and two fried herrings for 5 Marks. But of course that is not something we can afford more than once. In your letter you are saying Horst should not work so much, and I totally agree, but he really wants to keep us going. If we were over there, we could eat our fill. You have certainly heard on the wireless what it is like in Berlin, who knows what will happen? Totally unexpected Grandma arrived on Horst's birthday, she has been travelling since May 15th to come over to Werner, and now she is going to try it from here, she cries such a lot, she's so old, and she doesn't think she'll make it over, which makes me sad and wears me out. However at least she was able to care for me for a few days, and she will try to move across as soon as possible. I feel so sorry for her.

Now my dear boy, stay healthy and sending you lots of love and kisses from your mum and your brother Horst. Horst was very disappointed that he did not get birthday wishes from you. Best wishes to Jean and your mother in law.

Pickwell

May, 26th 1949

My dearest, darling Jean,

Just a short letter tonight, sweetheart. I shan't get into Leicester on Saturday at 2.12. Tonight I lost the crown of my watch. You know the thing to wind the watch up. That means I have to go to Melton first and then catch the 2.15 from Melton. So I shall be able to get it mended by Wednesday and collect it again when I come over on Wednesday. Tonight I was careless. The hunger drove me to it. I really didn't know what to eat so I bought us a 7 ½ lbs hen. It was lovely and believe me we enjoyed it. Of course that doesn't mean we finished it all for one meal. We had the legs and save the rest for Sunday.

~~Saturday~~ Friday 8.00

I am sorry, darling I didn't finish the letter last night. So I'll bring it along tomorrow. Young Gordon came in last night and started talking and I couldn't very well tell him to go. He stopped till 9.00 and I had to go shutting up. When I came back it was too late.

Well, instead of the letter I rung you tonight. Who was on the phone? Your cousin?

Are you listening to the Light Programme? "Faust" is on. It's lovely. I shall have time to hear it all. It finishes at 9.00.

As I said on the phone don't be jealous, darling. There's no reason at all. I love you and only you and I am not even thinking of anybody else. And please, sweetheart, never get the idea into your head that I could possibly like anyone better than you. Life will give us everything and we'll make as much out of it as ever we are able to. You certainly are the loveliest girl under the sun.

Why ~~do~~ people are so glad to have baby girls? I couldn't think of anything better and nicer that the first one being a boy. Do you agree? Can't you ask Joyce to let a few rooms to us if the house is so big? We could do with them. Have you had a look around in Leicester? What about the place we went to last Christmas? Won't they let us have a flat for a couple of bob rent per week? You'd better make inquiries.

I inquired about pictures in the afternoon and don't want to forget you are right. One of the picture houses starts at 2.00 p.m., but Helmut said there are too many children about to enjoy the picture. So that's another point to you. I don't know anything yet about the Whit break. I'll see how to arrange things best. Do you want me to stay the night at your place? You can tell me tomorrow.

Well, darling, I'll say goodnight and God bless you. Be good. See you tomorrow so till then

> All my love and kisses
>> Forever yours, darling
> Hans.

> 92 Wharf St
> May 30th

Dear Hans

Do you wonder what has happened, but I suppose you can tell that I am writing this at the office.

What I am really writing for is to ask you if you can possibly get a rabbit and bring it with you on Wednesday. If you can not get one don't worry. I won't starve, so don't get a chicken. I ought to have thought of this last night, but forgot until I thought what we would be having for dinner.

I have been and gone and done it. Now are you wondering what I have done. Well I have booked two seats on a bus to Skegness for Sunday. It leaves Humberstone Gate (top of Wharf St) at 7.30 and leaves Skegness at 6.0 gets back into Leicester at 9.30 so if all goes well you should be able to get into Melton by 9.0. I am not sure about the time it gets back but the bus is to leave at 6.0 and then the bus usually stops for a drink so you can please yourself whether or not you get off the bus at Melton or come back to Leicester and go back to Pickwell on my bicycle!!!

Now, I thought if you brought your old mac so you could roll it up in your bag and I would give my old one a scrub. I also thought you could put your khaki shirt on so if you bring it on Wednesday I will wash it. I am not going anywhere Friday I have the half day. So I could wash it then, I have some of my own to do.

I arrived home safe and sound. How is Helmut today have you found out what was a matter with him. I hope it was because you answered him rather sharp. You must admit that it does not take much for you to get on your high horse. Remember "a still tongue keeps a wise head". it is for your own good that I tell you.

I will see you Wednesday

    All my love

    Jean

    ___.

Jean and Hans at Skegness

16/6.49   Aschersleben, 31.5.49

My dear Hans

Thank you very much for your lovely letters dated 15.5.,
25.5. and Horstel's birthday letter, all of which arrived yesterday. Horst and I thank you from the bottom of our hearts.
Horstel was very pleased to receive your lovely birthday
card. Also say 'thank you' to Jean for her lovely note, it made
me very happy. Her style of writing seems a bit strange, is
she still a little shy? It will be five weeks ago tomorrow when
I went for my operation and I have been home now eleven
days. I am still no good at all. I just can't get back to normal.
Horstel's friend has a cleaning lady and she is still cleaning
our flat as well. The entire last week I stayed in bed except
for one hour during the day. Since last Sunday, I have been
staying up a bit more. I can now cook our dinners but have to
lie down every now and then and have a rest. I am still in a
lot of pain. I think all my organs have to 'rearrange themselves and settle down'. An operation of this kind is not an
easy task. When they have to take all the organs out, one has
one foot on earth and one foot in the grave. I had those dreadful pains with a high temperature for 17 days. All the other
women in the ward started to get better after four days. My
body has been subjected to so many trials and tribulations
during the last four years, so that it is totally and utterly
worn out. I look painfully ill and pale. My legs are shaking
and I always feel nauseas when I am awake. I am sure if I had
the right food, I would perk up a bit quicker. I have not heard
a word from Uncle Erich and Auntie Grete, even though they
know all about me from Mrs Zieman. They are alright – so
why worry about others? Oh yes, Horst has always done
everything he could possibly do for me. He was and is totally
devoted to me, and when he came to the hospital every
evening after work, the first thing he had to do was comb the
nurses' hair. They took advantage of him because he could

never say 'no'. The competition in Halle has not taken place. It was postponed until June. Why do you have to dig 50 cm deep down? I quite believe that you had a lot of hard work to do. Have you got a date for your wedding yet? Horst is very unhappy about not being allowed to come. He says 'I only have one brother and I am not allowed to attend his wedding'. It's a very sad world we are living in, where one cannot visit each other anymore. But don't forget to send us a nice wedding photo. We have to have something to remember your wedding by. I shall be with you in my thoughts on your wedding day with a heavy heart, because you are so far away from us. We had a lot of rain last Saturday evening and the water came again through the roof into our flat. My bed was saturated and I had to go into Horst's bed. Horst took all his bedding into the kitchen and slept there. Grandma went to the West on Ascension Day. She crossed the border with some other people who wanted 50 Marks from her. She said however, 'just the once and never again'. It was too stressful and exhausting for her. They had to cross the border during the night, there was a storm and they got soaked to the skin. She fell down twenty times and the others kept pulling and dragging her along with them. It is very upsetting if one cannot see one's loved ones in one's homeland. I wonder whether it will ever change. It is absolutely dismal. I hope she will settle down now, and is happy being together with Werner. She was living alone for a long time and I think everybody likes to have their relatives around them.

Now my dear boy, I want to finish my letter for today. Stay healthy. Give my best wishes to Jean and your mother-in-law and thank her for her best wishes to me for a speedy recovery.

To you especially we are sending all our love and kisses, your mum and your brother Horst.

Pickwell
June 2<u>nd</u> 1949

My dearest, darling Jean,
Thank you very much for a nice evening, sweetheart. I enjoyed the picture very much and hope you did, too. It looks to me as if we always get down to talking when going to the bus. Funny, isn't it. And the last minutes go so quick.

How was the rabbit? We made our meat last till today. I told you I was getting a dozen eggs so I asked the boss today for fresh ones on Saturday. He said "if it isn't every week, alright". We could boil a few and take them along, couldn't we? We'll see on Sunday about how to get back here best. If I come back on your bicycle I don't know how to get it back to Leicester again. And you know yourself how it is. Helmut will keep asking to go to Little Dalby on it. And I shan't give it to anyone. By the way have you got a light on it? It'll be dark by the time I get here. "Jeany with the light brown hair" is on again.

It's 8.45 now and another half an hour to go till the Woodcock-Hills fight. The Irishmen are coming over. I hope there's some hitting in it. And of course, a knock-out.

The boss told me this morning the meter has been installed in the workshop. I asked him what was on the circuit and found the egg washer is on, too. So I reckoned it out straight away what was going to be deducted for using the washer every day. Taking your advice I didn't say anything else. The hut will cost us 3d. Well, we'll save electricity now we have to pay for it.

Well, sweetheart, I'll close and say Goodnight and God bless you. Please, give my regards to your mother.

All my love and kisses to you

Forever yours

Hans.

Pickwell

228

My dearest, darling Jean,

How are you today, darling? Fine, I hope. Hasn't it been a lovely day again. Of course, I only mean the weather. It would've been so much nicer to spend these lovely days together. Well, our holidays are still to come and our honeymoon will be the time of our life. Let's find out where to go and let's make that date I was talking about last night. It is a waste of money to run two places. Please, sweetheart, let's talk things over with your mother and please, let me have my word in it. I don't want you to do it all by yourself. If anything turns up we can all talk it over straight away. I, for instance, could save quite a bit of the income tax. We still have to be married, by law, darling. Think of it. This time I'll leave to you to name a date and we'll see if we can agree. Think it over and make a suggestion on Saturday

It's so warm today and we decided not to cook any dinner and just had some egg pancakes. Potatoes are on the fire now, but for tomorrow night.

When you told me last night what that funny milkman of yours said I was a bit upset, but didn't say anything because I didn't want to spoil that lovely weekend even if it was for the last minutes. What does he think he is. I hope he starts talking to me about it when I am there. I'll tell him my point of view about other peoples affairs. Nobody asked for his advices, so he'd better keep them to himself. We know ourselves what to do and what we want. I know elderly people do get that way of seeing things, but they should keep their mouth shut. It really is much for the best of both parties. Well, that's that!!

I was going shooting after finishing this letter, but the Irishmen are still working so I have to wait for the gun. I hope it won't be too late. When I left here at 9.10 last night I still found all the birds out. No need to go before 9.30. That means getting back before 11.30.

In future I shall give you so much money every week to put

in the bank. You remember me talking about those parcels to Germany? I'll get the postal orders on Saturday and send the letter off to Pretoria for those tickets. My mother has lost 35 lbs till now and she has to have something solid to make it up again.

Well, my darling, I'll close now and please give my regards to your mother.

Goodnight and God bless you. Be good and think of me. I love you more than anything else in the world.

      So all my love and kisses

        Forever yours

    Hans.

    92 Wharf St

    June 8th

My dearest darling Hans

Just a few quick lines. It is 11.15 and it is way past my bedtime. I have been to Birstall to see my Auntie and Gertie and I did not get home until 10.30.

Thank you so very much for your letter. I too had a lovely weekend, the best I have ever sent. I wonder what on earth you meant by the funny milkman. You can hardly call him the milkman when he brings it for nothing. If he does say anything to you at any time it would be best to keep your tongue between your teeth. Because darling it is really for my good that he wants to know what your prospects are for the future. I know it isn't anything to do with him but before you lose your temper remember that my mother, Betty and Cyril like him. I know he has his eyes on me, but there is nothing darling, even if I had not you. I would never think him anymore than a friend.

Look darling, you want ~~to~~ me to fix a date when we can get married. I will see when we can save a bit of money. I know I have some money, but if we spent that we would be penniless and I am not doing that. You never know I might have a baby.

Now darling let's talk about your future what you intend to make of yourself in life. I for myself don't like the idea of being a farm labourers wife all my life, but surely you don't want to be working all hours God sends, for the most you can get is £7. I know that is quite good wages, but the hours are too long for it. If you intend to stay on a farm why don't you learn as much as you can about all types of farming then may be some time you will be able to get a job as manager. I may be a snob, but I have never classed myself as working class and don't intend to. Hans there is another reason I want you to get on, because people think that if I marry a German I will have a hard life and no future. I would love to be able to show them how wrong they were.

Maybe we could work hard together and get something on our own. You know I love expensive clothes and things, anyway you now know what you are marrying

Aschersleben, 8.6.49

My dear Hans

Another Whitsun has passed. I was not in the mood for Whitsun this year and it did not feel like it either. Horst worked again on both Bank Holidays and today he is in Halle. He has to buy fabric for a new suit and there is a lot more choice in the bigger towns than here. It's time he got himself something decent to wear, otherwise, one has to ask why he works so hard and for what? Yesterday he was completely stressed and exhausted. I hope you did not have to work over the Bank holidays. We have to have typhus injections again. I went to the doctor yesterday to ask for an exemption certificate. I am still so unwell I can hardly stand on my feet and I don't want to have any injections. It would be a lot better if they gave us more fat and meat instead of inoculations! For the Whitsun Holidays everybody received 100g meat and I got minced beef for us. Half of it was bones. Vegetables are not rationed but they are no good. From 10.6.

onward Curd cheese and other cheeses are not supposed to be rationed. This means that we will never be able to get any. We don't know whether the situation is ever going to get any better, neither do we know where this is leading to. You really notice it the most, when you are unwell and can't look after yourself properly. Heaven only knows how the talks in Paris will end. We don't have a lot of hope. We are having extremely warm weather at the moment, which is very uncomfortable for us under the roofing felt. I received a parcel yesterday from Auntie Lina. She sent us asparagus. We were very pleased with it because I have never seen any here. Edith is now living with her husband. She managed to get over to the West. We would be really happy if we could have another go. It's a completely different life style over there.

I will close my letter for today. Stay healthy. I am sending you all my love and kisses,

your mum and your brother Horst.

Give our best wishes to Jean and your mother-in-law.

Klawitter
Home

Farm

Hans

Pickwell

Melton   Mowbray/   Leics
Great Britain.
My dear Hans
We are sending you all our best wishes for
your birthday. May the coming year bring
you lots of happiness and health, with
best wishes from our hearts. Your mum and
your brother Horst.

92 Wharf St
June 10th

Dear Hans.

I have to write in a hurry and go and post this at the G.P.O. Mr Rudkin the milkman has given me 2 tickets for the agricultural show at Stapleford Park so could you either ring me tomorrow, that is if you get it Friday, otherwise you had better call me Saturday morning and let me know if you want to go. You may wonder why I put Dear Hans well my mother was looking so I will put it now my dearest darling Hans.

If you want to go I could come over to Somerby on the 1.15 from Leicester then you can see how far it is from Pickwell and how we could get there.

All my love
Jean

——.

92 Wharf St
June 10th

My dearest darling Hans

I thought I had better try ~~and~~ to explain myself a bit more, because I doubt if I would be able to tomorrow.

First thing if you ever see Mr Rudkin (the milkman) please darling be ~~nice~~ kind ~~and~~ polite and a gentleman, let me be the one to be rude if necessary. At one time it had used to bother me when he brought the milk bacon etc then I thought to myself "well if he wants to bring the things he can, but he will never get anywhere with me" though I will say this for him he is really very kind to everyone and has helped quite a few people.

If you ever think that because people say things about marrying Germany will make me change my mind I can assure you never need worry about that. I know what I want and no one will ever change my mind no matter what they say. Please, darling, when anyone judges you as the ex enemy and not as a human being, please try to understand, some people have lost much more in the war. It is easy for me not to hate the Germans, the war has never affected me in any way. I never lost anyone, neither Betty nor I were called up to the forces or put to work into a factory. We were not bombed or anything. We have been very lucky, but I do try to understand others. I know if I went to Germany I would find the same thing, I would expect it. You can't have a war and then expect at the finish everyone to love each other.

If you think I have got my big ideas since Mr Rudkin said those things, I can assure you you are very wrong. It is not big ideas it is just me. I have always had those ideas about my life. You should know that I like expensive things and not cheap ones. You wonder why I have never said anything before. Well I have never thought it necessary. I have hoped you were ambitious and I thought you knew that I was. Let me put it this way that when you asked me to marry, you thought I would be a good wife and mother and keep the house nice. So it is only natural that when I said yes I thought you had about you to get me a decent standard of living and it is not always money that can bring that. Quite a lot of people I know have money and live a very low life.

There is another thing I would like to say, when I fetched the milk off Helmut you said you only help people that help you. Well let me tell you what I think. If you help people you may not get your reward from them, but you do get it in some other way. And I believe it is the same if you do or say something wrong. You may think you have got away with it, but in some way it is always evened out. So if you can help anyone no matter what they have done to you you will get through life alright.

Now I have that off my chest. I will close and remain your ever loving wife, because that is what I am in the eyes of God. and I will remain that.

All my love

Jean

____.

What do you think it looks like
Mrs Johannes Klawitter
Or Gertrude Jean Klawitter

Pickwell
June 13th 1949

My dearest, darling Jean,
How are you today, darling? Did you get home well, last night? You'll probably be surprised to get a letter tomorrow as I told you I wouldn't write before Tuesday night. Well, I had to change my plans. Tomorrow night will be washing night. The boss asked me this morning if I mind going round the lot tonight with the poultry foreman having a good look at the birds. And guess what time! After he's finished his shutting up at 10.30!!!! I'll meet him out at Sandhams, the big field. I wonder what time I shall be back. Not before 12.00 anyway. Well, if the day isn't long enough take the night too. In future I have to shut up the sitters when shutting up at night to make sure I've got them all. That means it'll take it a few hours going into every house every night. The next thing I am waiting for him to let ask me to go shutting up myself every night. Nothing doing anyway.

Thank you, sweety, for a nice weekend. I really enjoy everything being with you, even an Agr show. Still, it wasn't bad at all.

I hope I shall meet the funny milkman on Wednesday. Still, we'll see. It makes me feel happy to know Whitsun was the best weekend you've ever spent. You know I like to see you happy- always. So Mr Rudkin only wants your best when he asked what my prospects are for the future. Well, what do you think I want? Perhaps lure you away from home? Well, darling, I am sure you know I won't. We have talked quite a lot the last weekend and I think almost everything is clear. I am really waiting for the boss to ask me about that house. Tuesday's my lucky day. Have a look what the stars say for me this week. He said to me this morning that he hopes to fix me up with something shortly, but nothing definite about that house. I told you I shan't asked him in any case. If he really is interested in keeping me he'll do something and find me a place. You know I am ambitious. When I started to learn at home it only took me 2 years to run a department myself. I hadn't even finished my three years I had to learn. Believe me I found it very hard for a start but I saw it through - successful. We had those stations for air raid alarms, too, during the war and one was in our building. People always wondered why I volunteered for night watch. Only my mother knew I was working. Many a time I worked all night to keep things going properly. Because I knew it made all the difference to me for I got permission to have my first exam at 24 instead of 27. That alone saved me three long years practising. It always was my ambition to get further in life than my father. He only was police sergeant. And also in the Labour service and army it didn't take me long to find my way up. Believe me, sweetheart, I'll do whatever I can to get us a good standard of living. I know I can work and £7 is not at all the best wages one can get. I told you I don't mind working hard as long as I earn my money in an honest way. We'll show them that marrying a German doesn't mean to be a work slave. I love people to be envious and be something better myself. As I told you even if we had to spend most of your money the only thing to do is save up after we've settled down and put some money in the bank again for the case of emergency. After that we could start again on fixing our home to make it comfortable. We'll too make most of life, darling, I am sure.

I also thank you very much for your explanation (the letter you gave me on Saturday). If I see Mr Rudkin on Wednesday I shall thank him for the tickets. You want me to be a gentleman, don't you? I'll try my best. I know nobody would make you change your mind about marrying me. I hope nobody ever tries to take you away from me. He'll have a bad time.

Of course I understand if other people judge me as an ex-enemy. People who have lost relatives or their homes can't judge because hate is stronger than love. I never hated anybody so I can't tell what it's like. Why can't one expect to have a war first and then love each other? Look at us, for instance.

I am sure you'll be a good wife and mother and am not in the least afraid that anything might turned out different to how it was planned. Of course, money alone doesn't make you happy, but it I can assure you that it gives a certain feeling of being more or less independent. One day we'll call that "certain feeling" our own.

Now it's time to close. I was going to write to my mother tonight, but this letter is longer than I expected and I hope it doesn't bore you, so her letter will have to wait till tomorrow night. It's 9.00 gone and I am listening to " Among your souvenirs"

Well, my darling I'll say goodnight now and this time I remain your very loving husband and always will remain that. Please give my love to your mother.

Be good, sweetheart and think of me.
    All my love and kisses
      Forever and only yours
    Hans.

P.T.O.

P.S.

5 pages, almost like old times, isn't it?
    Love
     Hans.

My dearest

Thank you so very much for your lovely letter

I don't know what to think about the house, that is if it is offered to you. I'm not very keen on the idea of having a house with the job. I would not mind if my mother still kept a home so that we would have somewhere if anything happened. Then my mother is another problem, what am I going to do? You will be saying I married you not your relations. I suppose I could live at home in the week and live at Pickwell at weekends, because it does seem a long way to travel especially in the winter and I really have to come out to work for at least a year. Anyway we'll see what happens.

I have to go tonight for those horrible German lessons, but still I have to learn.

Cheeri'O

    Love

     Jean

     ——.

My dear Hans   Aschersleben 13/6/49

Many congratulations on your 24th birthday. I wish you all the best, good health and a speedy Wiedersehen. Let us hope that soon we can all be together again. Now the Whitsun holiday is over and all the hard work has been completed. It was almost impossible to achieve. Mum is still not very well, she is still very weak. Of course we have nothing much that would help her to recover. But how are you, Hans? And how is Jean? We so regret that we cannot be there for your wedding, it being a one off event. The hairdressing competition has been cancelled because of too few participants. Nobody can afford it as it costs over 100 Mark to enter, and where should the money come from? We would so much like to move to the West. A space for living, as here it just keeps going downhill. The standard of living sinks all the time. Hans, do you have plenty of work? When have you fixed your wedding date for? I would like to thank you very much for your dear birthday greetings. In the evening I had several guests over for coffee – it was very cosy. Mum had just returned from the clinic at lunch time, I had big bunches of flowers from mum and a pair of trousers, from the Hohls, 300 grams of wool and from a customer a silver cigarette case and some other bits and pieces. Please excuse the writing, the paper is not that good. Please do not let us wait too long for mail, now I will finish, lots of love to you and Jean, and kisses from your brother Horst. Here's to a speedy and healthy Wiedersehen

Dried flower inserted in the letter

92 Wharf St

June 16th

My dearest darling Hans

Well darling, I have told my mother. She was waiting when

I ~~got~~ arrived home. It took me ages to pluck up courage enough. My mother was just going to bed so I thought I had better get it off my chest. She was saying something about ~~this~~ yesterday afternoon. I thought here is my opportunity so I said, let me get it right " Do you like Hans" she said "yes I have nothing against him" so said I " He wants to marry me" "OK" said my mother "I'll have to think about that" I told her what I intend to do about living at home in the week and going out there at weekends. I told her there was nothing for her to think about, it was that I hope she would fall in with the arrangements. She has not said anything today about it, I don't think you had better come on Sunday because you would not have any time to talk to her. Anyway you can ring me at work tomorrow if you like I will not be able to say much. If you don't I'll ~~ring~~ be there on Saturday

All my love

Jean

.

Pickwell

June 20th 1949

My dearest, darling Jean,

Thank you very much, darling, for the lovely birthday card. Well, the day has almost gone. After all, only two birthday cards arrived, yours and my mothers. Still, I really couldn't expect more. Who else should think of the day? Did you get home well, last night? You weren't the only one to stand up in the bus. There was no seat left for me.

By the way, I still wonder when and where you posted the letter. Haven't you a cheek!! At home I saw you putting the envelope in the bag, changing it into your pocket before we got on the bus, but then lost sight of it. Still the post stamp says "Melton". I can't make it out. Did you post it whilst I fetched the chips?

I also want to thank you for a nice Sunday afternoon. You

know what I noticed? Your mother looked funny at me. I hope she isn't mad with me. We aren't asking too much ~~?~~ are we? I hope to get a chance to talk to her the next time I come over. I would like the situation to be cleared.

The new fellow has arrived today. Still, I don't know if he starts working tomorrow. If he does, I will have to take over the tractor. I don't mind what kind of work I am doing. The time passes just the same.

Oh! I am sorry, sweety, I just found out I haven't got any stamps left. It's too late now to get them so I have to wait till tomorrow to post it. Well, darling, I'll say goodnight. God bless you always. Be good and think of our big day to come. Please give my regards to your mother. All my love and kisses to you.

<u>Tuesday 21st June, 49</u>

Hello, darling, how are you? I really like the warm weather better than rain, but it's just enough now. After all I had to change the 10/-s note today to get some stamps. My cigarettes will be finished tonight and then I shall see how I get on without smoking. Anyway I didn't smoke all afternoon. It was too hot!

You would have had a good laugh last night. When I came in at 5.00 I just waited half an hour to cool off and then had a bath. I stood beside the ~~tub~~ tap in the yard and Helmut kept pouring cold water down my back. I felt lovely afterwards. You'll have to do that later on.

Wouldn't it be nice if we were somewhere at the seaside now. If only there was a pool around here to swim in. I would go every night. It's too far to Melton when I am shutting up. That new fellow hasn't started yet. I heard him talking last night and think he's welsh. That's what it sounds like. Anyway as far as I know up to now I'll continue with the job I am doing at present. That fellow takes the new lot (20 house) and I am allowed to keep my 67. Nicely organised isn't it? Just like "leave John to it, he'll get it done alright '. People must think I am a saboter.

My washing is boiling. Half an hour and I'll have a go. I've put it on the cooker. Well, darling, I'll close now.

Be good, sweetheart and look after yourself. Remember, I love you more than anything else in the world.

Please, give my regards to your mother.

All my love and kisses to you

Forever yours, darling

Hans.

R 4/7.49   Aschersleben, 20.6.49

1/7.49

My dear Hans

Our thoughts are with you, today, on your birthday and we are sending you our very best wishes for the coming years. At the same time, we also want to thank you from the bottom of our hearts for your lovely letter dated 7.6.49. Were you annoyed that I wrote to you about the parcels? I did not mean to be nasty to you. In that case a lot of post must have got lost because we do not hear from you very often, and Jean has written too. Well, there was no letter from Jean among them either. We only received her letter dated 21.5. which you had translated for her. I have been home four weeks already now and I am feeling a little better. I can do all my housework, but I am still finding it very exhausting. On Saturday I queued up for 1½ hours in a free shop to get some herrings. They were 2.80 Marks for two. It was almost my turn and the herrings had been sold out. I would have loved to get something to put on our bread. It's always the same, if you can't queue up for hours, you finish up with nothing. As soon as I got home, I had to lie down again. I went to the clinic today for my post op check-up. The doctor is satisfied with me. All the wounds seemed to have healed quite well, but I have to still be very careful. I cannot lift anything heavy and I am still walking quite slowly. This is rather difficult for me when I am used to always walking very fast. Because of my aching legs, I had to bathe my feet in camphor salt for nine days. Today the doctor prescribed me some heart tablets and also something for my hot flushes and sweating attacks. I hope I can obtain these tablets today from the pharmacy. Most of the time they don't have them in stock. Grandma wrote to us as well, finally. She is sending her best wishes to you. She is now living with Werner and both are well. They were allocated a large room and she has already received her permit to stay. What else can they wish for! I wished we had got documents now. I don't think there is any point in hoping we could get back to our homeland one day, but we cannot live like this forever. It wears us down. If only our wish would be fulfilled!!! It would be so much better for Horst!! The Streeses sent us the two photos. I posted the money to them. It got very expensive for us. We had to pay 20 Marks because our money is almost worthless. Gertrud did not write to us for four months!

Now my dear Hans, I want to finish this letter for today, I still have to go into town.

Stay healthy and give our best wishes to Jean and your mother-in-law.

To you in particular, we are sending all our love and kisses, your mum and your brother Horst.

92 Wharf St

June 21st

My dearest darling Hans

I hope you have had a very Happy Birthday. I am sorry I did not write yesterday, but we decided to wash the other two blankets and then by the time I had ~~had~~ my wash I was too tired.

Mr Rudkin rang yesterday afternoon. On Saturday I decided not to speak again but, when it came to it I can't really be mad with anyone for long. I had never told him you worked for Maclean but he knew my mother must have told him. He asked me if you knew any dairy work other than poultry, as he said if anything happened at Macleans you would find it hard to get a job in poultry and that if you started a small farm it would be useful as poultry was too risky. Then he said had you thought of trying to go to Brooksby for a course. I told him I thought it would be impossible to get there without a government grant, he asked if we'd made inquiries. I told him we'd never thought about it. So he said he would find out. A few minutes later he rang back, he had been speaking to Mr Edwards. He told him he would not say who it was he was inquiring for, but somehow or other he told him it was you he had in mind and Mr Edwards gave you a very good character. While he was telling me what he said Mr Edwards rang me, he said if you were interested the best thing you could do would be to write to the Home Office and tell them you were going to marry an English girl and settle here. I told Mr Edwards that you knew nothing about it and I did not know if you were interested. but if you are the best thing would be to see him.

Well darling I will close now

All my love

Jean

.

Pickwell
June 23rd 1949

My dearest, darling Jean,

Thank you very much for your letter, sweety. In fact, I have spend a very happy birthday, starting work at 7.00 a.m. till 5.0 p.m. Wasn't that nice? Still I have to get going to catch up with your savings. It's only a matter of a couple of years.

That new fellow has started work today. The foreman showed him round on feeding and collecting. I took my old Ford again and went watercarting. It was quite a change sitting on the tractor instead of walking the whole round. I asked the foreman how we go on for weekend work now. He made the same suggestion as you last Saturday. So in future the new chap takes a weekend and I the next one, having Saturday afternoon and Sunday off. So if he's a decent fellow he'll work the coming weekend. I am not sure yet, but I'll find out and let you know tomorrow night at 5.00

It looks as if Mr Rudkin gets into action. He must be interested. I bet Mr Edwards was surprised to hear from me through him. I haven't been to see him for some time. Anyway I don't think it's a bad idea and good ideas have to be thought over. That's what I shall do. And we can talk it over, too.

This morning I received another letter. Those 2 tickets for the parcels. I'll send them home on Saturday. Still I wonder who's going to collect them in Berlin. Perhaps my brother. The main thing I have got the tickets.

Well, sweetheart, I'll close now. Be good and remember that I shall always love you, no matter what happens.

Please, give my regards to your dear mother.

All my love and kisses to you

Forever yours, darling

Hans.

Pickwell
June 27th 1949

My dearest, darling Jean,

I thank you ever so much for a very lovely weekend, especially the Sunday morning.

I would love to come over to you every fortnight when I am off. Of course, it's for your mother to say yes or no. It would be nice if you could fix it. So your mother gets used to me coming over any time I can after we get married. Only 95 days to go. I am crossing every day off now.

How are you today, darling? Nice and hot again and will be for the next few days. Wouldn't it have been nice if we had got married last week and had our holidays at the seaside now in this lovely weather. By the way, I shall have to teach you to swim so we can have a swim together when we go to Bournemouth. Imagine, miles out in the sea, just the two of us!!! Well, sweetheart, I know we'll have a lovely time. I am really longing for the 30.9.49. What a day it'll be!

I thought I was off this week, meaning the shutting up. Now the boss came and ask if I mind helping Doris tonight with shutting up. She can't get the birds in. Still, it's overtime and more for us to save, isn't it. My washing has to wait until to-morrow night. Please, darling do Lucy's hair on Wednesday. Please, give my regards to your mother. Remember how much I love you

> All my love and kisses to you
>> Forever yours, darling
> Hans.
> 92 Wharf St
> June 28th

My dearest darling Hans

I will finish what I was saying tonight on the telephone. I could have stayed hours talking, but there was a girl outside the call box and she kept giving me such a look that I had to say cheeri-bye.

I did thank you for your very nice letter. I did not know if you would write, as I told you on Sunday I was going to write. You can imagine how pleased I was when I saw your letter.

I would really love to have a baby, but I know it would be best to wait a year or two so we can save to get a nice home.

I won't ask my mother now if you can come every fortnight but will ask when we get there. I think it will be alright.

I thought I would walk down Belvoir Street and look in the shops on Sunday, but at the bottom of Friar Lane I saw Elsie Cox. I used to work with her at Corah's in fact she was over me. I told her I had just been to see you on the bus. I told her you were a German and she was very surprised. She said she thought I would end up married to a Duke. I think I must go around as if I have a good opinion of myself!

Do you think you could possibly finish the clock.

My mother asked me what I was going to wear on the great day I told her I had thought about a costume. She said why didn't I borrow Betty's dress, but I have definitely made up my mind that I am not having a big wedding very quiet just a few relations and not white. I think we have just cake and wine, then go away about 1 hour after we have been married. Anyway we will have to plan that later

I will close now

    All my love and kisses
    Jean.

Wednesday

Hello darling,

I have just got back from Lucy's. I have given her a Toni perm and it looked as though it had taken. I did not have time to stop to set it, as I had to catch the last bus at 11.00. Do you think that you could do mine (hair) for me sometime? I think Betty would do mine if I asked her, I will have to think it over.

What do you think about what I was telling you about going with my mother for a holiday? I myself would rather be independent of anyone, but on the other hand I know my mother could really do with a holiday and she is not able to afford one and I think she would like to go. I have just split the ink on the table cloth I hope it will come out .I have put it in milk and water. So I better get going to bed before I do anything else

    All my love
    Jean

    —— ·

Pickwell
June 30<u>th</u> 1949

My dearest, darling Jean,

How are you, today sweetheart? Another lovely day! If only we have such nice weather in September. Let's keep our fingers crossed for a late summer. It's 9 o'clock now and I am writing this in the bedroom. I couldn't stick it in the "kitchen". It's the first day we're having a hot dinner this week. And with the fire going it is awful hot in there. Just sandwiches day after day don't satisfy me. We had some meat left, so everything was alright. Some sweet finished the meal off.

Have you been busy last night? I was thinking of you all the time. You'll be surprised to hear that I've been out last night. Of course I only had 3/2 ½ s left and the bus fare and pictures amounted to 3/2. So I had a halfpenny left for the next week. Or could I have a few more shillings? I have to ask, haven't I? This weeks wages will only be just over £5. No weekend work and no shutting up. Next will be better.

I don't know what happened last night. I just was really fed up with sitting here on my own. It was 5.50 when I decided to go to Melton and the bus leaves at 6.00. Still I made it. And guess what was on? "The paleface". So I enjoyed it for the second time. But remember the supporting pictures about "Highlanders"? I saw that again, too, or rather had to as it just started when I got in. Those lovely bagpipes!!! Bonzo is sitting beside me. We both want somebody to make a fuss of us. Coming? It shan't be long before I go to bed. Are you ready?

I've got something to fix the ceiling in your (our) room. I only hope it'll stick to ~~eat~~ it. Have a go when I come over next weekend. We'll at least make that room comfortable, be sure. Are you getting some curtains?

Only another day and a half to go till I see you again. It was exactly 3 months yesterday darling. We're getting nearer after day.

Well, my sweety, be good and remember how much I love you.

All my love and kisses to you
Forever yours, my darling
Hans.

"My darling"

I thank you so very much for the lovely letter I received today. Well, Friday is gone, but this weekend shan't be as nice as the last one. No staying in bed till 9 o'clock and nobody to come and wake me with a kiss. Or should I ask Helmut what he could do? Still, I'd rather wait another week.

The poor girl waiting on the call box, we were only talking for half an hour. Still, as you said, I had to pay for the call we certainly made the most of it.

You sure have a good opinion of yourself and also let other people know it. Would you rather marry a duke? Perhaps there's a spare one about somewhere. Plenty of money those folks have and a – car. They don't bother with motorbikes as I do.

You're right darling, if you want to get married in a costume, let's stick to it. I really don't like the idea of borrowing one if one doesn't buy one himself. We'll make our plans before it's time. Don't let's cancel the champagne. I myself like it. We shall see what time the London buses leave. We can get one from Leicester can't we?

Why shouldn't I be able to do your hair? Remember my brother is a lady's hairdresser!

Well, darling, I've thought about what you're telling me. Take that holiday Mr Rudkin offered you. It's the best to let your mother have a change. I bet she also would love to go away for a week, so take the opportunity. I know it is a bit funny to have somebody pay for it but never mind darling. And go as long as the weather keeps fine.

I shall be busy tomorrow afternoon and evening. The boss has asked me to take my turn and go shooting crows at the chicken field. So we'll have a nice afternoon out. That's all overtime.

Well, my sweetheart, I'll say goodnight and God bless you always. Be good till I see you tomorrow.

I love you more than anything else in the world.

So all my love and kisses

Forever and only yours

Hans.

Aschersleben, 2.7.49

My dear Hans and Jean

We were so happy to receive your letter dated 16.6.49 and also your letter dated 25.6.49 which you sent by registered mail. We thank you from the bottom of our hearts. We were so pleased to receive both letters. The latter arrived here completely intact, with the two parcel vouchers. This will help us tremendously and I am sure I will recover much quicker now because the fat, meat etc. are what we miss most of all. We can collect them in Berlin and bring them here. Horst will probably go there by himself. He has a few customers with cars who often go to Berlin on business and I am sure he can get a lift. This would be good because he does not have to pay the train fare. Since yesterday, the Suburban Trains have been put into operation again in Berlin, which makes it much easier to get around. I am feeling a little stronger already and have put on some weight, but I want to go back and see the doctor quite soon because I suffer so badly from perspiration and still get these unpleasant hot flushes and sweating attacks. They are horrendous. I get so wet and look like someone who has pulled me out of a pond. They come day and night and I also have my heart problem. Perhaps these are still the after-effects of the very strong anaesthesia? They gave me two injections. I think that was more than enough. On the other hand, I feel that the after effects of the operation should have gone out of my body by now. You are writing about a heatwave. We cannot complain about this, we have already had autumnally weather for weeks now and everybody is waiting for summer. Let's hope that when your heatwave is over it will come to us, although I am not too keen on a heatwave, my body is already hot enough and also, living directly under this roofing felt does not help my problem. I am amazed how you can cope with this extreme heat! Horst and I have often talked about this. If I remember rightly, you never really stayed in the sun for long back home. I see that you have now definitely fixed your wedding date. If you want to buy all these things, you must have saved a lot of money. Have a nice suit made . Do you have the same custom as we have: a white dress with a flower wreath made of little flowers on the bride's head and a veil? We are hoping for a very pretty wedding photo. It all sounds very plush – and going straight after the wedding ceremony to your honeymoon. Why are you waiting until the autumn? I hope the weather will be nice for your honeymoon. Are you waiting for the harvest? We shall be praying for nice weather. There will be plenty of time for us to make the wedding cake. On Monday it is our Papa's 40th Birthday. I wonder what he will be doing on his birthday. Eight years ago we were lucky enough to all be together and celebrate his birthday. I have been quite restless a while lately and wonder if he is thinking of us a lot. So many soldiers are coming home. Why do I have to wait so long and still in vain! This week we had a letter from the Eichhorns who live in Steinach. They wanted to get me a job as a housekeeper. One of their neighbours who has a smallholding lost his wife. They asked me if I wished to move there. You should have seen

Horst. He was beside himself as you can imagine. I declined their offer, of course, with thanks. What would Papa say to it, if he came back, and Horst really needs me. I am sure, however, that the Eichhorns meant well. I also heard from grandma today. She is very well and is sending her love to you.

Now, my dear boy, thank you very much again for everything. We are looking forward to receiving all those lovely things.

Stay healthy. Give our love to Jean and your mother-in-law, and to you we are sending all our love and kisses,

your mum and your brother Horst.

We are hoping for a happy reunion.

Pickwell,
July 4th 1949

My dearest, darling, Jean,

How are you today, sweetheart? Fine I hope after this lovely shower we've had. It was just 5 o'clock and believe me I would've loved to put my trunks on and stand in the yard if it hadn't looked a bit funny. Everybody is feeling sorry for me today for I've had my shirt off all day and look dark red. Still, it doesn't hurt. One gets used to it I think. As it was cool I started the fire and cooked us some dinner.

Did you get home well last night? I was thinking of you when I went shutting up. Just the time you arrived at home, 9.45. Got back at 10.40. And believe me I was ready for bed. I am so much longing for Saturday to come over. That lovely Sunday morning. Be sure I'll stand in the yard on Saturday to wait for the clock to strike 12. And off I go.

I was watercarting again today. Not a bad job when the sun is shining. The time passes away ever so quick.

Well, darling, I've again thought about the wireless set. It's best to buy it straight the way and have done with. If we can't get that particular Decca set I think the best one we can get is His Master's Voice. Or can you think of any other good make? Still, there's plenty of time on Saturday afternoon to have a good look around. We'll sure find the right one.

We are back again where we first started our outings only the scenery is not so nice. We'll go to Croxton again one day. If only our great day and with it our holiday would be soon. Only 87 more days. I am striking one day off every day. You can do it when you come over again.

Well, darling, I'll close now and say goodnight. God bless you always. Be good my darling and think of me.

Please, give my kindest regards to your dear mother.

      All my love and kisses
        Forever and ever yours
        Hans.

92 Wharf St
July 5th 1949

My dearest darling Hans
It is only 9.0 and I am in bed, there did not seem to be anything on the wireless worth listening to. Speaking of radios I think myself it would be best to pay straight out for it but it is going to put us back quite a bit because without that I don't think we will be able to manage on what we save. I don't mind getting some out of the bank but not a lot because it will take a bit putting it back, because I know what we will keep needing after we are married.

Now about this milking business, I know you were annoyed because no one asked you, and I think I would be annoyed too. I don't expect you to do anything you don't want to do, but don't you think it would be best to gain experience in all things while you can, because I don't think you can get very far doing poultry alone if we had something of our own.

I don't know whether or not you intend to do farming. You have never said, but if you do it would be best to do it well. Mr Rudkin in the course of the conversation said that he would help us to get a farm or a small holding. I don't mean buy for us. I know if we did we would both have to work very hard. I don't mind that so long as we were getting somewhere, but darling, it would not be any use if you were not interested. We would soon be in debt and I would rather you stayed as a farm labourer at £4.14.0 than get into debt. All I really want is a happy family life with you always loving me and me you.

I wish I had a radio in my bedroom so I could switch it on and listen to some nice music.

I told Lucy about how we went to the chicken field on Sunday. I quite disgusted her when I told her I took my dress off to sunbathe. It has been quite a joke, Margery said it was no wonder you did not want to go home to Germany. Lucy said I was just asking for trouble (is it really my fault you did not keep your promise) and that I would give you ideas. I don't have to take my dress off to do that. I didn't tell her that.

Well darling I will say goodnight and God Bless. Please darling think what you want to do, not what anyone else wants, not even me.

All my love and
Kisses
Jean

.

Pickwell,
July, 7<u>th</u> 1949

My darling

I am so sorry, my sweet, for not ringing you. And I haven't even sent a letter. Do you mind? I was busy, believe me. Last night I started on the clock. From 6.30 till 10.00. Everything put on the right place and no parts left over. When I got to the balance, I got the shock of my life. The balance axle is broke on one side. Still I hope to be able to fix it up somehow. Another night's work will finish it up I hope.

You should've seen me tonight. Blimey I was in a hurry. It was 5.15 exactly when I got back. That meant too late to ring you. Straight away shopping. When I came back I cooked our dinner. New potatoes and beef, lovely. Then washing up and washing my head. Now I am waiting for the water to boil to have a wash myself. Afterwards shutting up and then it's time to go to bed. Still, only 5 more hours to go and I am off.

Haven't we had a nice chat on Wednesday night! Even the telephone operator would have laughed when you told me what Lucy and Marjorie said about taking your dress off.

Well, we'll see about the wireless tomorrow. I was really mad when I got my money tonight, 19/-0 income tax. It isn't worth working all weekend just to pay the tax.

About taking on farming, we'll talk tomorrow. We sure would have to work very hard, but it would be nice to call a few acres our own, wouldn't it. Don't worry about the happy family life. I am sure we'll always be happy.

Please excuse my writing but I am in a hurry. I have packed my briefcase and found it awful heavy. All the things in there.

Well, darling, I'll say goodnight now and God bless. Be good till I see you tomorrow.

All my love and kisses
Forever yours
Hans.

92 Wharf St
July 7th 1949

My dearest darling

You will be surprised to hear from me today but I had to buy a new writing pad this lunchtime and while waiting for someone to ring I may as well write a few lines to you. I have not brought my sewing today. I did not bring it because this morning it was raining rather a lot and I only have it in a paper bag and I would hate my cloth to get wet.

Hasn't it been cold today. My mother lit a fire first thing. I nearly put my vest back on but I have tried to be brave and so far I have left it off.

I had a peach given to me this morning by a man I pass on the way to work. I have not seen him for about 10 days because for about the past fortnight I have been early. He said he had brought some cherries but hadn't seen me. I am going to be late tomorrow to see what I get.

I think Nancy will be married before me yet. An uncle of her mother's has a small holding with a cottage, he is about 90 years old and wants to go to live with Nancy's mother. Nancy asked him about it and he told her she could have it as it stands. He intends to leave in September. So they will probably be married before she goes away on Sept 16th. She has booked 2 single rooms at Eastbourne. Should I book single rooms for us?

I changed my mind. There isn't much in what I have written so I think I will save 2 ½d. I have had a few expenses this week. 1/9 for this month's union fee, 1 packet of envelopes, 1 pad, they came 2 1/2 . 2/- to have my shoes mended. I only have 3/10 left. Haven't I been a spend thrift this week. I have not been out at all this week so let's try to go to the pictures.

Love Jean

Aschersleben, 10.7.49

My dear Hans

Today I want to send you my heartiest Sunday greetings. We

are having nice weather and I want to go for a walk later on. Horst will be going to Berlin during the next week to collect the parcels. We are looking forward to them very much. The car was supposed to go to Berlin this week but it was postponed. Last Saturday Uncle Erich came to see us unexpectedly. It was lovely to see him again. He is sending his very best wishes to you. He left us again during the night of Tuesday. He was not able to stay any longer because his hay was still outside and he also needs to pile the potatoes into heaps. As he put everything into the ground quite late because he had no horse and cart, everything is coming up a bit later. He had to look around for a horse, and finally, after a lot of driving, he has now bought one for 4,000 Marks. This is a horrendous price. Auntie Else has also written and is sending her best wishes to you. They are also very busy with their two estates. They have just started with building their house and they have to supply meals for the workmen, which is not easy nowadays.

I can say that I am now, thank goodness, feeling better. Horst has managed to get me loads of medication which will strengthen me and help to build up my blood cells, but I can still not queue for a long time, nor can I cope with these awful hot flushes. However, even those problems must get better one day. Yesterday another soldier came home again. Every time this happens, I am totally shattered. Have your harvests started already? The winter barley has already been cut. This is a sign of a good harvest this year.

Now, my dear boy, stay healthy and give our very best wishes to Jean and your mother-in-law.

To you, we are sending all our love and kisses, from your mum and your brother Horst.

Horst thanks you very much for your lovely letter.

Pickwell,
July, 11th 1949

My dearest darling Jean

How are you today, darling? Fine, I hope. I thank you so very much for a lovely weekend. Believe me I didn't feel like leaving you last night and not like work this morning. If I only could stay with you straight away. I love you more than anything else in the world and I shall make love to you – always. You are so lovely and the wireless we bought shows that you know what you want. It looks as if I have to listen to you a bit more. Still I rather like going into shops buying something and ask you if you like it. You know I love to see you happy and satisfied. The tea was very nice and I always enjoy it much more if you get it ready. Anyway it's just like being at home.

This morning my tractor broke down twice and I was on watercarting. It usually takes me all day to get round the lot. Well, when I got started it was 11 o'clock and I had to finish it because the tins were all dry. That, of course meant 3/9s overtime pay (2/6 income tax).

Haven't you got an uncle aged 90 with a smallholding? That's the way of getting somewhere easily.

I just and still wonder why Nancy is booking 2 single rooms. Is she afraid of her husband-to-be. I hope you are not !!!! Ours will be a double room, definitely. Don't forget to write this week and please think of the film. Shall you bring dog biscuits on Saturday? I got a postcard today from the radio people. The set is going to be collected on Thursday 14.7.49 after 5.00pm. I've packed and polished it up so everything is ready. The new set surely is good.

Well, darling, I'll do my washing now. Be good, good night and pleasant dreams. Please thank your mother for the lovely dinner and give her my regards.

  All my love and kisses to you
   Forever yours
    Hans.

 92 Wharf St
 July 11th

My dearest darling Hans

Did you get to Pickwell safe with the radio? I came straight home. I went down High St and had a look in the shop windows, I did not see anything I like. I listened to Variety Bandbox, wasn't too bad, did some needlework then I went to bed about 10.30.

I have just written to Bournemouth for a double room. Oct 1st to 8th. I signed the letter J.K. Klawitter. I don't want the people to know we have just been married. I think I am going to have a job to stick to a very quiet wedding, but I intend to stick to what I have said. I hope we can get married at 10.30 and catch a 11.30 train to London. My mother wanted to know who I was having for bridesmaids. I told her I did not want one because that would mean more expense. I wish we could be married in London where there would not be any bother. I have made up my mind I am not going to worry just take things as they come and hope for the best. So long as we get that piece of paper it will not matter about the rest.

We did not have that talk about the future. We did not have much time did we!!

I took the film in this lunchtime. I will be able to get it back on Saturday.

I have my income tax form to fill in, if I bring it over can you help me.

I want to post this tonight and I will take Freddy a walk. I don't think you need worry about Freddy and if other people think that I think more of Fred than you, they can, but I can assure you I don't.

All my love
Jean

.

My dearest ,darling Jean,

How are you today sweety? Fine I hope. I have just switched the wireless off because of the storm. It's raining very hard here. Drops as big as a sixpence. Anyway it comes just in time. It really is nice to sit inside and watch the rain without getting wet. But what about you poor darling over at Birstall? I hope you've made it in time and it stops for you to go back home. Shall I cross my fingers?

Why don't you want people to know we've just been married? That wouldn't make any difference to us. What about our or rather your identity card and ration book? Shall you have the name changed the day before? You could do couldn't you? Well, that's up to you.

Why do you think you'll have a job to stick to a quiet wedding? Did the relatives smell the joint before it was cooked? Well, darling don't worry, everything will turn out alright. It's just that piece of paper isn't it? We'll get that alright. Somehow I hope to be able to get hold of those words the preacher is saying. I don't want to say anything wrong and blush afterwards. That would be most embarrassing for me. Can you help me there?

Bring your income tax form on Saturday and I'll try to help you. Perhaps it's the same I've had. By the way, please bring a plug for the wireless like the one you brought before. I forgot to tell you last night.

Well, my sweetheart, it's 9.00 and I'll reply to my mother's letter. Please give my regards to your mother. Be good and God bless you. I love you very, very much.

All my love and kisses

Forever yours

Hans.

Aschersleben, 15.7.49

My dear Hans!

I am very happy to let you know that we received both parcels today. Two days ago Horst went to Berlin by car to collect them and he is now home again. He also came back by car and everything went very smoothly. We are so happy about all the lovely things you sent us and thank you from the bottom of our hearts. We are having very hot weather at the moment, around 30°C, but we badly need this kind of weather in order to get a good harvest. I am not able to work on the fields this year, but I am very grateful that I am slowly getting better and on my way to recovery. I have a lie-down every afternoon because it is too exhausting to be on my feet all day long. I still have to be very careful. If I overdo it I get pain from the wound. We had a letter from Uncle Erich yesterday. He is now safely back in Leyerhof. If you leave here at 1.15 in the morning, you can get to Grimmen (Vorpommern) at around 11 o'clock. This is by the Express train all the way, with only one change in Berlin. It is a very good connection. However, we cannot go there this year. I am not allowed to make such a journey just yet. Uncle Erich is sending his best wishes.

Horstel is so busy every day that he has not been able to answer your letter yet, but he will get around to writing to you. Auntie Else wrote that someone in Altentreptow is always enquiring about you. He met you when you were in captivity together. Do you know him? Has your suit been made yet? Horst's is finished now and it looks very good. The tailor charged 110 deutschmarks. If our Papa were here, we could save all this money. I am going to have a suit made for myself.

Now, my dear boy, I am sending you my best wishes, with lots of love and kisses from your mum and your brother Horst.

Give our best wishes to Jean and your mother-in-law.

Pickwell,
July, 17th 1949

My dearest, darling Jean,

How are you my sweetheart? Fine, I hope. I've just crossed

another day off. 73 to go. How time flies, still I wouldn't mind at all if there was only the last figure left, would you? Then, of course, we would be a bit more excited. Oh, darling, believe me I am longing for the 29.9. Well darling, as I said only 73 days.

Thank you very much for a lovely weekend. By the way, you forgot two things. First to bring me a few envelopes and second to take your "Sunday Pictorial" back, you were going to show it to your mother weren't you?

I had some expenses today 2/3 ½ s for stamps. However it'll stand me for a couple of weeks. The poultryman said today he is sorry but the boss wants to keep the cockerels. I take a good hen and pick it out myself. That's alright, too, isn't it?

About Saturday. I have decided to dress up properly. That first impression people get it always what counts. I'll press the trousers Thursday night and get everything ready for I shan't have much time on Friday. Shopping, getting the chicken ready, having a wash etc. Not to forget the shutting up. I wish it was Friday night.

You should've seen me this morning. I took a big trailer and fetched a load of feeding stuff from the top of the hill. On the way back down hill the drawbar broke and the full trailer got loose running after me. You believe I never changed into top gear so quick to get out of the way. Halfway down the drawbar went into the ground and stopped the trailer. By then I was on the gate. I wasn't half sweating.

Well, my darling, it's 9.00 and time to go my round. Be good and remember how much I love you. Goodnight and God bless you. Please give my regards to your mother.

> To you all my love and kisses
> Forever yours
> Hans.

Pickwell,

My dearest, darling Jean,

So you are going to leave me for a week. Is it just including the weekend I am off? Well, what does it matter. You enjoy yourself. Why should I mind darling? It will do you good.

I am surprised to hear that Otto is living in a hostel. I thought he was living with the farmer. It looks as if everybody wants to get married before us. Still the 16.7 is gone.

This is the last envelope I dug up from somewhere so if you want a letter on Saturday you'd better sent one along. I am not sure if I shall be able to ring you on Friday. I might be working late and then I've had it.

This week we have to see how we got on with our dinners. It'll have to bread and jam one day and jam and bread the next. Quite a change to our rich food. Still I'll make up at your aunties supper on Saturday. Ring her up to get something nice.

Well my darling, I'll say goodnight now. Be good and God bless you. Please give my regards to your mother. I love you very much.

> So all my love and kisses
> Forever yours
> Hans X (one special)

92 Wharf St
July 20th

My dearest darling

They are only 70 days more and I will then be Frau Klawitter. What a ghastly name!!! I think it's beautiful. I will be really glad when it is Sept 30th and it is all over. I wish we could just go away, get married, have a holiday and that is that. I hate a lot of fuss. I have a wedding present, or rather I will have. Mr and Mrs Dale (where my mother goes on Sunday) they are both in their 70s. Mrs Dale asked my mother if I would like what she gave to Charlie, 2 pillow slips and a towel. I thought it very nice of them, their only son was killed in the first war.

I'm worried again, but this time it is different. There is an examination called the last opportunity exam to be a permanent civil servant, I thought I was not included in it as it was for clerical officers but this afternoon Mrs Deacon asked me about it and said she would send me a note or papers I don't know. I told her I was going to be married but I added I hoped to be staying on, then she said it was a good opportunity for me. The only advantage I can see to at the moment is that I would not have the sack so easily. I think it would be a waste of their time because it is bound to be a stiffer examination for officers' grade and I am hopeless. Anyway I have said I would think it over, I will see what the paper says. What do you think?

You can please yourself what you wear, as long as you put something on. There is one thing I wish you would not wear that is your ring. I do not like to see rings on men and I know they have the same taste as me. I put up with it but I wish for one day you will take it off. What was I going to show my mother in the Sunday paper? There was something in the week before's paper.

I have a confession to make, I have been to the pictures this evening. It was like this. It started to rain, it looked so miserable out we hadn't a fire and my mother was going out. I went to see 'Accused', it wasn't bad. I got back just after 10.0 and my mother was still out. When I came in Billy was there but no Freddy I called him and he came trotting downstairs, he had been on my mother's bed.

I am still answering Bernhard's letter, I have been doing it for the past month.

I will have to close now.

All my love and kisses etc

God Bless you

Jean

Thursday Lunchtime

I have just read your letter, thank you very much. It was on time today.

I won't bother to send an envelope if you want to write and bring it with you on Saturday, you can. That will save an envelope and 2 1\2 saved.

We have heard from Sheringham. We are going 13th August to 20th. That means you will be off on the 20th. Because you are off this week 23 on 30 off 6 13 and 20. Betty is coming to look after the shop, I don't know whether she will sleep here or not, but I don't know how Fred will go on.

I still have not written to London, but I will tonight. I have to get cracking now otherwise I will be late.

All my love and kisses
Jean

—.

Pickwell,
July, 17th 1949

"My darling"

I thank you so very much for your lovely letter I received this morning. How are you today sweety? Fine, I hope.

So, thank you very much for the lovely expression 'What a ghastly name' I know it doesn't suit you very much but still, do you think I should change it to Phillips? Then it wouldn't be so difficult for you to get used to a new name. Still, the 29.9 will come and only 69 more days.

It's very nice of Mr and Mrs Dale to give you a wedding present. Everything will help us.

You'll have to explain a bit more tomorrow what this Civil Servants Scheme really means. We'll have time to talk it over.

By the way weren't you going to bring that income tax form along last week?

Even if the advantage of the scheme is that you can't get sacked so easily it won't mean much to you. If they want to sack you, let them do it. Then you'll stay at home and later on make a very good housewife. Why do you think you are hopeless going in for an exam? Don't worry darling, let it come and just get down to it. There's no need to be afraid of anything!

Don't you like the idea of wearing a ring? I think the one with the black stone looks rather nice.

Look, sweetheart, you don't have to make a confession when you go to the pictures, you earn money, I told you I couldn't go on Wednesday because I had to shut the broody hens up.

Well, darling, I'll close now. I have still got plenty to do tonight. Just be good till I see you tomorrow.

All my love and kisses etc

Forever yours

Hans.

Aschersleben, 22 July 1949

My dear Hans!

We thank you with all our heart for your two letters dated 5.7. and 13.7.49. We are always very happy to receive post from you and hear everything is alright and you are keeping well. These are really the main things. I am a lot better now, thank God, although not quite the same as before. One has to be content in the knowledge that things are going into the right direction. I am sure with the new medication I have now got, I will soon be better, but I have to be very careful with it so that it lasts long enough. In any case, it is an enormous help for us. I do wish we could make it up to you. Maybe one day we shall get an opportunity to pay you back somehow.

You have now brought your wedding forward by one day. Do you think that a Friday is an unlucky day for weddings? Well, my first wedding was on a Thursday and I can say that

I did not complain about too much happiness! I don't think it means anything. It sounds like you have made up your minds to settle down in Leicester. Have you rented a flat already? And bought some furniture? It means it is not very convenient for you to get to work. But you have to know what's best for you. Does Jean think she will get too lonely out in the country?

We had a letter from the Streeses this week. Auntie Martha wrote that things have improved a lot since we were there but they still have to sign up regularly for unemployment benefits. They received the money we sent for the photos. What a pity Jean is not going to wear a wreath (on her head) and no veil either. It is always so lovely, but I don't want to tell you what you have to do. I dare say if you are leaving by lunchtime then there is little point. How many guests have you invited? You are very posh. You have even booked a double room. Is this a living room and a bedroom, or even two separate bedrooms? Well, I am very curious as to how you will furnish your flat. I wish we could have our own flat one day and furnish it the way we want it to be. It would be lovely because it is always such a bad feeling to live in other people's property and with their furniture. You are doing the right thing in getting a nice home together. You have had to work very hard for it.

I will bring my letter to an end. Horst has just come home from work and he wants to go for a little walk with me. Give my best wishes to your Jean and your mother-in-law and to you, my dear boy, we are sending our love and kisses. Your mum, who is always thinking about you, and your brother Horst.

92 Wharf St

July 25th 1949

My dearest darling Hans

I am sorry darling I did not write last night. thought I would have a look at the shops in High Street but it was too dark to see. I did not get in until later about 10.0 I put my hair in curlers then my mother came home it would look funny to start writing just after I had left you. Anyway I have not had a letter from you so you could not have written.

About the wedding ring. It is hard to explain what I mean about a ~~plain~~ gold ring looking too married. Well I will put it this way with a plain gold ring those I have looked at look as though they have just scrubbed a floor. Anyway we will see, if I have a silver one then I would like a gold, could I have one. Do you know what holiday you will be having? I have Monday only. I could either come over there if you are working or you over here. I forgot to say anything about ringing in the week. We will now be able to save 6d we can spend that on a relay radio. I will go to Cooks one day and book seats, do we have good ones? We will go on Thursday or do we do Friday (I hope we don't fall out this time when we go to London). I made some more enquiries about the trains to London by the LNER there is one 11.23 and 1.4. I think the 12.25 will be the best we could be married at 10.30, say one hour in the church, 11.30. I think ½ hour will be enough to cut the cake and have a drink of wine. I am beginning to wish it was the first week in September. Nancy is going to be married Sept 10th it is definite now but she has not got the small holding her uncle is selling it, she could buy it if she wished but she is not she is staying at home and is going to continue working. Don't you think it best that we keep being careful so we can keep on saving, if we could keep up our saving as we have been doing this last month we should have something, but if anything did happen I would not mind at all would you?

Well darling I will have to say goodnight and God Bless you.

All my love and kisses

Jean

Tuesday

Miggy rang this morning to say she was leaving on Friday for Scotland. Otto is going Sunday. She wanted me to meet her at lunch time tomorrow. I will get all the gen then!

You are a good boy making 2/6 overtime, I will have to see if I can put some overtime in, but what kind!!!

I won't be able to go to the pictures this week. Unless it is Friday when I get paid but I won't then. I will spend that on something for our tea. I will see what I can find.

Well darling it is nearly 5.15 and I don't want to work overtime I don't get paid for it.

Love

Jean.

Pickwell,

July 26th 1949

My dearest, darling Jean,

I was so disappointed when I came back for breakfast this morning – no letter for me. Well, I hope again for tomorrow. How are you today, my sweety? Fine, I hope. Do you know what a boy scout looks like? Come to Pickwell, look at me and you know everything. It was very hot again so as I told you yesterday my shorts had to come out with me. Fortunately nobody said anything or joked. My legs got a bit red and don't you think it'll look much better to be brown all over when we go on holidays instead of being on top and the legs snow white?

Last night I was going to get us some dinner as the whole week's meat ration was still there. A little surprise was waiting for me. When I got it ready on Friday night I wrapped a newspaper tight round the pan. He had some meat on Sunday and just put the paper loose on top. You may know what's happened. The meat was walking around the pan. I was mad, but don't worry I didn't lose my temper. I don't know what to cook this week. We had some 'pudding' to-night!!! It's time we got a home ourselves and organise things properly. Otherwise I shall die of starvation soon. Tonight I was busy. At first I got the pudding ready, then washed two weeks things, washed up and now (10.00) have to shave.

Well, my sweetheart, I'll get cracking and say goodnight and God bless. I love you so very much and am always thinking of you.

Be good.

Wednesday, 7.00pm

Hello, darling, how's life treating you? Thanks very much for your letter. Of course I know it looks a bit funny to write an hour after I've gone back. So you can't write if you haven't got a letter from me. What about me? I start writing first every week. You certainly like window shopping don't you? We only need bags of money to buy everything we like!! Just wait and see when we get cracking.

It'll be quite a treat to come back Saturday and find the tea ready. But you'll have to hurry up as I shall be early. A lot of those hens at Sandhams are going to be sold this week so that'll make me earlier.

I know alright what you mean about a gold ring. You'll have a nice platinum one you may choose yourself. I've told you that I want a plain gold ring for myself.

When you go to Cooks to book our seats for the London show please book good seats. Don't worry about us falling out it would be a shame *one day * after being married.* I also think the 12.25 is the best train. Remember that we have to be there and call for our room till 7.00 at the latest. It'll give us plenty of time to cut the cake and have a drink, getting married at 10.30. Be sure I wish it was the first week in September. Still it's too late now as we have reserved the rooms. It was up to you to make it the 16.7.49 wasn't it?

You're right darling, let's be careful for the first year still I wouldn't mind after the marriage.

You'll be surprised to hear that even this short week I've put 10 hours overtime in. I hope to put £4 away again.

Please darling, do me a favour. Get a 7/6s postal Order, cross it and send it with the enclosed form to the following address: To the Office of the Clerk of the Traffic Area East Midlands, Grosvenor House, Friar Lane, Nottingham. Put the number of the postal order on the form at the place I crossed. I had the form with me last Saturday but forgot all about it. Please, get it and send it off before Saturday otherwise I have to have another provisional licence. I want to save those 5/-s. Please take the half a crown, change and go to the pictures Thursday night. Look darling, it's alright if we save our money and keep it together, but don't let's get avaricious ~~look~~ like Scotchmen. Life gets boring if you stick at home every night. It's different if I don't go as I am glad to seat down after a day's work.

This morning the boss sent me with the tractor to Somerby to fetch an elevator. The rest of the day I was 'creasoting' (I hope it's spelt right as nobody can tell me how it's properly spelt).

I received a letter from my mother today. Horst has been to Berlin, fetched the two parcels and got them safely home. They got a shock when they unpacked the parcels and saw all the nice things. Anyway they're very happy.

It looks as if I have to go chicken house moving next week. The big lot at Sandhams has to be moved to Cold Overton field.

Well, darling, I hope you don't mind if I close now. Does it bore you?

So good night and God bless you. Be a good girl and think of me if you can spare the time and be sure I love you more than anything else in the world.

All my love and kisses

Forever yours

Hans.

PS My mother and Horst send their kindest regards to you

and your mother. Love Hans.

92 Wharf Street

July 30th

Hello darling

I have posted that thing to Nottingham today. How long will it be before he comes to give you a test again?

You are a darling really saying I could go to the pictures with the change, but I was bored staying in, though I have been out this week. Monday I stayed in, Tuesday I did the same thing and messed about, Wednesday I had a bath, I went to see Gertie and brought 3 bathing costumes to try on. I know you want me to look nice even when I go bathing so I had a 2 piece. Gertie said I could have it 25/- it was 34/11. I took the others back Thursday lunchtime but I did not pay for the one I had, it was a good job I didn't. When I went in to today she had reduced them again to 15/-. I also bought a bathing hat, that was 5/11. If you have Monday off and it is very warm we can go to the pool. Now back to what I have been doing the rest of the week – Thursday I washed my hair and tonight, Friday, I have been a good girl and a naughty one. I'll tell you the good part. I have cleaned this room out. And now for the naughty part I have had my hair cut, but there is a reason. I had it cut so that if I get it wet it will not look too bad. That is not all I had touched the front up a bit. I know you will not mind really because when I did it before you said it looked nice. I hope you do this time.

I am glad you did not lose your temper with Helmut. Look darling, please look after yourself and have plenty to eat. I don't want to marry someone half starved. I am sure darling we will get organised when we have a home of our own. I only hope I will be a good wife to you. I love you very much and I am sure we can be happy together. We have not long to go now, 60 days.

I have changed my mind again. I am going to have a costume. I think that will look nice afterwards if we go out anywhere.

I might change my mind again yet.

All my love

Jean

Aschersleben 1.8.49

My dear Hans

Thank you very much for your lovely letter dated 19.7.49. I expect you have, in the meantime, also received our letter, in which I told you that both parcels have reached us. It always makes us very happy to get these tasty foods and we are making them last as long as possible.

Uncle Erich bought the horse in Ludwigslust, not here. There was a horse for sale in Berlin at the cost of 11.000 Mark and the horse was blind in one eye!

Our harvest is also in full swing. Everything is very dry here too. If we don't get any rain soon, we shall not have any potatoes and sugar beet in the autumn. Have you put your new tractor into good use yet?

I assume you will have to meet all of Jean's aunts first. I am sure you are very tired in the evenings. Excuse my bad handwriting. It is such awful paper. I shall be taking all my washing to the laundry facilities tomorrow. I can still not manage to do my own washing. On Saturday I read in the announcements that every resettled person is supposed to receive 60 points to spend on textile goods. I went there first thing this morning and was told that, in household of only two people only, there are no points, only families with three persons and more qualify. Well, I gave them a piece of my mind. That's how it goes: just empty talk. It makes your blood boil. Today is the anniversary of grandma's death. It is already four years ago when she closed her loving eyes forever. She had to endure such a lot of hardship, I think of her all the time.

Now, my dear Hans, I want to finish this letter and take it to the post office.

Stay healthy and give our best wishes to Jean and your mother-in-law, and to you, my dear boy, we are sending all our love and kisses, your mum and brother Horst

Pickwell
August 1st 1949

"My darling"
I thank you very, very much for everything. I only hope you enjoyed yourself and were satisfied with the teas and dinner today. You know I like to do everything as nice for you as ever I can. It's so nice to see you happy and satisfied and be sure I'll try to keep it up - always. You're so lovely, Jeanny. I wouldn't only cross the days off but every minute, if I was able to. Time goes slow, but it goes.

Do you want me to bring the suitcase over next weekend? I'll keep my things in the box for the week.

It's not too bad if Helmut leaves. I could get things done as I want them and also keep everything clean and comfortable. Still, what worries me is the cooking. I know I shan't look after two after myself and cook proper meals. If I want to do more overtime then I don't have to consider Helmuts meals. We'll see how things turn out.

Well, my sweetheart, I'll close for now as I am tired. The bed is the best place. Don't you agree? Goodnight and God bless you. All my love and kisses to you.

Tuesday Aug 2nd 8.15 p.m.
Hello, my darling, how are you today? Don't you agree that I have to save money where ever I can? Well, Gordon came and asked me if I had a pair of boots to sell as his aren't fit for work anymore. You know the second pair I have had were only size 7 and really too small as I want 8. They always hurt my feet keeping them on all day. As his size is 7 and the boots were in good order he gave me £1. That means if I put a few

bob to it I'll get a pair of new ones on Saturday.

I am sure we would get on alright if we started a business of our own. Anyway I know how to make a profit. The best would be buying and selling property.

There's quite a lot of shopping to do on Saturday. Shirt, Tie, Shoes, Boots, Tennis shoes. There the money goes. Don't forget to book the seats for the London show, sweetheart. Do you think we'll manage with the money we've got? Still I only want a few shillings to make up for the boots. I think the are about 28/- s.

Well, my darling it's 8.45 and I'll get ready to go. Be good, take care of yourself. Goodnight and believe me I would love to be with you. Please give my regards to your mother.

> All my love and kisses
>> Forever yours, my darling
> Hans.

> 92 Wharf St.
> August 2nd.

My dearest darling Hans

There were plenty of buses after the one I caught. Nancy came on the 9.0 She said there was another at 9.30 from Oakham. There was a lady speaking to someone at the back, she said that the conductor told her that there were 4 buses at Oakham and it did not look as if all of them got on it. So maybe it was as well I caught it, only we did not have our little talk. I forgot all about leaving the ration book with you to see if you could get a tin of Salmon, but if you could use your coupons for it you could have my ration book the following week. I have just thought I will need my book, but if you could take them loose I would cut them out and send them on. If that's O.K. let me know.

Well darling thank you so very much for a lovely weekend. I hope I have not eaten you out. I really did love being with you. I wish we could have a place of our own, but it would

be useless if we did have one at the moment. If we could manage for about a year so we could save, then there is my mother. We would still not be on our own. I hope in some ways that Helmut does not get that job. Besides the 15/- and Bonzo (no one to look after him) you will be alone all week. Then it would be nice not having to bother about him.
I will have to close now Goodnight and God Bless you.

All my love and kisses
Yours
Jean

—.

Pickwell
August 3ʳᵈ 1949

My dearest, darling Jean,
Well, How are things going today? Everything alright? It won't be long now till Saturday. Only 2 ½ days and 57 days till our own great day.
Tonight I told the boss about my holidays. He had a look at the paper and quite surprised said: 10 days? He also said he can't spare me thay long. So I said: I am sorry but I have reservations for rooms for 10 days and you told me the first time we're talking about holidays if I wanted 14 days. Of course what else could he say then. Well, then you have to have 10 days. So that settles that. Blimey, what's going to happen when I leave here. Looks as if he has to give up his poultry. Doris has also had 10 days. Do you think we'll have enough time if I come over on Wednesday after finishing work at 5.00? Still we have all night to get ready!! Do you think it would be alright if I stay at your place for the last night (alone in a double bed!!!) and in the morning go over to your uncle's or Betty's? Betty's would suit me better, but still I hope you'll be able to arrange something.

I've changed my mind about buying a pair of boots. Last night I had a look at my wellingtons and found there are holes in the soles. For dry weather my boots will be alright so I've asked the boss to bring me a pair of rubber boots. I'll manage alright for money. I don't like to take any of Friday's wages.

The G.P.O. has put a new pillar box up in the village. On the church yard walk almost opposite our gate so isn't far to go for me now.

Well, my sweetheart, I'll say goodnight now. Time for shutting up is coming on.

Be good and pleasant dreams. I won't forget to tell you that I love you more than anything else in the world. God bless you, my darling.

Thursday, August 4th 1949, 6.00 p.m.

How are you, darling? I thank you so very much for your letter. I received it this morning. Sorry to say, but I had to have a nice little chat with the boss. Everybody is going out working at night, but nobody asks me to go. You remember that I told you I was going chicken house moving or out with the tractor harvesting. Well, so I told him am I only good enough to do weekend work and shutting up at night when other people go to bed. And you know what he said? I once said to Tom that I have to pay so much tax and so the boss thought I didn't want to do overtime. So I've made up my mind, if he doesn't give me a chance of making overtime I shall stop working on weekends and also the shutting up. Perhaps that'll suit him better, then he can do my turn if he likes. I don't think it's fair. Other people do the overtime the easy way and I am allowed to go if the others don't want to. He's had that, definitely. For these last 7 weeks till we get married I want to make as much money as I can get so we don't have to take much out of the bank. Of course it would help us if I could get up to £7 clear a week. It means plenty of work, but still it doesn't matter. It's all for us.

When I go shopping tomorrow night I'll ask that fellow if I

can bring him loose points and if yes I'll get a tin of salmon for you.

You haven't eaten me out over the weekend. Only one day till the rations come in and there's enough butter, cheese etc left for tomorrow.

Why do you hope Helmut will not get that job. Just because of those 15/-. I hope he goes. What do you think I am? His servant? No!! He goes out every night and I have to do the washing up and cleaning. I remember when Herbert was here Helmut always grumbled he didn't give a hand. Now, however, he's turned out to be just the same. I don't have to bother about him when he goes and it doesn't make any difference to being alone all week. He's hardly in at all nowadays. And I shan't have half the work being on my own. Those 15/-s will come in on overtime. It's just as it was tonight. He went off at 5.30 saying "I shan't be back before 10.00 leave my dinner on the stove". I have never said anything to him, but I will when he leaves. A little reminder may freshen up his memory.

Today I was cleaning out all day. With horse and cart. My tractor has to pull a binder with Mrs Hawkins (Tom's wife) driving it.

Well, my darling I'll close now and get something to eat. I am hungry. It's only 1 ½ day till Saturday. So be good till then and pleasant dreams tonight. I love you very much. Please give my regards to your mother and to you.

    All my love and kisses
      Forever yours
    Hans.

    92 Wharf St
    August 3rd 1949

My darling Hans.

I thank you so very much for your letter. By the way I forgot about this, I do not wait to hear from you before I write, it is just that it is quicker for me to get a letter from you than you from me. I usually write Monday, post it Tuesday and you receive it Wednesday. Where if you write Monday and post it Tuesday morning I get it Tuesday lunch time.

I was very satisfied with the whole weekend. I only hoped I left you something to eat for the rest of the week. You certainly do look after me well. I will try to do the same for you one day. I can't promise that I will be a good cook like your mother but I will try to do my best. So far I think we have had a nicer courtship than most people. Although we have only seen one another at the weekends. Other couples see each other 2 or 3 times or even every night but they could not say they have had such a wonderful time as we. Picnic in the rain at Croxton, walking round Nottingham, going to Saltby, Stathern, and Redmile. I would not change any of it. Would you?

If Helmut leaves you will have to look after yourself, please promise me that. You will make yourself ill if you don't. I want you to cook a hot meal every night, because you will need it working outside all day. I would love to come ~~and~~ to look after you. But you know darling it would be best to stay here for awhile so that we can start well. But until I can look after you I want you to look after yourself well.

I have been to see Betty tonight and she is not sleeping here, but will come in the daytime. I do hope Freddy is alright. I think Betty will train him while we are away, poor little thing.

Will you bring your case on Saturday, also the camera then if we want to take a snap we can. I hope I do not spend very much. All I need is my train fare because I don't think there is anything to do at Sheringham but sit on the beach. I will try to get as brown as you darling. Will you let me go away without you when we are married?

Look darling I have been thinking, I could go and have a look around Saturday lunchtime to see if I could see a costume. If I did see one I would need the money. I could draw it out of the bank, but then if I did not see anything I would have it lying about the week I am away. If I did get something you will have to leave your shirt and shoes until later on. But you must get a pair of boots that is important, and tennis shoes. Let me get your tie please.

I have been looking at wedding rings and I still do not know what kind of ring I want. I keep looking. I think I had better have 2 to solve the problem. About your ring darling. Please if you must have a plain ring have a thick one because it would look so funny if you had a woman's. I wish you would have one with a plate on top, anyway we can look in the shops on Saturday.

Well darling. I will close be good my darling

     All my love

     Jean.

     Same address

     August 5th 1949

My darling Jean,

Well, I have spoken to you, but I know you like me to bring a letter along. For a start I thank you very much for your lovely long letter. I really was surprised to get a second one.

I am happy to hear you were satisfied with me the last week-end. Don 't worry, you haven't eaten us out. We managed nicely and a warm meal every night. You should know how much I love looking after you and I am sure you'll do the same for me. Don't be afraid of the cooking, it's easy to be picked up when one is interested. If things get burned for a start it won't matter, as one get's better every time.

We certainly have had a lovely courtship. I couldn't miss a single thing of it. Think of us stopping out in the cold weather and rain. Don't you think there was always some excitement in it. Though you forgot to name one place. In fact the most important one. Grantham.

Don't worry, darling, I'll look after myself alright when Helmut leaves. I promise as I know for myself I can't keep up with hard work if I don't have proper meals.

I still don't know how you dare to tell me it doesn't matter what time I get into Leicester. You should know every minute I get into town earlier means one more minute together with you. I don't know yet if I'll let you go away on your own after we are married!!! Why don't you want to take me along if you go anywhere?

Well, darling I am sorry I have to close now. The water is boiling and I'll wash my hair.

So be good till I see you tomorrow.

> All my love and kisses
>> Forever yours
>> Hans.

Aschersleben, 7.8.49

> My dear Hans

Thank you so much for your lovely letter dated 27.7.49. Today is Sunday and I want to write back to you. I am at home and on my own. We went out for a walk this afternoon and in the evening Horst went dancing. He does need some distraction after a hard day's work.

I have become quite restless since I came home from hospital. I cannot not find inner peace. I wonder if our Papa thinks a lot of us or what can it be? When I have finished this letter I shall take it to the post office right away so that I can get some fresh air. It is dreadful here at the moment, 30°C again

I can imagine what a nice tan you have, no wonder if you are working outside in the burning sun all day. You must be deep in the middle of the harvest. Does this mean you have to work on Sundays too? It should really be enough if a man works hard throughout the week, without having to work Sundays as well. Next time I write to Auntie Else, I will give her your address so that they can pass it on to the young man in Altentreptow. Horst wore his new suit today. It is dark brown and fits him perfectly. There we are. 110 marks for the making of it is no trifling matter. I am so pleased that he has, at last, something decent to wear. He managed to save the money from his private clients.

From now on he is not allowed to work for his private clients on a Sunday anymore. This applies to all his colleagues as well. The Master hairdressers had a meeting. They are worried in case they don't make enough money. All employees are being taken advantage of. They have to do a lot of extra hours in the salon without overtime pay. Also, working conditions in the bad air, with seven apparatuses all switched on tat the same time, all day long, leads to very poor working conditions. The refugees, in particular, are not popular. The bosses begrudge them their success, they don't like to see them getting on in life. Oh well, I am sure this is not the end of it. Horst is taking eight days leave in a fortnight's time. He wants to go to where Edith lives and suss out the job situation in there. Keep your fingers crossed. I hope he has some luck. We would be very happy if it worked out for him. It would be so lovely if you and Jean could come over to visit us! Well, we can only hope for the best. To carry on like this is, in the long run, quite pointless. Horst is good at his job and will find another one. Today we enjoyed an excellent cup of coffee made from coffee beans, and in the evening, we shall have cocoa – simply wonderful! It will be four years tomorrow, when Horst and I started on our marathon trip of 200 km from Rosow on the river Oder to Vorpommern.

We shall be thinking of you on your wedding day and hope you have good weather on your honeymoon, so that you can enjoy every day. It would be so lovely to see you again soon. Well, I doubt it will be 'soon'. I hope you can decipher my poor writing. I am sitting by the window sill so that I get a little bit of fresh air, but it makes writing rather uncomfortable. I have a lot of pain in my hands and arms these days. My hands suffer from pins and needles, which is horrible. It is worse at night. I wonder if these are the side effects of the operation or could it be rheumatism? I hope it will disappear again. Sometimes I cannot even hold the needle when I do my darning.

Now, my dear boy, I want to finish my letter. Stay healthy and pass on our best wishes to Jean and your mother-in-law. To you especially, I am sending you my loving greetings and a kiss, which comes from the bottom of my heart. Your mum, who is always thinking of you, and your brother Horst.

We are looking forward to a healthy reunion.

Pickwell
August 7ᵗʰ 1949, 9.30p.m.

"My darling"

Here I am, back again. If I could've only stayed with you. Still three times I shall come over to stay for a weekend and when I come the fourth we'll go away and be together for 10 days. Believe me I am already afraid those ten days will go so quick. It doesn't really matter as it is only the beginning of our life.

Monday, 8.9.49

Well, the fellows from Little Dalby has been to see the place. The farmer advertised £7 a week and a lovely cottage. When the fellow spoke to him it was only £6 and the cottage was terrible. Not too bad from outside, but rats inside. Hole beside hole all over the place. So that means there's nothing doing. He specially asked for a German, and I bet he thought the Gerries would be glad to take anything looking like a house. You know, there are some funny people about!

I had some fun today. First thing this morning I went cleaning a few empty houses out. There I found some chicken lice. Coming back at dinner time I smelled like a paraffin drum as I washed and soaked myself with it. So I made sure I wouldn't get any on me. I told the foreman and he told the boss but nobody would believe it. So I didn't say anything, but brought a few back tonight and showed to the boss. Nicely wrapped up in cigarette paper to be seen from both sides!! The boss is taking them to the chemist in Melton tomorrow to see if he can get something that'll kill them. I couldn't help laughing when I saw the bosses face. He couldn't believe his eyes asking if they were dead. So I let them run around inside the paper. Anyway I'll ring you on Wednesday 5.00 sharp. Now I am going to enjoy a nice cup of coffee. Won't you come along and join me? If you were only here. I was naughty and took the cream off the milk for the coffee. Still, I have to look after myself, haven't I?! Helmut helps himself to the butter so I take the cream. That makes it only even. When I come over in a fortnight I shall have enough money for my shoes. Just in case my suit should be ready by then and you aren't back I'll wait with fetching it, till you come. Of course I have to go for a hair cut.

Well, my darling, it's 9.55, time to go to bed. So goodnight and God bless you always. Be good and pleasant dreams. I love you more than my own life.

Please give my regards to your mother.

> To you all my love and kisses
>> Forever yours,
> Hans.

92 Wharf St
August 8th

My dearest darling Hans.

I am very sorry for being so horrible to you on Saturday. I do not know why I should have been. Maybe you will have to put up with that occasionally. I will try to be good in future. Did you get back to Pickwell safe and were you in time for the 8.0 bus. Freddy and I arrived back safe. I dried Fred and then he lay in his basket all night. I think it was the shock of his bump. Anyway he seems alright today he has been as gay as usual. I hope you are not too disappointed that the car missed him!!! Poor little thing. I know I make an awful fool of him. You should see him now he is asleep in the chair in our bedroom. I am writing this in bed, I have been very busy this evening. I have given the bedrooms a good clean out, washed the floor and the windows. And I have even put my shoes away into a drawer. I was in a working mood and that mood does not take me very often. I thought I had better leave the place looking a bit tidy on a Saturday.

Well darling it looks as though I shall be saving my railway fare to Sherringham. Mr Rudkin rang up this afternoon and asked if we had made any arrangements about how we were going. He has just come back from a week's holiday in Suffolk near the coast, his daughter has a cottage for the month and he is going back again on Saturday. He said there would only be Mrs Rudkin and himself in the car so he could take my mother and I as far as Sherringham, so we will not be walking after all.

Well my love I will say good night and God Bless you

    All my love

      Jean

      ———·

                        Pickwell

                        August, 9th 1949.

My dearest, darling Jean,

How are you today, my sweetheart? Fine I hope and as satisfied as I am. Believe me, I couldn't be more pleased with myself. Remember I told you in my last letter that the boss said something about moving chicken houses. I asked him why I didn't go before. He answered that he tried it himself, backing up to the houses with a four wheeled tractor and it's almost impossible. It took him 20 minutes to get the house ready to move. Well, after all, tonight I took my tractor (four wheeled) and went out. We shifted 3 houses till 8.15 and it took me exactly 2 minutes to get every one of those houses ready. The foreman was a bit surprised, too. Well, darling, I hope every time I shall be able to show people something different to what they think.

It's 9.15 and I still have to do my washing. It is boiling. I haven't eaten anything yet as I went out at 5.20. So I'll close for now. Be good and God bless you. All my love and kisses, yours Hans

Wednesday, 11. 8. 49. 9.00 p.m.

Hello, my love, how are you? Fine I hope. I've just come back, as I found that fuming doesn't kill those little beasts. Now I shall wait till the morning to see what it looks like and if it works alright continue in the morning. It is something like gas, small cubicles to be lit and as it burns it gives the gas. I kept well away as it affects eyes and nose.

Well, darling, I was really mad when the boss asked me to go out, but I didn't let him see it. I'd put everything ready for a quick change and really waiting to see you, and then - work. Still I shall see you again ~~and~~ week on Sunday. I'll bring a chicken.

By the way, darling, how am I to get my cigarettes this week? Shall you send me 20 by post. Put them into an envelope and please post them on Friday so I'll have some for the weekend. Well, my darling, I'll close now and say goodnight. God bless you. Darling, I love you very very much. Be good and think of me, if you can spare the time

>All my love and kisses
>>Forever yours, my love
>
>Hans.

>92 Wharf St
>August 11th 1949.

"My darling"

I have just had a bath, I do not want a dirty neck when I wear my bathing costume. Honestly it's like a hard day's work to have a bath here, what with lugging the water on and off the gas stove then emptying the bath. On top of that I had to wash the floor. I did not have to, but thought while I had some hot water I would do it. I was going to give this room (down stairs) a good clean out and have a bath tomorrow (Friday). But as I am phoning you it would not be wise to have a bath then go out afterwards. A little bit of paper has come away from the ceiling on one side. I think it was the gale on Sunday night, because it was going up and down with the wind. You need not bother about it, it still looks as good. I have switched the wireless off, there is a boxing match on. I honestly cannot understand how people can sit and watch two fools hitting each other, don't tell me there is any skill in that, because I have never known a boxer yet to have any brains. The only smart ones there are the ones that get them to fight.

Last night when I arrived home (Wednesday) my mother had visitors. My Aunt Cis and two people from Canada, a mother and daughter. I knew the mother she came over 14 years ago. She went out to Canada 39 years ago. She used to be a friend of my aunty in Birstall when they ~~whe~~ were young. She married a Canadian had three children 2 girls and a boy, he left her I think (the dirty dog!!!). They are here on a 6 week visit. They left a little parcel here it had a tin of pineapple, tin of meat (I think), a jelly, some rice a packet of cake mixture and some sweets for Susan. I think it was awfully kind of them. ~~I~~ We must look hungry.

I have posted the cigarettes

Speaking of being hungry. I was tonight after having a bath. I could have eaten some fried steak with egg and tomatoes, but all I had to eat was bread and cheese. Don't you think you could possibly find any Danish relations so we could go and live there. I told you about the person that had been there on holiday. Let us eat well, even if we get as fat as pigs. I wish we could go to Denmark, Don't you.

Thank you darling for your letter. I suppose that it will be the last this week, but I will be speaking to you tomorrow night. I am sorry we could not meet last night, it would have been rather a long journey for me to come out to Pickwell. I was quite looking forward to having some chips in Melton. I will send some cigarettes on, but I thought you took the extra cigarettes last week. You had 40. Are your nerves getting bad?

Isn't my writing a mess I ~~have~~ am trying to do it the other way for a change, I hope you will be able to read and understand it.

I have had the invitation to that 21st birthday, so has Lucy. It is on September 21st 7. till 11.0. I will have to ask Lucy if she wants to stay here as she will be unable to get home at that time.

Well darling the next time I write it will be from "The Bijou" Sheringham. We leave here at about 12.15 all being well, it should take about 4 hours. It will certainly be better than the train. I wish we had a car for Sept 29th, but still maybe one day we will have, until then we will have to use the railway. Be good while I am away

All my love and kisses

Jean.

Mr J Klawitter

Home Farm
Pickwell
Somerby
Leicestershire

Dear Hans
We have arrived safe. Left Leicester
at about 1.0 arrived 5.15. Quite a nice run
The hotel is very nice. The lounge overlooks
the sea. The place is very quiet. I think
The people must be half dead We have just
had a cup of tea and are waiting for dinner
7.0. I could do with it. I will write. Jean

92 Wharf St
August 14th

My dearest darling Hans.
You will probably get this the same time as the postcard. Anyway you will know we arrived safe. It is much better in a car, than on a train.
I have my two piece on while I am writing this, sitting in a deck chair. I should be as brown as a berry or as red as an Indian I don't know which. I am still like a lilly.
How has work gone down with you? Do you miss me very much? I wish you were here with me, it is a bit boring sitting here. I will have a rest if nothing else. Last night (Saturday) we went for a walk along the prom, then called in The Lobsters for a drink. I had cider. There is not very much to do here, there are two picture houses. There are a few shops and lots of Cafes. It's much nicer than Skegness, we'll come here when we have our family ! ! ! I'll write again this afternoon love and kisses Jean.
Hello darling, I have just retired to the lounge to finish writ-

ing this. It's quite a nice little writing desk, it has three drawers, need I tell you I have looked into them.

This afternoon has been a bit more exciting than this morning. I have actually wet my new 2 piece. It was lovely in the water, I had a float. That is a float with paddles. I was a bit nervous at first, but after a while I did not want to get off. I wish you had been with me, one can not have as much fun on one's own. I am like a red Indian. The tops of my legs are burning hot, and the tops of my arms.

I wonder how Freddy is. I wish we could have brought him because you can have some fun with a dog on the beach. With you and him here it would be perfect. I hope you don't mind being with Fred, but you know what I mean. Susan cried when we left, she wanted to come along. I think Betty feels it because she could not take Susan on holiday. But it is a bit expensive now there are four to take. So let us be careful for a couple of years. I have been thinking darling, it would be best even if you did find a house near Melton. I could still continue to work by getting a job in Melton, but I would not get paid as much, I don't know what I could do, perhaps scrub someone's floor. Anyway darling let us save hard. So we can get the things we want, but I don't suppose we will have all we want.

I have just noticed that I have put the wrong address at the top. The correct address is "The Bijou" Sheringham, but you should know that I have put it in a letter I sent last week. Cheeri'O and God Bless be good

All my love
Jean

Pickwell
August, 13th 1949

My dearest, darling Jean,

Thank you so very much for your letter and the cigarettes, both arrived this morning. I really was looking forward to meeting you Wednesday night and it was a shame I had to work. I felt miserable all night; but still the next weekend I'll be with you again. It's only 48 more days and that means 3 more weekends at your place before we get married. I have to see the vicar some day next week, definitely. We'll have to settle that before Sept 8th to make sure it's three weekends. Shall you go the week after you come back?

Tomorrow we shall have our first hot meal since last Monday. We'll make pigs out of ourselves. You should see us, but I don't think you are much interested, laying on the beach sunbathing. If I could only be with you. Enjoy yourself, darling and all I can do, is to think of you all the time.

Just before I started to write I fetched myself a bottle of lemonade to take out this afternoon. It certainly is warm. The weather forecast till Tuesday next says sunshine everywhere. I keep my fingers crossed it'll be all week.

Well, darling, I'll close now and get "my old horse ready". Shan't be long before I get back as I have the white one. Be good. I'll write a few more lines tonight. xxx

5.45 p.m.

Here I am again, darling. I was back from collecting at 3.40 and have been busy since. At first I washed up everything and cleaned the room out. Then I had my tea, boiled egg, Stilton cheese and jam. It didn't taste half as nice as it does when you're here. The teapot is standing beside me and I just keep sipping. It won't be long before it's empty.

The weather is just lovely. Are you sunbathing already? I wonder what you're doing this minute. People find it strange that you aren't here. Herbert and Tom have asked me where the "missus" is today. You are popular around here, it seems.

Now I'll try to answer your letter. Helmut has just come back (rather early). When I come over again I'll see if we can stick that paper back again where it belongs- on the ceiling. Listen, something about boxing matches. Get one thing straight, boxing is a profession and brings quite a lot of money. Besides that one has to have skill and technique and lots of experience to fight. So it looks as if boxers also have brains. Nevertheless I couldn't care less if they have brains or not, as I am not a boxer. And I never will be, if that satisfies you.

It looks as if you have quite a few relations abroad. I think it was very kind of them to bring you a little parcel. What was the remark "dirty dog" for. If her husband left her, well, as you always say "you never know why". Anyway you can be sure I shall never leave you. Perhaps you looked hungry and look at your figure. People must think you are starving. I'll see that you eat more when we get a place of our own.

I am awfully sorry, but I can't oblige you with Danish relations! When I was there it was as occupation forces and I don't think they'll like to see us again although I haven't done them any harm. Shall we go for a holiday next year or do you prefer to go to Germany.

I also wish we had a car when we go on Sept 29th. Still, there you are! I haven't saved enough and that means I have to make up for it now. Be sure we'll have one one day.

Well, my love, I'll close now and write to my mother. Be good and look after yourself. All my love to you. I'll write again tomorrow.

Sunday, 1.15 p.m.

This morning I overslept and it was 7.15 when I woke up. Still I was back at 9.15. Helmut is working on a binder all day today and as I didn't know what time he was coming back I had the dinner ready at 11.30 and went to sleep. After all he turned up at 1.00. This afternoon I'll do my washing and ironing write to you and it'll be shutting up time again, I told you we're going to make pigs of ourselves today. Fried onions are lovely. Please remember it for later on. And I like quite a few.

What are you doing now? Just having your afternoon rest? And then continue on the beach? My beach will be around the chicken field. I took my shorts out again as it is hot here today. So if you want to see "legs" you'd better hurry up.

It looks as if we have finished moving houses at night. On Tuesday we'll be on it all day and then there are only 14 left, but still full of hens. I've asked the foreman yesterday for a good chicken for next Friday. It's alright. Well my love, it's 1.45 and I'd better get ready. Be good. Have you ever before had a long letter? You'll get one next week.

<u>7.45 p.m.</u>

Well, my darling, it looks as if I have done my days work except shutting up. After collecting I got us some tea ready, then did my washing, washed up and had a wash myself. Now I have finished ironing. Everything in proper order.

Was the water warm enough to bath? And your lovely two-piece bathing costume! You really should have taken it out for the first time when we go away. I've just had a look, it's exactly 45 days. Half the time is gone since I started crossing the days off. This weekend has gone and now I have some-thing to look forward to - the next one with you. Now I'll get myself something to eat before I go out. Be good, my sweet-heart and think of me if you can spare any time. My thoughts are always with you. All my love and thousand kisses to you. Please give my regards to your mother.

Monday, 9.15 p.m.

I've just come back. Gassing houses out to get them ready to be moved tomorrow morning. That makes another ¾ hr overtime. I wonder only how much income tax I shall have to pay this week. Otherwise everything is running smoothly.

Well, now I'll get myself something to eat. I am starving. Hoping to hear from you in the morning. Be good, my dar-ling, goodnight and God bless you. I love you more than any-thing else in the world. Remember it always.

Tuesday 1.25 p.m.

Received your card and letter this morning. Y I thought I'd better write a few lines at dinnertime and post it straight away so you'll get it tomorrow. Your letter will get answered tonight after I've finished work at 9.30

It looks as if you are enjoying yourself.

Well, sweety, be good and God bless. Take care of yourself. Please give my regards to your mother.

All my love and kisses etc

Forever yours, my darling

Hans.

P.S.

What a long letter

92 Wharf St,
August 16th

My dearest darling Hans.

What no letter today? I hope there will be one in the morning,

The weather has not been too good today, it is really a good job because my arms and thighs are burnt. I am not as tough as you are. I went into bathe twice yesterday in the morning and in the afternoon the sea looked so lovely that I gave the boys a treat and went in again, by giving the boys a treat I mean I have been undressing and dressing on the beach, but those days are over for this holiday. I will now have to be satisfied with sunbathing and see if I can get a nice golden brown.

I am just going into dinner. I will write afterwards.

Well darling, I have had my dinner (dinner in the evening). I am now in bed. For dinner we had soup, then fish. They have given us fish 4 times, twice for breakfast. Fortunately it is fresh. We have had very good meals so far.

Have I told you what I have been doing? I told you about Sunday. Monday we were on the sands (pebbles) all day. In the evening we went for a drink, I had cider. Today Tuesday it rained, it started about 9.30 so we sat in a shelter on the front until 11.30 then came back for our coat, then went and had a coffee. This afternoon we went to Cromer. I did not like that as much as Sheringham, the streets are very closed in and there seems to be a lot of old empty buildings. Besides that you seem to find a different type of people there. You know the kind, eat chips in the street!!! There is a nice beach there, it is sand, but I think the pebbles are cleaner. There's sand at Sheringham when the tide goes out. I wish you could have been with me yesterday. The sea was perfect. I was actually swimming. I forgot we went out in a motor boat yesterday morning. I think we had better put a yacht (a boat) down on our list.

I have been to have my photograph taken, there is a place here that takes them straight the way. I thought I will have one to send to you so that you will not forget me. I have not seen you for a fortnight, it seems longer than that. Have you missed me very much being those extra few miles away from you. There seems an awful lot to do before Sept 29th. I will get cracking when I get back. I am coming home Friday so on Saturday morning I will see about the cake and also see if I can find something for myself.

I don't think you had better write again here. Could I ring you Friday night at 10.0? I will ring then but if it is not possible for you to be there don't worry I will know

    All my love
    Yours
    Jean

    ___.

Time Wednesday 10.0
Place - on the beach at Sheringham.
It really looks as though it takes awhile for letters to get here. I received your letter this morning, it really is very nice to have such a long letter I read whilst having breakfast. I let my mother have the paper first.
What did Herbert and Tom think had happened to me? Did they think we had had a tiff or something. While I think of

it, don't ever call me the missus or the wife to anyone, either call me Jean or Mrs Klawitter.

I have not taken my jacket off to sunbathe because I have some sore places on my arm caused by the sun on Monday. I have my red dress on at the moment, the one with the staggs on it. I have also tied a handkerchief around my arm to keep the sun off. I will survive.

I have got faith in children again. There are 2 sitting at the next table to us and they are very well behaved at the table. Of course I do not know what they are like when they are at home.

I am now going to see if I can brown my face So cheeri'O All my love kisses etc

      Jean

                    Pickwell

                    August, 16th 1949

My dearest, darling Jean,

Hello, my sweety, are you enjoying your holidays?

Well, how has work gone down with me? It has almost got me down. It's 10.15 and I am only back half an hour. Another 5 hours or 10/- s. I have copied my time sheet and let you see when I come over what a good boy I've been whilst you're away. Today is move houses all day. Only 11. Believe me I wish I could be with you and I wouldn't even mind being mentioned with Freddy in the same breath. We certainly take our family out there once we have got one and that won't be long.

I was really surprised to hear you paddled around on a float. Well, as you are an expert, we'll take a float when we go to Germany one day and cross the channel that way. It's not so expensive!!! You can do the paddling and I'll look out for the other ships to make sure we don't collide.

Well, if Susan cried when you left I wouldn't blame Betty. It's up to Cyril to get them away on a holiday. If it was my family I would work hard enough to make it possible for my family to go away, at least for a week.

By the way, darling I've just remembered somewhat!! Next Saturday is the day the football season starts. Shall we go in for the football pools and try our luck. It comes up to 3/- a week. Of course, that is if we can afford it. Oh, there's still something else I have to give you a lesson about. Remember always- my wife is not going to scrub other peoples floors! I don't want to hear that remark again and I am serious. It's good I am coming over this weekend. One hot meal a week is not enough. Well my sweetheart I hope you don't mind me finishing. I'll have a wash and then off to bed. The next letter will be delivered by myself. Goodnight and God bless. I'll always love you so

 All my love and kisses
 Forever yours
 Hans.

       Pickwell
      August, 17<u>th</u> 1949

My dearest, darling Jean,

This letter will be delivered by myself and that means this long week is over and I am with you again. Oh, darling, how I am longing to see and speak to you. Still only 2 ½ days to go. I've made my timesheet out tonight. Not bad at all. Of course it would be much better if there wasn't that confounded income tax. It'll be more than a pound this week.

Today I was laughing. Just before 5 o'clock the boss came back with a lorry load of feeding stuff. He asked the new chap and I if we would give him a hand with unloading it. So we got cracking, he also gave a hand. After we got a few bags down, someone had to go on the lorry to hand them right to the back. So I jumped on and the boss looked strangely and said " you know a good job don't you"? He kept going carrying the bags to the shed.

How are you, today, my love? I don't want to be selfish, but I am glad to see you back on Saturday. Now I would love to ring you and talk to you, but you are too far away. Well, my sweetheart, I'll have to wait a bit.

Well, darling, I'll close now. It's 10.00 time to go to bed. Pleasant dreams and good night. God bless you always. I love you so very much. Love Hans.

Friday, Aug. 19th 1949 7.45 p.m..

Hello, my darling, how did you get back? By now you'll be at home I hope. I am looking forward to your call at 10 o'clock. I am sorry I couldn't write last night. It was just 7.30 and fetched the writing pad when Mr Cooper came and ask me if I would do him a favour and bring a fuel tank out to one of the caterpillars. So I went out hoping to shut up whilst I was out there. When I got out I was asked to take a load of oats back to the yard. I got back at 9.15 and then went out again shutting up. Having a wash and something to eat finished the day off.

Something else. Last night at 5.45 I had a date. Wonder who with? The Vicar. That means I have settled that. It'll be read for the first time day after tomorrow. The certificate about no objections can be collected from the vicarage on Sunday Sept. 4th. Fee - paid last night 3/6 s

I am really in a rush tonight. The chicken is cleaned and plucked. I'll get the eggs tomorrow morning.

Thank you so very much for your lovely letter and that wonderful photo. I'd better answer the letter tomorrow. Now I'll wash my hair then shutting up and a wash, your call, washing up and I'll be ready for bed.

So long, my love. See you tomorrow.

I love you very very much, in fact, more than anything else in the world.

>   All my love and kisses
>   Forever yours
>   Hans.

92 Wharf
Street
August 22nd

My darling

I am writing now in my lunchtime, because I forgot to ask you how you spell your names. I don't want to get to the vicar and find that I cannot spell them; it would be rather funny. You had also better have a look to see what the name of the Pickwell church is.

I started back this morning and it has gone down not too bad. I soon got back into it.

Mary came in this morning to say Iris has gone into hospital, she went last Thursday. They have to turn the baby, she has had it done once, but it went back again. Now she has had to go again. She should have had it on August 20th Sat. With her being so fat I think they'll try to bring it on, at least that is what others think.

I keep wishing that I had my ring so I could have another look at it. I will have to wait until next Sunday before I can do that.

I will have to say cheeri'O and get ready to go again. So please let me know as soon as possible.

    All my love
    Jean.

Pickwell
August, 22nd1949

My dearest, darling Jean,

To begin with, I thank you very very much for a lovely week-end. You thanked me for your ring so I thank you very much for mine. At first I thought you got the idea about the rings when I spoke to you on Friday night. Then I'd made up my mind to oblige you and take a signet ring. You should have noticed by now that at the end your ideas and tastes are expected. I always like to see you happy and satisfied. Believe me, love, I'll always try my best to fulfil your wishes. If you would only not be so much against me having a motor-bike. It would be alright if I could get a secondhand bike on weekly pay. The only difficulty would be the deposit even if it wasn't more than £15. We shall want the money for some-thing else. It really looks- and I am sorry to say it- as if I have to give up to have one. I really would love to get one.

Did you get on the third bus alright? It's a shame there's no later bus this way.

Today I was watercarting all day. Wasn't it hot again today, but in spite I really felt like work. Of course I made it last all day so I didn't have to start another job before 5.00. Tonight I shan't bother with a hot meal. I mean potatoes. I made some custard with sultanas and put it in the next room to get cold.

It's 8.30 now. Helmut came back so I stopped for the time being. We had our pudding and now he's off to the pub. It won't be long before I go to bed tonight. As soon as the pro-gram "Our Mr Meredith" has finished. I always listen to it.

By the way, darling, don't forget to fill in that form for the cake. And please book the theatre seats for Friday, Sept. 30th. After all, it's fortunate enough you hadn't booked the seats yet as we changed our mind about the day. Alright, lets make it Friday and keep Thursday to ourself.

Something else, please get me a pipe. Cheap 2/6 will do. You know the kind. I showed you at Melton not a big ~~hat~~ head. A nice small pipe is alright.

Well, darling, I'll say goodnight and God bless you. I wonder if I shall get a letter tomorrow. Remember, my love, I love you more than anything else in the world.

Please, give my regards to your mother.

> All my love and kisses
>> Forever yours
> Hans.

P.S.

I have just had a look at our rings. Lovely !!!

92 Wharf St
August 243~~thrd~~

My dearest darling Hans

I thank you so very much for your letter and for calling. I will go to see either the verger or the vicar on Wednesday or Thursday. I have not been to Birstall since we went together so I thought I had better go there.

Betty asked me about the cake tonight. I told her what you said and she has plenty of stuff, marg etc. If it is that you would rather get a cake made say so, I will not mind.

You make me feel so mean about the motorbike, but I have never liked them. It is just lately I have hated them, but if you really want one it is not anything to do with me as long as you can afford to run one as well as buying it. You also please yourself about having it weekly, but myself I would not want it until I could pay for it. After we are married I want to save hard so darling if we do find a place on our own we would have something to buy the furniture with. I would hate having it on the weekly. Having things like that is like getting into debt. I know you do all you can for me, I only wish I could do more for you. I will try to be a good wife to you. I will try to make you proud of your home and family. I will do my best for that. That is all I can do in return for how hard you work for me.

I nearly went to the pictures tonight. I do not say to myself is it worth can I afford it. I think 'is it worth it' or could I do something better with the 1/9. And if I find I can, I do not go, and now I have something better to do with it I do not mind staying in. So long as we both try to save I do not mind. I would like those shoes I showed you, but £7-7-0 is rather a lot and maybe there is something I could do better with that.

I will have to close now All my love

I will always be yours

Jean.

Same address

My "darling"

How is everything with you, alright I hope.

At last I have got moving. I went to see the verger this evening, but he was out so I will have to go tomorrow lunchtime after I have had my dinner.

I have also settled the bridesmaid problem. I went to Birstall tonight and Gertie said she would go with me as she thought I ought to have someone to go with me. I asked Betty if Cyril could be best man, she will ask him, but Mr Riley, his boss will be away sometime in September so she could not say. My Aunt Gert said tonight that Charlie would go as best man if Cyril could not. Today I also put in an application for 3 day's marriage leave. I thought I may as well apply so I can keep 3 days in hand, then I can have another holiday later!!! I feel really mean about the motorbike, but if you really want one I can't stop you. I have no right to say you can't do this or that anymore than you have me. We can only advise each other of what we think. I hate motorcycles I always have done, no matter how careful anyone is on them there is more chance of an accident on one than anything else. There is another thing you must think of. Is it important saving for a home? Because I will not have a home on the weekly (I mean the furniture etc) I want to try while I can to keep out of debt. I would rather stay in every night and be bored ~~than~~ so I can pay for what I want. So darling after we are married we will have to save hard and be careful not to think just because we are both bringing in something we can throw it about on things that are not needed. I think the best thing would be not to touch the money I earn, put it away as if we never had it, then try to manage on yours and try if we can to save out of that. Anyway we'll get married first and have a good holiday. Then we <u>have</u> to save.

I don't think I will have those shoes. I would like them very much, anyway I will let you come with me to fetch my shoes. Then we can see if they are alright. Well darling I have to say goodnight it is 11.30.

Darling I want to thank you for how hard you work, well, for the long hours you work. I only wish I could do more. I will try to make you a good wife and make you proud of your home and family. That is all I can do in return for what you do for me.

> Good night God Bless
> I will always
>   Be yours
> Love
> Jean
>   —.

<u>P.S</u>

<u>ERGENT</u>

I have been to see the verger. I have a form to fill in and I will have to know your father's name in full and profession. Will you ring me tomorrow Friday sometime before 7.30.

Pickwell
August, 23rd 1949

My dearest, darling Jean,

I really was surprised to find a letter this morning. Well, I thank you so very much.

100 more birds went today so I went cleaning out at once and got the houses ready for moving. I think we'll get cracking again soon. Though I don't know if anymore go this week. Wasn't it close this afternoon. And imagine inside the chicken houses, I was baking.

Talking of baking. For Sunday I've cancelled our two sandwich cakes and decided to make one myself. Keep your fingers crossed that it may turn out alright. I hope to be able to get some sultanas on Friday.

How was it that you didn't mind talking so long last night . Was your aunty out?

I found out last night that the Sunday service at the church is at 7.30 p.m. there's nothing in the morning except Sunday school. It lasts 1 hour so we can't go. In spite of it, please come for the day and make up for not coming Saturday.

The first bus from Melton to Pickwell leaves Melton at 10.00. I don't know about buses from Leicester to Melton. Please, darling, come on that 10 o'clock from Melton. It really isn't too early. In the afternoon you can come collecting with me.

Have you gone tonight to see the vicar? I hope so anyway.

Well, my love, it's 7.30 and I'll say cheerio. Write a letter to my mother and then off to bed. It'll be early again and I can do with it. Be good and look after yourself well. Please give my regards to your mother. I love you more than anything else in the world and am quite sure.

All my love and kisses etc
Forever yours

Hans:

P.S. The rings look lovely

Pickwell
August, 26th1949

My dearest, darling Jean,
Thank you so much for your letter I received this morning. Well, darling, today work got me really down, for the first time. It was awfully close and I was cleaning out all day. The last chickens from the big field were sold today and I wanted to get them cleaned straight the way. After being empty for a few days I daren't go in. The houses are full of flies. We disinfect or rather gas all of them. Of course that meant get going and keep going all day. The sweat was running down my face. Anyway I got done what I wanted.

Have you brought the form back to the vicar? It's only exactly one month on Monday. How time flies. ⅔ of the time is gone since I started crossing the days off. It's a shame I can't continue as Bonzo has had a good look at my writing utensils this morning. I could've killed him. Oh! It looked a mess. My other writing pad has had it. The two letters about our rooms were amongst the things, but fortunately he didn't touch them.

It's nice Gertie coming along as bridesmaid. We'll see about Cyril or Charlie I myself don't mind who it is as long as we get that paper. Everything else is only formality.

So you want another holiday!! On your own again or are you coming to spend it in the country (Pickwell)

Look, darling, let's not mention that motorbike again. I don't want to fall out with you about a silly thing like that. You're right, saving up for a home is far more important. Because that's what we really want and also need. You should know by now what I think about getting into debt. That word does not exist for me. Even if we start saving it doesn't mean we have to stay at home every night and get bored. I always like to make you happy and what other people can afford we can. That's what I am working for. Right! Let's do it as you said. Save all your earnings, manage on mine and save from it as well. Then we'll know how we get one. We'll certainly enjoy ourselves on our honeymoon. And I want to see you smiling all the 10 days. About the shoes we'll have a talk on Sunday.

Don't thank me for working hard and long hours. I love doing it for you. You yourself do more already than you should do. I am quite sure you'll make a lovely wife. In fact, the best wife in the world. Oh Jeanny, I love you so very much. I am very proud of you.

I was going to make a cake tonight, but found I had no eggs left. So I'll wait until tomorrow afternoon. Then I've got something to do, being on my own. Keeps me out of mischief. Also have a wash tomorrow.

Well, darling, it's 9.30 and I'll go to bed thinking of you. Be good and good night. God bless you always. See you on Sunday.

      All my love and kisses etc.

       Forever and ever yours

      Hans.

<u>P.T.O.</u>

Please darling get 2lbs dog biscuits and don't forget the cigarettes.

Love

Hans.

                      Pickwell,

                      August, 27th 49.

My darling,

How are you today sweetheart, have you been busy? Well, I hope you're successful in getting blouse and hat. Do you after all want new shoes to go with the costume? I thought you'd made up your mind about those lovely tan shoes! You have them, love, if you want them.

It's 6.30 now and in an hour's time I hope to be able to go shutting up. We've changed over. Broad Meadow and the new field go together. Also with feeding in the morning but collecting all round. It isn't too bad as I got back at 3.45 today.

The cake is ready and I washed my hair straight away after tea. I am lonely darling. It's only good I don't have to wait till tomorrow afternoon to see you. Shortly after I arrive back from feeding you'll be here and cook us a first class dinner. Don't think I've been lazy last night. I got some jelly and custard ready. Beside that we'll have rhubarb if anyone fancies some and for tea there are pears. So everything is fixed and I hope you'll enjoy spending the day with me. I only hope it'll keep fine so you can come along collecting in the afternoon. Have you been to the pictures last week? "Treasure at Sierra Madre" was on at Melton but after looking over my money I decided to stop in. Helmut went out on Wednesday to Melton and met somebody from Leicester. Still, don't ask me who, as I don't know. Do you want to have a look at the ring? Well, my darling, I'll say cheerio now and be good. See you tomorrow morning.

All my love and kisses
Forever yours
Hans.

R 30/8.49   Aschersleben, 21.8.49
                                    28/8.49
Edith's address: Edith Jachner, 23 Kirchwistedt, Kreis Bremervörde (Hannover)

Hedwig Schünemann

My dear Hans

We received your lovely letter dated 14.8.49 two days ago and thank you with all our heart. The letter only took five days to get here. We did not have any post from you for two weeks. I am now going to be completely on my own for eight to ten days. It will be very strange. Horst went away this afternoon with four women. I hope everything will work out alright. If only he had some luck! He wants to go and see Elsbeth in Pinneberg near Hamburg and also Edith. We had a postcard from Edith the day before yesterday. She is sending her best wishes to you. Edith has settled into her new abode very nicely and has made her home really comfortable. I think she will be rather pleased to see Horst when he arrives on her doorstep unexpectedly. We couldn't get all the money together to pay for train fares, so he is doing most of the journeys by car. He badly wanted me to come with him but I am not confident to undertake such a long journey just yet. It would be far too strenuous for me.

I am now getting two salt water baths charged with carbon dioxide gas twice a week. Every treatment costs 5 Marks, but it is paid for by the medical health system. It is good for the heart and rheumatism and it suits me, without a sign of any side effects. It is always a long walk for me to get there and back (45 minutes each way). But, I don't mind, I need the exercise too.

Dear Hans, guess how much weight I have put on through eating all the lovely things you sent me, and having indulged in lots of rest? I now weigh 133 pounds. Well, don't you think it is a record to put on 21 pounds? I have nearly regained my old weight since we left home. I am feeling quite alright, but when the weather changes I get a lot of pain in my scars. It feels like someone is sitting inside me with a sharp knife. I suppose I shall have to put up with it for a long time. Horstel hasn't been quite himself lately either. He had a painful right shoulder and was worried in case it had something to do with his lungs. I told him right away that it is probably rheumatism and it proved to be right. This is a genetic problem. Rheumatism runs in our family, what with me, and our grandfather also suffered from it. I suffer badly from pins and needles in my hands, it is dreadful! Horst is now getting hot air treatment and massages, which are doing him good.

I can see, dear Hans, that you had to work extremely hard during the harvest. Oh, we could do with some rich uncles like you have now, who would buy us a whole bedroom suite. I am sure you are both very pleased to receive such a gift. Have you not secured your flat yet? We thought it was all sorted. It sounds like you will be on your own this Sunday too, just like me. Wouldn't it be lovely if we could find work and accommodation over there! And then you could come and see us with Jean, it would just be wonderful! You managed to get your shirt again, it is almost as expensive as here in the 'free shops'. I bought one for Horst this week in dark blue silk and paid with 20 points plus 10.5 Marks. We can't really get anything special here, it's not like it used to be at home.

Now, my dear Hans, give my best wishes to your Jean and mother-in-law and to you, we are sending our love and kisses. Your mum, who is always thinking of you and your brother Horst.

    92 Wharf St
    Aug 29th
Dearest Hans

Well darling a month to go, by the date of the 29th I will have had it, so will you, then you have a heavy load on your shoulders do you think you can manage it.

I arrived home safe. Nancy was on the bus with Bert, they get married on Sept 10th. She is having 6 bridesmaids and all that goes with it. Even with all that it will not be as nice as our little wedding and I am sure could not be as happy.

I have been cleaning my wardrobe out, the moths have been in my skirt, the one my mother made last winter. I have tried to mend it as best I can, but it still shows a lot. I was annoyed. I have been going to do it for a month, I felt sure there would not be any in it. I know it is always best to make sure.

I have been to tell Mr Taylor the name of the church and he said they were called last Sunday.

Darling do you think you could possibly mend that clock before we are married. I know you have a lot to do and I hate having to tell you. I would not bother if the clock belonged to me. If you don't think you will have time let's take it to a watchmaker, anything, but let's get rid of it. I feel awful when I ask how's the clock going.

I rung Peter Conway's to see what time they have for lunch and what time they close. I will have to go at lunchtime as they close at 5.30.

Well darling I will have to go to bed, think this time 29th and we will go to bed together. Can I put my cold feet on your back? I will write a few lines tomorrow if I have time.

Love and kisses

All of them

Jean

Tuesday

Thank you darling for your letter. I did not wait for it before I sent this, it just worked out that way.

I have not fetched your suit this lunchtime because I forgot to take the money with me. I am going at 5.15.

Iris has had her baby, a boy at 2.0 yesterday she is calling him Philippe.

I will write again. I can't get on very well, Lucy is talking to me.

Bring your shirt, tie and shoes, then we can see what you look like.

Tuesday evening.

Well darling I have fetched your suit and it looks very nice, the fellow said he thought it would be OK but if it was not to bring it back and they will put it right.

I seem as if I have done an awful lot of correspondence today. I have answered the invitation I had to the party. Also sent my leave sheet in to be altered and also had to write a letter stating that I will continue to work at L.A.E.C. so I could have the 3 days leave (marriage). I have sent the application form for a permit for the cake and I have been told it takes 2 weeks, don't give up hope we can always have bread and cheese.

I had better close as I have to take this to the GPO. I'm going to have an early night I feel dead tired.

Love and kisses Jean

Pickwell,
August 29th 1949

My dearest, darling Jean,

It's 10.00pm but I know you are waiting for a letter so I shan't keep you waiting. I've only just come back. Working till 9.45 that's the spirit. It adds another couple of bob to our account anyway. We have been moving those small houses and then I went shutting up straight the way.

Today I went watercarting but finished 3.30. So when I came back Mr Cooper asked me if I could give a hand with harvesting till 5 o'clock. So I went out to the field and relieved one of the Irish men who was loading the wagons. Believe me the wheat isn't half heavy. And then on piece work. As soon as one wagon is loaded the next one is there. The sweat was running down my face in streams but I didn't surrender. My arms were nearly dead. One has to get used to that kind of job.

I hope you got back safe last night. I'm sorry I couldn't see you off and you know yourself how I hate to let you go on your own. This morning at 10.30 I have been thinking of you. It was exactly a month to when we get married. And what will we be doing by this time? Having a nice rest after a day full of excitement. Darling, I am longing for the day. I'll always love you very, very much and try my best to make you always happy. Let other people think you'll have a hard life. We both know better don't we?

Did you go for my suit today? I wonder what it looks like. Do you like it?

Well, my love, I'll say goodnight and God bless you. I am really very tired. I don't feel like eating so off to bed I go. Be good. Please give my regards to your mother and Betty.

To you

      All my love and kisses

         Forever and only yours

            Hans.

                    Pickwell,

                    August 31ˢᵗ 1949

My dearest, darling Jean,

Thank you ever so much for your letter. So you've also been thinking on Monday of the day exactly a month to go. I don't worry about that heavy load on my shoulders. Don't you think they are strong enough to bear it? If you can't remember how strong they are, have a look at the new jacket. They just fit in there.

Nancy is only having 6 bridesmaids? Still if they are as happy as we are without then I call them lucky. Even if it is only once in life it just concerns the two of us and not hundreds of other people. We'll be alright sweety, never worry. Not even about the things the moths have been in. I remember what the yanks shouted across to our lines in France to make us surrender. They said: 'Throw everything away, come over to us and you'll get everything new. Just bring a blanket.' Rather nice wasn't it? But nobody went.

So the banns were read in Leicester last Sunday. I have only next weekend to go, that'll be the third time and another job is done with. About the clock. Tonight I am doing my washing, get us something to eat and then I'll have another look.

If I can't do it I shall take it to Melton next Wednesday and have it done there. Anyway I'll let you know on Sunday.

So in a month time you want to warm your feet on my back. Cheeky aren't you? I thought you're the one who's got all the heat. Still I won't mind if I've to be the hot water bottle and only hope you don't insist on putting one of them into the bed. Terrible things they are.

I'll bring my wedding utensils, shirt, tie and shoes so you can have a look what your husband to be will look like. Can I wash my neck before I put the white shirt on?

Yesterday I had a letter from my mother. She told me she has gained 23lbs and that only because of those 2 parcels. She still can't get over it seeing all the nice things. Believe me she's more excited about the wedding than we are, mentioning it in every letter she writes. Horst went over to the Western Zones last week to see if he can get a job and accommodation there. If so, they are both going to move over somehow. She said it will be alright then for us to come over and visit them. I am sure she is anxious to meet you.

Today I really got down to work. I was cleaning out. Only did 10 houses and 15 nightharks. It took me 1 ½ hours to unload the wagon. Still I went early enough to finish at 5.00.

Don't worry, Jeany, we'll get the cake in time. I am not so much used to bread and cheese than to bread and marmalade. So if you don't mind let it be that.

You have been tired? What about me? I have to get going and keep going all day.

Today I got a letter about the driving test. On September 26th, 5.30pm the fellow will be coming. That means another provisional licence and so another 5/-. Still, doesn't matter. You'll have to get me a new one just before then.

I'll do my washing now. Be good, my love and think of me if you've got the time.

Please give my regards to your mother.

Cheerio my sweet and to you

All my love and kisses

(Soon) forever yours Hans

Oh, darling, I am done in. I've just come back from shutting up. 2 hours only. This afternoon they put more chickens in the big field. So half way to the field the storm caught up with me and I got wet through. It got dark in a couple of minutes and about a dozen hens were out. Chasing those in took me an hour. Anyway I earned 5/-5 the very hard way. Still doesn't matter. Now I shall be off it bed. Good night and God bless you my darling.

Thursday Sept 1st 9.05pm

Hello, my love, how are you today? At your best I hope. I am really sorry darling but it looks as if you are not going to get your second letter this week. Tonight I went again to the post office and found the people have gone away for a week's holidays. That means I can't get any stamps as the Somerby PO closes at 5.00. Don't be too mad with me. I'll bring this letter along on Saturday. Of course I have to keep my mouth shut this week if I only get one.

Well, today I was watercarting and put a few hours overtime in again as we moved some night larks. I am glad it's only another day and a half to go till I see you again. Have you been busy again corresponding or is everything settled?

Helmut was on piece work all last week and got £11 on the time sheet. He starts shopping on Saturday. Shirt, boots and rubber boots. It's time he had a new shirt anyway. The old one is only collar and sleeves but one can't see it if he wears the waistcoat.

Well, darling, Be good and pleasant dreams. Remember our great day is coming nearer and I love you more than anything else in the world.

Goodnight and God bless you always.

All my love and kisses to you.

Friday Sept 2nd 9.10am

Well, darling, I've been speaking to you but it didn't sound as if you believed I couldn't get any stamps. Still, I really couldn't as those people have gone away. I am just back from shutting up. It wasn't as bad as last night but I got wet through. The shower just caught me on the way back.

I wonder what time I'll be ready to go to bed tonight. The meat has to be done, washing my hair and the body wants a scrub too. It'll be 12.00.

The boss came by and started talking keeping me off for half an hour.

As I have to get cracking I'll say goodnight and God bless.

> I love you very very much
>> All my love and kisses
>>> Forever yours
>> Hans

92 Wharf St

September 5th

My dearest darling Hans

Is your cold out now? I have been sneezing tonight (3 times). I blame you but it is worth it. Did you feel any effects of the cycle ride? I can feel where the seat has been when I sit down, but my legs do not ache.

Hasn't it been muggy today especially this morning, it was sweltering. I wished I was at Bournemouth lying on the beach in my two piece, with you of course.

I have a German station on the radio at the moment. I think it is or Dutch, it is light music and the singing is very nice.

I was annoyed this morning with Freddy. It was about 8.55 when I left here, going by the Green up the street I saw Fred have a look around, he saw me before I saw him and after me he came, I shouted and told him to go back, he waited until I was nearly at the top of Wharf Street and after me he came. I gave him a good hiding and sent him off, he still would not go back. You will never guess what came along and saved me from having to take him all the way back ,his girlfriend, while he was looking her over I was off like a shot out of a

317

gun.

I have been working this evening. I washed your shirt. It is dry too, but I will not be ironing it. I wish I could but my mother is going to do some in the morning. Of course I forgot to take those bones out of the collar until I had put it in the water and given it a good punch, but you need not worry there are alright. I washed the dusting mop then I polished the floor, my mother rubbed it this morning so I got cracking and it looks a lot better. I have had a good wash, I am ready for bed.

You would have laughed last night, well maybe you won't especially if you were going to sleep with me. Freddy got on my knee and I saw a flea on his back. I caught it between my fingers and while I was having a look it jumped, but not back on Fred and fortunately not on me either. So that poor little flea was all alone in the world with no one to bite.

Do you think we will do for Sept 29th? I will be very glad when is it 12.30 and all the fuss is over. Then we can start our holiday, that is what I am longing for. I am dreading the wedding. I hate being the centre of anything I would much rather be at the back.

That programme I was listening to was from Leipzig Oh dear I will be hopeless at spelling German I know I am at English. After we are married we will try to find the first lesson book in German.

Well darling goodnight God bless.
I will always be yours.

> All my love
> Jean

On NAVAL MESSAGE paper

I have just been trying to make a survey of what money we shall need on our holiday. Here it is:

Railway fare £2.4.10 ea   4.9.8

London hotel 24/6 per day	2. 9. 0
Bournemouth hotel £6 ½ gns	13. 13. 0
	£20. 11. 8

Does not look so good, then we have for a while we are in London. Heaven only knows what that will be if we have champagne.

Here are some more things we have to get for the 29th:

Cake, wine, flowers, cars and the expenses church.

Anyway let's hope we get through alright.

One of the girls in the office upstairs has been to France for 8 days on the coast for 5 days and to Paris for 3 days. I am wishing now we were going somewhere like that, maybe one day we will go. Far away places I am longing to see. Do you?

Lucy is not here this morning she had half a day of her leave to tell the baker what he could do with his bread on Saturday. He left it on the doorstep instead of in the bin left especially for the bread.

Pickwell,
Sept 5 th 1949

My darling

How are you today dear? Did you get home safe last night? Only just a bit more than 3 weeks to go. How the time flies. Remember when we settled the date it was 3 months to go. I'm so much longing for it aren't you? Still I guess we both will be glad to sit in the train and say "it's over now, thank goodness".

I just thought of something. You wanted the wedding at 11.00. Don't you want to change your ration book and have the identity card altered? We can do it on the way to the station can't we? Whereabouts is your food office? I never noticed it anywhere. We can call a taxi for the station and go there on the way.

Well, darling, I thank you very, very much for a lovely weekend. Believe me I even enjoyed the ride out on that funny bike on Sunday morning. It wasn't nice to start moaning was it?

Your dress and hat are lovely really. I don't know how come but I really like that hat. It suits you. I truly hope I can stand beside you without blushing. Don't forget to bring the prayer books, socks on Saturday.

The new chap told me that the vicar has gone away this morning for 12 days. That's why he asked me to collect the certificate last night. I still hope he's posted it to me. I shall see it in the morning. Otherwise it'll do when he comes back. Plenty of time.

Oh! Wasn't I tired this morning. Good thing I was watercarting today. Tomorrow I am on moving houses on my own. If I could have gone moving today there would've been no chance of getting the houses wound up. Last night at Melton I had to wait till 9.15. Our bus was 15 minutes late. I was ready to drop any moment. When I came back last night the boss came along again and told me all about the new carburettor they've put on my tractor and about moving houses tomorrow. So, of course, when the foreman told me all about moving he was ever so surprised when I told him I know.

Well, darling, it's 9.30 and believe me I am ready for bed.

I hope to get a letter tomorrow, that's if I'm lucky.

Be good darling and look after yourself. Goodnight and God bless you.

Please give my regards to your mother.

I love you very, very much, more than anything else in the world.

> So to you
> All my love and kisses
> Forever yours
> Hans.

R 6/9.49   Aschersleben, 27.8.49

6/9.49

Hedwig Schünemann

My dear Hans

I want to write to you again today.

Horst came back from his travels on Wednesday. He left on Sunday and on Tuesday I received a card from him to say that he had arrived safely there (in the West). All the more was I surprised to see him back home again on the following Wednesday. Unfortunately, he was unable to go and see Edith because she lives so much further away. The train fare from Hamburg to Edith's would have cost 15 West Marks, in our currency about 100 Marks. He did not have that kind of money. He travelled in a lorry from Helmstedt to Buxtehude near Hamburg, but there was no practical motor connection like that to get from Hamburg to her house. He arrived in Pinneberg where Elsbeth lives, on Monday at 9 p.m. They were so unkind to him and did not allow him to spend the night there, they wouldn't even let him sleep in the kitchen on a chair just for the night. They said they had no space for him. They could see how tired and exhausted he was but they made him leave their home at 11.45 at night and told him to find a hotel. I think the least Elsbeth's husband could have done was to go out with him looking for accommodation. They live on the edge of the town and it takes half an hour to walk into the town centre. Everywhere was, of course, total darkness. The hotels were all booked out and Horst did not find a bed anywhere. He decided to go to Hamburg, from there to Harburg and from there he immediately found a lorry which took him to Helmstedt. He did not find any work or accommodation. Yesterday he received an offer from Braunschweig. He has to have another go in September. If only something would come up. The doctor keeps telling him that he needs a change of air. As soon as the weather changes, he develops bronchitis. If he does not do anything about it it is likely that he will finish up with asthma. Dear

Hans, what do you think about Elsbeth? And she calls herself a relative. She has had it with me. As long as we lived at home and kept giving them things, we were okay. Oh well, we will get over it. We are experiencing an extreme heatwave again. It is almost unbearable up here and also where Horst works in the salon, without any windows one can open. They don't get a breath of fresh air and have to work under electric light bulbs, and when all seven motors are running, you can imagine how bad the atmosphere is in there. He comes home quite distraught. There's no way he can stay healthy under these conditions.

I should think that you too have been feeling very hot this summer. You have to sit on a tractor all day long in this burning heat. This is no mean feat. Your wedding day is drawing nearer by the day. I imagine Jean has returned from her trip by now! Give my regards to her and your mother-in-law and to you, my dear boy, we are sending our loving greetings, your mum and brother Horst.

We are looking forward to a healthy reunion.

Pickwell,
Sept 6th 1949

My dearest, darling Jean,

I was unlucky today. No letter from you, but in spite of that one from my mother and one from the vicar. That settles it. No objection on my side. You'll have the next Sunday to go and the church will have given their permission for us to get married. That seems to be the first stage. Everything else will follow quietly as you wish. Three weeks the day after tomorrow. It won't be long now. The day will be within reach when I come over again to Leicester.

How are you today my dear? Fine, I hope. I really feel done in tonight. Moving those houses got me down. It isn't easy to wind 18 ctw up and that's 9 times. Anyway I managed to get one more done then with the foreman.

I was just listening to a boxing match. Poor Dick Turpin was knocked out in the first round. The other fellow was tougher. Still I know you aren't interested.

Well, my darling, I'll close for now. It was late last night, but it'll be earlier tonight. By the way, I repaired my briefcase yesterday and think it looks decent, I'll leave the judging to you.

Look after yourself and remember I love you more than anything else in the world. Goodnight and God bless you.

Wednesday 6.30pm

I am very much disappointed darling. Not even a letter on Wednesday morning. Still I think you'll have your reasons. Perhaps being busy or are you going to take revenge for last week? I hope not, otherwise I shan't get one before Saturday.

Today was a rotten day. Believe me I looked a mess at 5.00. When I finished. I gave a hand to the land and not as easy as last time. Threshing, and of course, carrying the short straw away. The threshing set was just standing nicely so I got all the dust. I was washing for half an hour to look a bit clean. Still it's a change and I'll be watercarting again tomorrow.

Mrs Cooper gave us some apples yesterday so tonight it'll be stewed apples and custard.

This week isn't very much on the time sheet, but it'll be £3 just the same.

It was hard work yesterday, winding the houses up. The boss is going to have it altered for next year so that one man can wind the houses up easy. It's time he found out as he hasn't tried it himself. I am always a fool in saying 'yes I can do it.' Because I think it's worth trying everything once. Anyway up to now I always showed that I could do it, in fact, at least as good as anybody else here.

People are fixing the flat up next to the yard. I only wonder who is going in there. It looks as if they're painting it all over.

Well, my sweetheart, it's 7.00 and I'll get cracking with our

dinner. Helmut will be back at 8.00. Be good and think of me. I'll go to bed again early tonight as I can do with it.
Goodnight and God bless you.

Loads of love and kisses

Forever and only yours

Hans.

Thursday Sept 8th '49

I was lucky today, after all. I thank you very much for your letter. It was a bit late but it found me alright. I only wish you would put the proper address down as it is on top of my letters. Somerby is always crossed out when I get them.

So after all you agree that our music is nice? Well, I am glad to hear it as I naturally like it too. Then it settles the problem of listening to German stations.

Wasn't Freddy lucky to meet his girlfriend at the top of the street? Unfortunately I have further to go but I don't mind at all. For you it wouldn't have been too bad taking him back if it hadn't been for 8.55.

Thank you very much for washing my shirt. Don't bring it on Saturday. When I come over again I'll bring the white one I was wearing last weekend. But, please don't forget the socks. It doesn't any harm to those little things in the collar if you don't boil the shirt. I wish you would understand me if I say it isn't nice having Fred on the bed. When he goes out he of course picks flies up and there you are. I feel very uncomfortable having any on me.

What a funny question to ask if we'll do for Sept 29th. I've told you I like your costume and hat very much and you like my suit. Nothing to say about the two people wearing those nice things.

Look, sweety, don't fear the wedding ceremony. What shall I say as a foreigner? This is only once in a lifetime and after being the centre of everything for an hour we'll be off and it'll be quiet again around us.

Don't be afraid my darling. I am not. Even learning German

won't be too difficult. We'll have a go when we come back from our holidays.

I was surprised to the list about the things we have to pay for and still to get. I don't know if we shall do it, but I certainly do my best. It would be nice not having to take any more money out of the bank. Still, we'll make up for it again if we're to take some out.

Well, everything is alright for the cake, wine, flowers and cars can wait another fortnight. When you go and take my certificate to the vicar you can ask about the expenses and if possible pay it.

Today I was watercarting all day. Not too bad as there was a breeze. Don't know yet what's happening tomorrow. Anyway it's Friday and only another 1 ½ days to go till you come again.

Well, my sweetheart, I'll close now. It's 7.30 and my washing has been boiling whilst I wrote. So I'll get cracking. Be a good girl. Goodnight and God bless you.

I love you very very much, more than anything else.

  All my love and kisses

   Forever yours

  Hans.

PS The fellow on Radio Newsreel just said: 'The last Great German Richard Strauss has died.'

Of course he didn't know me. Don't blame him.

  Love Hans.

  92 Wharf St

  September 9th

My dearest darling

It is now 10.24am. In 21 days time we shall nearly have had it. Just 2 hours more we shall be on our way. 'Thank goodness.' I have been making inquiries about the cars. Do you think one car will be sufficient? I think it will be, because if he fetches you and the best man at 10.15 he should have time to make 2 more journeys. Anyway why worry as long as we get there.

I have been in to order the cake and I have paid £1 deposit. Aunt Gertie said last night, 'I hope you are not disappointed with the cake, Enid's mother had a Christmas cake from there and it was just like sawdust' aren't people cheerful.

I went to see Gwenn last night. They are trying to get a small holding and sell their house. They have written after 2 but have not heard anything yet. Gwenn would like to get it out of Leicestershire if possible. She thinks it would be better for her little girl to go where they're not known. They are doing the house.

This is as far as I have got and it is nearly 5.15, so cheeri'O.

Love all of it

Jean

PS
What no stamps!!!

92 Wharf St
Sept 12th

My dearest darling Hans

I arrived back on Leicester all in one piece. It seemed as if I was waiting hours for the bus. I went round to the village to wait, there was quite a crowd. There was plenty of room on both buses.

On Saturday I intended to catch the 2.45 bus from Melton to Pickwell but because I didn't get into Melton until 2.15 I didn't think ½ hour would be long enough to look around, as I was looking in that nice dress shop (it usually has the blinds fasten to the window) the bus came along and I got on it, it was a good job I did. It would not have been until after 7.0, I would have to have walked oh dear!!!

Did I tell you we have to leave the showroom by the end of the month. Lucy, Margery and Arthur are going to the Phoenix buildings and I am going into Eagle House in an office on my own. I will be lost to death on my own. The office where

I'm going is a very nice one, it is where the old Labour department were. I believe you went up there when you were a POW. I'm in Barker Swains old office. I hope we don't move until after the 29th.

We have our first wedding present, 2 pillow slips and a towel from Mr and Mrs Dale, it is really very nice of them, they are an old couple and have not very much money.

Iris's husband has just been in. Lucy went upstairs and found him wandering in the corridor looking for Mr Whiteman, the ministry of Labour had sent him there as a cook. Lucy brought him in to see me it was painful speaking to him he knew only a few words in English,

All my love
Jean

——.

92 Wharf St
September 12th
My darling Johannes
It is only Monday evening and I'm writing again, although I have not very much to say.

My mother has just gone to bed, she has gone early, 8.45. I'm following too in a few minutes. Until a few minutes ago I had a German station on with some very nice music. I seem unlucky like that. I find some music, sit down, get comfortable then they start talking. I listen for about 5 mins then get up and find something else.

I told you Iris' husband came for a job as cook, he did not take it, at least I don't think so according to Shilton he wanted to live at home and travel backwards and forwards not live in the hostel. I hope he is able to get something here, I doubt if Iris will go to Paris.

I am longing for something nice to eat. I would think I was having a baby if I had not got the pip already. I have had to do with a piece of bread and cheese. I will have to be satisfied with that for tonight.

I'm going to bed now, I will think of you all night through. I will write a few more lines to this. All my love and kisses Jean. Goodnight and God bless.

<u>Tuesday</u>. Nothing new to report. I still love you and I have not changed my mind.

<u>Evening now</u>.

I have just been listening to a play, it is a serial, this is 5th instalment it is the last one next week so I will have to listen to that, it is called 'Death --- and Mary Dazill.

I have been with my mother tonight to see a representative for a firm of hardware manufacturers. I have ordered a pair of scales, they are rather nice green and cream with weights up to 2lbs. I have got it wholesale for £1.1.0 it will sell in a shop at £2.2.0. It will probably be a little while before they send them. I can't wait to try them out. I also saw a slicer, like a small bacon slicer that came to £3.15.0 it would slice bread tinned meat etc. I was wondering whether to have one but my mother said I would not want one so that stopped me wondering.

Now I will answer your letter, You are right darling it is silly to worry beforehand but I can't help it. I don't intend to worry, it's just that I can't help wondering and hoping that everything is alright now and there will not be any need to bother again.

Darling you and I must be born under a lucky star. Mr Rudkin was here when I came home, he had brought some milk, bacon and a few plums (they will not keep until Saturday I would keep them if they would) he asked me if I was having a reception after the wedding I told him we were having cake and wine so he said he would get me 2 bottles of sherry and 2 of port, that is one less expense we have to bother about. I know it seems rather funny that he should do all he does but if he wishes to be a fool he can be, he's old enough to know what he is doing. You never need worry about me falling for him or anyone else, you never need be jealous of anyone. I love you and that is enough for me.

What have you to get on Saturday? I want some dress shields and we will have some Yardleys talcum powder to take with us. I want to get an uplift, I want to show what little I have got. I will make a list of what we will take with us. What wants washing bring with you. Will you take the khaki shirt with you?

I have just had my milk and I'm ready for bed. So goodnight, God Bless.

> All my love
> for ever yours.
> Jean

PS Don't bother with a chicken we will manage.

<u>Wednesday</u>

Thank you darling for the lovely long letter

I'm so glad your mother has moved to the British zone and we will go next year for a holiday, (so just you be careful). I do want to learn German but you must remember I'm not very bright when it comes to picking things up, so if you have a little patience

I have been in to book seats and I have to go again on Monday to collect the tickets. I have paid a £1 deposit, they should be good seats in the balcony 13/6 each.

You are definitely not having any wine before, I want you to marry me sober then you cannot say 'I did not know what I was doing'.

You are a lucky boy 8 pages. I hope you can understand it

> All my love
> Jean

> ——.

R 13/9.49   Aschersleben, 4.9.49

13/9.49

My dear Hans

Thank you very much indeed for your lovely letter dated 24.8.49, which we were very pleased to receive. I have some fabulous news to tell you. Horst left here on Thursday and on Friday I received a telegram to say that he was offered the position. I was so very pleased for him and have already sent off some things out for him, because he has stayed there already. This was the advance arrangement. I am sure he will write to me and let me have more details. They are paying him already in order to make the start a bit easier for him. We are allowed to send parcels up to 14 lbs. now. This applies to the inter-zones as well, and via a shipping company the crates can weigh up to four hundredweights. You can imagine how busy I am now. Tomorrow I have to go and see a carpenter to get a crate made, because whatever we can possibly take with us we will be sent over there. Everything is very difficult to come by. I don't know anything yet about accommodation. I am sure Horst will try his best. If nothing comes up, I shall go through the refugee camp.

Tomorrow will be very difficult for me because I have to tell Horst's boss. It will be quite a battle. He knows nothing so far. I have to get the papers from him. He did not want to give permission for him to leave. I had quite a confrontation with him yesterday and subsequently Horst just left and went. I am sure that he now thinks he can just get rid of him. Well, he has another thing coming. These men only think of themselves.

You could have spent your honeymoon here. Perhaps you will introduce your young lady to us soon. It won't be long now until your wedding day. A rest will do you good after all the hard work. I collected my suit from the tailor yesterday. It is very nice but he charged me 82 Marks. The photos from the Streeses arrived yesterday and I shall go and order the duplicates now. I wonder how our Horst is spending his Sunday today? He was finding it really difficult to leave me behind but the time will pass very quickly. The weather has changed. It is extremely warm again.

Now you both have your wedding outfits together – well, you are all ready to go then. Maybe I will be living with Horst by the time your wedding day comes along. It would be nice so that we can have a little celebration together as well.

Now, my dear boy, I am sending you all my love and kisses, your mum.

Give my best wishes to Jean and your mother-in-law.

Horst's new address:
Braunschweig-Bebelhof
Salon Lüders
Hans-Porner-Str. 23

Pickwell,
Sept 13th 1949

My dearest darling Jean

I thank you so very much for your nice letter. I sure was surprised honey to get a letter this morning. The more as I had one from my mother too telling me good news. Horst went over the British zone I think it is. Didn't I tell you about the offer he got from Braunschweig? I think I did. Well, Horst went over the second time on Sept 1st and the next day my mother received his telegram saying that he's got the job and staying there to start straight the way. He's a good boy and knows what he wants. So my mother has started packing and sent some things over at once. She was waiting for him to tell her about accommodation. She'll know by now. Do you know what she said? By the time we get married she'll have settled down and if we'd known earlier we could have spend our honeymoon with them in Germany. It would've been nice but we'll try to spend the next one in Germany, if you like. That, of course, means to get cracking to learn a bit of the language so you can at least make yourself understand when you talk to my mother. When we come back from our honeymoon we'll have a go. It'll be alright and easy enough if you are serious about it and interested. There always is a day when one gets fed up with learning but if you're sticking to it then it's quite easy. I remember when I was in Amerika I got fed up with it and threw all the books I could get hold of away. The next day, however, I picked them up again.

See what difference it makes putting the proper address on the envelope. You posted it last night and I received it this morning.

Poor girl I really feel sorry for you if you have to be all on your own in Eagle House. Where is your relief going or are they going to finish with that? Still, don't fall asleep.

So the first wedding present has arrived. It sure is very kind of Mr and Mrs Dale. When we come back we'll go and see them one day and say thank you. I still wish somebody would give us a house or flat as a present. Furnished of course! Wouldn't that be lovely. It looks as if that so-called rich uncle from the U.S. hasn't been born yet.

So you've met Iris's husband. Do you appreciate how lucky you are to marry a foreigner who at least can make himself understand?

Did you remember to book seats? Please, don't forget it darling. Have you made up your mind now about the shoes? We'll see on Saturday about that and the wine. Can I have some before?

It is a long time since I had the last, if I remember right it was in the army. At that time I always kept a bottle of Red Burgundy in my wardrobe. Only for special occasions.

Well, sweetheart, it's almost time to go shutting up. Only on the chicken field. It takes me ½ an hour. Though there's plenty to do tonight. My washing is boiling and I'll do it when I get back.

Be a good girl and look after yourself. Good night and God bless you.

All my love and kisses

Forever and only yours

Hans.

Pickwell,
Sept 15$\underline{th}$ 1949

My dearest, darling Jean,

Thank you darling thank you so very much for your lovely long letter I received this morning. See, if you were able to understand German you could leave the station on and listen to it. No getting up when you're comfy.

What's Iris's husband doing now? Not working at all? What does he think a cook's working hours are? The only thing I can't understand is why Iris doesn't want to go over to Paris. People usually think much about France.

That play, Death and Mary Dazill is not too bad. I've been listening to it all the time.

You are a darling buying a pair of scales. Did you listen to 'Ray's a laugh' this week. If you didn't, don't miss the repeat broadcast. You'll be surprised where she gets the money from to buy things. She (Kitty) might give you a hint.

Bless Mr Rudkin. You know what I think about him getting anything for us for our wedding, but still you're right. He's old enough and if he doesn't know what to do with all his money let him buy it. After all it looks as if we'll just make it having those expenses less. I hope we don't have to draw any more out of the bank. I know well enough I never need worry about you falling for him. I don't know what I would do if I found out he wants to attract your attention this way. Blimey, he's had it. I'll never be jealous if there isn't any reason. Still it may show you that I love you and don't want anybody else messing about.

You also know that I am hot tempered if it comes to anything like that. Of course I am sure there'll never be any need to lose my temper. You are the only girl in the world I love and I always will love.

Well what do I have to get on Saturday. Dog biscuits, flexible plaster dressing and a bandage. Can't think of anything else yet. You'll wonder why I want some bandage. Well today I was watercarting and as it was raining this morning the ground was wet. When I filled up the last time just before 5.00 I slipt and caught my left knee in the barbered wire. It looks smashing. The trousers had a nice red colour. The boss just came across the yard and sent me over to the foreman for some iodine. I didn't have anything left myself. Doesn't matter about the trousers because it's those with the zip you don't like.

There's something in your letter I don't understand. You said something about taking some talcum powder along and you wanted to make an uplift to show what little you've got. I don't quite get it.

There's nothing on washing to bring along on Saturday except the white shirt. I'll also make out a list of what I want to take along and then we can go through it together. I don't know yet about the khaki shirt.

I'll be careful, or rather, we both will have to be and then go to Germany for our next holidays.

It won't matter about you learning German. You'll pick it up alright. I have plenty of patience as I know myself what it looks like to learn a foreign language.

So the seats are booked. 13/6 should be pretty good.

Oh! I am not having anything to drink before the wedding. Alright!

Don't worry I know what I am doing. I was thinking of it all today at 10.30. By now (7.30) we'll be somewhere in London.

Well, my darling, 1 ½ day and I'll be with you again.

It's fine now for shutting up. I'll say cheeri'o and God bless you. Be a good girl till I see you on Saturday.

I'll be off to bed as soon as I get back, think and dream of you all night.

All my love and a thousand kisses
Forever and only yours
Hans.

Pickwell,
Sept 19th 1949

My dearest, darling Jean,

Thank you ever so much for a lovely weekend. Darling I just enjoyed everything. The christening, too. It was the first time I've been to a christening. Still one has to be sure how things go. One day we'll have to go to have our little Johnny christened. But, as you said, not just yet. Next year we'll go over to Germany and see what it looks like there. I am sure you'll enjoy yourself. Darling, if only the weekends wouldn't pass so quick. It'll be the same of our holidays or rather honeymoon.

It's only 8.15 now and I have finished my Monday night jobs so far. We have had our dinner, I washed up and did my washing and now the milk is about to boil. That'll mean a glass of ovaltine. I wish you were here and have some too. When we have our own home, sweetheart, we'll be able to share everything.

I am just listening to Family Favourites. The German love song is on. Are you listening too? How do you like it? That's my favourite song. Translated: 'Do you hear my secret calling' I hope you hear it!!!

By the way darling, I forgot something. Some time ago I told you if the driving happens to be after 14.9.49 I have to have another provisional one. That means I'll get a form to fill in and could you possibly get the license for me and bring it along on Saturday as the test is on Monday next. I'll see if I can get the form tomorrow so just nip round to 14 Friar Lane and get the license please. It's 5/- sh.

I've asked Mrs Cooper tonight and she's quite willing to look after Helmut whilst I am away. That settles that. It really wasn't my business to ask her but it doesn't matter. I've also told Mr Cooper about my last week's wages and the holiday pay. He said he would see the boss tomorrow about it.

Well, darling, how are you today? Fine I hope. I was water-carting again today but don't know yet what's happening tomorrow. Perhaps moving the rest of the houses as Gudger has marked the places today where they're to be put.

Tonight I did my washing your way and it looks quite clean. I think it's one of your handkerchiefs here. It's a little one with a broad red band and little blue pattern next to it.

Well, my sweetheart, I am tired and go to bed. Did you get something for your mother? What a shame, we forgot about it on Saturday.

Be good love and remember I love you more than my own life. I would do everything for you.

> All my love and kisses
>
> Forever and only yours
>
> Hans.

Betty with Sheila

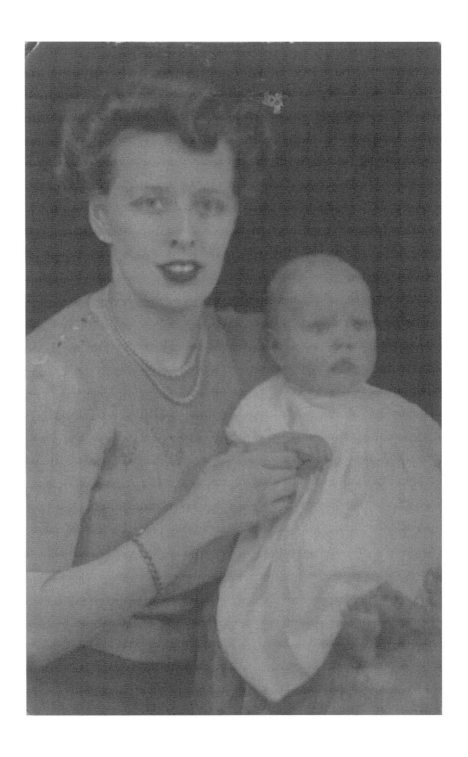

Aschersleben, 12.9.49

My dear Hans

I am sure you will be quite surprised. When you read this letter we will no longer be in Aschersleben. Horst came home on Thursday telling me that he can start his new job in Braunschweig on 15 October. He has not found any accommodation yet and he has to go through the refugee camp first. As I also want to go and stay with him in Braunschweig, we shall be going through the camp together, so that we can get registered together. How it will work out with being allocated a flat – I don't know. Maybe it means a long stay in the camp for me. If we had some money to pay towards the building costs, things would look quite different, but we don't have this kind of money. We can just manage to live off our savings for a few weeks. The move has cost a lot. You know my boy, if I did not want to live together again with Horst, and also bearing in mind that this move brings us nearer to you, I would never have undertaken any of this. I am at the end of my tether right now, I did not close my eyes for one minute last night because it is a step into the unknown. Once we are settled things will be fine, I am sure. So many people are leaving, most of them without any help or security whatsoever. When you have left the 'roof over your head' behind, you can feel very low even though things did not run very smoothly all the time before. The Streeses wrote again reminding us to come over as living conditions are so much better there. I trust in God that he will protect and guide us as always. I am asking myself why I am suddenly so despondent. It is the uncertainty that bothers me the most. I worry what will become of us. We shall have to save as much money as possible and maybe one day we'll get a deposit together to pay towards the cost of a flat. If only you would be nearer here and give me some moral support. It would be lovely. But your wedding is here soon and I don't wish to spoil your happiness. My heart gave me trouble during the night just thinking about everything. I hope we'll manage everything and stay healthy. I want to gather all my energy and put it into this project so that it goes well. God willing, we shall be on our way tomorrow. We shall be with you in our thoughts on your wedding day. I will write to you as soon as we get there. Horst is very worried about me, but I only want what's best for us all, because the thought that you and Jean would never be able to come and see us was unbearable for me. Now, we are going from one place to another restless and homeless. Keep your fingers crossed that everything will be alright for us . Stay with us my boy, I beg you, your mum.

I am sending you and your Jean our love and kisses, your mum and your brother Horst.

Give our very best wishes to your mother-in-law.

Here's to a healthy reunion.

Pickwell,
Sept 20<u>th</u> 1949

My darling

How are you today, sweety? Fine, I hope. I wasn't as lucky as last week in getting a letter Tuesday morning. Still I know you've been away to that party last night. Did you enjoy yourself? I hope so, anyway. It is only just over a week till we have our little party. I only wish it was Saturday. Now it is getting nearer I am much more longing for it. These few days will go soon, too.

Today I went out moving the last 7 houses and therewith finished that job for this year. I really couldn't care less who's going to do it next year. Perhaps it's I again, but I doubt it very much, Many things can happen till then.

I hope by then we have settled in our own little home somewhere. We'll work up to that for a start. And we'll show people what a real happy family life looks like.

I received a letter from my mother today stating that Horst has come back to fetch her. They were going to leave the Russian zone on 13.9.49. Horst hadn't found any accommodation so they probably will have to go into a camp again to start with and be registrated there. My mother has sent everything over they possessed. That gives a bit of a start at least. She said it always was an unbearable thought to her to know we (you and I) would never be able to be with her. As it was impossible whilst they're living behind the Iron Curtain she decided to move over. We won't disappoint her will we? We'll go over next year and make sure everything goes alright.

So, let's say goodnight and God bless you.

Remember darling, I love you very very much and always will do.

> All my love and kisses
> Forever and only yours
> Hans.

Wednesday Sept, 21st 1949

How are you today, my sweety? Anything wrong over there or was I just unlucky again today? Anyway – no letter. So it'll be Thursday once more. And that means only 7 days to go. By this time tomorrow week we'll be somewhere about town, meaning London.

In fact as I said no letter from you but a small parcel from my mother. Guess what it is? Our wedding present and a card. You want to know what she's sent? Well it's something you put on the table or somewhere else if you like. Little table cloth (lace) a set of four - 2 big round ones, one oval one and two small round ones. It looks very nice. I was surprised as I came in for breakfast a bit later and Helmut had fetched paper and mail. And there the parcel was. You'll see on Saturday.

I'll enclose the form for the license. Just take it round to No

14 and take 5/- along. Please don't forget to bring it on Saturday. Otherwise if I don't have it for Monday the examiner won't take the test.

A couple of days ago I asked Mrs Cooper if she would mind looking after Helmut whilst I am away. She said it would be alright with her but I had to see the boss first about him going to have his meals with the Irishmen. Well, I asked him last night and could see he didn't like the idea. Of course, I told him Helmut isn't able to look after himself. His answer was that Mrs Cooper has got enough work to do looking after the Irishmen. So Helmut won't have his meals there and has to get something himself.

I figured there was another reason for the boss refusing it. When I went for the milk tonight I asked Mrs C if she's seen the boss and how it stands now. So, of course, a bit of gossip and she told me all about it. On Monday night he went along with Pickwell's dart team to Oakham, 4 of the Irishmen belong to the team and they all went on a private bus. Of course, he had one over the eight and started trouble already at Oakham. A girl came to see one of the Irishmen and Helmut went outside, took the valves out the bike and the poor girl had to walk home about 3 miles. When one of the Irish fellow told him off about it he wanted to give him one on the nose. The others separated them and on the way back in the bus he started trouble again. They got him home safely and I woke up when he came in. He didn't notice me being awake. Twice he knocked the table over and fell down. In the morning he was sleeping on the floor beside his bed.

So, of course, they won't take him along again and won't have him at their quarters. It's his fault if he can't behave himself. Nothing to do with me. I am not his guardian and he's old enough himself to know what to do.

Well, my sweety, I'll say goodnight and God bless you. The next job is ironing a few things.

Be my good girl and think of me. I love you very very much.

All my love and kisses

Forever and only yours
Hans.

92 Wharf St
September 20th
My dearest darling Johannes
First of all I am very very sorry you have not heard before this week. Last night, as you know, I went to the 21st birthday and did not get home until late, then all today I have been too tired, I still am but I really can't leave it any longer. Thank you for your letter, it was waiting when I came home at lunchtime. I am glad you enjoyed yourself at the Christening. I hope our wedding goes through as quickly.

That handkerchief does belong to me, actually, it is my mothers, have you washed it with your things or have you waited to see who it belonged to.

Will you send the form on so that I can fetch the license, when is it you have to have another test?

I have been to Birstall this evening to see auntie and Gertie to make the last arrangements, Gertie is bringing her things here on Wednesday, it will not be long now 7 days more to go. I will go about the cars tomorrow. I rang up about having a bo (can't spell it) a bunch of flowers and it would cost £3.3.0 a bunch. I think that is throwing money away so I will have a spray of roses. I will go across to Adams for that. I think that is all I have to do. You will be pleased to know the vacancy for best man is filled, Cyril is going to be it. So there was any need for you getting on to me. I may as well warn you now, never hurry me up, you waste your time. I am sorry I shouted but you would not let me explain. I know what you meant, that it would not be fair to Charlie to ask him at the last minute, on the other hand I can not go around demanding other people to make up their minds. I would not have any friends left, after all it is they that are doing us the favour.

We have another wedding present 1 pair of sheets, 1 pair of pillow slips from Auntie and Gertie.

I have been everywhere to try to get some shoes, I could not see any I liked. I will go to Melton and have a look around.

I am in bed and would love something to eat, would you be a darling and fetch me something.

I almost forgot I am going to night school to learn German. Some of the girls at the office are going and I asked them what books they have. They have asked me to go tomorrow night with them so you see I do intend to learn.

I smacked Fred a little while ago. He went downstairs and has not come back, he has the puss to keep him company. We've a mouse somewhere so we have left him in so he can catch it.

Well darling I had better get some sleep so God bless.

All my love

Jean

Wednesday

And I'm still tired. I must have been born tired. I am not going to the German lesson tonight. There is a class on Tuesdays at another place and Tuesday will suit me better then if anytime I want to go to Melton on Wednesday I will be free. I forgot to tell you I won a prize at the party on Monday. To get it I did not have to do anything 12 girls had to sit on a chair then 12 men had to make a hat out of coloured paper. The girls had to parade in front of the judges, my hat was the best. I had a tablet of soap given to me.

I will close now and I am sorry you have not had a letter before.

All my love

Jean

My dearest darling

I am not going to post this to you because it is Thursday and if I posted it tomorrow you wouldn't receive it until Saturday morning and you will be here at lunchtime so I may as well save 2 1/2d (look after the pence the pounds will look after themselves).

I have been catching up with my correspondence this evening. I have written to Iris to congratulate her. I believe I did tell you she has a son. When Frances rang they were having to give it brandy and oxygen. It has started drinking at an early age. She has named him Philippe Taylor Giogetti, poor little devil. I wonder if he speaks French or Italian.

I have written to Muriel. I said I hope she was sitting down, I had a shock for her. It will be a shock when she reads that I am marrying a German!!! I saw Mrs Batt she is the telephonist at Corah's she is between the age of 50-60. I told her I was getting married. She said I hope you have thought about what you would do if there is another war? I told her I would not mind as long as the internment was in a big hotel or on Isle of Man. That is where most aliens were interned last time. You never need bother about me being upset about what people say to me marrying a German, I used to be but now it amuses me and I could not care less. I know it is not wrong to marry Germans, and who are others to judge whether it be right or wrong. I know we will be happy as long as we love each other like we do now.

We may not have anything to start with but just wait. That will be the day when we can drive up in our very modern car, I in a mink coat and a string of real pearls with a dress on as well with 4 kids in the back. That will be the day.

Did you have a first class dinner on Sunday my sugar plum? You wait. I will try to do that one day, first I must get myself a cookery book and a pair of scales.

I hope you see a difference in the bedroom, I cleaned them out last night and I gave our room a good polish. I also polished the floor so you had better be careful you do not slide in. I hope I do not untidy it before you have been on Sunday.

Well darling I am dead tired, I have been these past few days, it must be the weather, it has been very close. I will trot off and have a good night's sleep so that I am wide awake at the weekend.

On Sunday we will have a dress rehearsal that is if you want to see what I am wearing on the great day.

I love you very much and I hope I can make you a very happy husband.

Pickwell,
Sept 22nd 1949

My darling

I thank you so very much for your lovely long letter. It was a bit late but still better late than never. I really was very much waiting to know if you go home safe on Sunday night.

At first I thought they had drowned you in liquor and so you weren't able to write for a few days as I know you don't refuse a drink as I do. Never mind, my love, it's the main thing you enjoyed yourself and I'll be blessed you even won a prize. Of course you had to have the best hat as the loveliest girl always has the best things.

I am sure our wedding won't take long I bet we have to keep our ears open to get the right moment when saying 'I will'

The vicar certainly has got a good speed on. He must've heard something about jets.

I hope you got the form today and also got the license. The test is on Monday 5.30pm. Anyway it's just in time before we go away.

Believe me darling I would have loved to help you make all the arrangements. It was a lot for you and be sure I admire you doing it all on your own. About the bouquet, do as you think it's best. £3-3-0 is rather a lot, but I certainly wouldn't have minded because I want you to look your very best. What about the buttonholes? Do we arrange that later on?

Good thing the vacancy for the best man has been filled. That settles that. Don't let's mention the Sunday afternoon incident again. That's gone.

Nice the second present is. It looks as if we shan't have to worry about sheets and pillow slips when we have a house of our own.

So you are going to have German lessons. Good girl. I think that's the best way and I can help correcting you as I think it's good to get the correction from someone who speaks the language.

It's 8.00 and I'll get cracking.

Be good, my love

Always yours Hans.

Friday Sept 23rd 1949, 7.45pm

Hello my sweety. Everything alright, I hope. We certainly are getting nearer. It won't be long now. Just the weekend and 2 ½ days to go. I've arranged so you can take the eggs along tomorrow.

By now you'll have arranged the last things and all is set for the great day.

Today I was really busy. The boss asked me this morning if I possibly could get round cleaning out before I go away. This time I didn't say yes, but I'll see. So I got cracking this morning and at 4 o'clock this afternoon I had done 30 houses. It was close and I was perspirating all day long, my shirt wet through. I think I'll do it till Tuesday night.

Well, my darling, the water is boiling and I'll have a go. Be good till I see you tomorrow afternoon.

Remember I love you more than anything else in the world and hope it'll be Thursday soon.

Goodnight and God bless you.

All my love and kisses

Forever and only yours

Hans.

R 10/10.49   Weferlingen, 18.9.49

23/9.49

My dear Hans

I am writing to you today from Weferlingen, where we are

staying with Frau Lehmann's parents, who have very kindly allowed us to stay a few days. We arrived here last Friday evening and have to get on our way again tomorrow morning.

My dear boy, it is all very difficult for us at the moment. If only everything was behind us already. There's no going back to Aschersleben now. We left it behind us on Wednesday afternoon and managed to get over the border alright after a very strenuous experience. We went to Braunschweig first, where Horst had to collect a parcel which he had to sign for. Then he went back to his new boss who needed some help and afterwards we got a lift from a lorry driver. He took us along the motorway and drove 135 km to Uelzen, where the refugee camp is. The camp is overwhelmed with refugees. Only a few get registered, the others are turned back. Conditions are shambolic! We were so desperate that we wanted to go back again. We spent one night in the camp and went back to see his boss, who gave him a letter to say that Horst can start to work for him on the 15th. But, of course, we have no accommodation yet. I shall have to find out if grandma can put me up for a while in Ascheffel near Eckernförde. She lives in one room together with Werner. You may now ask 'why did you give up your home?' Yes, I agree, but in the R. zone all young men between the age of 18 and 25 have to do compulsory service in the Armed Police Force and you know what this means. I am sure you have heard about this on the news? Do I have to lose Horst as well? I would not be able to survive! How will everything work out for us? If Horst starts earning money from 15.10. things will start to get a little better. Lots of young men are coming over the border and again and again they are being sent back. Many of them are on the edge of despair. God might have mercy and make things better for us. We shall have to stay in the camp for ten to twelve days and if we are not registered by then, we don't know what will happen. We cannot go back again and winter is upon us. We must not think any further ahead.

Little by little our money will have been spent, and what then? What can we do without any finances? I must not dwell on things too much, it does not help. Perhaps grandma will put me up for a while!!! Frau Lehmann's parents and sister gave us a lot of moral support: 'Don't go back again under any circumstances'. If we did, what would become of Horst and me? We shall have to go through with it, however hard it is. If only you could be here with us and give us some encouragement! Apart from one crate and three parcels, all our possessions are here. We would not be able to return anything because we are running out of money. Please God stay by us and give us strength to get through this situation. Tomorrow we are going back to Braunschweig, again via the motorway, where we hope to hitch hike with a lorry back to the camp in Uelzen. I shall write to you again when we are there. Give my regards to Jean and your mother-in-law my dear boy, and to you we are sending our love and kisses. Your mum, who is always thinking about you, and your brother Horst.

Werner Schünemann
Ascheffel Krs Eckernförde
Holstein

Pickwell,
Sept 24th 1949,
9.30pm

My dearest, darling Jean,
Well, sweety, that was a short Sunday afternoon we had together. Just 4 hours. Still, my darling, it won't be long now, just 4 days to go.
Good thing it didn't happen to rain whilst I was shutting up. When I came back, it was as dark as inside a bag and I couldn't see a thing. I am just listening to "Round the Shows"

excerpt from "Annie get your Gun". Oh, it's smashing. Perhaps you're listening to it too.

Did you get home alright love? I hope so anyway. Did you know that last letter you'll get from me as Miss Jean Phillips. The next one will be addressed to Mrs J Klawitter. How do you like it? Not bad, is it? Well, sweety, I'll say goodnight and God bless.

I'll have another grapefruit and then off to bed. Stay well and pleasant dreams.

All my love and kisses
Forever yours Hans

Sunday night, 9.00

Hello, sweety, have you done your ironing? You certainly have been very busy today. What a shame you stayed at home today. It was lovely warm this afternoon. Yesterday, of course, it had to rain. The shutting up took me 2 hours tonight. Those blinking hens. It's always the same when we let them out for the first time. And funny, it usually falls in the week when it's my turn. Never mind, only two more nights to go and I couldn't care less who has the trouble afterwards and only hope all the empty houses have been filled up till I come back.

Did you notice we talked half an hour on the phone? Well, darling, draw as much spending money as you think will be alright. We'll manage alright. I meant something else and I am sure you understood me wrong when I said if the money was mine (in the bank) I would draw £50. I'll tell you on Wednesday what I meant. I would've a reason for drawing that much.

Never mind, sweety, all will be alright after Thursday. Then we won't have anything else to worry about than not missing our meals. I know you'll be glad when it's all over. Does that include our honeymoon? I hope not. I wish it would last at least 365 days. Just the two of us at faraway places. It'll be our first, but in no case the last, trip. I hope many more will

349

follow.

I've just got a German station on. Wouldn't it be lovely to sit in our own house on the settee. There isn't much more to do for me till Wednesday. Just keep working and do my washing tomorrow night. It's in soak already. Of course I'll wash my hair on Tuesday and have a good wash myself.

In case any letters from my mother arrive here I'll leave Helmut a few stamps so he can send them on to Bournemouth as I like to know how she got on.

Well, my love, I'll go to bed, thinking and dreaming of you and our great day. Believe me I love you so very very much. Goodnight and God bless you.

Till Wednesday all my love and kisses

      Forever and only yours

      Hans.

Pickwell,
Sept 29 th
1949

My sweet little wife

Well, darling when you read this letter everything will be over and we on the way to London. How do you feel? I hope it won't be too much of a strain to you. Anyway, sweety. I thank you very very much for all the lovely hours we have been able to spend together till now. Believe me I enjoyed every single one of them. It was a dark time as a POW but still it didn't matter as I always looked forward to those hours and then life was much easier. Now my only wish has been fulfilled and herewith I promise you always to be your loving husband and a good father to our children.

Now will enjoy our honeymoon and when we come back I'll have to get cracking and put some of the money back in the bank. Just in case, darling. And, of course, we shall want some for our first holidays abroad next year.

Well, my darling, I'll close now. It's only supposed to be a short one.

I shall always love you
Only yours

Hans.

Hans and Jean's wedding, and honeymoon in London and
Bournemouth

THE LONDON COLISEUM

EMILE LITTLER'S

ANNIE GET YOUR GUN

PRODUCTION AND CHOREOGRAPHY BY
HELEN TAMIRIS

MUSIC AND LYRICS BY IRVING BERLIN
BOOK BY HERBERT AND DOROTHY FIELDS
THE RODGERS AND HAMMERSTEIN
NEW YORK MUSICAL SUCCESS PRESENTED
BY ARRANGEMENT WITH CHAPPELL AND CO. LTD.

DIRECTION AND LIGHTING BY
CHARLES HICKMAN

Charles the Second

Theatre Royal
Drury Lane

Oklahoma !

6ᵈ

This design is copied from the original
Charter granted by King Charles II to
Thomas Killigrew in 1663 the original
document is still in existence.

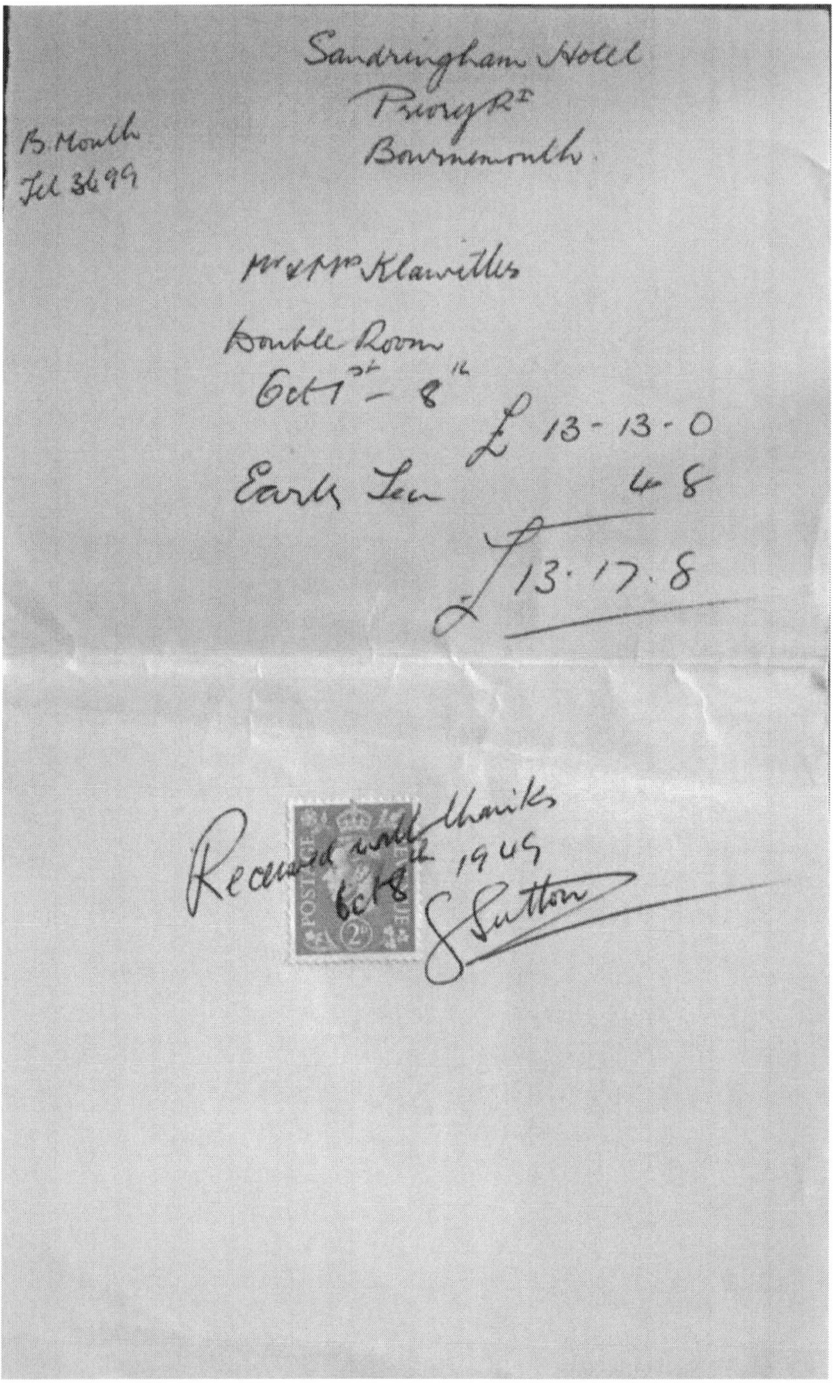

Sandringham Hotel
Priory Rd
Bournemouth.

B.Mouth
Tel 3699

Mr & Mrs Klawitters

Double Room
Oct 1st – 8th
                    £   13 - 13 - 0
Early Tea   4 8
                    £ 13 · 17 · 8

Received with thanks
Oct 8th 1949
E Sutton

Weferlingen, 25.9.49

8/10.49

My dear Hans

We have left the refugee camp in Uelzen and did not get registered. They sent back literally thousands and only allowed politically persecuted refugees. However, nobody goes back to the Russian zone once there. I'd like to know how they can survive and cope with the forthcoming winter. Horst has tried so hard to get a room which has not been confiscated but no luck. Tomorrow he will go out looking again. If he can't find anything, it means we shall have to go back to Aschersleben this week. Dear Hans, you cannot imagine how we feel. Our nerves have been exhausted and tested to the limit. Day and night I am sweating with fear. I don't know what will become of us. If only somebody could help us! I am so sorry that I have to burden you with all my troubles on your wedding day but to whom else can I open my heart? All this is too heavy for me to bear! Our possessions arrived in good condition and it looks now that we shall have to send them all back. However, it is not as easy to send crates and parcels back from here to the Russian zone as it was to have them shipped and posted from East to West. The only thing we can do is to send them from here to the Western sector in Berlin and from there they need to be collected. But where will we find the money for all this? Oh my dear boy, how did our lives get turned upside down into such turmoil? We weren't too badly off until the job offer came along from Braunschweig, and then there is the (seven-year) compulsory national service. All this has ended up in nothing but sorrow and grief apart from my strong wish to meet up with you and Jean one day, If only I knew what to do! Mrs Lehman's parents and daughter are strictly against us going back. We are now up the creek without a paddle. What we could do with is some really good advice.

We want to wish you all the very best on your wedding day.

This comes from the bottom of our hearts. We shall be with you in thought, my dears. May God bless you both. Write to us as soon as you can to this address. Should we not be here anymore, the post will be forwarded.

Now, for today I want to finish my letter and send you and Jean both our love and kisses, Your mum and your brother Horst. We are looking forward to a healthy reunion. Did you receive our registered package?

H. Schünemann
Bei (c/o) Robert Hensel
20 b Weferlingen
Über Wolfenbüttel b. Braunschweig

Pickwell,
Oct 9th 1949

My sweet little wife,

Well, darling, in a few minutes you'll be at home. It's 9.40 now. I arrived back here just after 9.00. There's one thing I want to tell you. I hate this place like nothing else in the world. It's so quiet and I am lonely. We've had a taste how nice it could be. Still, let's hope it isn't for long that we have to be separated. We'll save hard for a while and I'll see if I can find anything around here. If not, well, it looks as if I have to get a job somewhere near Leicester so that we may be able to lead a normal married life.

Well, my sweetheart, be good and look after yourself. I'll write more tomorrow when I've done my first day's work.

Goodnight darling and I love you more than anything else in the world. Sure? Yes! How sure? Quite sure! So, all my love and kisses to you. God bless you.

<u>Monday Oct 10th 8.00pm</u>

Hello, my darling, how are you? Fine I hope. Did you get home safe last night? With a bit of luck I should get a letter in the morning. Keep my fingers crossed, anyway. Oh, sweety, I am lonely. I am so used to being with you that I can't be on my own any longer.

The first days' work has gone down alright. I feel a bit tired, but not done in. After all it wasn't watercarting today, but cleaning out. Of course I didn't get as much as usually done, but that's only because I talked too much finding out the news.

Now my report. The farm still stands at the same place as before. You'll have noticed that yourself I guess. But something else now. The new chap is leaving on Saturday morning as he's found a better place. He told me he had a nice little row with the boss as he gave his notice. Still he insists on leaving. That means the cottage will be empty again and to be honest I am after it. Some people here have asked me already if the boss has offered it to me as I am married now and as good as anybody else on the farm. Of course he hasn't yet, but I did let people know that if he doesn't offer it, I might consider finding a place with a cottage somewhere else. I know he gets to know it somehow and I shall see how he reacts. It really wouldn't be fair if he doesn't ask me. Don't you agree? I am no fool to be pushed aside every time it comes vacant. Now still something else. I spend some money and hope you aren't mad with me. I bought a bike (pushbike) and a bath from the new chap. The bike is in a very good condition, 3 speed gears, dynamo and lamp, pump. Price £2. The bath is a metal bungalow one, full size. Price £1. It is almost new as he's only bought it when he came here a few months ago. I thought of us that is if we get the cottage we shall want one in the other case you also haven't got one at home. Am I a clever boy or not? Tonight I started shutting up straight the way to put some overtime in. It isn't too bad now I have got the bike. It only took me 1 ¼ hours starting at 6.15.

Well, my darling, how did you get on at the office? It takes some getting used to again, doesn't it? My back ached quite a bit by the time I finished. Did you put your name down alright? I am sure you remembered alright.

Everybody here was joking. 'Long Harry' or rather 'John' asked me if I feel weak in my knees after the weeks holiday. He said he heard the boss telling the poultryman to give me a 'taxidrivers' (easy!) job for the first day. We had a good laugh. I shan't get my holiday pay before Friday as they haven't had my timesheet in for last week. That'll make it a bit more on Friday.

This morning I put a mousetrap down and when I came back for breakfast the first one was in. At midday I found the second one. Now I am waiting for the next one. No more yet.

Well, my darling, I'll say goodnight. It's 9.00 and I have to write to my mother. Be my best girl and look after yourself. A good night kiss to you. Please give my regards to Mamma. God bless you.

> All my love and a thousand kisses
> Only yours
> Hans.

92 Wharf St

Oct 10th 1949

My dearest darling,

Did you miss me last night? I was very lonely no one to put my cold feet on or to get close to if I was frightened. I missed my Pappa so much did Pappa miss Jeannie

How did work go down for you? I am getting used to it once more. Everything is upside down here, some of the offices are changing round. Labour and Hostel are going to Phoenix Bldgs, Machinery is coming into Labour. You should hear some of the remarks that have been passed to me today such as "How do you like it" "What do you think of it" and so on. It is very embarrassing it should die down in a few days.

The office I'm in now is not too bad, though I miss the company. I get a few visitors in. I have not anyone to argue with. Lucy has been across twice. Margery and Arthur once Nancy is coming sometime this afternoon. There is one thing being on my own I am able to write to you so you may have this in the morning.

It seems a terrible long afternoon. My!!! I have just had a rush Well darling, I did intend you to have this tomorrow, but there it is I did not post it, but you will have one Wednesday and a longer one at that. I have been busy this evening. I feel done in. Mamma did the washing this morning. I told her to leave it when I got home at lunch time she had done it, was my face red, may be she did not notice but still it does not matter if she did we have that slip of paper. I thought I had better have a go at ironing, and believe me I had only done 4 handkerchiefs and doing your white shirt I was fed up already I could have thrown the iron out of the door, but I kept going until I was nearly asleep then my mother finished them off. I probably would have been up all night doing it. I think I had better learn housekeeping before I learn German. Well darling, I thank you for such a wonderful holiday. I hope we can always be as happy together. I can't say how much I love you much much more than anything else I thank you too for being so good to me. I hope that I can be as good to you. I will try.

I did not have to sign my name in the book this morning, but when I received my wages and had to sign the slip I put Phillips I manage to do the other right. It will take a bit of getting used to.

I will have to close, I'm nearly asleep. I wish I had someone to cuddle to.

Be a good boy

All my love and

Kisses

Your wife
Jeannie

Pickwell

Oct. 12<u>th</u> 1949

My sweetest, little Wife,

Thank you so very much for your letter. I wasn't lucky enough ~~this~~ yesterday morning, was I? Believe me I was longing for the letter. Oh, Jeannie, Pappa is so lonely. Nobody to cuddle up to and nobody to put arms around me. I got so used to and it didn't take me long to fall asleep. Last night I lay awake for an hour. Daddie loves his Jeannie so very, very much.

Don't worry about the funny remarks that have been past on to you. It's the same here, but everybody who gives funny remarks, ~~gives~~ gets a much funnier one back. Up to now I've always been the laughing side. Though, it has died down already. Well, now you'll have plenty of time, writing to me.

There's one thing I can't understand. Time goes so awful slow. A day seems like a week. Anyway, only 2 ½ more days to go till I see you again.

So Mamma did the washing. I would've loved to see the red face. Don't matter darling. If anybody says anything show them that little piece of paper.

Never worry about the housework. I'll give you a hand where ever I can. Remember when I was on leave and did the ironing for all of us. I can't say I got fed up with it. So there you are. If you do the washing, I'll do the ironing!!! Don't for heavens sake, throw my iron outside.

I also want to thank you so very much for the lovely holiday. I enjoyed everything. We'll always be as happy as we were since we are married. I'll do my best, believe me. I shall always be good, very good, to you.

Now about the house. The boss stopped me this morning

and said "you'll have heard about Mr Warwick leaving and so the house becomes vacant". I said "yes, I was waiting for you to say something" well, after quarter of an hour he was far enough in explaining to let me know we certainly have to have somebody in his place. So he said "even if I give you the cottage one good man like you can only do one man's work". Of course, that's that and you needn't be afraid of leaving your mother and stopping work. He's still trying to get a house for me and said he wouldn't like anything than getting me a house and see me settling down. Still that's only talk. I know him by now.

I hope you got over those "horrible German lessons" alright. Nevermind, darling, bring your books along on Saturday and I'll see what I can do for you!!

My mice catching-business goes alright. I've caught 7 within the last 3 days. Isn't that a record? I haven't seen any since lunchtime. They are getting rare now. Bonzo is on my knee. He asked me to give his regards to you.

I have just finished our dinner. It's only milk soup with raisins. There isn't enough time to do anything before shutting up for I have to leave at 6.10 p.m. Today I went cleaning out again. My back wasn't half aching. Nevermind I have to get used to again. The new chap was going to bring the bath over at 8.00, but he hasn't turned up yet. It's 8.45. Well, he'll be busy packing.

Helmut has gone to Melton again to those funny meetings. It looks as if the people are successful in reforming him. I didn't think anybody could

Well, my sweetheart, I'll have something to eat now. I haven't had anything to eat since midday. So I feel mighty hungry.

Please give my regards to Mamma.

You be a good girl and look after yourself. I'll ring you to-morrow night if all goes well.

Good night and God Bless you.

Your ever loving husband

Hans.

1. <u>P.S.</u>

When I went shutting up last night I had to seat down half way round. My poor foot!

I have also painted my bike for the first time tonight. It'll get the finishing touch next week when I don't have to go out on it at night. Love Hans.

2. <u>P.S.</u>

Please, don't forget the snaps and wedding photo's when coming on Saturday and dog biscuits. Remember our second anniversary? More love Hans.

92 Wharf St

Oct 13th

My darling Husband

I have been for my lesson in German and I honestly don't know where I am with it. I do my best to keep up with them, I can't understand. So please darling help me I feel such a fool and I really do want to learn. I am going to the person's home on Monday for a lesson.

I am glad you have bought a bicycle, you were a very good boy. Have you had a bath yet?

I'm glad you have caught that horrible mouse, my mother had in her bedroom last night. Fortunately it did not pay me a visit I would have died.

I have had a good wash and put my pins in. I wish I had someone to fetch the pins out again I am ready for bed.

So my darling I will have to say good night and God Bless you

From your very
loving wife
Jeannie

Wednesday

Here I am again. Isn't it a beautiful morning? I have the window wide open (I'm writing at the office now) the sun is shining in, this office is really better than down below but I miss the laughs and arguments that we all used to have. Lucy has just rung me to read a letter she had from a pal in the army. We usually manage to ring each other at least 4 times a day and talk for about ½ an hour. I do not know what we find to talk about, but never seem to have finished our conversation off.

Nancy is not getting on too well at home, so they (her and her husband) are going to buy a house if they can get one, within reason. They answered an advertisement in the paper. A cottage at Desford, on Monday night they went to see it. Nancy said it was lovely, but the owner wants over £2000 for it. So that was the end of a cottage in Desford.

I am sunbathing at the moment. I could almost do with my glasses on, the sun is so strong.

I have just remembered it is our second wedding (2 weeks) tomorrow. Are you glad you married me? Do you still love? - are you sure? - how sure?-. As for Jeannie she is <u>very</u> sure that she loves Pappa.

cheeri'O

Love all of it

Jean

Pickwell

Oct. 13<u>th</u> 1949

My sweetest, little Wife,

I thank you so very much for your letter. Don't despair about the lessons darling, I certainly will give you a hand. It won't be long before you're the one at the top.

I am glad you approve of my buying that bicycle. I've painted it and though the colour looks funny it looks quite decent. You'll see on Saturday. You know Friday is the day I have a good wash, so instead it'll mean a bath tomorrow night. Still, I don't know yet, where I shall get all the hot water from. All the saucepans, kettle and bucket will have to do.

You'll be surprised to hear that I've catched another 2 mice, making it up to 9. Not bad, is it? I am surprised myself as I expected perhaps two or three.

The weather was lovely this afternoon. Of course I went cleaning out. Got on with it alright. If only my back wouldn't ache so much. Before I never felt anything at all. Just like a rubberback it was and now it's stiff. Never mind it'll make me keep my shoulders back. I sure had a look at my watch at 10.30 a.m. today and was thinking how it was 2 weeks ago. Isn't it a long time? Married two weeks already. And no family yet!!! I <u>am</u> glad I married you yes - yes - quite sure!! (do you understand the code)?

Another question! Are you glad you married me and are you satisfied with Papa? I hope the answer is yes.

This morning I also had a letter from my mother posted at Aschersleben (Russ. Zone) that means they are back. She told me how everything went. It's awful. Now once again they are homeless without a penny as they spend almost all the money on the trip to the British Zone and the time they were there. On our wedding day they had to go back. I'll show it to you on Saturday.

You poor little darling have been waiting for my call tonight and nothing happened. I am sorry darling, but it wasn't my fault. I was back here in the yard at 4.50. Enough time to fill the tractor up and be at the phonebox by 5.00. Still just as I was filling up the boss asked me if I would run up to the far field with the trailer and bring four crates of cockerels out there to be put into the houses tonight, also by me. I didn't say anything, but ~~it~~ I was mad. It was 5.45 when I got back. And at 6.15 I went shutting up, got back 8.00 p.m.. Dinner tonight was potatoe pancakes. I certainly enjoyed it. The only trouble is, it's so awful late when I get something to eat. Nothing from midday till 8.30 p.m. Never mind, as long as I get something at all it's alright.

Well, my sweetheart, I'll say goodnight and God bless you. I am ready for bed for I can't keep my eyes open any longer. 10.15 p.m. I'll think of this time a fortnight ago.

Be good my sugarplum and look after yourself. I'll try my best to do the same.

Thinking only of you I give you
     All my love and kisses
          Your very loving husband
                    Hans.

R 15/10.1949   Aschersleben, 1.10.1949
                    13/10.1949

Hedwig Schünemann

My dear Hans and Jean,

You will now be astonished to receive post from us from Aschersleben again. Yes, it is sad but true, there was no alternative for us, other than to return, even though it is so difficult for us. I did, after all, write to you twice from Weferlingen. We tried everything we could to get accommodation but unfortunately, all was in vain. Horst's manager could have made a bit more effort about it as well, but the main point is, that when you're at rock bottom no-one cares about you any more.

You can probably imagine how we feel. But if we had stayed a few more weeks over there, we would have lost our rights to residency over here and what would have become of us then?

So then on Wednesday evening at about 10 o'clock (on the evening before your wedding day) we left Weferlingen and set off on our way. Frau Lehmann's sister came with us right away, as she wanted to visit Frau Lehmann. At half past one we began our march from Schoeningen. There was such a thick fog and after one and a half hours we had to turn back because we couldn't orientate ourselves any more and didn't know where we were. After a long trek we came to an

English check-point where the man told us about the route along the railway line. By five past five in the morning, after an awful lot of effort, we nearly reached the border.

Three times I fell so heavily because of my heavy rucksack, that the impact completely tore my stockings and I was bathed in sweat. Once we were standing at the water's edge, it was a mystery as to how we were going to get across with our heavy baggage. Horst summoned up all his courage, took his shoes and socks off, rolled up his trousers and then carried me through the gurgling water. Then it meant I had to climb up the opposite bank, which I did, scrabbling like a pig.

I was now standing in the Russian Zone, and Horst and Frau Fuchs were still in the English zone. Then Horst managed to get the baggage over and I took it from him, with my heart in my mouth that at any moment they could catch us. Horst was groaning with pain, his feet were so badly cut, as glass shards and barbed wire were lying in the water.

Then we picked up our things and went at a pace to the railway station, anxious always about our few belongings. Just as, with relief, we arrived at the station, we found that the train had left 10 minutes before. At that point we felt really beaten, the next train was not due till half past three in the afternoon.

Because of the police we couldn't stay at the railway station. So we had to hurry on another 3 Km further and could hardly manage it. It was such cold, foggy weather. Our thoughts were continually with you, because it was your wedding day. When we could go no further, we sat beside a ditch at the side of the road. Then the sun burst through and the weather became lovely and warm.

Just at the time when you were being married, we sat in prayer and so were able to experience everything in our thoughts with you. Then we got a few jacket-potatoes from a woman, and had them with salted herring and for pudding, a pot of water as dessert. That was our wedding feast. At half past three our journey then continued.

At about half past eleven we arrived at Aschersleben. We went to Horst's friends, the von Hoffs, who warmly took us in. All our acquaintances were very pleased to see us back there again. We are now destitute, in spite of my sending a telegram – on 16th September, the second day after we had to leave here - saying that we would have to come back. Early yesterday morning I was promptly at the Housing Office and described our plight to the men, regretting our ill-considered step. They were all very pleasant to me, though couldn't at that point offer us any help. I am to go back again on Monday. If only it would all come right.

Horst must now get a job straight away again, so that he can earn something as, in one fell swoop, we have lost the money we saved so carefully and we will have to start from the beginning all over again. Oh, it is so bitter when you get into such a desperate situation all through your own fault, and, especially as we only wanted to do what was best, so that if you were to come and visit us, we could offer you a little piece of Heimat*.

We had no idea that everything would become such a cruel failure. We have one bed and we have brought a large part of our clothing back here again, but we had to leave all our household items and crockery behind, we can't simply post it. Today all my limbs still feel as if they are shattered. I'm not able to carry anything heavy and now I have enormous agony from carrying the heavy rucksack … I hope it doesn't have any bad consequences.

While writing, I want to thank you warmly, my dear Hans, for your two lovely letters of 4th and 5thSeptember 1949, which we found waiting for us when we got back here. I hope, from the bottom of my heart, that you had a really wonderful honeymoon. Write to us as soon as you can, we love hearing from you. For today, I shall now end my letter. With much love and kisses from your mum and from your brother and brother-in-law Horst.

I should pass on to you warmest congratulations on your marriage from Uncle Erich and family and Aunt Erna, Uncle Gustav and family and Edith and her husband, Erna Schüne- mann and Grandma and Werner, not forgetting Frau Leh- mann, the von Hoff family and the Ziemann family as well. Best wishes to your mother. Did our little parcel for your wedding arrive at all ? I sent it on 12.9.1949.

It's very likely to be a cruel winter for us, without any sup- plies and without any adequate heating. But worrying and grieving is no help. I have lost a lot of weight again. But, after all, the main thing is that we stay in good health. Once again, much love from your Mum.

* Home

Pickwell
Oct. 14th 1949

My sweet, little wife,

Are you waiting to get a few lines tomorrow afternoon? Well then, here you are. How are you today, my darling? Fine, I hope and let me tell you I am so much longing/long- ing so much for tomorrow afternoon to see you again. Time seemed to have stopped on Monday morning last. Never be- fore a week went as slow as this last one. Anyway I am glad it's only a few more hours to go.

How are things going at Leicester? Has the joking at the office died down? I hope so and also hope you've taken my advice in giving a good answer to every remark passed.

I felt a bit done in tonight. It really was a rush these last two days. Tonight again I went shopping at 5.00, and came back at 5.50. Ten minutes later I had to leave again- shutting up. Back at 7.45, I did the meat, washed my hair and had a "bath". It was smashing and I really feel clean now. The shutting up took such a longtime because we got 30 new cockerels and I have to count them every night as they are very valuable. 10

guinea each.

Believe it or not I've caught mouse no.10. That's a record, isn't it. I'll put the trap up again tonight just to make sure I've got them all.

Well, my sweetest, as it is 9.45 Papa is off to bed. Be a good girl, good night and pleasant dreams. God bless you.

> Till tomorrow all my love (sure,-quite sure-)
> And thousand kisses
> From your ever loving husband
> Hans.

Saturday 4.45 p.m.

Papa has hurried up and run nearly all the way to get back early. I was back at 3.50, but no Jeannie here. A minute ago I went up and had a look on the bus, but again nothing. So what else can I do than wait and be so disappointed as I'm looking so much forward to this afternoon.

Well, I hope you'll be on the 5.20 from Melton. The tea is ready since 4 o'clock.

Love Hans.

Saturday, 7.45 p.m.

Well, my sweetest, here I am back from shutting up. I received your telegram at 5.15 just when I was on my way to have a look at the 5.20 bus from Melton. Mr Cooper came and told me. He said something like: have you got a mother-in-law at Leicester? (Funny question, anyway). So I said yes. Well, he replied, message has just come through, she's in bed with a cold. I asked who and then he said "Jean". Of course then I knew what he meant. At first I thought Mamma was ill and you wanted to stop home. I would've rung you after that bus had been through. When you weren't here when I came back I thought you'd been window shopping at Melton and missed the bus.

Well, darling it'll be a very dull weekend if you have to stop in bed tomorrow, too. I wish I could be with you now and comfort you, get the tea, supper and wait on you. I'll be quite honest, Jeannie, I am fed up with working here and you being at home. I've made up my mind it won't be long before I am leaving here. If I can get hold of the newspaper man on Monday morning I shall ask him to bring me "The Stockbreeder" on Tuesday and from then on I shall be on the lookout for a job as tractor driver somewhere near Leicester. Then I'll be able to be at home with you every night. That, of course, if Mamma doesn't mind me living over there. I'll have to ask her when I come over next weekend. What do you think about changing the place? Warwick told me yesterday there are lots of vacancies in "The Stockbreeder" especially for tractor and caterpillar drivers. So I'll have a go. Wouldn't it be nice if I could seat on the bedside and read a book to you or have our wireless upstairs and listen to the nice music? It won't be long, darling.

How did you get your cold? I only hope it'll be better by tomorrow morning so you can come over tomorrow afternoon. I am longing for you, darling. It wouldn't have taken much and I would've come over on the bike tonight after shutting up. It only takes 2 hours, but it would've been against the wind all the way and perhaps raining in the morning. If I don't have to shut up I would come over tomorrow afternoon just to see you.

Well, my lovely, I'll say goodnight now. It's bedtime. You promised me to look after yourself, but it almost looks as if I had better do that for you.

In case you don't turn up tomorrow I'll write a few more lines so you at least have a letter Monday morning. Be good, my love, and get better soon. I love you more than anything else in the world.

All my love and kisses from your ever loving husband.

Sunday Oct 16th1949 4.15 p.m.
Well, my sweetheart, it looks as if you had to stay in bed for another day. This place be damned. I have to seat here and

you are ill. See if I had a motor bike now it wouldn't take me long to be with you. Still, I haven't got one so I have to stay here. If I could only find somebody to go shutting up for me tonight. I would come over on my pushbike and go back in the morning. Gordon and the poultryman have gone out and Doris has to do the second half shutting up. It will be too late when I come back (7.45) Ah! It's a blinking nuisance, and I am definitely going to have some alterations made.

How do you feel today, darling? I hope it's much better than it was yesterday. I've just been to fetch the milk and had my tea, but no appetite without you. Another long week to go before I shall see you. It's awful, darling. Poor Bonzo and no dog biscuits, poor me and nothing to smoke, still never mind, I had to make it last the previous week and I didn't spend the 2/7 s I had left last Sunday. No smoking on Friday was alright, too.

Bonzo was a good boy this afternoon. I saw a nice big rabbit coming across the next field and showed it to him. He went across the fence and finished it off. I hoped you were here and could've taken it along.

Well, my sweet, little wife, I'll close now. It's getting on for 6 o'clock. I have to get going to earn some more money for my little love. Be good, and, darling, promise me to look after yourself more. Please give my regards to Mamma.Sure-yes-how sure- quite sure.

Goodnight now and God bless you always.

> All my love and kisses etc.
>> Forever and only your
>> Ever loving husband.
> Hans.

> 92 Wharf St

> Oct

My dearest darling

I am so very sorry I could not come but I felt so bad I couldn't have got there. I ~~went~~ have not felt too well since Wednesday. I went to Birstall Wed. and I came straight to bed (I had tummy ache) my mother brought me a drop of Brandy. I was alright Thursday apart from every time I spent 1d. Friday morning I had some einmers that just about finished me off. I went to bed early Friday, got to go to work Sat, I felt so bad that I came back to bed. I had a terrible headache I stuck it as long as I could, in the finish I took two aspirins and I felt a lot better then. I feel a lot better today. I still keep getting headaches but it goes and my back still aches. You should have heard Lucy when I told her I had back ache. I told her she need not apply for my job it was not that, she said having your visitor was not always a sure sign.

I was worried yesterday about letting you know. The phone next door was out of order, they could receive calls but not make them. So I had to wait until Betty came and she was late 4.30. Then to top that Coopers phone no. was not in the directory. Betty got the dog biscuit and I have the cigarettes. I still have no end to do. I have to go to the Ministry of Health to have my name changed, also to stop paying N.H. the only benefit you get by paying is sick pay which does not affect me unless I'm away more than 3 month and unemployment, do you think I had better that just in case.

I was so lonely yesterday I hope I would be able to come in the afternoon I was hoping to come today but I have been so hot my mother said I would be silly to get out of bed. Poor Mamma keeps struggling upstairs and you know how she likes that on her knees. You won't need your glass on to read this, you see I am lying down and looking sideways. Please forgive me for not coming my darling. I will have to see how I am in the morning If I don't feel any better I will have to have the doctor. I am only allowed 2 days without certificate.

Your very loving wife who must be misses you so very much
Jean

92 Wharf St

Oct 17th 1949

My dearest.

I certainly have missed you this weekend. I am sorry you had to let your tea get cold, but I could not let you know sooner. I am pleased to tell you that I am feeling a lot better today, but I have to stay in bed until Wednesday when the doctor calls again. You will never guess what I have wrong with me Oh dear, dear me. Cystitis to do with the badder, but that's not all. When he asked me my full name I told him I had changed it, he asked me how long, then he said "that accounts for it" it is what is termed honeymoon cystitis. Asked me quite a few embarrassing questions. Was my face red. You never need worry about me staying in bed if I feel well I hate it when I feel ill. I was just about fed up yesterday afternoon, if I laid down I had a terrible headache if I sat up the headache went, but my back ached. I took two aspirins with a cup of hot milk just before my mother went out, by 10.0 I was ringing wet though aspirins always do that to me. One thing darling you can console yourself with not seeing me this weekend, that is being in bed all day I did not sleep too well and you would have missed your beauty sleep. I made the best of it. Susan fetched me some grapes yesterday. So what with drinking water and eating grapes I managed to keep my thirst down.

I hope you will be able to read this I have been nearly standing on my head. Fred has just been in to see me. He has been a good boy, he brought the paper up this morning, then when your letter came Mamma put it in his collar he shook his head and out it came, upstairs he came to me, Mamma called I sent him down he wondered what was wrong. The second time was ok. I keep writing a bit then have a rest. Susan will be here in a minute I will ask her to post it.

Fancy you thinking I was window shopping in Melton you should know that only takes 15 mins.

Darling I will leave it to you about leaving Pickwell but darling I should not mention or hint about it to anybody. It is

377

a pity you can't get the stock Breeder from somewhere else. I know darling I don't have to tell you, but I thought I had better mention it. Even if you are leaving, don't do like most do and start throwing your weight about or tell people what they can do, because you may never know what you may want them.

I have now got to write to Lucy to send the certificate and to the German woman. I will have to sit up for that.

    Always and forever your loving wife
    Jeannie

                        Pickwell
                        Oct. 17th 1949

My sweetest, little wife,

I thank you so very much for your nice letter. Believe me I was so much waiting for a few lines from you, though I've been speaking to Betty and Mamma. You'll understand I wanted to hear from you yourself.

It's alright about not coming last weekend. You know I rather see you getting well again soon ~~in spite~~ than coming over here and being worse afterwards. Last night I asked Mr Gudger if he knew the train to and from Leicester. In the course of conversation I mentioned my wife was ill, but he didn't offer his motorbike to go along on. He, of course, didn't know what it means to me to know you're ill and I have to stop here.

Well, my sweetheart, I've just been speaking to Mamma and know you have to stay in bed till Wednesday. You'll be alright on Saturday and I'll be with you for a day. What a nuisance. This isn't the married life I've been thinking about. And I am going to change the situation into what it should be like. I'll find a place alright that'll suit me and is near enough to Leicester to come home every night if there isn't a cottage with it.

I hope you are not too lonely, my darling. I sure am. I missed the weekend with you, in fact I missed you every single minute since we came back. Well, sweetheart it won't be long before the changes are made.

Do you think it's worth paying N.H? Even unemployment won't affect you. If you get out of work before the next 12 months are over, you'll stop at home and look after Papa. Won't you rather do that than sitting at the switchboard?

I received a form from the Inspector of taxes day before yesterday. I'll bring it along Saturday as I have to have your work no.

Monday's gone. I've had one of those jobs this morning I like very much. In fact, I went feeding in the big field (tractor and trailer) and had to pick cockerels out as well. It was 11 o'clock when I got back for my breakfast.

That'll be all for the day. Mamma told me you've sent a letter today so I'll be lucky in the morning. Be good, my darling and keep thinking of the nice time ahead of us.

Goodnight and God bless you always. I love you more than anything else in the world and miss you very very much For tonight

      All my love and thousand kisses
        Forever your loving husband
    Hans.

    92 Wharf St
    Oct 18th

My dearest darling
Here I am once again still in the same place and by the look of the weather I think it is the best place. It has just been tipping it down. I hope it has not been doing it at Pickwell or my poor little sugar plum will get wet Come and get in bed with me we will see if we can cure my cystitis the same way I got it!!!

Thank you very much for your letter for a moment this lunchtime I was disappointed I thought there was not one for me Mamma said the postman had come, she went in the shop to fetch it, then she said one from the football pools my heart sank, then she said to Fred " Come on are you going to take it up" I don't know what his answer was. I called him and up he came with your letter. I was pleased to see him.

Did you really expect Mr Gudger to say "here Johnny boy take my bike and use my petrol ration" you poor darling. But I don't suppose he cares whether I'm ill or not anymore than if you care what Mrs Gudgers health is. There is another thing you have not a driving license or an insurance policy. You would need that on a motorbike. Think of poor little me and Johnny. I'm beginning to think we may be three, anyway time will tell.

I was hoping Betty would be coming so she would take this to the P.O. or rather Susan but it is raining hard and if it keeps on I doubt very much whether she will come.

Where do you get (or have) a work number. I have never heard of it, I guess I must have one if you want it.

It is Tuesday and I should be going to have a German lesson. I also should have gone last night to the teachers home. I ought to have written to apologise yesterday but could not find the energy. You know how you told me to say ich. Well the girl at work the one I went with, was saying that while I was away the teacher told her it wasn't the way you said it, but ish. It was a good job she did not tell me. Do you think she might not be German? Or maybe she thinks it would take far too long to teach the whole class (14) to say it the right way. Look what a job you have with me.

I have been meaning to tell you I am not Mrs Jean Klawitter but Mrs Johannes Klawitter. When you put the first it is when you are addressing a widow, so I should put J Klawitter. I don't suppose it really would matter, but we may as well do things right.

Susan has come so she can take this down to the P.O.

Darling don't despair we will be together soon. Don't do anything in a rush, look around. I can't go on forever. I always

love you
 All my love kisses
And everything else
　　Jeannie

　　　___.

Pickwell

Oct. 18th 1949

My sweetest, little wife,

Thank you so very much for your letter. Don't worry, sweety, my tea didn't get cold on Saturday. Everything was ready, except for the tea.

I am glad to hear that you feel much better now. To think that I am the cause of your illness makes me feel so low and ashamed. I am sorry darling and I promise only to make you happy. It certainly won't happen again. You poor, poor girl answering his embarrassing questions. I bet you felt very uncomfortable. I wish he had asked me about it, not you. The name of the illness itself doesn't mean anything to me. What exactly is it?

I really am sorry you had to go through with all this. Never mind if I wouldn't have got my beauty sleep last weekend. I just wanted to be near you and see that you're comfortable and have everything you wanted. Shake the pillow up for you and just comfort you etc. now I'll have to wait till Saturday.

I got "the Stockbreeder" today. There wasn't much in it this time except 2. One was an assistant to a farmyard manager. With modern bungalow (bath) and garden. Doesn't say where, it's only a code no: the second one is: Young married gent, anxious to learn farming, excellent old-world cottage. Mansfield The Grange, Ashby -de- la- zouch.

Do you think it would be worth having a good look at the Leicester Evening Mail for vacancies near Leicester? Be on the look-out, darling. Of course if there's anything worth trying I'll have to be quick. Or what do you think of putting an advert into the Stockbreeder? I think that wouldn't be a bad idea.

I've been asked a few times if I get the cottage. As my answer was "no", people always said: "we can't blame you if you leave, then he'll (the boss) have to look for 2 new men instead of one. You ought to be the next one on the list for a house". And I agree if he doesn't appreciate my work and thinks I like to live in a stable all my life, well he's had it.

Don't ~~be~~ worry, I won't start telling people off or tell them what to do with their jobs. If I want to leave I will and that's all. Remember I might want a reference for the time I've been working here. The best thing is to ask him for a reference straight away.

Well, how are you today, my darling? I hope you feel so much better. The doctor will see you again tomorrow and then we'll see how things are. I'll ring up again at about 7.30 and perhaps might be able to have a word with you. Oh! How I long to talk to you again.

Well, my darling I'll close now. I have to sew some buttons on trousers and jacket.

Be good my love and goodnight. Pleasant dreams and God bless you.

> All my love and a thousand kisses
>> Forever your loving husband
> Hans.

Pickwell
Oct, 19th 1949

My sweetest, little wife,

Thanks so very much for your letter. I hope there'll be another one for me in the morning to tell me what the doctor has said today. You really seemed to be better yesterday according to the way you wrote your letter. Don't you agree it has improved as you are joking again.

Be sure the bed was the best place yesterday. Your poor little sugar plum got wet through. Still, that day is gone and finished with. Today I was lucky as I was able to shelter when showers came on.

I don't know if it would be advisable to try to cure your illness the way you got it. Darling, I am only thinking of you every single minute since I know you are ill. The first thing I did when I finished work, was starting on a letter. At the moment it's the only way of connections between Pickwell and Leicester.

You think we may be three after all? Oh, it's wonderful. Don't you like it? Of course I agree we could do without, but think, just think of it. Our little family of three and all very happy. Time will help with a home of our own, I hope.

Tonight, I asked the boss for a reference. The first thing he said was: Are you leaving us? I replied not just yet. Well, he said he would certainly give one, but not before I leave. As otherwise I could just walk out and his reference wouldn't be true then, after all. I told him that if I find another place I might have to produce it before I can start. All he said was: you can have it when you leave and everybody who's done his job alright and in a fashionable manner gets a reasonable reference. So when I leave and it isn't anything decent he can keep it with my best wishes.

About your work no. I am sure you have one. I mean from the L.A.E.C. it should be on the wages slip. We'll see on saturday.

Do you know what I would like to do? Go along to one of your German lessons and see how that woman gets on with it. Spelling "ich" as "ish" isn't too bad, but certainly not right. How long is that lesson going on. I mean how many hours?

Thanks for telling me you are Mrs Johannes Klawitter. I would've put it right, but, sorry darling I didn't know. I don't want to address you as a widow.

Well, my sweetest, last night I got a shock standing in front of the mirror, combing my hair when I saw something white. At first I thought it was a bit of the blanket. But it was a long white hair. My hair is getting white. All that worrying in the past years is showing. Nevermind. As long as the hair stay put, not matter what colour.

How are you today, my sweetheart? If it only would be Saturday soon. I am so much longing to see you again. Are we going to the pictures on Saturday?

Tonight I've started a fire in the bedroom, too. It's very cold. In fact, I didn't sleep well at all last night. Woke up half a dozen times and felt cold. If you were here it would be different. Somebody to cuddle up to. Please, come!!!

Well, my darling, I'll say goodnight now and God bless you. Be good and look after yourself. I love you more than anything else in the world. Sure-yes-how sure-quite sure.

Please give my regards to Mamma

     For tonight all my love and kisses

        Forever and only your loving husband

   Hans.

   92 wharf St

   20.10.49

My dearest darling Johannes

I have two letters of yours to answer, I received them both today, one first thing this morning, the other this afternoon. The doctor came yesterday morning, he told me I could get up, but wasn't to go out until Friday then I have to go round to visit him. You need not feel low or ashamed, because I'm ill. Who was the worst? And who had to say NO! Anyway the doctor said it was quite a common thing "honeymoon cystitis". Cystitis is inflammation of the bladder. Do you know what a bladder is? It holds water.

I got up yesterday lunchtime, stayed up until 10.0 after listening to "Have a go" and got up today at lunchtime. I'm by the fire and cosy while writing this. Lucy has just called me, so I went in next door to have a few words with her.

I suppose I have a number on my wage slip one moment I will have a look. Yes, 89. What do the tax people want that number for? I'll do this if they cut your tax and put mine up.

I am wondering how I can get this to the P.O. Susan will not be coming this afternoon. Maybe Mamma will take it, but her poor knees are not too good, they have had rather a lot of exercise these past few days.

Charlie's in bed today he had to have the doctor this morning. He has penicillin poisoning caused from the infection he had. He has been having treatment at the infirmary for the poisoned finger, he cut it on a rabbit bone. My Auntie Gert has gone to Blackpool she will be back tonight. She only went for the night left early Wednesday morning. Edna had this morning off but went to work this afternoon. Uncle Roll is nursemaid to him.

You would laugh at Fred when the doctor came, both times he comes up with him, but got turned out. When he went he came straight to me to make a fuss. Whether or not he thinks the doctor does the same as you.

There is not much more we can say on paper about you leaving so we will have discussions in bed on Saturday night.

The German teacher did noy say spell it "ish" I meant pronounce it that way.

I have been looking at the book this morning. I am going to again when I finish this. I don't know what I will say if she asks me to go to her home for a lesson, because Elizabeth the girl at work used to go to her and was charged 4/- per lesson. I don't know how many hours. It is 2 hours when I go on Tuesday and the 4/- I have paid lasts for the winter month.

Well darling I am sorry but I can't think of anymore to say only I have just remembered can you bring any eggs. Also Alfreds and Ellens address and anyone else you would like to send a piece of cake to. I will fetch some boxes on Friday, then at the weekend we can do it.

I love you

Always

Jeannie

———.

Pickwell

Oct, 20<u>th</u> 1949

My sweetest, little wife,

I am so glad you feel much better. All week I have been longing to hear your voice again. I really hoped your uncle or
aunty would say "just a minute I'll fetch Jean". And so it was.
Do you think it worth starting work Saturday? What about
a good idea. You come over here Saturday morning and we'll
go back on the usual bus. Please, darling if you're allowed to
be up and out. It makes a few more hours for us to be together. I'll ring your tomorrow about 7.30 to get the answer
"yes". We can have our dinner together when we get back.

Are you listening to the radio. Songs from the shows is on,
and just now they are singing the songs of "Oklahoma". It's
from 9.00-10.00. It's lovely. Especially as we have seen the
show. It's 9.52 and too late to hear anything from "Annie get
your gun". Next week same night same time is the second
program of this serial.

I hope you aren't mad about this short letter. I just got the
idea about Saturday. Please, darling come and be here about
11 o'clock. It isn't too early for you is it? Well, my darling,
till tomorrow night.

Be good, my sweety, goodnight and God bless you. Remember I love you!!

All my love and thousand kisses

Forever your loving husband

Hans.

R 28/10.49   H Schünemann, Aschersleben/Harz,

Hedwig Schünemann

My dear Hans and Jean,

It's been a long time since we heard from you, now we assume that you are back from your honeymoon, I want to write you a few lines.

We've been through hard weeks. I wrote twice from Weferlingen and once while we were living at Horst's friend's. Since Monday we've now had a flat again, two lovely rooms, the larger as a bedroom, with two white metal bed frames, a large wardrobe, table and chairs and in the small room there is a sofa, table and chairs, that we have set up as kitchen-diner. We pay 30 Marks rent a month for the two rooms and cellar-space. The flat belongs to a widow, she has one room and a kitchen also, it is all beautifully clean just as though it's been newly painted.

She seems to be an agreeable woman. I am just about at the end of my tether after all the turbulence. How wonderful it would have been if it had worked out and you had been able to visit us. I am sometimes so down because everything fell apart. As is Horst. He has got so thin, it makes me really very sorry. When you see what goes on both here and there. Because of it we have become poor and everything that Horst so carefully earned from his work, has gone. I shudder when I think of the winter. Without wood, flour etc, with the few potatoes and no money to buy anything additional. Before, we were able to allow ourselves occasionally to buy 1 Litre of oil. But what use is all that, we must keep ourselves above water. Horst walked eight days to find work. His boss had stirred up all the hairdressers, so none of them would take him on. So, I went to the employment office and told the gentlemen the whole story. He was very indignant about it and told me it was unheard of that he should make things difficult for Horst, Horst shouldn't put up with it and should take him to court at the Work Tribunal.

Last Saturday Horst took a job in a small salon, he really likes it a lot, he has a nice boss who is very pleased that Horst came to her, she has always liked his work. But at the same time he can't earn any extra as they are waiting to catch him out. That is a great shame and makes it very difficult for us to improve our situation. If only I too could at least earn something. It's very hard for Horst. If only our Papa would return! We live about 20 minutes away from the town centre. They are all settlement houses (Siedlungshäuser), but lovely in the countryside. Let us hear from you again soon. Two weeks' ago today, it was your wedding, we had brilliant weather then too. Stay in really good health. With very warm greetings and kisses from your mother and from your brother-in-law Horst. Warm greetings to your mother-in-law. Looking forward to when we see you again.

R 7/11.1949

Aschersleben, 20.10.1949
29/10.1949

Hedwig Schünemann

My dear Hans and Jean,

Many thanks for your lovely letter of 10.10.1949 which Frau Fuchs from Weferlinger has forwarded to us. Unfortunately, the letter you wrote to us previously has not reached us. We were so looking forward to receiving a few lines from you. The day before yesterday I was washing with Frau von Hoff and I was told by our co-tenant that day two letters had arrived for us from Frau Fuchs, this the postman also confirmed yesterday. When I got there, there was only one letter. No-one knows who took the letter, but it was certainly the youths (scum) from the street - our post box is mounted in the porch. You can imagine how angry we are about that. Your previous letter was dated 14.9. which we received it 3 weeks ago, when we got back. Did you tell us about your wedding and your presents in the lost letter? If so, then please write and tell me everything again. So you are safely back from your honeymoon. What is happening about your wedding picture? We are waiting impatiently for it. Yes, dear Hans, you write that we shouldn't go back. But we had no alternative. I told you about the difficult weeks we had. You have to try to imagine what it was like. We were both mentally exhausted. We couldn't go to Grandma because permission to go to Holstein was blocked even for short stays. I was so sorry for Horst, but are we expected to exist over there without any money and on the street? You can't expect help from anyone else, everyone has to look out for themselves. Yes, it is bitter, we feel so deserted. If only I were also able to work, but the exertion is too hard for me, I can't get anything. We should have been able to lead a different life over there : they get 2000 grams of butter each month; here, it is 300 grams. And then one could buy anything one needs, and **here** ?

Last year we still had an additional 12 hundredweight of potatoes that we had foraged, but this year it's only 5 hundredweight in total. We can't buy anything on the black market. Otherwise, we would still be able to buy oil at least. Oh, what is the use of talking about it at all, we are not able to change anything. We can't go to another camp, as Uelzen is the only processing camp.

We are very pleased that our little package has arrived – did it get there in time for the wedding ? Haven't you got a flat yet? I thought everything was already sorted out, as you are both working, you should be able to catch up with your outgoings. Dear Hans, if you come next year on holiday, and we want to meet over there, Frau Fuchs will gladly make her room available for us, she offered it to me immediately, it is a lovely big room. It costs only 1,90 West Marks per person to get from the border to Weferlingen, that is as manageable as going to Luebeck.

Now I must end my letter for today, my landlady is going to the Post Office and will take it with her. Stay in good health, be warmly greeted and kissed by your mum and your brother and brother-in-law, Horst. Warm greetings to your mother-in-law.

Pickwell
Oct, 23rd 1949

My sweetest, little wife,

Thank you so very much, darling for a lovely weekend. Believe me, I didn't feel like going away again and I am so much relieved to have seen for myself you're better. You poor darling. The doctor might find things alright again when you go tomorrow. I hope so and keep my fingers crossed.

Now what about tonight. Nobody to cuddle up to. Oh, sweety, I wish I was with you or you're here. I only hope I'll be able to get something for us in the near future. As I said last night, I shan't stick it long, stopping out here on my own.

Well, my love, it's 10.00 and I am tired. I've had my usual supper again. Please, darling, come on the 12.05 in any case.

Good night and God bless you. For tonight all my love and kisses, your ever loving husband.

<u>Monday Oct 24th 8.00pm</u>

Hello, my darling, how are you? Have you seen the doctor? What did he say? Everything alright again or has my poor little sweetheart to keep to the pills?

Well, the first day of this week is over and it certainly went quick. I kept going, of course cleaning out, and when I looked at my watch the first time it was 12.45, time to go back to the stables (not to be called "home"). In the afternoon it was soon 4.00 and time for unloading the trailer. At 6.00 I left for shutting up and got back 6.45. Then I got the meat and gravy ready. Helmut had done the potatoes while I was away. Mashed potatoes and I must say he did them very nice. He fried a bit of bacon and mixed it into the spuds and it tasted lovely. The washing up was also done. I knew he wanted something otherwise he wouldn't have bothered. When we finished our dinner he asked me if he could have my bike to go to Little Dalby on. I gave it, but told him it's once and not always.

It was 10.00 when I went to bed last night. He came home just before 10.00. And believe me I got a shock when he told me something! You never guess!!! He's getting married next year. No date fixed yet. He just mentioned that from now on he has to save money. I told him what it is like to save for a wedding. Cutting down in smoking and going off the beer. He'll be 22 and the girl 16. According to his talking he's asked her mother and the father doesn't know about it yet. They aren't going to ask him. So I told him something about marrying a girl under 21. Both parents permission etc. I am sure if he asks the courts permission he won't get it. They want to see something and find him capable of looking after a family.

It's all up to him now and I wonder how he's getting on with his savings. We have all that behind us, darling. For myself I can only tell people to get married. I am so happy to call you my wife. And I am quite sure I can call myself very lucky to have found you. All the years of hardship as a POW were worth it. I couldn't love anyone more than I love you. Though the present situation is not what I like but one day we'll start our life together "till death do us part"

Be good till I see you Wednesday. Remember what I told you of putting your warm things on. Bring your big coat along even if the sun shines. It's cold at night.

Good night and God bless you always
All my love and kisses
Forever and only your
Ever loving husband
Hans.

92 Wharf St

October 24th

My dearest darling Hans.

I have been to the doctors with my bottle and I still have something in my water. So I have to take the rest of the tablets (I should finish those about Wednesday) and go in to see him on Saturday then I suppose I will be starting again to work on Monday, what a shame, but I don't mind really once I get back. The doctor asked me if I thought I might be having a baby. I told him I had not had any connections since I had my visitor. He did not think that was likely. As for my-self I will not be sure until I have had my next visitor. I only have to wait another fortnight. I have to have the doctor's permission now, to tell me when I can have connection. I had to smile when he said "Don't have any connection until I tell you" I hope he does not forget to tell me when I can.

Freddy and I went into town, took the cake to the P.O. The fellow at the G.P.O. said the cake going abroad should be in a tin. I thought afterwards, should we have put our name on the back of the box. It cost 3/6 ½ to send them, so it has cost us nearly 10/- to send cake in a doz boxes, a good job we did not send 2 dozen out.

I have just done my good deed for the day. It started to rain so I went in to tell Aunt Gert it was raining, she had a line full of washing out. I started and gave her a hand fetching it in. That is more than she does for me, but I always think you get a reward in some other way that is why I never mind helping people that don't help me.

I have been a bad girl and spent some money. I bought some material to make a blouse. It is blue. I have to get another piece sometime, so I will have 2 blouses for the winter, one in the wash and one out.

I took the body belt back to Jones, but could not get a larger size. So I suppose I will have to go round the shops to see if I can get one.

I called in to see Gertie this morning, but she was out. She wants me to do the ends of her hair with a Toni perm. So I will go in again to see if she would like me to do it one afternoon this week (except Wed.)

Well darling I will say cheeri'O for now. I will be seeing you on Wednesday. I will try to be on the 12.15. 1.6 in Somerby I suppose it will only go as far as the village, so I should be at Pickwell at 1.20. Have a cup of coffee ready.

Be a good boy.

    All my love
    Jeannie

———.

> Pickwell
> Oct, 27ᵗʰ 1949

My sweetest, little wife,

How are you, darling, did you get home safe last night? I hope so, anyway I was back here 2 minutes after I left you. Your bus must have been still in the village as I saw no lights going down the other road.

Are you mad with me because I want to leave this place? Look, darling, I wouldn't mind if I got told off for doing wrong, but it's nothing like that. I have got pride too, perhaps more than the boss. He's gone too far in saying things like that. We'll have a good look when you bring the advertiser on Saturday.

Now I'll get some supper ready (cocoa, bread & cheese). And then off to bed. I'll close now and wish you a very good night. "Songs from the show's" has just started.

Be good and look after yourself

All my love and kisses forever your loving husband.

Friday Oct 28th 1949, 8.00p.m.

Well, you'll see the doctor again tomorrow. I wonder what he'll say this time. Perhaps you'll get permission.

Thank goodness , another ½ a day and I'll see my little wife again. This week wasn't too bad with coming over Wednesday, compared with the last fortnight.

This morning I received my new income tax code No. before it was 35, now it's 70. Guess how much deductions for tax I had today? On the timesheet was 5-15-4 and in my wage packet I found £5-14-1. Only ⅓ s in spite of 10 hours overtime. I should've some money to come back, shouldn't I? On the form it says code No 70 for 1949-50. I wish it would mean from April 5 th.

My leg hurts quite a lot tonight. All day today I was shifting houses on my own. It was a bit too much, I think.

Tonight was the usual Friday rush. Coming back from shopping I went shutting up, back 7.15 and had something to eat. Helmut bought chips but I couldn't face them. He went out and I got something ready I fancied. A bit of fried beef and tomatoes. That was much better.

Now I am waiting for the water to get hot to wash my hair and "myself".

Well, my love, I'll say goodnight and be good. God bless you.. Pleasant dreams.

All my love and kisses forever and only yours from the one who loves you more than anything else in the world.

Hans.

92 Wharf St
31.10.49

My dearest darling Hans.

Well I am back slaving away and so far it isn't too bad. I started well, 5 minutes late. I'm turning a new leaf tomorrow.

I arrived home safe and sound, listened to the last part of "Variety Bandbox", Frankie Howard was very funny. I had a bit to eat, a cup of milk, put Freddy out and up the stairs I went. It was 12.0 o'clock with big ben, I have not had time to put it back. I have to take it right round.

Now what I really want to know is, how is my poor darling today. Is your leg still painful? I wish I could do something for you so it would not hurt so much. If it does get too bad don't go on working, because it might do more harm to your leg.

I am not mad with you for wanting to leave Pickwell. You do what you think best. It does worry me a bit, but you know me I worry over nothing and I will get over it. There is one thing I hope I never have to do, that is ask anyone for help. Also, I don't think it is a tragedy because I may be having a baby, but I would like to have been a bit more settled and have saved a bit of money, because although we are able to live with my mother at the moment, if anything happened to her, where would we be, half belongs to her as well as me. I wish we could get somewhere on our own especially if we are having a little Johnny or at least away from my Aunt Gert next door. She speaks terrible and I don't want John to speak like her, Susan did. I know she does not speak too well now, but it was a lot worse when she lived with us. There is one thing I do like, that is for a child to speak nicely and of course to be well behaved.

I had to pay out 2/6 almost as soon as I got here, it was for 5 weeks football lists. I managed to pay it. I now have about 2/2 ½ left. I have just looked in my purse and find I only have 2 ½ d. That will buy a stamp and I have a stamp at home. I have just found 1 ½, so that will see me through the week. I don't think I have any expenses, I have my hat to pay for so I will go in to see if I can get it cleared up.

I have had a letter from Miggy this morning, also one from Otto written in German. I would love to know what he has put, both letters are to both of us. I will put the one in German in the letter to you. The one Miggy has written is 12 pages and I think will be too thick to put in but I will try. I will have to close now, but just look after yourself all my love and kisses I hope your leg is OK

Jeannie

Pickwell,
Oct 31st 1949

My sweetest little wife

Well, darling here I am. I have finished my first day's work and I am sorry to say I don't feel better. In fact I was limping all day so Doris asked me at 5.00 if I wanted her to go shutting up tonight and take any other day for her when I feel better. It was very nice of her but I refused. If it doesn't get better within the next day or two I'll have to tell Gudger I can't do all those jobs on my own any longer. Not for the time being anyway. I really don't like to go to the doctor because then I am sure I've had it for a couple of weeks. Knowing how much I can stand I am sure I shan't collapse just yet. If I could get hold of that Frenchman who shot me, I would strangle him. Not because of the pains but because of all the trouble it gives me. Please, darling, don't you worry your little head. If it gets too much for me I'll ring you and come home. But I don't think that'll have to happen before Saturday.

Jeannie, how I wish you could stop at home. We'll have to try our luck at the football pools and see if we can get some easy and quick money that way. I am sorry I haven't got relations that went to America and are going to leave me a couple of thousands. We certainly could do with it and most of the bother would be over. Still there you are.

By the way, please remind me on Saturday to get a birthday card for my mother (17.11).

I've put my washing in soak and have a go tomorrow night. After this I've to darn my gloves. Do you mind if I close now? It's 9.00 and I want to get off to bed. It's the best place to rest that confounded leg. So be good my sweet and I love you so very very much. Good night and God bless you.

All my love and kisses forever

Your husband Hans (who causes you all that

trouble).

Photo in Hans's wallet through which he was shot in his leg

92 Wharf St
November 2nd

My darling husband Johannes

How is my angel's leg today? I wish I could kiss it better for you, is there anything I could do?

Thank you darling for your letter. I did not get it until this morning as you know I usually have it on the lunchtime of the morning you post it. There is another letter for you today from Kurt. It is rather a stiff one so I will keep it until I see you Saturday. Also don't forget to bring Miggy's letter back with you then I will answer it sometime next week. What did you think to Otto's letter? I could not read it of course. I hope to be able to one day. I did not go last night to the German class, I am such a long way behind and I don't particularly want to let her give me private lessons at 4/- a time. I may as well try to learn myself with your help.

I am all on my own some. Mamma went out at 8.0 with them from next door. I still have my pal Fred but he is asleep in the chair. When I sat down to write he wanted to get on my knee but I wasn't having any.

Have you got "Have a go" on? I have, it is just finishing though or has my poor darling gone to bed to rest his leg. Do you think you will be able to go into the town on Saturday? I have to get you 2 shirts, you will have to have 2 so we may as well get them together. We had better go to the bank. I will make inquiries but I am sure we have to go together to open a joint account and I will have to get my name changed on the bank book, though I don't suppose that will make any difference if I don't.

I got a recipe (is that right) out of Lucy's book Life and Home. It was a sponge cake it was called One Year Old but it sounded rather nice so I thought it would do for a 24 year old. I wrote it out but it will have to be a special occasion cake because it takes 3 eggs. About eggs can't you get some eggs from Hills at Somerby. They would be cheaper than buying them from Maclean.

Did you have the play on last night about Queen Victoria? It was quite good. She was married to a German so we have something in common.

Lucy and Margary are still nagging me about being away after being married. Lucy keeps saying it is these foreigners they are hot stuff. I could not say it was the foreigners, it is the English they marry. Then this lunchtime I saw a woman from finance dept she asked how I was then said 'he soon did you in.' I am standing up to it. I take it all as a joke and I even don't let my temper get the better of me when Lucy says the German must be hot stuff. I simply tell her she does not know what she has missed by marrying an Englishman.

I know I would not change my German for anyone else in the world.

Well darling I will close now and find myself something to eat. I feel very tired. I wish I could cuddle up to you and show you how much I love you but I only have to wait until Saturday.

Goodnight and God Bless you. Your loving wife and faithful.

    J. Klawitter

Pickwell,
Nov 2<u>nd</u> 1949

My sweetest little wife,

Well, sweetheart about myself. The leg is a bit better but I'll be glad when it's Saturday dinner time. I just keep rolling along till then. I have been naughty tonight, spend some money. I was so fed up with sitting here on my own so I went to Melton to the pictures. It was "Beyond Glory", American not too bad. It was about a Westpoint Cadet.

It's just 11 o'clock my bedtime, but I don't want to let my lovely wait again. Rather stay up for another ½ hour. Good thing it'll soon be the weekend.

Don't worry about my leg darling, it looks as if it does it good if I keep on walking.

I quite agree with you about having a baby and then live at Leicester. Aunt Gertie's language is not the best anyway. We'll get something somewhere darling, don't despair.

How are you today my sweet? Fine, I hope. Helmut just told me he has asked for a job at Little Dalby where his friend works. The foreman there is going to let him know tomorrow night. If everything goes alright he's giving his notice on Friday. Well, we'll see.

Well, my love, it's 11.20. Don't be too mad about this short letter.

Be good and take care of yourself. Goodnight and God bless you. I love you more than anything else in the world.

For tonight all my love and kisses etc.

Forever and ever your very loving husband

Hans.

replied 14.11.49   **Aschersleben 30.10.49**
14.11.49

      My dear Hans and Jean,

Today I would like to thank you warmly for your lovely letter of 15.10.1949. I hope that Jean is better now. For a few days now we've had night frost already, it's come particularly early this year and not all the potatoes for cellar storage are mature enough. Each sack will cost 60 Marks. Up to now we have only got 2 hundredweight per person since August and that will mean a real shortage as potatoes are still the staple diet. We can't afford to pay the black market price of 25 Marks. Horst is making every effort to get us through, but it's too hard. Wheat costs 85 Marks a hundredweight once again. Who can manage that? Those are all the kind of things we could previously allow ourselves, when I was able to forage for potatoes. We could even allow ourselves to have oil, but these days we are fat-free again, and the meals taste thoroughly disgusting.

When will things change? It would have been so nice if everything had worked out, at least we would have had something to eat. Dear Hans, you write that, with his talent for hair-dressing, Horst would soon be able to find a job again, but it has been made very difficult for him, because his manager secretly stirred up other hairdressers not to hire him.

But he is happy in his new job, even though the salon is smaller, he has a good manageress, who appreciates his work, his clients are all with him again, they kept asking until they found out where he was hiding. Have I already told you that his former manager, with the head of the craft guild, came to see him and threatened to take him to a labour camp if he drew away the clients? You can see from that what fools they are, being afraid of a 20-year old urchin. Clearly it shows he is more able than they are. Competitive envy will always exist, so he'll have further battles to win. I feel very sorry for Horst, he has already had so much trouble over this at such a young age.

We will have to sell our household goods and crockery over there, as otherwise we'll only bring back broken fragments.

We haven't had any mail from Uncle Erich for a long time, they are probably also up to their ears in work. The same goes for Uncle Gustav, they still have a lot of extra work with the two settlements and then with their own building, I do think they will move in well before winter. Aunty Lina also wrote recently. She sends warm greetings to you and Jean and wishes you lots of good luck. Bruno spent 6 weeks in hospital. He fell badly in the barn and fractured the bones in his left hand. His hand is still stiff. The doctor says it will be fine again in a few months. Bruno is a really unlucky person, given that his leg already makes it difficult for him to walk. We are waiting impatiently for your wedding photo and a report about your wedding. Please don't make us wait too long a time for them. Now I must finish my letter, Horst has just come home starving. Give my best regards to your mother-

401

in-law.

Greetings and kisses from your mother and from your brother and brother-in-law Horst.

Pickwell,
Dec 11th 1949

My dearest darling Jean

Hello, my sweety, how did you get home? Alright, I hope. Well, my sweetie pie I am miserable and so terrible lonely. Those last five week have been perfect except when we didn't agree. Still, all that doesn't matter. Helmut hasn't come back yet, it's only 9.30. Believe me I felt awful when you went on to the bus. If I could've only gone with you. I hope it won't be long before we can be together forever. I am listening to "Musichall". It's quite good. Howard keeps me laughing. But the trouble is nobody to cuddle up to tonight. Nobody to put the arm around me. Good thing you're coming again on Saturday.

Well, my darling, I'll have some bread and cheese and a cup of coffee off to bed and a good rest,

A thousand kisses and remember I love you more than anything else in the world. God bless you always.

Monday, Dec 14th 1949

Hello, my sweetest! Here I am again. The first day work in the life of a "G.F.W" I feel as if they've done me in today. Don't be surprised I woke up at 6.10, that is 5 minutes before the alarm went off. Good show isn't it. What about you? Did you make 7.50? I bet 2/6 you didn't! Well, now the report of the day. First thing feeding with that young chap from Melton. After lunch watercarting. It was 1.30 when we got back. Out again at 2.00 and continuing watercarting. Including shutting up I finished at 5.30. My foot felt just like 5 weeks ago. The boss just came by so I told him straight away I shan't be able yet doing the shutting up as I am not taking the risk of having another 5 weeks on the sick. He told me it'll be difficult as the others have taken my turn already when I was away. Cheeky, isn't he? Taking my turn whilst I was ill! Sound funny.

Anyway I'll have to tell Gudger in the morning. It's no overtime in it as we go before 5.00.

Well, my sweet little wife, I feel awful. Ask Mamma if I can start at home as charwoman or shop assistant.

Imagine what time Bonzo came back last night? Helmut brought him back from Little Saltby at 12.30. He's found a bitch down there and that's where he goes. Just before we fetched him he was away for 3 days and a farmer from L.D. told Helmut he'd run his sheep.

But I myself think he's been after rabbits in the hedges and of course when sheep see a dog in the field they go off. Still, tonight I took him up the road and he was alright. He'll have to stay in for a bit now. Our beds are here now. When Helmut came back last night he went next door and no beds. Still he wasn't tight so he found them alright. He has had his dinners at Little Dalby and at Christmas he goes down there and stops there from Sunday till Tuesday night. So if I get the first days off you could come back with me and stop here if you like. Think it over.

Ring me on Wednesday at 8.00pm.

I'll close now, sweetheart, be good. Goodnight and God bless you always. I love you so very, very much.

Loads of love and thousand kisses

Forever and only yours ever loving husband

Hans.

R: 20.12.1949

403

Aschersleben, 1st December 1949

13.12.1949

My dear Hans and Jean,

Thank you very much for your lovely letter of November 24th, 1949, which we received today. That came really quickly again. In any case, we are always very pleased when a letter from you arrives. I am really concerned that your foot isn't better yet. Just don't strain it so much, such things need a lot of rest. I fell over the day before yesterday and well and truly sprained my left hand. It is hurting a lot today. But then I can still shake hands with your mother-in-law. I have also been so affected by rheumatism that I could hardly move last week, because it was so bad in my knee and ankle. It's quite awful.

Horstel is not at all well and also has so much work to do before the festivities. He looks so dreadfully pale. But that's no surprise. It was quite different when I was able to go foraging. We were able to buy ½ a pound of Margarine for 9 Marks in the H.O. weekly. You can't afford that very often. We got 25 hundredweight of unprocessed coal delivered and I went 4 times to the wood yard at half past six in the morning and had boards cut down at 8 Marks each, for firewood. Previously, we didn't need to buy it at all, as I was always able to go to the forest.

Horst came for dinner and went straight to bed. I made him a chest compress and wrapped it round him to make him sweat. I am really so worried about the boy, he is so susceptible.

Dear Hans, we are so very happy that you have ordered a package for us, can you really afford it, when you spent so much on the wedding? After all, now that you are sick, you aren't earning anything. It would be wonderful if it arrived in time for Christmas. I would go to collect it.

Horstel's manager seems to have calmed himself down now. We'll just leave the fool alone.

Now get well soon. Warm greetings and kisses to you and to Jean, from your mother and your brother Horst. Warm greetings to your mother-in-law.

92 Wharf St
December 13th

MORNING

My dearest darling Johannes

I will start to write a few lines now and hope that I will receive a letter at lunchtime. I doubt if I will because the last time, I did not get it until the next morning they seem to have changed collecting times.

 You had some money come this morning £1.10.4 from the National Health. I thought they had paid up to date still every little helps, will you be able to go to Somerby Post Office to collect it? I would go but it has to have your signature on it. I could forge it, *J Klawitter* is it good!!! For that I would probably land in jail.

I washed my hair last night, that took all night, Mamma altered Enid's skirt. I tried it on, I did not think much to it, and believe it or not it fit me, a bit tight, so I could not be any bigger than her around there.

It has just started to rain. I do hope it is not raining at Pickwell. I would hate you to get your new hat and Wellingtons wet.

I still cannot make up my mind whether to go to this dance they are having, I somehow don't think I will. I may as well save my 3/- and go somewhere nice with you.

I have started to write this at home but it will only be short. I have been waiting for Mamma to go to bed so I could get cracking but she has only just gone 10.0.

The man has been today to see about the gas stove, he did something to the meter in the shop and there has been a terrible smell of gas all day.

I have been a busy girl tonight. I mended your socks and sewed the coat up. You should hear Fred at the moment. He is just like a pig, speaking of pigs, Betty fetched the pigs feet, 2 for us and I for herself she is going to try it. I will see if I can get you 2 on Friday and 1lbs of sausage.

I need you to come back and keep me in order, I don't have time to make the bed in the morning (what would Gertie say?) I just straighten it a bit and hope for the best. I have not fetched the bottom out yet so I will manage.

I was so lonely last night I just wanted you to put your arms round me but I will try to make the best of it knowing that this is giving us a chance to get a home of our own some day. I am sure it will be worth it in the long run. I would much rather wait until we can have things nice and comfy than to have a place now with only a few things. But if we were able to get a place to rent privately (not tied) I would take it and hope for the best. There is one reason I do not want to take a tied cottage is because if you were ever ill with your leg we would be out and a home is the main thing no matter what happens that wants to be permanent. You don't want to have to worry about your home if you're ill.

I will have to say goodnight God bless you, Mamma is calling me, I love you very very much and need you terribly darling will be seeing you on Saturday.

I will write some more tomorrow when I get your letter.

<u>Wednesday</u>

Thank you for the letter darling it arrived this morning. It is stamped 9.0am Dec 13th. It is probably the train service that has changed.

It isn't the not agreeing that bothers me it is the not speaking. We can't expect to agree on everything can we?

It wasn't 'Music Hall' you were listening to – it was 'Variety Bandbox'!

I can't remember what time I got up on Monday morning but

if you look at the last letter I sent you will see, if it was be-fore 7.50 I will take you on, if not forget it.

Why do you call the fellow from Melton the young chap? He looks as old as you. Don't tell me he is 15.

Probably the Boss thought you did not want to go shutting because there isn't any overtime. Would you like a job as a char (man) woman? Do you think you could manage that, think of the brain work – trying to get a bucket through a small space almost as hard as getting a tractor through a gateway.

<u>Afternoon</u>

I have been home for lunch, had pig feet and rabbit. The poor rabbit got cooked a bit too much. I told you they have been to fix the gas stove. Someone looked at the meter yesterday and another person came today. This one has been before ages ago, he came the other day to see what was to be done. Anyway, when he came today he went round the back and serenaded her. I should think that is how the poor rabbit got burnt, it was very nice though.

You are a lucky boy to have such a long letter. I have been writing with an ordinary pen and I can get on much better. I'll bring the worm tablets on Saturday.

About staying at Pickwell, you had better start catching those mice, it would send me mad to lay there with them about.

I will have to close now otherwise it will cost more than 2 ½.

All my love

Jean Klawitter

Pickwell,

Dec 13<u>th</u> 1949

My sweetest, little wife,

I thank you so very much for your lovely long letter. You know how much I was longing to hear from you.

The second day is over. It wasn't too bad. Cleaning out all day. Though tomorrow will bring a change. The whole lot is to be blood tested. That means a few very busy days.

Oh! I lost 2/6s. Believe me I still can't make it out how you got up so early. Never mind, the 2/6s is yours. Mamma's suggestion about coming back if it isn't better, nothing doing. Now once I've started no going back. Gudger went shutting up himself last night.

Please, darling, keep to your old handwriting. It looks so much better. Your new writing paper looks very nice. A complete change in colour. Don't you like this one? Bring Freddy on Saturday if it is nice.

Well, sweetie, if those teddy's you saw are good ones get one of them. You'll want something in any case. My mother's letter arrived also this morning. Last night I asked Helmut if there were any letters from my mother during the last 3 weeks. He said there were 3 or 4 and he gave them to Mrs Cooper. She said that was right and sent them on to 96 Wharf Rd, Leicester. Now I know where they went. Certainly back to the sender. Isn't 96 that paper place. No wonder I didn't get any at all. Mrs Cooper said she thought that was the right address. Never mind it'll be alright if my mother gets the letters back as I've kept writing from home.

Helmut went out at midday to Melton. As he told me he was going to the Labour Exchange. He told me so a long time ago.

I spoke to Eileen today. She was surprised to see me back. She said almost everybody here thought I would only come back to serve a week's notice. We talked about Christmas and she said if I was working and egg washing at Xmas as people might expect me to after being away so long. That means she's heard something or somebody has mentioned it. If Gudger thinks so too he's had it. I said to Eileen there is nothing doing. I am not going to spend Christmas in this hole. She said if she was in my place she wouldn't spend a single night at this stable. Anyway nobody is keeping me

<u>here over Xmas.</u> I'll mention it to Gudger in good time so he knows where he stands. I don't mind taking my share in work but he shouldn't get too big ideas.

Last night there wasn't any time to go shopping so I went tonight. The butcher hasn't had any meat in at all so when he gets it tomorrow he'll send it over. All the outstanding bills (except the coal bill) are paid. I have about as much left as you. A few pennies. Enough for a couple of 2 1/2d stamps. I don't like to keep Jeannie waiting. Another thing. I remember now to have a good wash (warm water) every morning and night.

Bonzo is just having a look what I am doing. He sends his regards to all including Freddy. Well, my sugarplum, I'll close now. Please give my regards to Mamma. Be good. I love you more than anything else in the world and only hope you're here with me. Good night and God bless. All my love and kisses and I'll always be your loving husband

xxx Hans

Pickwell,
Dec 15th 1949

My sweet little wife,

Thanks so very much for the nice long letter. I really was happy when I received it this morning and only 12 hours later miserable and disappointed. You know what I mean, don't you? About Christmas. I kept thinking of the best way, giving up Xmas eve and -day and when I asked you if it was the best I just heard a very poor 'maybe.' Now I am sorry to have given you all the bother about the holidays. I don't want you to wait with the turkey. Never mind me, look after yourself and everything will be alright. It seems to me as if you don't understand the new arrangement and hope I don't bother with explaining it again. If I work this weekend that means work on New Years weekend as well as Xmas. However if I take this one off I shall have time off for the next three weekends. And that also means the next three weekends together with you. Tell me, what's the big difference of having the first 2 days or last 2 days off? I know, I said yesterday I'll definitely take Xmas day off. But you yourself always say to me to keep out of trouble. I can tell Gudger I shan't be working at all at Christmas and that's that. We'll talk about it on Saturday so to have something to argue about!! See you at the usual time 2.15 isn't it? It'll be a bit earlier if I come Melton-way. Never mind getting the things for me if you haven't got the time.

As I said on the phone yesterday, I'll cash my post order on Saturday afternoon. That'll be soon enough for me. Your forged signature would certainly land you in jail.

Thanks for mending my socks. I bet I couldn't have done it better and I am not joking, but meaning it. There's a clever girl!

You're telling me about being so lonely. You are able to dream and remember everything. I, however, when I dream and wake up the only answer I get is Helmut's snoring. That makes me get my senses back pretty quick, believe me. It tells me that I am at Pickwell anyway. This situation doesn't give us a chance of having our own home some day. I want it as soon as we can afford having it. Don't you know of a place we could rent privately? There wouldn't have to be any bother about Christmas.

Why do I call the fellow from Melton the young chap? Because I am at least 6 years older. Well preserved ain't I?

I certainly wouldn't mind a job as a charwoman, if I could be with you all the time. Could I possibly be your charwoman and personal servant? No wages, just your love and only yours. I know, it takes some brain work. Think of the poor bucket getting knocked!!

Well, my sweetest, it's 9.00 and I feel very tired. Goodnight and God bless you. I love you so very, very much. All my love and kisses

Your ever loving husband, Hans.

Pickwell,
Dec 19th 1949

My sweetest little wife

How are you, my sweetie? I hope fine. The first day's over again and it'll soon be Saturday. Still I wish it was tomorrow. I felt so lonely last night getting on the bus and leaving you behind. If you could have only come along. I got into Melton at good time to catch my bus, but it went round the long way and so I got back at 8.35, started the fire again as it was icy cold in here. Of course my egg and bacon followed as usual. The sausages went down the way of everything eatable at dinner time today. The pigs feet are cooking and will be ready tomorrow night, I hope. Remind me not to forget to put the peas into soak. So it'll be pea soup and stewed apple pudding tomorrow. The mince tarts will have to wait until later on in the week. I've had my wash and that might finish the reports of today's work and food problems.

. At dinnertime I put the lock on my bike and as Helmut was going to L.D. tonight and went to fetch it without asking. He certainly was surprised to find it locked. I told him it doesn't mean that if I buy anything he can use or wear it as well. He knew what I meant and I hope he'll remember it. It's only 8.00 now, but I still have plenty to do tonight. My gloves (woollen) want mending and also the pockets in my black trousers. Then there is a letter to be written to my mother. I didn't write last week but still I haven't had any more since the one you sent me.

Now after all Helmut is going away Christmas Eve. So if I could only arrange for us to get to Melton or John O'Gaunt station then you could stop here on Saturday. Can you find out if Melton Taxi service runs on Sunday. It's only 10/-s that way and he could be up here by 6.15 to take us down to Melton station. If you want to stop here, ring up Melton and if they run order a taxi for 6.15 to wait at Pickwell against the pub. Let me know straight the way how you think about it. Of course, if Betty has invited you for dinner please yourself. Well, my angel, I'll say goodnight now and get on with my mending. Be good and God bless.

        All my love and kisses forever your
          loving husband
              Hans.

      92 Wharf St
      December 19th
My dearest darling Joannes

I hope you arrived back at Pickwell safe and sound. Were you in time for the 8.0 bus? If so I suppose you were able to listen to Variety Band Box. It was good, especially Reg Dixon, I listened to that and Palm Court.

Freddy and I were soon back, Uncle Roll brought the papers I had a look at them. When Mamma went out I thought I had better get cracking with my correspondence, I wrote a letter to Bernhard 3 ½ pages and it did not take me long. The next on my list is Muriel. I intended to do it last night but when I finished Bernhard's I was hungry so I had my supper and listened to the radio.

I have been home for lunch, I've had the same as yesterday with pigs feet. They were quite nice but I can't eat an awful lot of them.

We had a Xmas card from Dora.

I will see what Gertie has in nighties but I will leave the shoes until the spring. I might see something else I like better.

There isn't anything to bring with me on Saturday is there? I had better bring the things you will need back with me. Let's get things clear about Bonzo before we start so we don't fall out. First of all if Susan is there and plays with Bonzo leave them, if Betty does not want her to go near it let her keep her away not you keep Bonzo away. I always do that with Freddy. I don't mind him touching her kids so if she minds she can keep the kids away that is her concern. Second, don't keep hitting him and telling him to go in the corner, let him sit near the door if he wants to. Above all don't lose your temper with him. It all put's you and me in a bad mood. I forgot the worm tablet again. You had better give him some just to make sure.

I will try to make some nice mince pies this week. I would love to have a go at making some of the things in those books but not knowing what is available to use, but you wait until I get organised in our own home.

Well my darling I will have to close be good

All my love

Jean

.

Pickwell,
Dec 20th 1949

My sweetest, little wife,

Hello, my sweetie, are you enjoying yourself at Susan's party? Did you really want to come down to Melton tomorrow? It would've been nice but hardly worth for you coming all the way. Or do you think it worth?

About Saturday and Sunday. Never mind, sweetie, if you'd rather stay at home I won't mind. It's not a nice place to stay the night at, anyway. Just please yourself. I only got the idea of the taxi service from Melton and thought I'd better let you know just in case.

I've just had a shave, have written a letter to my mother as I was so tired last night. Helmut came back only 10 minutes after I went to bed but I didn't hear a sound. Cleaning out is a tiring job and I haven't had anything else to do yet this week.

When I came back from calling you the dinner was ready. In spite of soaking the pigs feet for 36 hours they're still pretty salty, but still we enjoyed our washer-woman-soup. The boiled pudding turned out lovely. I only hope the mince-meat tarts will be as nice. Would my face be red if they weren't. After giving you all the advices and then can't do it myself.

I made my 20 cigarettes last from Saturday till including today and tonight fetched a packet of tobacco. That'll last me till Saturday.

You'd better get used to the holidays now, getting 4 ½ days off. Is it worth starting again in the new year? Doris said to-night there's no entertainment on Xmas day, but plenty of work for us. Bless the hens, they let us earn our living. Well, my love, I'll get myself a round of toast and go to bed. I am ready for both. Good night and God bless you always.

I love you so very, very much. So all my love and thousand kisses forever and only yours.

Thursday Dec 22nd 49

Hello my darling? How are you? Well, I have been speaking to you on the phone so there isn't really much to say. It's almost 8.45 and I still have plenty to do. I've done our mince-meat tarts. I'll save a couple for you. No excuse eating them as I've eaten yours too. And those you're going to do this week will be perfect, I know.

Many thanks for the letter I received yesterday morning. How was Susan's party? Did you have a good time?

It hasn't been raining here lately. Thank heavens it didn't. And also be thankful as I've finished cleaning out tonight. 4 days in the big field. Watercarting tomorrow and odd jobs on Saturday I hope. And that's that I am ready for a couple of days off. Alright about Bonzo, but one thing, if it gets too bad, I'll just put him outside and everything will be quiet. Agree?

Look, Jeannie, don't rely on those cookery books too much. Let it give you a hint or idea. Oh! Don't let's talk about that.

The kitchen is your department and everything will be alright.

Well, my darling, it's 9.00 and I'll close now. I am going to do my boots with lino polish to keep the wet out. Be good, goodnight and God bless you. I love you more than anything else in the world.

Please give my regards to Mamma.

All my love and thousand kisses.

Forever yours loving husband

Hans.

92 Wharf St

20.12.49

My darling Johannes

I will start this today, finish it tomorrow. That is if I get a letter from you.

Well my darling how are you? And how is Bonzo? Is work going down any better this week? I hope so.

I did not go to the pictures after all. Instead I took Susan's birthday present, the cardigan. Betty was busy getting ready for the party, not many are going my cousin Joan and her two children, 2 girls, and a friend of Cyril's children are going, 2 more girls 'What no boys!' that makes 4 children then there are 2 mothers (with the kids) Mamma and I. 2 more that is 4 adults if I am counted as one!!!

Cyril's aunty in Leeds has sent Sheila a teddy bear for Christmas but it is not as nice as the one I got fortunately. Mamma, Fred and I will go round about 6.0 after we have closed the shop. I could have done with this evening a home. I want to wash my hair, scrub the floor and polish it and a thousand one things to do this week. I will probably do the house on Sunday morning,

Nancy has just nipped out for a few minutes with Bert they have gone to see if they can buy a house that is for sale, that is if it doesn't fetch too much. I will know when she comes back.

The pigs feet were 2/6, sausage 1/6 this is 4/-.

I will bring you clean underwear on Saturday.

I wrote to Muriel last night. I have post the xmas cards to Germany. I will do the rest tonight.

The house fetched £1725, far too much for Nancy. It wanted a lot of cleaning doing to it. They thought they could do it themselves if it went cheap.

Wednesday

We had quite a nice time at the party. I went home first to do myself up. I could not let the Jerries down and I don't think I did. I wore my fawn dress and brown high heels. Freddy enjoyed himself. When we were home he didn't want to leave us, he came upstairs when we went to bed then again in the middle of the night. You need not worry he went down again.

I am going to ~~Birstall~~ Evington tonight.

About staying at Pickwell Saturday night – it is rather hard to decide what to do because I know you would like me to stay there but I have rather a lot I could do at home on Sunday morning, not only that, do you think a taxi would be reliable I would rather you took a taxi to Melton than a motorbike especially if the roads are like they are today, icy. Well darling will close.

All my love and kisses

Jean.

My dearest darling Hans

I thought if I put this on paper I could explain better but I still find it difficult. I will try –

I want you to choose your job to make up your mind what you will be happy doing and I will try to help you the best I can and I promise to try to be contented with what we have. When you look for a job look for one with prospects that is one you can gain experience in. Not a job like lorry driving that you already know but if that was your choice I will understand. It is up to you to choose what we will do. I am sorry I can't help you there.

In the new year we will really have to start saving. We will have to go without things that are not really necessary, luxury things like all our sweet ration, grapes etc: and going to the pictures a lot and lots of other things. I want you to help me to save Hans. It is the only way we will ever get anywhere.

You know I would like to start a family, but I hate the idea of having to wait for the week's wages before we can get the rations like so many people nowadays. And I sure I will be able to budget it out whatever we get coming in. Love Jean

24/12.49   Aschersleben, 7.12.49

My dear Hans and Jean

Thank you very much for your lovely letter dated 28.11.49. You wrote this letter exactly on the date of our wedding anniversary. It seems you had to wait for a long time again for post from us, but I am sure you must have received some in the meantime. We also received your letter in which you mentioned the parcel and we are looking forward to it very much. I answered this letter immediately. I shall go to Berlin and collect the parcel. Horst is very busy before Christmas. The poor boy looks really ill at the moment. He has been working extremely hard. If you could have seen him you would have felt sorry for him when he was fighting to get his breath. It was frightening during the Sunday night.They gave him some asthma injections and because his heart has got so weak, the body did not respond to the treatment. Yesterday, he went to see a different doctor, who gave him a thorough examination. Today he had another X-Ray. Thank God his lungs are healthy, but the problems with his bronchial tubes and his heart continue. I am always so worried about him. There is only one solution: a change of air and better, healthier food. I shall be very happy when the parcel arrives. Horst will be able to consume some good quality food. The doctor advised him to drink as much coffee, made from coffee beans, as possible to stimulate his heart. He does too much, always offering to help out – if only he got better again.

And how are you, my dear boy? I hope your leg is better. I dreamed of you both last night. I was with you and it was so lovely for me to be able to talk to you again. I always take Horst's lunch to his shop, because it takes about 20 minutes to get there. I don't want him to be outside too much in this inclement weather. I am really enjoying my galoshes – they are serving me well at the moment. We are on good terms with our landlady. She is very grateful that Horst does her hair every day, and he is happy to oblige. He decorated the shop window beautifully again this year. He created some lovely hair styles for the Christmas Season. You have no idea how pleased Horst's boss is with him. Her tills are always happily ringing, whilst other hairdressing salons complain about the lack of profit and are struggling to make ends meet. Uncle Erich is sending you both his love. He was very happy to receive your letter, but has been unable to write back as he has too much work. Then, when he did get around to it, he discovered that he had mislaid your address. He has now asked me to send him your address and he intends to write to you immediately he gets it. Uncle Erich went to your grandma's grave on Totensonntag *. Auntie Berta and Uncle Albert still live in Rosow on the Oder and he also went to see Hannchen Werner in Angermünde – I am sure you remember her? She came to see us often when she lived in Stargard. She has a little girl of one year and two months and now her husband has left her for another woman. This kind of thing happens almost on a daily basis nowadays. Mrs. Fuchs has sent us four parcels packed with our belongings. Everything has arrived so far, but there are quite a few parcels still over there, in addition to the crockery. I am going to the doctor's tomorrow morning to get a prescription for a massage to help ease my rheumatism. My hands get very numb at times with pins and needles.

Dear Hans, please don't forget Auntie Erna's birthday on 23 January. I am sure she would be very happy to receive a card from you. Ursel's birthday is on 19 January and Lina's on 12 April. They would all be very happy to receive post from you.

I am sending you, my dear Hans, and your Jean, all my love and kisses, your Mum, brother and brother-in-law Horst.

Also kind regards to your mother-in-law.

* Sunday of the Dead' - the Sunday before Advent to commemorate the dead

R 24/12.49

Aschersleben,   3rd [Sunday of] Advent, 1949
24/12.49

My dear Hans and Jean,

Today on the 3rd Day of Advent we send you our love. Outside there is a storm and it is snowing, so the best place is in a warm room. How's your leg, dear Hans? I very much hope that it is better again. In 14 days, we will be celebrating Christmas. If only our greatest Christmas wish could be fulfilled and our dear papa would come home to us! This one hopes from one year to the next. Many people are coming who haven't registered yet. We both fear Christmas coming because we'll be so lonely again. If only you could at least visit us! Thank goodness Horstel is a little better. I have to go to the Occupational Health doctor tomorrow. I need to get Disability stamps, so I have to make a sworn declaration to say where I have worked. I will have to write to Hermann Wentland, who is in Itzehoe in Holstein and to Frau Theel, near Luebeck. They can best give me the confirmation I need. I can't keep on expecting Horst to keep me fed.

419

I had collected 11 years' worth of stamps at home. The worst thing is that in 1945 all the papers were taken away from me, but it wasn't my fault.

According to the regulations, I need another 3 years' worth of stamps, that would cost 108 Marks. Where can I get that from ? In that case, they shouldn't have taken all of my papers away from us.

Aunt Lina has asked me to send you her warmest greetings. I just cannot understand why Bruno hasn't visited her at least once. He could have got an Interzone Pass a long time ago. Our landlady travelled to Rheidt near Cologne on the Rhein early yesterday with an Interzone Pass to visit her Sophie. By 22:00 she was already in Cologne. She was able to pay with East Marks for the trip as far as Cologne, it cost her 41.30 Marks. Then she had to pay for her return back here with West Marks, but you have to give a valid reason. Dear Hans, I hope that you are giving your Jean language lessons so that I can talk to her when we meet again and you introduce your young wife to us! I am now getting a hot air massage so that my rheumatism should improve. You must surely be pleased that you don't have to sit on the tractor in this awful weather. First, just get yourself really healthy, otherwise working is no joy. Haven't you got a suitable flat yet? It will be a very busy time for Horst at his work over the two weeks before Christmas. Now my dear ones, we wish you a very joyous, happy and healthy Christmas, the first in your young marriage! Spend the festive days as best you can, we'll be with you in our thoughts. Heartfelt greetings from your mother and from your brother and brother-in-law Horst. Warm greetings to your mother-in-law. With hopes for a healthy reunion.

Pickwell,
Dec 27th 1949

My sweetest little wife

I got back safe and sound. Bonzo was no trouble at all. As there was nobody sitting beside me on the back seat I put Bonzo on and he stopped there laying down all the time.

Well, my sweetie, I thank you so very very much for a lovely Christmas time. Even if it only was for 2 days it was great. Believe me I enjoyed every second.. You made me so happy night before last. I shall love little Johnny. I hope I was able to make you happy too. Oh! I'll be lonely tonight. Thank goodness it's only 4 days to go till I be home again.

So be good and if you should happen to dream, dream of our family.

Goodnight and God bless you always I love you more than anything else in the world.

Wednesday Dec 28th 49, 7.30pm

Today I received 3 letters. 2 in the morning, one from my mother and one from Gertrud. My mother told me in hers that she was in possession of the parcel coupon and was going to collect it the same week. In the letter which came this afternoon she said she'd got the parcel on the 16.12 four days after the coupon arrived. She thanks us very much for it. Both of us as she knows my money is yours as well.

Gertrud thanks us for the cake. She couldn't write before as she has had an operation and was in hospital for 5 weeks. Operation on the lower part of her abdomen. I know when I was there she always had pains in what she thought was her stomach. I didn't have a close look though.

Tonight I'll mend that little hole in my brown socks and have them ready again for the weekend.

Are you listening to "Marriage Guidance"? It's interesting, but we won't be one of that divorce that happens every 10 minutes. Aren't we perfect? Oh, Jeannie I love you very, very much. I hope to be able to make you very happy, believe me I'll try my best.

Well darling, I'll say goodnight and God bless you. Pleasant dreams to you.

All my love and thousand kisses
Forever your loving husband
Hans.

Ashersleben 12.12.49
28/12.49

My dear Hans

We have just received your lovely registered letter with the parcel voucher dated 5.12.49, and thank you both from the bottom of our hearts. We cannot not tell you how happy we are. I am intending to go to Berlin in two days-time to collect the parcel. The train leaves at 1.30 in the morning and I shall be home again in the evening of the same day at 8.45 pm. I shall put the parcel into the rucksack, so I am sure I will be able to carry it. Alas, my dear Hans, why have we become so poor! How much we would love to give you a gift for Christmas. If only I could go out to work and earn some money. I posted my letter to you this morning but I am writing to you again immediately so that you know we received the voucher. I spent all morning at the doctor's and am glad that it is behind me now. I paid my membership fee as well, 3 Marks per month. We are very happy to hear that you are better again, but please, do be careful and don't work too hard. You must not get ill again.

I really don't understand that you have not received any post from us. I have written to you so many times. I posted the last few letters to Leicester, but will now send them to your old address again. We always receive your post very quickly. Or do you have another suggestion? I am so pleased that I have my galoshes, because today we have the most awful snow slush. I am sure Horst will have got wet feet today.

Well, my dear Hans, I want to finish my letter for now. This afternoon I have an appointment for another heat therapy session.

My dears, please both stay healthy. I am sending you all my love and kisses,
your mum and your brother Horst.
And thank you again, from the bottom of my heart.

R 29/12.49   Aschersleben, 16.12.49

28/12.49

My dear Hans and Jean

I am confirming receipt of your parcel today. We are so happy about all the lovely things you sent us and thank you from the bottom of our hearts. We are now able to celebrate Christmas. Yesterday afternoon I returned from Berlin. Everything went very smoothly and without any problems. It is always a big and happy day for us, when we receive your parcels. On Tuesday I left in the night at ten past one. I did not have to pay the extra fee in Güsten for the fast train, because it was overfilled and I had to wait for the next train which came at six o'clock in the morning. I arrived in Berlin Wannsee at 11 a.m. I then had to take the City Railway to the Lehrter Station and afterwards I walked to Lotti's. They were very welcoming. It was seven years ago when we last saw each other. Her husband returned home from the war captivity in April. After we had taken lunch, Paul and I went out for a walk and did some window shopping. Then we went by underground to the Lützowstrasse to collect the parcel. We should really have gone to the Grosse Hamburger Strasse, which is our allocated post office, which is in the East Sector. But I would not have been able to get there by 3 pm because it was already nearly 3 pm. I begged the lady to let me have the parcel because I would not have been able to stay until tomorrow afternoon in Berlin, because I had booked the laundry room for the next day. The lady must have taken pity on me and handed the parcel over. I was beaming with joy and left. I had intended to catch the train at 6 pm in order to get home by 4 pm the next morning, but Lotti and Paul did not let me go. I had to spend the night at their house and take the 7 am train, which got me home at 4 pm in the afternoon. Lotti and Paul are sending their best wishes to you. They are doing well. They and their children have sufficient to eat. I wished we had enough too.

My dear boy, you have given us so much pleasure with your wonderful Christmas parcel. We shall enjoy everything and will be thinking of you all the time. The only thing we long for now is that our Papa comes home. It would make our Christmas complete. We hope you will have a lovely Christmas. It is 9 pm and Horst has still not returned home from work. I did all my laundry today. I am always glad when I manage to finish this task, because Horstel's white overalls give me quite a headache each time. I shall make a nice cake for Christmas now.

I hope, dear Hans, that you have – by now – received all my letters. I have written seven since 18 November. Dear Hans, have the photos not yet been developed?

Now, my dears, I want to finish my letter for today. Many, many thanks again for everything. Stay well and have a lovely Christmas and a blessed New Year. My best wishes also go to your mother-in-law. We are sending you all our love and kisses, your mum, brother and brother-in-law. We are hoping for a healthy reunion.

I am enclosing the table of contents.

11552

In case of any claim whatsoever, the original form of this table of contents needs to be sent to the;

Caritas Head Office

Luzern

Switzerland

We would ask the parcel recipient to please confirm receipt of the parcel to the sender immediately, so that further parcels/shipments can be executed without delay.

Name of recipient:---

Land and Province --

Town, postal district

And post code _____

Street   _____   No.
_____

Caritas Head Office Switzerland

Lucerne

Type Caritas C

1 tin lard – 2 pounds gross weight

1 tin margarine – 2 pounds gross weight

1 tin beef in in brine 2 pounds gross weight

1 tin pâté de foie 115 g net weight

1 tin pork in brine 1 pound gross weight

1 tin ham and beef roll 1 pound net weight

2 bags of coffee 1 pound each

2 bags of sugar 1 pound each

2 bags of rice 1 pound each

1 tin condensed milk, sweetened 400 g

1 tin condensed milk, unsweetened 413 g

1 tin honey 400 g

½ pound of chocolate

½ pound of cocoa

1 tin of jam 900 g

2 pounds of wheat flour

1 pound of raisins

Pound = English pound = 453 g

Christmas Wishes

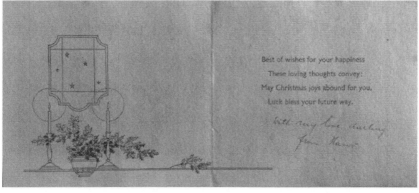

Best of wishes for your happiness
These loving thoughts convey:
May Christmas joys abound for you,
Luck bless your future way.

92 Wharf St
28.12.49

My dearest darling Hans

Did you get back to Pickwell safe and was Bonzo with you?
I am tired this afternoon. Mamma and I finished the remains
of the turkey and pudding and now I feel like I did yesterday
after lunch. Take me all my time to keep my eyes open.

How has work gone down with you today? Were you up in
time? Big Ben has stopped, it stopped at 12.30 last night so
of course I did not know what time it was, it wasn't too bad
a guess, 8.10. I lit the fire and a good one at that, but not as
nice as the one you lit. I need not tell that I did not get here at
work on time. I am going to start the new year right, be here
on time and walk not run.

I have just had a little nap. I had to be careful that I did not
fall to sleep and believe me that wouldn't take much doing.

They are going to close the hostel Mr Chandlers is at. I wonder what he is going to do?

Did you have a good Christmas darling? I did. I had a beautiful one. I was miserable Xmas Eve, it did not seem like
Christmas but the rest of the time more than made up of
that. I only hope we can always be as happy together as we
are now. Maybe I do not tell you very often but I do really
love more than anything else in the world.

I have just had a drop of sherry sent in by Mr Percival, so I
asked one of the girls in the typing pool to share it with me.

It is now 4.45 and we still have not had any tea, it doesn't
look as though we will get any. They have just brought it
thank goodness.

I'm not going anywhere tonight. I will do a few odd jobs and I
will have an early night.

Well my darling in 10 min time I should be on my way to

post this.

So until Saturday all my love and kisses
Jean

Pickwell,
Dec 29<u>th</u> 1949

My darling

I thank you so very much for your lovely letter I received this morning. Believe me I was surprised

I wasn't very tired these last few days. Of course I haven't had such a lot to do. Today I went watercatering with Mr Lewis or whatever his name is. You know the old chap from Burrough. Since yesterday I do my shutting up turn again. It's not too bad going you asked me if I was up in time yesterday morning. Since I started to work here I have been late once and that means once in 15 months. Pretty good record I think.

Oh! Jeannie Christmas was wonderful. It's a shame the nice time goes so quick. Don't worry, we'll always be so very happy. Even if you don't tell me very often but I know you love me. Still, like you, I always like to hear you say it.

The boss asked me this morning if our bedroom is empty as he saw the beds in here. He wanted to put some wheat into that room as he has got nowhere else to put it. We can have it back any time we want it. I haven't said it to him but I don't think I shall sleep in there again. I won't be here that long. We shan't go in there anyway as long as it is cold.

John told me yesterday that they are going to build 6 council houses here directly. He said it was in the Melton Times a week before xmas. He asked if I was going in for one of them. I am getting wiser now. I didn't answer and changed the subject instead.

Bonzo had his worm capsules this morning, but I didn't notice any action at all. So I gave him something to eat tonight.

He was hungry. Poor chap didn't get anything for 1 ½ day.

Well, my sweetheart, it's 8.45 and I'll write to my mother now. Be good and think of us and our little family.

Goodnight and God bless you. Sure? ------- Quite sure!! All my love and a thousand kisses.

Friday Dec 30th 1949, 8.50pm

Hello, my darling, here I am again. I've been very busy till now. Cooking dinner, washing up and washing my hair, getting the chicken ready and after I've finished this I'll have a good wash myself. Then of course, off to bed. The day went pretty quick. First thing I went moving half a dozen nighth-arks and then – as lately – carrying straw for the rest of the day.

Did you listen to "Family Favourites" tonight? Harry Lime Theme and "Never Trust a Woman". That second one was silly. One should always trust the woman one loves.

Well, sweetie, only ½ day to go. Oh! I am longing for it all. You're so sweet and I loves you so very very much. What about Jeannie?

Be good darling till I see you tomorrow. Goodnight and God bless. Pleasant dreams.

> All my love and kisses
> Forever your loving husband
> Hans.

> 92 Wharf St.
> January 1st
> 1950

My dearest darling

We have at least begun the New Year together. Darling, I love you very, very, much and I hope I can make you very happy. I will try always to be understanding and I will always be faithful to you and I hope I will be able to give you a beautiful son (to start with). I think we had better wait until we have had a holiday in Germany before we think of him again. Because we could not afford to go if that happened and I would not want to go looking like the back end of a bus. Having a baby is a big expense and you know I want everything nice. Darling, when I start saying we can't afford this or that does not mean I am dissatisfied and unhappy because believe me if you owned the bank of America I could not possibly be happier than I am right now. Oh, Hans I am so glad I married you. You make such a wonderful husband and I am not just saying that to please you. You are so wonderful in helping to do everything,and I know that is very unusual for a man. I know most men think that women are here to wait on them.

I am all alone Mamma has gone out, Fred and Bill are here, we will not get stuck for conversation.

You should be back at Pickwell now, 9.15. I have "Variety Bandbox" on, so far it is very good. I have roasted some chestnuts, one has just gone pop and the dogs nearly shot out of their skins. I will put the nuts away for a fortnight and the bar of chocolate (the Pickwell pub one) then we can have another Xmas. I hope all our lives will be Xmas.

My darling I will have to get going with your pullover now. So God Bless you and keep you safe.

> All my love ~~and~~ kisses
> And a very happy new year
> Jeannie

MONDAY

I have the registered letter You are married to a dope! I got the registered envelope from the Post Office lunchtime, I never thought about how wide your book was and of course the envelope was too small, but I could not waste 7 ½ I had written the address on it but with a bit of manoeuvering I managed to get it in. You need not worry I did not bend your photograph I will post it with this tonight.

I have been spending this lunchtime, I bought 2 pairs of knitting needles size 10 & 12 and a packet of soft collars 3/ 10 1/2 . Stamps etc 1/ 1/2 . We will have to get the dog license

this month.
Well darling Cheeri'O happy New Year
Jean.

Pickwell

Jan, 2nd 1950

My sweetest, little wife,

I arrived back here safe and sound at about 8.40, started the fire, but didn't bother to get myself some supper. I felt full. It looks to me as if I always over-eat myself when I am at home. You make everything so nice and in your company it tastes much better than it does when I cook it here.

After all it was 11.00 p.m. when I went to bed. I stayed up too late to see Helmut coming in. I had to say something to him and if I had waited till the morning I might have changed my mind. He had been sleeping in my bed again and messed it up with his wellingtons. I was mad, believe me. Well, I told him I don't want him to sleep in my bed again and the next time I go away for the weekend I'll lock the blankets and pillow case away. If he wants to have a go on the bare bedstead, he can. He knew he was in the wrong so he didn't say anything at all, but helped today where ever he could. When I came in at dinner time the fire was lit and tonight he peeled spuds and even dried, a thing he hasn't done for weeks. It looks as if he has to have a telling-off occasionally.

Did you post the letter to the H.O.? How's the pullover getting on? Sorry, darling I shouldn't ask, but wait till you tell me. I still have to learn a lot. I'll try my best to learn from my mistakes.

How's work gone down with you today? Another fortnight to go till I'll be able to come over again. I only wish it was tomorrow. When will it be? Not long sweety, I hope. Because I can't stand it much longer. Think how nice our life could be. I daren't think of it and then remember the fact of sitting out here in the wilderness. Well, darling, this year will bring some changes.

Now I'll say goodnight and God bless you.
All my love and thousand kisses
Forever your loving husband.
Hans.

Pickwell
Jan. 3rd 1950

My dearest, darling Jean,
Thank you, darling, thank you so very much for your lovely letter. The best one I've ever received.
Look, my darling, if the first one is a girl instead of a boy I'll be just as happy. Don't think because I keep talking about a boy that I would be disappointed with a baby-girl. It'll be our baby and that's really all that matters. Be sure I'll be happy whatever it is going to be.
Was I laughing when I read about "looking like the back of a bus". People in Germany look at these things a bit different than here. Still, sweetheart, I for myself wouldn't ~~back~~ mind owning the Bank of America. Still, you are right, we certainly couldn't be happier. Only the financial situation would be slightly different. A couple of big cars, a lovely big house and so many maids that there wouldn't be anything at all to do for my sweet, little wife. That's what I would like to get to one day. Jeannie just driving around in a smashing little M.G. sports car. And our children growing up like organ-pipes, but not just as many. That's the castle in the air I like to build. Let's hope one day it'll be true.
You can't imagine how glad I am I married you and I shall always be very proud of my English wife. No other girl in the world could be lovelier and better than you are. What's Margaret Lockward got, that you haven't got. Nothing at all. To me you are the girl I was hoping to call my wife one day. And

that wish has been fulfilled.

Even if it is unusual for a man to do the things I do, I'll always hope to be able to help you with everything. I certainly don't mind what it is as long as I can see you happy. Do you understand when I say that it would be nice if the meals were ready when I come home from work but that's only so we can have more time for ourselves and the children afterwards. But if it isn't we'll get it ready together, right?

I am listening to "Cinderella". It's very nice. It has just finished and now "Take it from here".

Wasn't it awful today? Till lunchtime I stopped in the yard doing odd jobs, because it was raining too hard. For the rest of the day I went cleaning out. Thanks for posting the reg. Letter. I should hear from the H.O. within the next fortnight. Jeannie, now my wife, isn't a dope, please get that straight. She just forgot to think about size of the envelope.

Well, my darling, I'll close now. Be good. God bless you and keep you safe. Please give my regards to my mother-in-law!!! (The best one I can think of).

> Goodnight and also a happy new year to you.
> All my love and kisses
> Forever your loving husband
> Hans.

92 Wharf St

4.1.50

My dearest darling Johannes.

Thank you for both your letters. The post office seems to have gone back to their old time. I received one on Tuesday and the other today Wednesday.

"Have a go" has just come on ~~the~~ das radio are you listening? I did listen to "Cinderella" also the play "His house in order" did you? I thought it was very good. I have not been out at all this week so I have listen to most programmes and doing your pullover, last night I washed your vest and pants and my vest. I was only going to wash mine, ~~but~~ because I will need it at the weekend only having two vest I knew you could wait having 4 lots but I washed them. I also darned your socks. Mamma washed them, I told her they did not need it but it was too late.

Miggy called into the office this morning, she was on her way to catch the train, Otto had gone to the station with her mother, another German came down from Scotland with them. They came down on Friday and have been staying with some friends at Nuneaton where her mother is living now. She has spent most of the time looking for a place to live as they are coming back to Leicester in three weeks time and have both got jobs at John Bull rubber Co.,they have not had any luck this time, so Miggy is coming down a week before to have a look around. She showed me her wedding photograph and said she would send me one.

So poor Helmut has the push, where will he live after next Friday if he is unable to find accommodation? What about you my darling being on your own. Do you think you had better pack it in too or wait until you hear from the Home Office. It is up to you, but whatever you do try to leave without any bother no matter what you think of the place.

Freddy and I are alone. Mamma has gone out with Gert. I'm just going to have a wash, I would hate to come to Pickwell dirty.

Well my darling I have to do my hair so good night and God Bless you.

> I love you very much
> Your Sweetie

———

P.S.

> I am having Monday off to help Gertie move in
> Jean.

R 10/1.50   Aschersleben, Christmas 1949

My dear Hans

I would like to send you all our love today, at Christmas. Thanks to your help and generosity, we were able to enjoy a lovely Christmas celebration. We had such fine delicacies! But, the festive season is coming to an end. Our thoughts were always with you.

Last night, the Rückbrechts and the Ziemanns came to see us. It is always nice to have some company here. When we can talk to other people, it takes our minds off all our worries. I was always hoping we would get the photo of you by Christmas, so that we would have felt your presence even more, but it was not to be. Your photographers seem rather slow.

It will be four months this week since you got married. How was your Christmas? Was Father Christmas kind to you? We hope he was really busy! We are very pleased with everything. Horst gave me a nice piece of material, from which I can have a dress made. I also got a ring etc. All the HO shops were very busy with lots of long queues. The prices have already gone down quite a bit, but are still too high for ordinary people like us. How was your first Christmas together as a married couple? We hope, dear Hans, that you did not have to work during the festive season. I am sure everyone would like to be at home over Christmas. I was hoping and hoping that our beloved Papa would be home for Christmas. When, oh when, will our wish be fulfilled? So many soldiers are coming home now, from whom their loved ones did not receive any news.

Horst was very busy over Christmas. He did not know whether he was coming or going at times. Had he been able to serve his clients yesterday or today, he would have earned himself a lot of money, but jealousy is the root of all evil!

Everyone is envious of each other.

Horst went out for a while to a dance. He needs a little distraction.

We haven't had any post from you, but now that the holiday season is over, deliveries should get back to normal again.

Now, my dears, we wish you a very happy New Year, and all the very, very best for you two.

Lots of love and kisses from your mum and brother Horst.

Give our love to your mother-in-law.

92 Wharf St

10.1.50

My dearest darling Hans,

I have not started to write at a good time, Jack on the lift has been speaking to me. I have to chat to him because he brings me his paper every morning. Just as he had gone in came the telephone engineer, one of the old ones and he talks a lot, always about what he told people, he bores me stiff. Since writing that I have had two girls in talking and the engineer has gone, the girls were here so he did not stay to talk thank goodness.

I will tell you about my day off. Gertie asked me to be there about 10.0 and I was just on time. Their house is very nice. There is one long room downstairs, a bay window one end and french doors the other. The kitchen is a nice size too. The sink fits into a bay which makes the kitchen light, there are two big rooms and a small one, a bathroom in black and white, the lavatory is in the back room. It was a job to know where to put all of the stuff. Gertie has to buy a sideboard to put the china and glass in, also a new bedroom suite for herself. They are going to have a garage built, but they cannot have one built until they are in the house, so until then the mangle will have to stand in the back. The garden looks awful at the moment, anyway you can go and see it for yourself. I too wish it was our place, but I am sure if we save hard we will have a place like that. We went to Doris for lunch, but we had tea at the new place just with Gertie and Aunty and I set the table properly.

Do you think we could manage to sleep 2 in your bed, because if you cover up, rather block the mouse hole up, I would love to come for the weekend Jan 21 + 22nd. I would then have a chance to cook one dinner. We can talk about it this weekend. That is if you would like me to come. It would be fun.

Mamma had a card from your mother this morning. I think it was a New Years card.

Has Helmut got a job yet? You should hear from the Home Office next week sometime. .

Be good and remember I love you very very much

 All my love and kisses

 Jeannie.

Pickwell

Jan. 11th 1950.

My sweetest, little wife,

Are you lucky, or rather am I lucky!! I've just had a look and found 5 x ½ stamps left. So it'll just be enough for your letter.

I thought it over and now rather like the idea of having one big room on the ground floor. It sounds nice, anyway. You like the french windows, don't you? We'll have one, one day, be sure of it. And with a big bay and French window.

There was no need to tell me that you set the table. I know you can do it properly.

Why shouldn't we be able to sleep 2 in my bed. It'll be fun, and everything has to be tried once. You know I want you to come. If the place was only something better and decent I would keep you here and no switchboard on Monday morning. Or I myself come home and take over the place, meaning you to stop at home.

Well, sweetie, yesterday I thought I was going to die. A good thing I know it takes more to die. In the morning I took tractor and trailer and moved the shaving stuff into our bedroom. After lunch Mr Bromwich (Doris's father) and I carted a few more loads of straw into another shed. Well, one cart was unloaded, I got one from the back whilst Mr. B. just put his hand out to get hold of the reins, the horse suddenly pulled and off I came. Hard ground and flat on my right side. From hip to the foot. I got up straight away, but had to sit down for a few minutes, the leg is still the same, but now the foot hurts awfully. Never mind I'll have a rest on Saturday and it's only 2 ½ more days to go. Thank God when this week is over.

Helmut went down to Melton again yesterday and he's got the job after arguing with the Labour Exchange. They asked him why he hasn't taken that farm job at Kirby Bellars. He had a look there and found it a dirty place, far away from anywhere. So he told the fellow at the L.E. if it was a decent place that farmer would have had somebody a long time ago. After all he got the job at Melton. He'll be living at Little Dalby (with the Jerrie) and as he told me his wages will be £6, carrying milk cans and stacking cheese. Not rolling it to the station!! So he's fixed up alright.

We (Gerald and I) had some fun today. We went watercarting after lunch in the big field. From underneath one of the houses I saw a rabbit dashing out making for the hedge. It was about the middle of the field. Bonzo was in front of us so I called him and he went after it. You should have heard us shouting. Gerald for a bit of fun, and I thinking of a nice dinner. So as loud as ever we could: "Get him"!! He chased it across the whole lengths of the field and gained space every second. Then suddenly he turned a somersault and when he got up again the rabbit was in his mouth. It made a lovely dinner or rather two. Gerald was surprised when Bonzo brought it back.

After all it looks ~~after~~ as if I'll have to bring Bonzo along on

Saturday. That is if I can't fix anything else up for him. I hope you and Mamma don't mind.

Well, my darling, I'll say goodnight now. Be good, and think of S- day. I'll be with you then.

Pleasant dreams and look after yourself well. Remember I love you more than anything else in the world.

> All my love and kisses
>> Forever your loving husband
>> Hans.

<u>P.S.</u>
 No reply from the H.O.
Love Hans.

> Pickwell
> Jan. 12th1950

My sweetest, little wife,

It's Thursday night and the weekend is within reach. Only day and a half to go. Believe me I am ready for it. My leg feels quite good tonight. Should be after such a lovely day and the weekend so near.

Well, sweetie, it's 8.15 and I've been very busy till just 10 minutes ago. In fact I've painted my bike black. The second coat tomorrow night and then it has time to dry over the weekend. I am going to take the other old bike tomorrow so it'll keep mine klean till it's properly dry.

Do you think it's worth posting this letter? I think I'd rather bring it along on Saturday.

Helmut is gone out tonight again and for the last time. Yesterday I asked him if he wasn't going to pack his few things together before Friday night. He said he's just jamming his things into the kitbag and everything he possesses is packed. Still that's a way of doing it, too.

I am still hungry after dinner. When I came back from shutting up Helmut surprised me saying there are no potatoes left. So we had to have bread and the rest of the rabbit.

Darling, I am longing for my Saturday dinner. It's always so nice. But I am still more longing for the dinner on Sunday week for Jeannie will be cooking that. Everything is left to you for these two days and as you know what my rations will look like, bring what you think will be right. That includes breakfast, tea and also supper. Eggs will be here, also bacon. Are you going to bring your cookery books along? If you do, pick something nice.

Well, my sweetheart, for now I'll say goodnight. Be good and remember I love you so very very much. God bless you and keep you safe.

All my love and kisses.

Friday, Jan 13th 1950. 9.30pm

So Helmut has left at about 8.00 and as I told you as I was going to have a go at the place. And so I did. A good cleanout, the wash will follow one night next week, before you come over, anyway. This time I want to show you the room look quite different. Of course, things have been moved around a bit. My bed stands against the other wall now. At least it won't be so hot having the fire going. Don't be surprised, I even cleaned the three shelves. It looks tidy now.

Packing my bag will finish the day off, but don't worry, I am not worn out yet. Anyway, let me tell you how much I'm longing for the weekend. Still, it's only a few more hours to go in the morning.

Well, I'll bring Bonzo along tomorrow. The only trouble is that I have to go back an hour earlier.

My bike has also had the second coat and looks rather nice. No compliments on the job, please. I am not a painter, so there are some places that don't look what they should look like.

Well, my darling, I'll say goodnight and God bless and keep you safe. Be good and my sweet little wife. The fact is, the best wife in the world. I love you more than anything else.

All my love and kisses

Forever your faithful and loving husband

Hans.

92 Wharf St

12.1.50

My dearest darling

Thank you so very much for your letter. When I saw the half penny stamps on the envelope I thought that you had run out of stamps. You poor darling, falling off the cart. I hope that nasty horse falls on his hip. You had better bring Bonzo with you on Saturday, it would be best at least you would know he would not get into any trouble.

I have been knitting and listening to the wireless. I started to listen to " Florence Nightingale" then put it on to "Rays a laugh" Last night I was very busy.. I darned the hole in your brown socks and other odd bits of sewing.

Nancy heard there was a cottage to let at Frisby so she rang the post office about it, to find out who it belonged to. After a lot of inquiries she wrote, but it had already been taken.

I am sorry this is not a very long letter, but I will make up for it Saturday and talk you to death.

Well my darling be good. See you soon

All my love

Jeannie

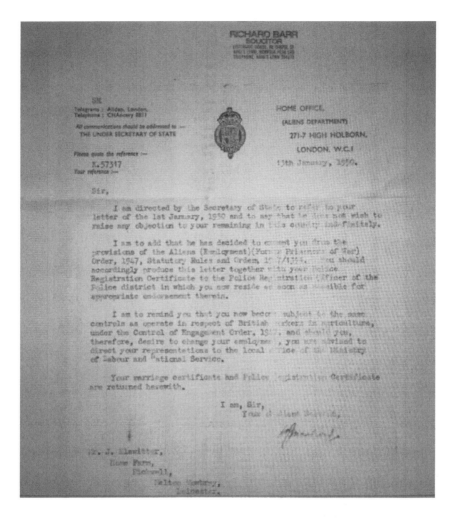

The awaited letter from the Home Office.

Pickwell

Jan. 15th 1950

"My darling"

Here I am, safe and sound. I arrived back at 7.30, started the fire and on the way in fetched my milk. Mrs Cooper had left it ready on the doorstep. Still, I knocked and asked her if it was mine. Fortunately, there was a letter from my mother, as well. Came yesterday afternoon. When I got myself ready to get off the bus (at the church), Bonzo got up and ran to the door and straight off the moving bus before I was able to call him back. I saw him overturn a few times and then he chased after the bus. Good thing the bus doesn't go fast round those corners. Anyway, he's alright now.

It certainly is a bit different now when I get back here. At least the place is as clean as I left it yesterday. And Helmut's boots don't smell anymore. I've fixed the electric fittings. Don't tell Mamma to buy one of those switches. She can have my old one. It'll be alright for her room. At least I've done away with all those wires hanging on the lamp. When I come over again in a fortnight time remind me to measure the distance to the kitchen and I'll put you a light in there. We'll buy the cable on Saturday afternoon and fix it Sunday morning. So you can see properly when you do toast on the gas. It'll cost a few bob, but I think it is worth it. We shall want cable, junction box, switch and bulb holder. Of course some cable tacks. Don't get anything yourself. Wait till I come over again.

I was surprised when I read my mother's letters. She has got a hen and 4 pullets. As I am a poultry specialist I'd better go and start a poultry farm there. Well, at least, they'll be able to have a few eggs. The price of eggs is 30 Mark (£1-10-0) for one.

And now off for "Variety Bandbox". It's just before 9.00. Nice and cosy (warm) in here. I only wish you're with me. Still another 6 days hard work to go. Never mind, I am looking forward to Saturday. I'll get a nice hen and we'll have a smashing Sunday dinner. Can you remember everything you have to bring along? Don't forget the pepper. The little man will have some I'm sure. If you don't remember everything, I'll put a list into the next letter.

  So be good and pleasant dreams: All my love and kisses

Monday, Jan. 16th, 1950, 7.20p.m..

After I finish this I'll write the letter to my Aunt. Perhaps another one to my mother.

Helmut might be coming over tonight. Before he left on Friday he said he had to come again tonight as the "P-Form" wasn't ready. Never heard of it. Do you know what it is?

Oh! Listen, Jeannie, please bring us half a packet of tea back. I just had a look and found there's not enough left to last us two days. I don't want to miss my Sunday morning cup of tea. I've had my ½ pound for this period.

Did you listen to "The Piddingtons"? It was quite good. I don't think there's any foul play in that thought transferring. I went over to the shop tonight and fetched a packet of tobacco, 2 lbs of apples (to save the plums) and oats. One night I'll have stewed apple-suet pudding.

Well, sweetheart, I'll say goodnight and God bless you. Pleasant dreams and keep dreaming of our dream house.

Be good and remember, daddy loves you more than anything else in the world.

> All my love and kisses
> Forever and only yours
> Hans.

92 Wharf St

15.1.50

My dearest darling Johannes.

I have started to write straight the way to you to make sure you hear from me by Tuesday. I was mad with my uncle Roll, they came (him and Gert) to fetch Mamma. You know how Fred goes to the door barking. Well just as Fred was at the door (Bill went too but not barking). He closed the door rather sharp, the dogs jumped back and over went the pot of water. I wasn't worried about the water really. I thought he might have hurt Fred. It was a good job he did not squeak out I would probably have thrown something. Because they were in the wrong. Uncle Roll knew I was annoyed, he said "I thought he was going to bite". In which case if they are afraid of Fred they should knock on the door and wait until we answer it. It's their own fault he barks at them, they tease him with their feet and making noises. Well that is enough about that I have almost cooled off.

Another weekend has gone, this week will not seem so long, because we will spend the next weekend together. I am really looking forward to it, being alone together I will try to make things as nice as I can. If there is anything you wish me to bring let me know.

Hans darling, it is up to you what job you take. You know what you are capable of doing. But I would not want you to take a job where there was not any head way. But if you should never make it I would love you just the same. So long as you have a good try. I will always be proud of you. I sometimes think I would like a change in places, but then I suppose I would be like Miggy. I would like to live in the country, not on a housing estate. I am sick of living in the town. In the town you may be near shops and cinemas but you don't want to get to the pictures every night or round the shops every day. Time will show what is to happen to us. So until then all my love and kisses Goodnight and God Bless you and help to make up your mind and to find what you want.

Your ever loving
sweetheart
Jeannie

Aschersleben, 2.1.50

My dear Hans and Jean

Thank you very much for your lovely letters dated 20.12. and 24.12. and for your Christmas card as well as the Christmas card from your mother-in-law. We were so happy to hear from you all. I also sent a Christmas card to your mother-in-law. Christmas is gone now and we are getting back into our old routine. I wonder what 1950 will bring us. I hope it will be a better year than 1949! I have just received your letter which you wrote on Christmas Eve and want to answer it right away. Yes, my dear boy, we were just as lonely as you over the Christmas season. I already mentioned this in my letter to you dated 26.12. On New Year's Eve we felt dreadfully lonely and 'deserted'. The Rückbrechts intended to come but something cropped up last minute and they had to cancel. Horst was so overwhelmed with work that he slept on the corner settee until 11 pm whilst I did the ironing. Then I made us some lovely coffee, which we had with a piece of cake I had baked. You need very little fat for this type of tin. Afterwards, both Horst and I went to the train station to see if our beloved Papa might be coming, but unfortunately!! From there, we walked through town and listened to the church bells which rang the New Year in at midnight. You were constantly in our thoughts and we talked about you all the time. My heart was so heavy over the holiday period. It was the tenth Christmas without my boy. There are so many soldiers returning from the war, in our neighbourhood. You can imagine how I feel – always missing out. When will this happy day come to us? I did want Horst to go out and celebrate with a friend on New Year's Eve. But I could not persuade him. He said to me that he would feel ashamed if he left me at home all alone on New Year's Eve. But I do want him so much to have some fun!

Dear Hans, please can you write to Auntie Erna on the occasion of her fiftieth birthday on 23 January. I know she would love to hear from you. She has not had many happy moments in her life either. With this inclement weather, it is very hard for her to be outside.

Dear Hans, long distance driving is a very hard and dangerous job and I am already worrying about you, especially when you are often plagued by the fog over there. You must take care of your foot and take the matter very seriously. Your mother-in-law should try heat therapy one day. They use this kind of treatment a lot here and it would be relavent in her case too.

Did you never receive my letters in which I told you that I had collected the parcel from Berlin before Christmas? The health insurance is now 36 Marks per month. Horst pays 50% and his lady boss also pays 50%. We now have 18 Marks less per month to budget with!!! It will get harder and harder for us!! Where on earth are we supposed to get all this money from? How can we build up a home from the money we have? People who can slaughter animals are not too badly off food wise. It would be great if one could scoop up something from their proceeds. We had lovely food over the Christmas period, it was wonderful, a real treat! I have gained some weight again. A year ago we had our forthcoming reunion before us. It was so lovely and we are looking forward to the next one. Mrs. Fuchs is still looking after our 25 pounds of flour. I want them to stay there so that we have something extra when we need it. Rosow is not in Poland, it is situated this side of the river Oder. The river Oder is the border between Germany and Poland.

Does your boss not carry on paying the health insurance stamp when you are off sick? I don't understand Bruno either any more. Auntie Lina wrote to me that she has not heard from him for four weeks again now. We have not heard from him since February last year. I can hardly believe this. I am convinced that he does not send anything to Auntie Lina. Is it right that his mother lives in such poor conditions? I do know that Auntie Lina is very poor, and I feel that it is Bruno's duty because Christel has not got the means to pay for everything. I would love to give him a piece of my mind. He could easily go to see his mother with an inter-zonal pass.

So many people come over by these means. It is a lot better than coming over illegally. I already told you that we have had some chickens since mid-November: One hen and four younger ones. They were very tiny when we got them but have developed very well. The old hen will be laying some eggs soon. She bites the younger ones. I smacked her today because she should not be so unkind. We are very fond of the animals. We had to pay 30 Marks for them and I also bought some fodder for 27 Marks. It is quite expensive but, at least, we can look forward to eating some lovely eggs soon. An egg costs 1.50 Marks. Dear Hans and Jean, what is happening with your wedding photos? We are dying to see them. They should have been here before Christmas!! Now, my dears, I want to finish my letter. Do teach Jean German so that we can talk together when we see each other again. Stay healthy. I am sending you my love and kisses. Your mum and brother Horst

Pickwell
Jan. 17ᵗʰ 1950

My little sweetie,

So my little Jeannie almost lost her temper. Never mind darling, if your Uncle Roll gets too fresh, tell him off. That's one big trouble having relations living in the same house. They think they can do how they like.

Believe me I also look forward to the weekend. It'll be nice. Well, darling I'll leave it to you about the pictures. As long as we get back here to have a few hours sleep before I start work Sunday morning, everything will be alright. I've told Gudger today that I want a chicken for Friday night. By the way, darling don't forget my clean things on Saturday. You poor darling have to carry all those things yourself. It's a shame I don't get back earlier so I could come up to Somerby on the bike.

Now about the job. Well, sweetheart, I myself feel capable of doing a lot of things. You know yourself I want to get on in life, have something to call my own. Of course, if I want to stay in farming the best thing to do is try and get on a mixed farm. I know that just hard work won't get me anywhere. Knowledge is just what matters. Doing a dirty job and getting a lot of money for doing it, it's just a way of making a living but not getting on.

Believe me, darling, I would like our children to say "My daddy is this or that". And I'll try my best to make my dreams come true.

So you yourself would like me to stay at a job in the country. I am not so much for living in a town myself.

It is wrong to say, time will show what is to happen to us. Happen to us will what we let happen to us. Sometimes it pays to go against the wind. Well, sweetie, we'll have another talk on Sunday.

Well, it's 9.00 o'clock now and it won't be long before I am off to bed. As usually I've been busy again tonight. I had a nice dinner and finished my meat off, also stewed apples and custard. After all, I'll make the bacon last two days. Over the weekend there is the chicken so I'll be alright. Remember I told you a long time ago I was going to have a go at my sheep skin gloves. Well, I've done that tonight and also got Sunday's milk ready for cream cheese. It's draining now. Sorry I can't keep it till Saturday. Tomorrow I'll wash the floor, Thursday night make a cake, Friday pluck the chicken and have a wash and then the weekend will be there. Well, my sweet little sugar plum, I'll say goodnight and God bless you always. I love you so very very much. Be good and look after yourself.

> All my love and kisses
>> Forever your loving husband
> Hans.

Wednesday, Jan. 18th 1950

Hello, sweetheart, how are you? The boss just came across the yard to ask a question and as the door was open he said "that certainly looks decent". You'll see for yourself on Saturday. Remember where to find the key? Open the right half of the window and you'll see it to the right on the inside of the frame.

I just thought of something. Don't you have to give particulars about the set when you get a wireless license? Well just in case: Type 3710/15, Phillips, No. M 21443. Please, darling, get the license and bring it along. That keen copper keeps snooping around too much. Day before yesterday he was here and told Mac to build the gateways up that come to a public road. He's even sent people back to clean the road after loosing dirt from cartwheels. So when I come back from the fields I always come in the back way. No road sweeping for me.

Well, my darling, it's 9 o'clock gone and I am really very tired. Been working pretty hard today. Cleaning out is finished but if he doesn't have anything else to do for me I'll have to start again. Never mind, Wednesday is over 3 ½ day to go.

I'll close for now. Be good my darling and look after yourself well.

I am so much longing for the weekend and love you so very-very-very much.

Please give my regards to Mamma

      All my love and kisses

        Forever and only your loving husband

      Hans.

    92 Wharf St

    17.1.50

"My darling"

Poor Bonzo I hope he is O.K now. I fetched his license last night and the wireless license. I asked for 2 dog licenses and a wireless. He wrote your 2 out first, he asked me what I wanted on the other so I said Mrs Jean Klawitter and I could say the address, he put Home farm Pickwell. I did not like to say anything, I thought it would not matter until I read a piece on the license about notifying the County Council of change of address. I had to get courage this lunchtime to go back to have it altered.

Did Helmut pay you a visit last night? A P-form, I believe is an income tax form. Does he like his new place?

Last night (Monday) I fetched the bread and milk from the little man and I felt very embarrassed. He started talking about you having to work some Sundays and so on. I do wish you had not led him to believe you were something that you weren't. I do not see any point in it, are you ashamed of being a farm worker. I would have told him what you did only I did not want him to think you were a fibber. So next time anything happens like that be yourself. I know that isn't really important, but I do hate it. I hope you do not mind me telling you.

The sweep has been and swept the chimney this afternoon. It is much better, no smoke blowing out. I have been busy clearing up after him tonight. I will do the washing tomorrow, I thought about getting up at six o'clock in the morning to do it. I only thought.

Freddy was a bad lad last night, he came upstairs and slept in the little chair. I would have sent him down, but I felt afraid I had been dreaming, frightening dreams I missed not having your arms around me I would feel quite safe then.

I think it would be best to have a list of things I have to get, if you have not already written it put it on a separate piece of paper.

Well darling I will have to say goodnight and God Bless
    All my love

                        Pickwell
                        Jan. 19th 1950.

My sweetest, little wife,
How are you, my darling? Oh! Jeannie I feel done in today.

Did I tell you in my last letter that I finished cleaning out? Well, Gudger found me a very nice job for the day. Building that road at the reservoir. With tractor and trailer. Loading that concrete stuff did it. At first I thought I was breaking in half. Just above my bottom. Believe me that concrete is heavy and then loading and unloading it all day. Never mind, hard work makes people hard. I really don't mind as it keeps me in good health. Anyway, I was glad when it was lunchtime. Wasn't it cold! You should know what it was like when you went to the office. Working without gloves. My hands were just like two lumps of ice. But I am alright now!!!

It's 8.45 and my days work's finished. As always - busy. The cakes been baked. Doesn't look much, but I hope it tastes better. I also did a few other odd jobs. Some additional cleaning like giving the frying pan a good scrub etc.

Why were you surprised when the P.O. clerk put my address on Freddies license. People expect us to live at the same place. I didn't see Helmut. Perhaps he's been here whilst I was in Somerby doing the shopping. Of course I locked the room and put the key away.

Now about the little man! Why were you embarrassed? I never said to him I was a lorry driver or even anything like it. And I am working weekends, am I not? For havens sake why should I be ashamed of being a farm worker? As long as I earn my money in an honest way, everything is alright with me.

You poor darling, having frightening dreams. What did you dream about? I'll keep my arms around you night after tomorrow.

Sorry, sweetie, I forgot to put a list in the last letter, now of course it's too late. You'll be alright without. If you forget something, it won't matter. We'll have enough to eat, anyway.

Don't you dare get up at 6 o'clock to do the washing. Washerwomen do that, but not-my-wife.

Don't matter about the butcher bringing the meat tomorrow. I want something for tomorrow in any case. The porridge is ready so I'll have another meal. Just bread and cheese and a cup of coffee.

Well, my darling, goodnight and God bless. Be good, I'll write a few more lines tomorrow night. Remember I love you more than anything else in the world.

      All my love and kisses

        Forever your loving husband

                Hans.

<u>Friday, Jan. 20th 1950. 9.00p.m.</u>

Hello, my sweetest, how are things going and how is my little sugar plum? Fine I hope and getting herself ready for a nice weekend. I am ready myself except for the work tomorrow and Sunday. Really, I don't mind as we want the money. Still, it makes a few bob more. Tonights wage packet wasn't to my liking at all. And £4-14-4 for a week hard labour? That turns my hair grey. Next week will be better.

Can you imagine what I did today? He sent me out moving those small chicken houses. The trouble started when I moved them last time. Remember? Still, no moving on my own again so he sent Gerald along. We tried four or five different ways and after experimenting for an hour found the best and easiest way. If anybody had watched us they would have declared us perfectly daft. We had to laugh ourselves. I've got a good stock in now. When I took the tractor out at lunchtime I went by the potato camp where the Irishmen are riddling and collected a bag of specially selected King Edwards. Ginger got them ready.

I think I am ready so far. Cake done chicken <u>un</u>dressed and the room looks decent. I hope you'll be satisfied.

Well, darling, I'll have a wash, some supper and off to bed. So be good, goodnight and God bless you. I am longing for tomorrow afternoon.

      All my love and kisses

        Forever yours

      Hans.

Aschersleben, 9.1.50

19.1.50

My dear Hans and Jean

Thank you very much indeed for your lovely letter dated 29.12.49. At the moment, we are enjoying the best spring weather, but I am sure we shall have to pay for it in February and March. It is quite an unhealthy climate and I can feel the flu in my bones already. All my joints are hurting and I have a headache and a cold. This week I fetched 1.5 hundredweight of coal twice. It is always such a long way to the coal merchant and going up a hill as well nearly kills me. I perspired a lot on my way home and then, when I unloaded the coal, I was in a draught which resulted in a cold and will end up being the flu. I always get a lot of pain from my scars when I overexert myself. The problem is that we don't have a coal merchant nearby. I wanted to have the details on our cards changed but it was explained to me that it is not possible. In March, when the new cards are being issued, I should be able to have the changes made. Oh well, why do it the simple way, when it is much easier to do it the more complicated way?*

It sounds like you had lots of guests over the Christmas holidays. I am sure you managed to conjure up some lovely meals. I have already told you about our presents. We were well pleased with everything, especially as you put a lot of thought into our wellbeing. Your Father Christmas was very busy as well, and I can well imagine that Jean liked the beautiful skirt you gave her. I am now rather sad that the promised photos have still not arrived. And you are not mentioning them any more either!! Last night I fetched our landlady from the station. She came back from West Germany. She loved it there.

Dear Hans, I wonder when we will see each other again. I am making a proposal and you can let me know what you think about it. How about if you came to see us in May and we could celebrate Jean and Horstel's birthdays together on 21

May, especially as it falls on a Sunday. Can you think it over and let us have your answer? May is a lovely month and it would not interfere with your agricultural duties as it won't be quite so busy then.

Auntie Erna is sending her best wishes to you. She sent us a letter and talked about the presents she got: one pair of pants and a few cookies. Everybody had a lot of presents and also a box of chocolates. She did not go into the room on Christmas Eve, because she felt quite hurt. I was very upset about it as well. She works all day and every day at Uncle Erich's and does not get a penny for it. I find it very mean to treat her like that. Anyhow, Horst and I decided to buy her enough material for a dress for her fiftieth birthday. We want her to have something new to wear. I had to promise grandma on her deathbed that I would look after Erna. It will not be easy for us, but it has to be done, and giving brings happiness, which will return into our own hearts.

Now my dears, I will have to finish my letter for today. Please stay fit and well. I am sending you all my love and kisses, your mum, brother and brother-in-law.

Here's to a reunion very soon.

Pickwell
Jan. 22<u>nd</u> 1950

"My darling"

Thank you ever so much for this weekend. You made everything so nice and believe me I enjoyed every single second of it. Up to now there's only the Xmas weekend that has been at least as nice. Well, darling, I have the one wish, let our life be just like these two weekends. Somehow I know it will be. The meals were lovely. Don't you tell me again you can't cook. It's taste was just marvellous. That tablecloth makes the room ever so much better. Still, it doesn't matter how nice the place will look like, I don't like it as long as we can't be together. I have to get down now to find another place nearer to Leicester. By the way what am I going to answer to my mothers suggestion about a holiday in May? Shall I ask her to leave it a bit longer or rather later in the summer? Well, what do you think? We really don't want to draw all our savings out of the bank again. Of course, if I could find a better paid job, things could get on better. If I could only make up my mind what kind of a job as I would then like to stick to it and settle down. No changing again if I can help it. "Variety Bandbox" is good tonight.

Well, my little sweetie, I'll have a bite to eat and off to bed. So be good and pleasant dreams. Goodnight and God bless you and keep you safe.

I love you more than anything in the world. For tonight all my love and kisses

92 Wharf St
23.1.50

My dearest Johannes

Here I am, back at the grind stone after a very lovely weekend. I arrived home safe, I was just in time to hear Frankie Howard.

Well, darling, I really did have a lovely weekend. It is much better than coming back Saturday and going Sunday. I wasn't really uncomfortable and I slept quite well considering it was a strange bed. I loved getting the things ready.

Mamma stayed at home for her lunch, she could have gone to Betty's or next door. She asked me how we went on for sleeping. I told her we managed when one turned we all turned.

I am not going anywhere tonight or any other night this week. I may go to see Gert, they have moved into their house now, before they were with Doris.

I don't think there is really any need to get dress up to go to the Rosen's for tea. It is not as though we were going for supper, but if you want to dress up do so. I wonder how long tea will take.

I have just been speaking to Mr Pickering, he said he wants inviting to the christening I told him he wouldn't receive it just yet, he always says something like that.

Well, will you have me as housekeeper. I will be very pleased to do it. I wish we could have a place of our own. But then if we had the money another problem would arrive. My mother. But we will have to have it settled sometime.

About going to Germany for a holiday. Ask your mother when it is most convenient for the people in the British Zone for us to go. As long as nothing happens we will be able to go. I will go into Cook's one day to make inquiries about the fare, we had better go by tandem. You peddle up hill and me down.

It I will write again so be good.

All my love

Jean

.

Pickwell

Jan. 24th 1950

My sweetest, little wife,

 Well, how are you, darling? Catched up with your sleep? I myself feel as fit as a fiddle now.

It's only 8.15 and I have finished my odd jobs for tonight. Darned 2 pairs of socks, my gloves, and did some alteration to my big winter gloves. Wasn't it cold today? And can you imagine what our job was today. Watercarting!!! 4 hours on the tractor, I was frozen when we got back at 1.00. Of course I had my great coat on and all the socks. Gerald was frozen too, the water froze as it went on the ground. Believe me we're glad to finish that job.

I am glad you liked the weekend and even enjoyed getting the meals ready. Be sure it was more than a change for me. I enjoyed every single second of it. It's just lovely to know you're there when I come back from work.

So Mamma asked you how we went on for sleeping. Well, I

bet she thought her part. Never mind, my sweetie, we know what to do, don't we. I am looking forward to week next Sunday!!!! Do you know what I mean? I hope I am right in thinking you're coming and staying again.

Oh! I think <u>we</u> had better dress up a bit. Not for showing off, but we want to look our very best, don't we? Show them it's worth marrying a Jerrie! Sorry the mink coat won't be ready for Saturday. And our Mercedes Benz (best car in Germany) is in the garage for minor repairs. If it only was true.

Good old Bill can't leave joking. You should have heard him at Stathern sometimes, he made me blush and that takes a bit.

You know yourself how much I would love to find a place of our own. It looks as if I have to be hard. I mean concerning Mamma. If I can get a decent place I'll take it and don't think of anything else than us. Otherwise we'll never get anywhere. Gertie was right in saying Mamma has to expect it one day and still it's not as if she was at a strange place all on her own. Next door is alright and Betty is only a few streets away. I am sure she didn't expect you to become an old spinster. Do you want to waste years of our lives? I don't think you would.

I'll write and tell my mother. She can see then and find out when it suits those people best! Alright, Jeannie go and inquire about the fares. See what difference it makes in price by plane or boat. The tandem idea is good, but we want to get there as quick as possible and not spend days on the road. I've been listening to "Mother Goose" and "Take it from Here" and whilst I have to eat my supper I'll listen to Freddie Mills fight. Then off to bed.

I've cleaned the bird up tonight and have meat for the next 3 days. So you can see I have plenty to eat.

Well, my darling, I'll say goodnight and God bless you and keep you safe. My porridge is ready for the morning. So off to bed I go. Be good and pleasant dreams. I love you soooo very much.

All my love and kisses

<u>Wednesday, Jan. 25th 1950, 7.30 p.m.</u>

Hello, my sweetie, how are things going and how are you yourself? Fine I hope. Isn't it cold? Blimey, I get no end of cleaning out done, trying to keep myself warm at work.

I've just been over to the Irishmen to have a look for another bedstead , but unfortunately found that they're far too big. So I'll try and fix the other bed up (the same as mine) and put that in here for the night. Spare mattresses to cover both beds are at the Irishmen's place. Well, we'll see.

I am just having one of the oranges. Oh! Lovely if you could join me and have half of it. Do you know how it is to be really tired? Oh! I am tonight. Just have a bit of supper and off to bed again. This morning I got up at 6.00 to put the porridge on. It was smashing made with milk and in fact it was so nice that the pot is on the stove again for the morning.

Now something about the bike. Mr what's-his-name took the 3 speed to pieces and found it is a very old model. So it might be very difficult to get spare parts. Gerald's father has some spare second hand wheels in the garage. I'll probably buy a cheap wheel that's cheaper than getting the spare parts. Anyway I'll see when Gerald comes in the morning.

Well, my sweet little sugar plum, half the week is gone and now it won't be long till Saturday. Be good, my darling and look after yourself. See you Saturday.

Remember I love you more than anything else in the world. Goodnight and God bless you.

      All my love and kisses

        Forever your loving husband

      Hans.

      92 Wharf St

      25.1.50

My dearest.

How are you today, and is everything alright with you? I hope it is. It is only two more days before we see each other. Mamma has gone out, but has not yet returned, I expect she will be in any minute. I have not been anywhere this week. I have mostly been knitting, last night I did the ironing, Mamma did the washing. I was very glad now I will not have to do it at night. Tonight I have been listening to "Barretts of Wimpole St". I thought it was very good. Did you hear it?

I have been a naughty girl today.- I have spent 14/6. 11/3 on a pair of nylon stockings, but I did need some new ones. One pair of mine have given notice and are only fit to wear with my boots. So getting this pair means I have two pairs to wear regular and one for a best pair. I got them from Morgan's, the shop opposite to L.A.E.C. Then I bought a ball of wool red to go with that I knitted Susan's cardigan with. I had to go into Johnson's so I inquired if they had some, fortunately they had so that was 3/3d more. I think I will have to have another ball of wool for your pullover I will call in tomorrow lunchtime to see if they have any.

I had a letter from the income tax office to say my code was 34. I don't know what it was before. I will ask.

My visitor should have arrived yesterday, but you need not worry it came today. I shall be worrying now in case I can't have any. We had better get more settled before we have another try.

I will leave it to you when you think it best we go for our holiday. Do you think you will be able to have the time off, if you start at a new place. I can only have 2 weeks off at a time so we could only go for a fortnight. I would very much like to go, because later on we may not be able to go. I will make inquiries as to how much it will cost from Cook's. We do need the money for other things.

Darling I will be glad when we can have a place of our own. I was so happy Sunday and I'm so glad you like me being there. If we did get a place, what about my mother? We may as well stay here for a while. This place could be made more comfortable, but I don't think it is worth spending the money on. There is no room to have children.

About your job I do wish we could get it settled because it is a worry. What do you want to do? I wish we could get away from Leicester. To somewhere near the sea, but that is only wishful thinking.

Alice is coming tomorrow for supper, I asked her to come for tea, but she wouldn't so it will be supper. Bread and cheese.

I am very tired so I will have to say goodnight my darling God Bless you and keep you safe. I love you more than anything else in the world

All my love

Jean

___.

<u>Thursday 4.30</u>

As you can see this day is nearly over and it will soon be time to leave. You are right in thinking I will be staying at Pickwell next weekend. I will leave it to you about fixing another bed up. Make sure the mattress is not damp.

Well my darling I will have to close. I have to buy a stamp from somewhere. Will be seeing you Saturday

Yours for ever

Jeannie

<u>P.S.</u>

The past tense of catch is caught not catched

Pickwell

Jan. 26<u>th</u> 1950

My sweetest, little wife,

Hello, my little sugar plum, how are you today? Are you at home and listening to the radio. I've got "Sleeping Beauti" Oh! It's nice.

Well, darling, another day is over and only day and a half to go. I am so glad!! I hope the tea at Rosen's won't take too long. We'll find out alright. The day went as usually, cleaning out. If it only wasn't so cold in the morning. It was really lovely today when the sun shone. But it doesn't last long. It's still freezing.

I wrote a letter to the Police Registration Office at Melton and sent the certificate and the letter to the Home Office to have the necessary endorsements made. I'll post it tonight, just ordinary letter. It might be back Saturday morning. Remind me I've got to tell you something. Rather interesting. Well, darling, the water is boiling and I am going to wash my hair. Be good, goodnight and God bless you always. Oh! I love you so much

All my love and kisses.

Marg 25
Butter 45
Lard
Sugar 29
Bacon 7
~~Cheese~~
1 los. Coffee D 1.8
1 Meatpaste I 8
1 Sardines A 109
1 Puffed Wheat P 89
1 Fruit   1.3
Eggs   105
1 Shampoo 35
Cigarettes 3.107
1 Matches 4
Cheese 2/6 Buto 9 3.3
Beans 11

‾‾‾‾
16.1

£ 5-19-7   less
Grocer   0-16-1
Baker   0-2-3 ½
Butcher   0-3-1
Eggs   0-7-0
Electricity   0-2-1 ½

```
               _____
                  4-9-0
Chain + Wheel    0-12-0
               _____
                  3-17-0
               =======
Papers           0-2-10
               _____
                  3-14-2
Bus fare         0-1-5
               _____
                  3-12-9
               =======
```

<u>Friday, Jan. 27<u>th</u> 1950, 8p.m.</u>

So my sweetie spent 14/6 . never mind. I'm glad you're able to get nylons. I also have been naughty spending 12/- on the bike. 7/6 for a new chain and 4/6 for the free wheel. Mr-what's-his-name hasn't been able to put it together because he can only do it in the shop and the boss was about almost all day. He might get it done tomorrow. I'll give him a packet of cigarettes for doing it.

Do you know your old code No. for the Income tax. You might get a few bob back if the new code is higher.

Please, my darling, don't worry your little head with funny ideas like not being able to have a baby. Everything will be alright. Perhaps we haven't picked the right time yet. We'll just see how we get on. I think it would be alright to get time off even if I start at a new place. Of course, I can only have the holiday once a year and it's left to me when I take it.

I know your place could be made much more comfy, and it might even be worth spending some money as the things we buy aren't lost, but belong to us, still, you're right, there's no room to have children. Of course the washing and cooking also could be made easier. Believe me, darling, I would like our children grow up in the country. It's so much healthier than in the town. I want people to say: "look at those children, healthy and strong just like their dad". (On the radio is "Oklahoma")

Well, what do I want to do? Never before it has been so difficult for me to answer a question. If I would only make up my mind. Look, it isn't only a wishful thought to leave Leicester and find a place near the sea. It's just a matter of writing. The "Stockbreeder" is full of vacancies down south. Let's talk that idea over. Then of course we have to have the money ready to furnish a house. Because that's we shall definitely want.

Well, my darling, I'll close for now. See you tomorrow. Goodnight and God bless. Daddie loves you soooo very much.

> All my love and kisses
> forever and only yours
> Hans.

92 Wharf Street
30.1.50

My dearest Hans.

What did you think to the weather this morning, when Mamma said it was snowing it took a great deal of will power to get out of bed, tomorrow I have a bit of shopping to do, not actually shopping. I've to go to the Midland Press to Mitchell's and the bank I will have to have about 5/- of the money I said I would put in the bank, because you only left me with 3d. I had 3/9. 3/6 of that for cigarettes and I had a cup of coffee with my 3d. I would not need any money until Saturday, but I will have to get the cauliflowers on Wednesday, they are dearer at the weekend.

It was a good job you had your wellingtons changed, you needed them this morning. It is thawing here the streets are awfully slushy I was glad you mended my boot they would have let the wet in.

I miss you terribly all the time, we only have to wait 4 ½ days, I can't work out the hours and minutes. Is there anything you will be wanting me to bring?

Well my darling I hope you will not mind this letter being very short, but I ~~won't~~ want to get on with your pullover.

Remember I love you ever such a lot. Be good my sugar plum

    All my love and kisses

    Jeannie

                        Pickwell

                        Jan. 30th 1950

My sweetest, little wife,

Here I am , my sweetie, safe and sound. It was cold in the Melton bus, my feet just like ice. When I got here at 8.30 I started the fire straight the way. It was about 9.45 before the room was really warm. Still I had a cup of coffee and some bread and that lovely dripping. 10.45 saw me in bed.

I thank you so very much for a lovely weekend I certainly enjoyed all of it, the tea at Rosen's too. If you ring Dora one of these days, please give her also my thanks and regards.

How are you, my sweetheart? I am so glad you can sit inside all day. Wasn't it awful today. First thing this morning I went with Gerald feeding and for the rest of the day watercarting. It wasn't half cold and the snow. Never before in my life I've seen such big snowflakes. As big as eggs. Still it's only about an inch of snow. I've just been out, it's dense fog. The weather forecast gave snow again for tomorrow. Everybody from the general farm gave a hand on poultry today, putting lamps into the houses to keep the water from freezing.

Another letter from my mother arrived today. She wants us to come in May or June, if possible for us, as in July some relations of those people are coming to stay with them. We'll talk about it on Saturday and see if we can reach final decision to let mother know. Can you find out about the cost of the trip, both- by rail, ship or plane. Let's see which the most reasonable price is. I'll write to her tonight and tell her that when we come it'll be for a fortnight.

I've been thinking if there's anything else to bring besides those things we talked about last night, but I can't find anything else at the moment.

It was 6.00 when I got back from shutting up. Some of the hens didn't want to go in because of the snow. Still, it wasn't too bad. They'll get used to it alright. It was the first time today I wore my great coat, Oh! It was lovely warm. But my poor feet.

Well, my sweetest, I'll say goodnight and God bless you. I love my little wife more than anything else in the whole world. Be good and look after yourself.

All my love and thousand kisses

Forever your loving husband

Hans.

R 2.2.50   Aschersleben, 20.1.50

30.1.50

My dear Hans and Jean

I thank you from the bottom of my heart for your lovely letter dated 10.1.50. We did not have any post from you for two weeks. I have not been feeling very well for the last eight days. The nettle fever is still bothering me. It started on my arms and then my face swells up such a lot, I looked really distorted. I went to the doctor's three times. Two days ago he gave me a calcium injection and I had another one today. The calcium injections are absolutely awful. As soon as one goes into a vein, the calcium dissolves in the blood and if it does not get done very slowly by the doctor, the result is that you – without wanting to – lose consciousness. You have no power over it at all. The calcium literally rushes through the vein and causes the heart to beat like mad. I don't know where all this is coming from. I am itching and my skin is 'burning' like I was sitting in a bush of nettles. I can only hope that it will get better soon.

Since yesterday, we are having cold weather again – minus 13°C. Oh well, I suppose winter will be coming. I imagine that our hen will stop laying eggs. We have had seven eggs so far. Auntie Emilia died in Berlin on 14 January. The funeral is on 21 January. She was 82 years old. Unfortunately, her biggest wish did not get fulfilled, because she never saw her son Erich Rindt again. They have not heard anything from or about him since 1945. This uncertainty is just awful.

Did you write to Auntie Erna on her 50th birthday? Horst received a letter from Braunschweig. They said that the shop is finished now and he can start his new job. Apparently, the boss has arranged for a room for Horst, but not for me. Horst does not want to go without me, he will not leave me here on my own, and he can not be otherwise persuaded. I agree, it is much better if we can stay together, and also it is so much more expensive to run two separate households. It would not be sustainable in the long run and we could not possibly afford it. I look after Horst a little like doing and mending his washing etc. and keeping things in an orderly fashion. What do you think about it, dear Hans?

I wonder what your photographers are doing. This would never happen here. We would soon get behind them. Or did the photos not turn out. If you want to change your job, what will happen to your holiday? Would you be able to come in May? And how long would you be able to stay, or would you prefer to come in June? I am asking because Whitsun is on 28 and 29 May and Horst will not be able to take any time of work the week before. Please think it over again and let us know whether you are coming in May or in June. In July, the sister of Mrs. Fuchs and her children are coming to Weferlingen. I imagine she will stay at Mrs. Fuchs' place. Can you not find work in the field for which you did your apprenticeship? I am thinking that you cannot carry on forever doing too much physical work with your leg. Do look after your foot. The days are already getting longer now. It is quite noticeable. I just hope the weather is not getting too cold because our coal reserve is going down slowly but surely. No wonder as I have to keep the sitting room warm from morning till night and also the bedroom needs some heat. It would be nice if you could find work in Leicester and could go home every evening. Now that you are married, it is quite different from being single. Horst is going to a Masked Ball this evening. He needs some fun in his life. He went for lunch today in a Gaststätte*, as I am unable to carry his food. In the evenings he goes straight there after work but he does not stay very long.

Now, my dears, I want to finish for today. Best wishes to your mother-in-law, and to you both we are sending our love and kisses. Your mum, brother and brother-in-law.

*(tavern/inexpensive eating place)

    92 Wharf St

    31.1.50

My dearest

Well darling half of my days holiday is over and I have quite enjoyed it. I will tell you what I have been doing so far. To start with I was going to stay in bed until about 8.45, but ~~how~~ who should start knocking at the door but Mrs Johnson to leave her pension book. I thought it was at 8.45 because you know she comes twice first thing first to leave her book, then her bag before she goes to work. Well to cut a long story short I came down to open the door and she had gone. I could have murdered her. It wasn't worth going up to bed again so I lit the fire, then messed about getting myself ready until 10.15. I went straight up to fetch the photograph. The fellow said to me "That is an unusual name". I told him it was German, he said he didn't recognise it, he told me he had been in Germany taking photographs in an internment camp. After my chat with him it was about 10.45, from there I had a look in the shops down the London Rd and Belvoir St. I took my costume into Sketchly's to be cleaned. I have to call today week. Then on to the bank where I deposited

£16.10.0 we now have £44.11.3. I have been spending again, but not on myself, on our home. £2.19.6. plus tax. This is what I bought.-

1 Prestige knife for carving	6.10
1 Prestige knife for Ham	6.3
1 veg knife (quite a nice little sharp)	1.8
½ soup spoons	6.3
1 box of tea knives ½ doz	14.6
½ doz of tea spoons	4 7 ½

On all of these there is 33 ⅓ % tax and I went rather rash and bought a cut glass dish 19/- with 19/- tax on it 38/-. They are sending on some scales and a pot dish that would do for fruit or veg . the scales were 21/- and the dish 4/- both have 33 ⅓ tax on. I hope I have done right. I also brought home with me an anti splash for the tap I could not bear to be told off again, anyway it is much better it does not splash. My old pal keeps having a growl and a bark at the neighbours up and down the yard. I am going to have an orange then get on with my knitting.

I will write a few more lines tomorrow when I receive your letter until then all my love.

Wednesday

I went into Cook's yesterday to inquire about the fare to Germany. From here, London to Brunswick by boat- 3rd class via Belgium £12.12.6 return 2nd class £18.12.3. Via the hook of Holland 2nd class £15.17.10 1st class £25.6.3. There is not an airport at Brunswick so I ask what it was to Frankfurt!!! That is £23.5.0.-then you would have train fares on top. There was a person there asking the fare from Berlin that's £19.9.10 odd, anyway a few shillings more. Then this morning I rang Dean & Dawsons to find out some more, they told me the best way was via Belgium, leave England 9.0 A.M. arrive Brunswick 6.0 PM same day. I asked about going by air- they said the only thing was to Berlin from there to Bruns. I will call in to Pickford's sometime to find out more. I did ask what you had to do. You apply to the Home Office, when you do that you can find out what I will want.

I forgot to tell you what else I bought, a rolling pin. I went to see Bob Hope it was a good program.

Well my love I will be seeing you on Saturday.

Your loving wife
Jeannie

Written on NAVAL MESSAGE paper

Thank you for your letter my darling. You have 2 letters today. One from Horst the other from South Africa. I have re-address them to you. I will post them with this.

You wanted to know how I was! I am fine apart from feeling a bit tired, but that is not unusual for me in the afternoon. I will have to get some knitting the day seems awfully long. How do you like my writing paper. It was the best I could do. I lost my grey pad.

Did you do anything about those stamps (5) missing off your card if not I think you ought. It would be best to put them on. There is a good picture on the Savoy it is "Look for the silver lining" I won't go, I will see if it is on when you come to Leicester I'll go then or may be we will see it in Melton.

I didn't write to Mr & Mrs Springthorpe last night after all. I was much too tired to bother. I will do it tonight also I hope to write to Uncle Frank. It is about time.

Well my love how are you today still working hard I wish I could have had your dinner waiting at 7.0 last night for you. Do you really want to go home on holiday? If you don't think it is worth spending our savings, say so. I would like to go because we may not be in the position another year to be able to go. We will have to get cracking next month if we are going. I will leave that to you.

Well my angel I will say cheeri'O

All my love
Jean.

My dearest, darling Jean,

When Mamma told you it was snowing I was out in the field, actually seeing the snowing. When I got up it was raining, the snow came later. Believe me I also was glad I got the wellingtons changed. It was thawing today and water all over the fields.

You poor darling have been very busy today, haven't you? Did you get your scales? and the photographs?

So I only left you with -/8d. If I remember right I left you with £3. You know, sweetie if you want some money you know where it is.

4 ½ days to wait is a long time. I wish we wouldn't have to wait at all, spending all our time together. It won't be long I'm sure.

It's 9.30. I am late tonight. As my bike hasn't been fixed up yet I had to go myself for an hour. It takes some doing. Those 3 speed are really complicated.

By the way, darling, please bring me a pair of socks to put in my rubber boots. You've got some in the shop. The size of my boots are is 7.

Well my sweetheart, I'll say goodnight. God bless you. I love you more than my own life.

All my love and kisses

Wednesday, Feb. 1st 1950, 8.30 p.m.

Hello, my sugarplum, how are you? I am proper fed up today. Wasn't it awful? After lunch I got wet through for the first time, in spite of my raincoat. The water was running down my neck in pints. So of course I was glad to get back here, hoping to find a job in the yard. Still, after dinner Gudger asked me to go collecting with Gerald and the rain was streaming down. So you can perhaps imagine what I looked like when I came back. But that's not all, after shutting up I was wet through again. I wasn't half mad.

Well, my sweetheart, I'll close for now. Be good, my sweetie, and again I love you so very much. Goodnight and God bless you.

All my love and thousand kisses

Forever and only your loving husband

Hans.

Same address

Febr. 2<u>nd</u>. 1950.

My dearest, darling Jean,

I thank you so very much for your lovely long letter. Thanks for asking, I am fine and proper fed up. Let's hope the rain stops soon. It kept fine all day, but when shutting up time came it was streaming down and your sugarplum got wet through again for a change. All my things are on the fire drying.

Don't you think that Mrs Johnson is going to be a nuisance. That woman gets up too early. Well, darling, the next deposit at the bank will cross the half century mark. I wish it was 100. And now to your shopping at Mitchell's. There's a clever girl and I mean it. If it wasn't for the furniture we could start our own home. We have got a rolling pin to keep the kids in order and-the father at a safe distance!!! Isn't the P.T. on those things awful. 100% on that glass dish. Still, you have chosen it so it must be very nice. Poor Jeannie, did I tell her off because of the splashing tap? I am sorry.

I've been over to the Irishmen tonight and arranged to fetch the mattress tomorrow night. I'll get everything ready tomorrow night, including the chicken. It'll be a late night. One bed will have to stand on bricks because it is a bit lower. I am sure it'll be alright.

We'll see and talk about the holiday on Saturday.

So you saw Bob Hope. it doesn't look as if I am going to see it, too. I don't mind, my sweetie! I won't see it when it comes to Melton. No money to go out during the week and really too lazy after a days work. If I don't go anywhere I don't have the trouble of coming back here. At the moment it is the best place against the fire.

Well, my darling, be good and goodnight and God bless you and keep you safe. Oh! I love you more than anything else in the world. All my love and thousands of kisses.

Friday, Febr. 3rd 1950, 9.45 p.m.

Well, my darling, most of my work is done. I am almost done in. For a start I got back from shopping at 6.30 then went over to the shop and fixed the bed I've put up. That means cutting a couple of inches off and weld it together again. Now it fits nicely in here. After that I fetched the mattresses and put the bed ready. It takes a bit of room but still I hope it satisfies you and the main thing you'll have a good nights sleep. The chicken is also ready and it really is a very nice bird. I don't regret (as I did last time) to pay the price for it. Now as everything is ready for my sweet little wife and I am longing to see her again tomorrow afternoon.

When I finish this letter I was going to write to my mother, but I'll have to leave it untill tomorrow. My gloves want darning again.

Tonight we had yorkshire puddin' it was quite nice. One each in those sandwich tins."Ain't I a pig" But I just had 2 little potatoes so only made up for it.

Please forgive me for this short letter, but it's 9.30 and I am awful tired.

Be good, God bless and keep you safe. Good night and pleasant dreams. I love you more than anything else in the world.

All my love and thousand kisses

Forever your loving husband

Hans.

P.S.

Nothing from the H.0 yet!

Pickwell

Febr. 5th 1950.

9.20 p.m.

My dearest, darling,

I am so lonely, my sweetie. Can't you come back to me? Do so straight away. If it only could be. Please, darling find out the address of those housing people in Melton and I'll write and ask what chance I would stand. I've set my mind on getting a home and I am going to get one one of these days. There's a feeling something is going to happen in this line. Well, my sweetheart, as I said I enjoyed every second of this weekend and I am really very very happy. We'll get a place and get it organised too.

Oh! I am ready for bed tonight. So goodnight and God bless you and keep you safe. Look after yourself, darling and be good. I love you more than my own life.

Monday, Febr.6th1950, 7.45 p.m.

Hello, my darling, how are you today? Oh! Blimey I felt done in this morning and best of all I had to go feeding on my own. I just couldn't manage to get back for 9.00. It took me 20 minutes longer. It is nice if one feels done in and then have to carry a few bags of wheat about. At first I expected my back to break. Good thing it didn't, otherwise I wouldn't have known which part to present to you on Saturday.

Well, the day went quick. After lunch we went watercarting and in the afternoon as usually- cleaning out. It was not too bad after all. It means the first day is over. Only 4 ½ to go.

Mr Cooper gave me the letter from the N.H. back this morning. He said he had looked it up and found that in case of sickness (illness) the contribution can be made. Noone, master or man, has to pay for it. So he said if I wanted the 5 stamps I had to pay the lot myself. Do you get the idea? That means the boss doesn't want to pay his share so if I am interested I have to pay it all. About £0-11-0 per week. Though if one doesn't pay it will be less sickness benefit the next time. Perhaps 1 or 2s less. So after all I don't think I shall pay that lot. That's getting too much for my liking. What do you think?

Gerald also was done in today. He had 2 nights out till 2.00 a.m. We agreed to have an early night. After finishing this I'll darn my gloves again and off I go without any supper. I am still full. Bonzo is sitting in front of the stove again, but I can't bother to tell him off. Too tired to sleep.

Well, my sweetheart, find out that address and I'll write and find out if there's anything to be had in this ~~area~~ district. We might have a bit of look.

Remember when you said you wonder how we'll go on being on our own all the time? I think we'll have to economise a bit. Don't you? We'll ~~sey~~ see, anyway. Can you tell I am tired? I'll close now. Be good, my sweetie, and goodnight and God bless you. Look after yourself. I would like to do it as I love you so very very much.

All my love and kisses forever your
Loving husband
Hans.

92 Wharf Street
6.2.50.

"My darling"

I arrived home safe at 9.45. Just in time to hear Frankie Howard. I could have left your mac there, I didn't need it this end, it had stopped. I hope you didn't get wet or at least it wasn't as bad going back to Pick as it was going up.

Thank you my darling for such a lovely weekend. I can't express how happy I was. I don't mind a bit coming out every weekend, but what about you it isn't going to be very nice for you not having time off. So you had better have a day off once a week so you can have a res.t I don't want you to wear yourself out. I wish I could do something to help, all I can do is to go shutting up which I like doing.

So we do not know what we are going to do for our holiday. I would very much like to go to Germany to meet your mother but if junior decides to come I will not mind, I am sure it would be worth giving our holiday up.

Today has been a usual day. Up at 8.10 out at a few minutes to 9.0 but I made it to the office before they put the stars in for being late. Don't be surprised if we have a runner in the family. We had the chicken for our tea with hard boiled egg. It was very nice, Mamma said she enjoyed her tea. I have decided to spend some money tomorrow. I have made an appointment to have my hair cut tomorrow lunch time 12.45. I thought it would look better having it done then for the weekend. I will probably fetch my costume Wednesday, then we will not have much to do Saturday.

Well I had better tell you this before I forget, I didn't think it was right you had to pay the stamp whilst on the sick. Getting 2/- in one hand and taking 9/1 from the other. So I ran the N.M.I. at Melton to find out how you stood. The N.M.I. issue a class 1 credit when you are on the sick. You were on the sick 23.7.48 to 6.8.48 then 4.11.49 to 3.12.49 and the 5 weeks you are short would be when you were home in Germany. You will have to pay 4/8 per week as unemployed that makes it £1.3.4. He said something about sending your card in. I could not quite get it but maybe you will make inquiries.

I don't know whether you ought to write to the Rural District Council or the Urban. I think Pickwell would be Rural in which case the address is Melton Belvoir Rural District Council, 10 High Street, Melton Mowbray, The housing Department. Write a very polite letter stating our case. You know if you go into an agricultural Council house you can't take a job in anything else as long as you live in it.

By the way you spell luck like that not look, that is to see.

The Midland Red bus Company did me for 1/2d coming back that is 1 1/2 d in a weekend. I will have the correct amount next time.

Well my darling I will say cheeri'o 3 ½ days to go
All my love
Jean.

Aschersleben, 29.1.50

7.2.50

My dear Hans and Jean

Thank you very much indeed for your lovely letter dated 10 January. In the meantime, winter has arrived. Today, the weather was very nice. We had minus 16 $^{\circ}$C and the sun was shining . Horst and I, together with Mrs. Ziemann went for a walk in the Stintchen. At 5.45 pm we went to the cinema. Horst just went to a dance and I am now happy that I can sit in the warm room and have a little chat with you. I hope you also had a nice, restful Sunday. Yesterday, we received a letter from Auntie Lina. She is sending her love to you. They have extremely cold weather there. They live very close to the river, and she doesn't have sufficient firewood. What do you think of this, dear Hans? Bruno has never helped Auntie Lina, not even a tiny bit. Apparently, he is worried in case it gets lost, but this is just a lame excuse. He should be smoking a little less and thinking a bit more of his mother. He should be trying a bit harder to make her life a little more comfortable. Where he lives, one pound of margarine only costs 1.22 Marks. Should he not be sending her one parcel a month, or does he prefer she eats dry bread? He can buy anything now without food ration coupons, except sugar. I couldn't wait any longer, because it breaks my heart. So, I decided to write to him, even though we had not heard from him for a whole year. I gave him a piece of my mind. He has no idea how much his mother longs to see him. He could have come to see her a long time ago with an inter-zonal pass. I cannot understand what he is worried about. Nobody here will eat him! Auntie Lina has always worked hard and tried to give her children as good a life as possible, but she gets no thanks at all for it. What do you think about it?

Auntie Emilie died on 14 January. She was buried in Berlin on 21 January. I was unable to go to the funeral. The fare would have cost 30 Marks, which is too much for me, and – of course – I have still not quite got my health back yet. My nettle rash is still bothering me. This morning, my face was very swollen again, and my entire body is itching. I am going back to the doctor's again on Tuesday. If only it would get better.

We keep getting a lot of post from Braunschweig, literally begging Horst to come. But Horst cannot make up his mind. Every time I mention it to him and say something positive, he says: " If you want to get rid of me and wish that the two of us will also be separated, then I will go". Well, what can I say to that? I shall not interfere any more. He must know what he is doing.

Now my dears, I want to finish my letter. Please stay well and write back soon. Best wishes to your mother-in-law, and we are sending you two our love and kisses. Your mum, who is always thinking of you, and your brother Horst.

Pickwell
Febr. 8th 1950

My sweetest, little wife,

I thank you so much for your lovely letter. There was also a letter from the Melton Police station. It has taken them sometime, but at last I got it back. They've made the endorsements.

Do you notice I've changed the pen? I could strangle myself, my good fountain pen was on the table when I got up and knocked it off. On the floor and the nib is flat. Well, I think I'd better bring it to Boot's to have it repaired. I bet they will have to send it away to factory.

Never mind, darling, I won't wear myself out working every weekend. Even if I don't have any time off during the week. I am only glad you don't mind coming over every weekend. If you come along shutting up it helps me so much. And it's much quicker even if I go on my bike.

Never mind our holidays, sweetie. I also would like to go and take you to see my mother and brother. Let's see first if, as you said, junior decides to give us the pleasure of his presents. On my side I ~~am~~ think it's worth giving up our holidays.

I'll check up about the N.H. payments. Better send the card down and ask what it is really all about. To the R.D.C. Melton we'll write on Saturday. The boss mentioned to me today that there are 3-4 council houses to be build here in the very near future. He said it might be worth waiting. Better a nice place at the end of the year than any old house. He also came to see how I had fixed the bed and when he ~~said~~ saw it he asked me to measure the the spare place and let him know the measurements in the morning so he can get me a proper sprung bed, any size I want.

Well, my sweetheart,it's 9.30. I'll have a shave and then to bed. Be good and pleasant dreams. Goodnight and God bless you always. Only 2 ½ days to go.

      All my love and kisses
        Forever your loving husband
      Hans

    92 Wharf St
     9.2.50

My dearest darling Johannes.

I hope you don't mind but I have said we will go out for tea on Saturday, I went to Gertie's last night and she asked, or rather Auntie said we will both have to go up sometime. So I thought if we were going we had better take this week in case you have to work the other weekends. I have been thinking that when you take your day off you could come home the night before. But I suppose you have already thought of that. We will have to find out which day is best for busses.

Jack has just brought the paper in "Daily Express". So I will have a read. We had better see how the budget is this weekend. We should have enough to pay for the things I bought this weekend. I fetched my costume from the cleaners, it was 3/9, I thought it would be more than that about 5/-. They have done it well but it needs pressing a bit. Remember that we have to get a birthday card for Sheila. I think a little dress would be the best thing to get her, because she doesn't need a lot of toys or more money, it is a good job I have ~~not~~ only 2 nieces.

What happened to your pen, how was it that it hadn't got the top on? Anyway it is too late now to bother about that. I think Roe's in Belvoir St would be the best place to take it to. You may not have to leave it, they usually have nibs in stock. You had better bring the broken one with you, they sometimes allow a little on the old one. I have just rung Brooks (they are stationers) to inquire the price of a new nib. It takes 2 to 3 weeks to order one, the price depends on what type of pen it is. The Jewell Fold which I think yours is comes to 18/4 , with the old one back, but it will not be any good going there as they close Saturday. I think it had better be Roe's.

When Mr Maclean brings the new bed I will bring some sheets over. Could you bring the blanket with you so I could wash it on Sunday. I don't know when I will do the washing when I come over every weekend I will have to do it in the evening.

Do you really mean you would be pleased if junior came or are you just saying that? When Betty came on Tuesday she said she had been awake since 5.0 with the baby, Cyril went into Susan's bed, then Susan went into Betty. Susan would be pleased the baby cried if no one else was, she loves to get in bed with Betty.

Well my darling I have to close now All my love

You're the nice sweetest strongest Brainiest Husband that ever lived

  Your sweetheart

  Jean

P.S. bring your diary with you Saturday

Betty with Susan and

Sheila

Pickwell
Febr. 9th 1950.

My sweetest, little wife,

How are you today my sugarplum? Fine, I hope in spite of the bad weather. Still, tonight I was wiser. All day my job was laying nest boxes so at 4.30 it would've been time to go and take horse and cart. As it was raining 90% of the hens were in so I stopped out there and shut up straight the way. It was dark (5.45) when I got here but I saved one way and getting wet through.

I am listening to " Straight from Trinidad". Are you listening, too?

Well, my darling. Thursday is gone and that means only 1 ½ day to go. Bonzo will be alright on Sunday. Gerald is going to take him along feeding on Sunday morning and feed him as well. So everything in that line is alright.

Now "Rommel" is on. I forgot all about it, till I read in the paper just now. Quite interesting.

Well, my sweetheart, I'll say good night now and write more tomorrow. My water for washing my hair is boiling. Oh! I am longing for Saturday and love you so very very much. See you Saturday.

Friday, Febr. 10th 1950.7.45 p.m.

Hello, my darling, how are you today? Fine, I hope. I am fit as a fiddle, that is because I had a break from shutting up tonight. Don't think I mind shutting up, it's alright if it wasn't for the rain. It is more pay and that is the main thing for me.

About may day off. I also thought about coming the evening before after I've finished up here. There should be a bus about any day of the week. And the service from Melton to Leicester is alright.

Our budget for this week is quite good, if that is what one can call good. £5 coming from me and yours is not too bad. It'll be like that every week once I get cracking.

Yes, my foot needs warming up. It wants company and as for company all the time and not only once a week.

What happened to my pen? The top wasn't on because I was writing to you and just put it on the table to do something else that moment and off it came. I asked at Boot's a long time ago and they said it would be 10/-s not 18/-!

I've given Mac' the measures for the bed, but he hasn't said anything yet. If he doesn't turn up with one till next Wednesday, I'll have to remind him. I don't think I'll bring a blanket tomorrow. The weather isn't good enough for drying blankets. Weather forecast said rain.

I can't make your "P.S." out. What the matter with my diary and which one do you mean? Sound funny to me. Well, we'll see.

When I say I'll be pleased if junior comes then I certainly mean it. You should know that by now.

Doesn't matter if he starts crying at 5.00 as I have to get up at 6.00 anyway. See! Just like that. I'll have one hour to nurse him.

This'll be all for tonight, my sweetie. I have to get busy again. Chopping some wood and packing my bag. Of course, a good wash. And you also are the nicest, sweetest, strongest and brainiest wife that ever lived. I love you sooooo very much

     All my love and kisses
       Forever your loving husband
         Hans.

       Pickwell
       Febr. 12th 1950. 9.30 pm

"My darling"

Here I am safe and sound, the place warm and I have even had my supper. Sausages and an egg. Would you have liked to join me? Oh! Darling I am missing you so much! Please come and stay with me. The pillows are on the bed so you'll be comfy.

Did my sugarplum get wet on the way home? Bonzo had been a very good boy. Nothing messed up at all. I took him out straight away and it looked as if he was waiting for it.

You know what I forgot? The petrol. Please, bring it next Saturday. That tractor petrol smells so much.

Well, my darling, I'll go to bed. Be good and look after yourself. Oh! I love you more than anything else in the world. Goodnight and God bless you.

Monday, Febr 13th1950, 8.30 p.m

Hello,my sweetheart, how are you? Fine, I hope. For me it has just been the 13 th. We were watercarting and the boss asked us if we would like a new longer pipe for the watercart. It is better for us so we said yes, not knowing what kind of a pipe it is. Tom fixed it on and off we went. Only 7 yards long. For a start I was glad to be the driver for the morning. After we'd started, Gerald began to use unusual words. So I had a try, and blimey, was the pipe heavy and then 7 yards of it. Well, we finished at 12.30 after calling everybody concerned the worst words. As we hadn't finished the field I had to do it in the afternoon. The pipe was full of muck and you may imagine what I looked like. Messed up from top to bottom. I wasn't half mad. Thank goodness, that day is over. Only 4 ½ to go.

Oh! Jeannie my pullover is lovely. I thank you so very much. The pillows are also smashing. I slept like an angel. Almost overslept.

By the way, darling, there's something else you could bring on Saturday. What about one or two tea towels if you have got the money. Also a Southwester for me. It's only about 4/11 s. I certainly can do with one now. What about that washer-up for yourself. Don't you think you'd better bring one? Did you remember my fountain pen?

Well, my dearest, I'll close for now. It's 9.00 and I still have to darn a big hole in my socks. My bike is alright again. Now the chain is too short and Gerald has to change it. Be good and look after yourself. Good night and God bless you. You are the best wife in the world and I love you sooo much.

All my love and thousand kisses
Forever your loving husband
Hans.

92 Wharf St.
13.2.50.

My dearest Johannes.

Did you arrive at Pickwell safe with your parcels. It was pouring with rain the whole of the time on my way back. I got in just about to take my coat off when I remembered the card for Sheila. I didn't go back to Betty's you had made a good fire, so I sat there feeling miserable. I looked through the paper to see if I had missed anything and listened to "Variety Bandbox". I had a nasty shock, just before going to bed. I let Freddy out for his nightly walk, he had been gone quite a while so I went out to call him, whilst doing this a man on the opposite side of the road said "he's been run over." You can guess how I felt. I went upstairs to put my boots on, I was almost ready for bed. I had myself dressed to go out, to see what had happened, just as I was going in the shop he started to bark to come in. I was pleased to see him, but if I could have got hold of that man I don't know what I would have done.

I have had a letter from the Inspector of Taxes to say I had £9.8.5 in post war credits. I had almost bought those shoes. When I learnt I cannot have it until I am 65 years old. I have something to look forward to in my old age.

Was Helmut's wife's name Hardiman or something like that. Nancy went to Somerby this last weekend and her mother in law was telling her about it. Just shows how news travels.

I have just been trying to remember the names off the picture houses in Melton, so I could find out what was on to tell you in this letter, but I can't think of them. I know the names now Plaza & Regal, but they are not on the phone. One picture is "Barkleys of Broadway" we have seen that.

Well my darling did you have a good night's rest. You don't seem to be able to have one when I am with you. I hope you didn't oversleep this morning. It took me all my time to get out of bed, I forced myself at the finish at 8.20. Then I had to jump to it.

I can't think of anything else to tell you, only that I love you very very much and miss you.

Be good and look after yourself.
All my love
Jean

92 Wharf St
14.2.50

"My dearest"

Thank you so very much for your letter. I want to know what you mean by a south wester is it a hat for the rain made of oil skin or something, a fisherman's hat the brim turns all the way down? I call it a sou-wester if that is what you mean I will get one and bring it Saturday I thought I had better make sure before I got it.

I took your pen into Boots. You will never guess how long you will have to wait 2 months, that is 11th April before you have it back. I left it. I hope I did right. I forgot to inquire the price.

I fetched 2 large envelopes for the photographs 3 d each I will get them ready for posting tonight.

I am longing for Saturday to come, I have written the things down you want me to bring. I will probably come on the 2.15, if I find I have plenty of time I will come on the 1.15, but it does not give me much time to have lunch and fetch the milk and bread.

Well Johannes my darling I will love you and leave you I will make up for it on Saturday. I love you so very much

All my love
Jean
P.S.

I meant to put the stamps on straight.
Jean

.

Pickwell
Febr. 14<u>th</u> 1950.

My sweetest, little wife,
I thank you so very much for your letter. I am sorry my sweetie got so wet on the way home on (Saturday) Sunday night. And then you had to go out and post the card for Sheila. Good thing I made your fire up before we left for the bus. Don't be miserable, sweetheart, I too was when I got back here all alone. Are you also getting fed up being on your own? Show me that fellow who told you Fred had been run over. I'll fix him for you. Still, you had the possibility of getting a frying pan from the shop.

Isn't it funny that you only get your post war credits when you are 65. Didn't they say you would get it back after the war.

I am sorry I couldn't tell you Helmut wife's name. It shows really how news travels. In Leicester already.

Something nice happened tonight. Remember last Saturday I told you I didn't feel well and hadn't eaten anything that morning? Well on Friday night the milk had a funny taste. Like disinfectant. I had some for supper after boiling it, but the taste still was the same. During the night I had to get up twice. Well, I didn't drink anymore and also didn't say anything because it was the first time. Tonight, however, it was exactly the same. At 5.00 I fetched the milk and when I got my bike ready I had half a cup of it. I spat it out again. So on the way shutting up I met Les and asked him what his milk was like. He said alright. Doris didn't notice anything unusual in hers. So I asked her to come and taste it. She agreed with me, meaning it tasted awful. So what did I do? I took the bottle over to Mrs Cooper. No losing temper or hot words. Just told her there must be something wrong with the milk and if she would please taste for herself. She went off straight the way and told me it was tonight's milk and that nobody else had complained about it. One of the Irishmen had a taste and said it was alright. So she was bringing it back, but I told her on Friday I had to throw the custard away and I don't want it back and would fetch myself some milk from the farmer next door for tonight. She said, well, if it isn't good enough for you the master can taste it in the morning as there wasn't anything wrong with it.

I, of course took my big pot and bought 2 pints of real milk. The woman at that place started asking questions. She knows I am working here. Questions like "don't you get any milk and do they still skim the milk?" I said I just wanted a bit more. And what a surprise when I saw Mr Cooper coming along. So that woman tasted and said to her "Oh! That is poor milk and no taste or flavour at all. If I wouldn't know it was fresh milk I would say it was skimmed". Mrs C didn't say anything at all. Some excuse like that aren't rich cows!!! I am only waiting for the boss in the morning. Wonder what he has to say.

The day went as usual. Watercarting and cleaning out. Gerald is off tomorrow that means feeding and collecting for me.

By the way, darling, can you bring a map for me?

Well, it's 9.00 and I'll have some darning to do. Be good my sweet and Good night and God bless you. I love you more than anything else in the world.

All my love and kisses to you.

Wednesday, Febr. 15th 1950, 7.45p.m.

You are right, you call it a sou'wester. It's short for southwester. Like the thing fisherman wear.

Blimey, I am surprised the fountain pen takes so long to be mended. You have done quite right leaving it at Boot's.

489

Clever girlie. 11<u>th</u> April sounds a long time, but never mind as long as I get it fixed. We'll see about the price when it's ready.

The boss has been speaking to me a few times today, but hasn't mentioned a word about last nights affair. When I came from shuttin up I went to look if Mrs C had put a bottle ready again. But no, she hadn't . If she's waiting for me to beg her for milk she's had it. I went and bought some again. Just a pint. I'll make that last, though I could have a gallon if I wanted. And the milk is good. This morning I had enough cream for my puffed wheat. You know what that means? I'll save some cream up for us for the weekend. Rather pay 5d but get milk and not water.

Today I was feeding, cleaning out and collecting as it was Gerald's day off. I am rather tired tonight so I'll be off early.

Well, my sweetest, I'll close and say Good night and God bless. Look after yourself and be good. I love my Jeannie more than anything else in the world. See you Saturday.

All my love and a thousand kisses
Forever your loving husband
Hans.

92 Wharf St
16.2.50

"Hello my darling"

How are you today? I only have to wait 1 ½ days more, then I will be with you. I have finished my jumper. I have not anything else to do but sit here to wait until someone rings. I have not been rushed with calls so far.

I will get the sou'wester tomorrow (Friday) lunchtime. I only have the sausage to get. Ernie brought a cauliflower.

Is Mrs Cooper trying to poison you? The old cat giving milk away that is usually given to pigs. You may as well pay for your milk to have it good than have it for nothing and no good, but what right has she to say whether or not you can have the milk. It isn't for ever, so why should we worry what they do with the milk. We will see what the next 2 weeks bring forth. If we are going to Germany for our holiday you may as well stay there until you have had a fortnight holiday. Don't you agree?

Here I am once again I am a nice clean girl now. I have just had a bath. Mamma has not gone out, her knee's are not too good today, she is in bed. I will have to take her a cup of milk.

I am having to use my fountain pen. You know the pen holder with the beautiful nib in, I said you could take to Pickwell? I dropped it and now it looks like your nose!!! I was annoyed.

Well my darling I will say good night God Bless I love you more than anything else

Same address
Febr. 16th 1950.

My dearest, darling Jean,

Hello, my sweetheart, how are you? Fine, I hope. I'll just write a quick few lines. It's 9.00 and up to now I've been busy (busy) and still have to darn my socks. The day went as usual, cleaning out of course. Still, I don't mind, it's only day and a half to go. Les is going shutting up again so I can go shopping straight away. That means a break for me.

Well, my darling, it'll be all for tonight and I have to get cracking. Be good and look after yourself. I wish it was Saturday. Oh! I love you so very very much. All my love and kisses. Friday, 7.45 p.m.

Hello, my darling, it's Friday night again meaning only a few hours to go in the morning and I'll have my sweetie here again. Tomorrow morning I'll be able to have my porridge again as I bought some treacle. Well, I think I've bought about everything we need for the weekend. Don't be surprised when I tell you the price for my 2lbs Beef and Pork-4/8. It almost knocked me out. But still it's nice. After all it's a low week in wages, but I still have more left than last time. Of course 5d. for milk every night, but that's only 2/6 a week and I'll have it because that'll be paid out of my so-called pocket money.

I didn't say anything to the boss because of the bed, but he's just been and ask me if it would matter if it was narrower, but longer. He can't get the exact size I've told him. The bedsteads are more or less standard size. So he's getting bedstead, springs and mattress. These mattresses will be too wide in any case. I only hope it comes soon. Don't think it'll be tomorrow.

Oh! I had an awful job today and it'll probably be for another few days. Cleaning the cobwebs in the chicken houses. You have never before seen ~~and~~ as much dust. My face was dark grey when I got back here. And the whole lot has to be done. All the best to me.

Are you ready for coming? Poor girl will have a lot to carry again. I wish I could get back earlier and meet you at Somerby. Still, you might be here on the early bus.

I'll close now and say goodnight. Be good, my sweetie, I'll do the looking after you for the next 2 days. Goodnight and God bless you always.

> All my love and kisses
> > Forever your loving husband
> Hans.

92 Wharf St

Feb 20th 1950

My dearest darling,

Another weekend has gone, now I am counting the days to the next weekend. Next time I will try to do better with the dinner. I'll buy myself a good cookery book someday in the near future, then if I can't get a dinner ready with the aid of a cookery book you should get yourself a cook.

I arrived home safe. It was raining, but it looks as though it had ~~by the look~~ been pouring. Mamma hadn't gone out her knees are still bad, she could hardly come down stairs this morning. She slept at Betty's Saturday night, Betty and Cyril went to an R.A. dance.

I am home, it is 9.0 and I have just sat down. When I got in at 6.0 Mamma wasn't in she had gone to the doctors. Betty was taking Sheila because she has had a discharge from her ears. Mamma has some pills and medicine to take and has got to rest it. She did not get back until 7.15. Betty and Susan came, and we did not have our tea until 8.0. Was I hungry. I fried egg and bacon. That is one thing I can do. Do you think you could live on love, eggs and bacon with tinned tomatoes. I noticed today those tomatoes are not on points. I will get a few tins.

I have been spending again, but not much. I bought a packet of relief nibs 8d. 7 in a packet. I bought a packet thinking it would be cheaper, but I found out too late, they had some a penny each. I would have had one more that way.

How have you been getting on today? Working hard. Please darling don't over do it. Don't try to do all Gudger's work, always think you may be in the same position yourself, and if anyone asks you if you can do it all on your own again, say you will try, then if you can't manage it does not look so bad. There I am again lecturing you. I hope you don't mind, but if you are sure of yourself, don't show it quite so much, be a bit modest. No matter what I love more than anything. I never seem to tell you so when we are together, but I do. I can't tell you how much I will try to show you by being a good wife to you. When I am with you at Pickwell that room to me does not look like a saddle room.

Well my darling I have to write to Mr & Mrs Springthorpe for the present, put the porridge in the oven and get Mamma some milk. I am a busy girl?

So goodnight and God Bless you. I love you and need you more than anything else.

All my love and kisses

    My one and only

    Jeannie

———.

Pickwell
Febr. 18th 1950.

My sweetest, little wife,

The place is so empty again and more than that I am so terrible lonely. The fire is out, but it doesn't matter as I will be off in a few minutes. You'll almost be at home by now and so I'll go to bed. Be good, my darling and look after yourself. God bless you always. All my love.

Monday, Febr. 20thth8.45 p.m.

Did you enjoy the weekend? Oh, Jeannie I enjoyed every second of it. It only was a shame I had to keep going most of the Sunday. Though it won't be so bad next weekend as the chicken sexer comes on Monday. That's less work for us on Sunday morning. I arrived back here in a few minutes and listened to "Variety Bandbox". It was alright again. Wasn't it awful this morning. Gerald and I were waiting till 7.45 before we got off, but when I got back at 9.30 it was still raining heavily and I wet through. That sou'wester is good. I put it on today and G. did the same. We really looked like fishermen. At 5.00 we went out again shutting up and got back from spraying at 7.00. My dinner was ready at 8.00.

Can you imagine how it is if you can hardly keep your eyes open? I made the round 4 times today. My feet feel as if they'll drop off at any minute.

Well, darling it looks as if we're going on holiday to Germany after all. Never mind. I really like you to go over and see for yourself what it looks like. I am sure we'll enjoy ourselves. Is it up to us now to be careful? Let's see how things go.

IBe good, my sweetheart and look after yourself. Goodnight, God bless and keep you safe. I love you more than anything else in the world and hope always to be a good husband.

All my love and kisses
Forever loving you
Hans.

Aschersleben, 10.2.50

21.2.50

Horst Klarwitter

My dear Hans and Jean

I want to send you a little note today. We have not heard from you for two weeks and are waiting every day. The weather here is terrible. It is raining every day and we have to literally wade through the mud outside. How are you both getting on? Have you started your new job yet? Dear Hans, I am enclosing two photographs, both were taken at the two masked balls I went to recently. Next Monday, there is going to be a big Hairdressers Fancy Dress Ball, for which I have created four evening hairstyles. One is called 'The Powder Hair Style' with Marie Antoinette in mind, whose face was always pasted with white powder, and the hair is coloured white. Another one is a lady wearing a replica of an old Hansa ship in her hair made of blue silk. Her hair is coloured blue. The third one depicts 'The Queen of the Night with the Golden Moon'. I have put a golden moon in her golden/bronze coloured hair and she is wearing a black veil. My fourth creation is the Chess Queen with a chess board in her hair. The hair has a hint of gold. All models are wearing an evening gown. You have no idea how much running around I had to do before I got all the 'ingredients' together. Mum and Mrs. Lehmann are also coming to the Ball. I am wearing my white dress tailcoat again. There will be seven prizes for the best seven hair creations. It means that one has to put a lot of effort into it. There will be motor cars available for driving us there. Maybe they will take a photo of us all. Dear Hans and Jean, what are your thoughts about coming to Germany? I need to know because of my holiday booking at work. The prices in the west have come down quite a bit now, also shoes with natural rubber soles have been reduced, but things are far too expensive for us. The currency rate of 6.7 is completely impossible for us. I will close my letter for now. I still have to put the finishing touches onto my historical wigs. I am sending my love to you both, yours Horst and mum. I am looking forward to seeing you again soon. Remember me to your mother-in-law.

Horst and his Chess Queen

My dearest, darling Jean,

I really was a little bit disappointed yesterday to go without a letter, but you certainly made up for it. You may believe that I also have started to count the time till next Saturday the moment you went onto the bus. No excuse because of the dinner Jeannie. Even if it was late it was beautiful. Do you think a cookery book would help?

So Mamma's prepared to see the doctor. She really should've gone a long time ago. My work has just been finished that means 3 hours overtime last night and tonight. My fire's gone out, that's the position at the moment. I can't be bothered to start the fire again, so just fry the meat up and have some bread with it. Yesterday my dinner consisted of bread and milk. Now I feel hungry but still, I'll be able to make up at the weekend.

Oh! I think I might be able to live on egg, love and bacon and you've forgotten one thing- plenty of work. Can you bring one of the nibs at the weekend. This one is on the "going"

I am getting on alright. Plenty of work keeps me out of mischief and what else can one expect here at Pickwell. Believe me I won't try to push Gudger out of his job. Even now if I do most of his jobs it's only for the time being.

Where was I? Yes, By now you should know that when I say I can do a job, I do it, even if I have to work all the time. Every day has got 24 hours plus 1 hour dinner break. Up to now everything has been managed to the very best. In fact we've got more time than before because of making jobs easier for ourselves. That's one thing G. has no idea about. If it comes to organising it's just nil. I really wish I had a chance to run the place myself.

Look, darling even if you don't tell me very often how much

you love me I know and I on my part will try to show you how much I love you by being a good husband. If we both try hard we should have a very happy life together. And somehow I am sure we will have. I am very happy when you are here, but still notice what this room looks like. A hole and it isn't what I think a place fit to live in.

We'll see about it at the weekend. As to our holidays we'll have to make up our minds and let my mother know. Horst also has to arrange his time off.

By the way, sweetie, there's one thing I would like you to get for me and bring along on Saturday. Remember I told you about the gear change and wire for my 3-speed? Well, Geralds father doesn't get to Leicester this week so could you get those things for me? The B.S.A. shop is top of Belvoir Street, on the left side opposite John Bigs. It's the wire that goes to the rear wheel and the things you change the gears with, fastened to the crossbar. It isn't expensive. I can't think of anything special for you to bring. So let it be it.

Well, it's 9.45, the porridge is done so it means I go to bed. When I was sorting eggs tonight I kept yawning and my eyes wouldn't stay open. I am really very tired.

So I'll close for now. Be good, my darling and look after yourself. Goodnight and God bless and keep you safe.

More than anything else in the whole world.

> All my love and a thousand kisses
> Forever and only your ever loving husband
> Hans.

92 Wharf St

23.2.50

"My darling"

Here I am again still waiting until the weekend comes to see the sweetest person in the whole world, my jerry husband. I wouldn't change him for anybody.

What have you been doing these past few days? Being a good boy I hope. I have been a good girl apart from spending 9/3 on wool and a pattern. I have bought some blue wool for a jumper. I picked a pattern out and I forgot to look at the size, it is for someone with a 33 bust mine is 35" I will either have to put more stitches on or get another pattern. I will knit you a sleeveless pullover when I have finished this one.

I saw some nice shoes this lunch time, I nearly bought them but I managed to stop myself. I have not any wellingtons yet. I saw some in Morgan's at 13/3. I will have a look around to see if I can see any cheaper. I have done our washing. Washed it last night, hung it out this morning. Oh! My poor hands it was cold again this morning, but the washing dried well. I ironed it ~~this~~ tonight. I will finish it off round the fire tonight then away. I have also written to Mr & Mrs Springthorpe and Muriel.

The fire is nearly out so I will have to close, I am getting cold. I will have to have cocoa made with water, we have not enough milk. I will not bring any milk on Saturday, we can get from Hill's what we want, it will make my load lighter.

I will write a few lines tomorrow afternoon when I hope I have heard from you.

Do you love me? Or have you changed your mind? I hope not and I hope you never will. I will do my best so you won't.

Goodnight my darling God bless and keep you.

Thursday

Thank you my love for your letter. I will fetch that thing you want for your bike tomorrow. After dinner I chopped a box up (we have run short of fire wood). I got carried away with it and it was 1.50 and I hadn't had a wash, I made here at 2.5. I will have to go to vote tonight. I am still not sure which one to vote for but will definitely not be Labour. I think it will be Liberal.

I will have to see how much I owe Mamma. I have not settled for last week's things. I will also get those other things settled. Then we'll see how much we have saved for this month.

You poor darling no one to feed you when you have been working hard all day. You must have a really awful wife!!!

I asked Nancy what happens on Sunday if you want a newspaper. They come from Oakham those two people deliver them for nothing, but only in Somerby so I will not have a paper to read.

I can't think of anything else to say at the moment. I love you very very much and longing to see you. For that I will have to wait until Saturday 48 ½ hours from now 3.20. I will be on the 2.15 and I will try to remember everything. So my darling until Saturday cheeri'O

> All my love and kisses
> I am your loving wife
> Mrs Johannes Erich Gustav Klawitter
> (Jeannie)

Same address
Febr. 23rd 1950 9.00p.m.

My sweetest, little wife,

Hello, my one and only. Here I am again with 1 ½ day to go. After lunch today we went laying nest boxes. The boss came and asked me what the nest boxes in the big field looked like. So I said I'd only done them one day last week. He said " in one day and done 12 boxes in every house?" I answered "yes". So he said then you must've been sweating or otherwise I don't know how you did it. I told him it was cold and I had to keep myself warm. And you know what the cheeky blighter said? He wishes it was cold more often. But I had my answer ready to that. I says I thought I'm doing my share at work. Oh! He said I was only joking and I know you're doing your share alright. Gerald was laughing. He seemed to be on the joking side these last few days. Yesterday he said we should bring at least 1200 eggs from the big field instead of 800, according to the feeding stuff Gerald takes out. I told him that we do the collecting alright, but not the laying. He didn't say anything just smiled. Gudger has been back for a few hours

hours today working at the incubator place. I think he's starting again in the morning. One miserable looking face more on the farm. Still, never mind. I guess I'll be cleaning out again tomorrow.

Well, my darling, I'll close for now. Look after yourself, good-night and God bless you always. I love you soooo very much
<u>Friday, Febr. 24th 1950, 8.15 p.m.</u>

Only a matter of hours now. The morning will go quickly.

I hope you bought a pair of wellingtons. Please, darling, don't always say you're going to see if they're cheaper any-where else. A good pair will last you longer. Even if it's a few more shillings, but it certainly is worth it.

You poor girl have to do the washing by yourself. If I could only give you a hand. It really was cold yesterday morning. How is it you are short of milk? I hate cocoa made with water. We'll get plenty at Hill's tomorrow.

Hasn't it been an exciting day. Everytime I came in here I switched the wire on to see how the parties were. Blimey it was a close chase. He just announced that the L.P. has the over-all majority with 313. So have another go with the same lot. Your poor party had to pay for it losing all the de-posits. Good thing you didn't have to deposit me. Otherwise you would've had it.

I had a letter from my mother today. It looks as if our going home is definite now. They expect us and have also got something for us they can't send, but want us to take it back. Wonder what that's going to be. Horst is very busy again preparing 7 models for a competition. My mother said you can't speak to him when he is busy with it. In Horst's letter were two snaps of him, I'll show you tomorrow. By the way I just thought of it. What's going to happen to Bonzo when we go away. It's hardly possible to leave Mamma with the two dogs. He's too big to be kept inside and she can't take him out. Looks as if fellow has to go.

Well, will see how to arrange things.

Well, my sweetheart, I'll say cheeri'o. Be good till I see you again.

Goodnight and God bless you. I love you more, thousand times more than anything else in the whole wide world.

> All my love and kisses
>> Forever your loving husband
> Hans.

> Pickwell,
> Febr 27th 1950

My darling

Hello, my sweetie, how are you? Fine, I hope. It was lovely out in the moonshine tonight, but it would have been much nicer to have a walk with you. That spraying powder (DDT) is deadly. My nose is all full up. This afternoon I had to go and spray all the houses in the big field first and tonight the hens. Believe me I've just had enough. Water to have a wash is on the cooker.

Did you get home safe and sound last night? I hope so. I arrived back here at 8.50, listened to Variety Bandbox (for the last ½ hour in bed) and dead 10 o'clock switched the light off. I knew you'll be at home by then.

This morning I fetched myself a hundred weight of spuds so we'll have plenty for the next weekend. When I went for my milk tonight Mrs Hill showed me the pig they've been killing today so we just got down to talking and I said it's a shame I can't keep one as one can't keep a bit of home cured bacon. You know what she said? I'll give you a nice slice of bacon. So when I get it I'll save it till Sunday breakfast and we can have a bit more bacon then. I didn't ask for it, but fortunately the conversation took that course.

Well, my one and only, I'll close for now and say goodnight. Be good and look after yourself. I love you more than anything else in the world.

God bless you and keep you safe.

> All my love and kisses

Forever your loving husband
Hans.
PS Please put a nib in the next letter this one has had it.
Love Hans

92 Wharf Street
February 27th
My dearest Johannes.
I arrived back in Leicester safe at 9.20. Just in time to hear Reg Dixon. Mamma was in, she had been round to Betty's for the day. I had a look in the papers to see if there was anything I had missed. I shall be as fat as a pig soon I had another cup of milk before I retired. What would you say if I did weigh about 12 stone in a few years time!!!
I did not think it was as cold today as yesterday. I put my boots back on. I ought to have put them on at the weekend, but I did want to look my best and show my stockings off, just think if I had put them on I would not have laddered my best stockings. I took them to work this afternoon to mend. I have done my best and they do not look too bad, I will be able to wear them.
Mamma has been to the doctor again tonight. About 20 minutes after she had gone I let Fred out because he was at the door, first of all he dashed over to the pub across the way. I thought he was looking for Mamma so I called him back, but would he come, no. He ran as fast as he could towards Betty's he caught up with Mamma in Clyde Street, she had to go to Betty's to leave him whilst she went to the doctors. Sheila has been very poorly again. Betty had the doctor on Saturday. She has been having trouble with her ears, they discharge, then yesterday she came out in spots but they have gone again today. What a worry, I would be grey in no time especially if you had a motorbike.
I have seen some material I rather like to have a summer

dress made. Would it be alright, if on Friday I bought some, it was 11/5 a yard I would want 4 yds. That would be £2.5.8 or maybe I ought to wait until the summer comes. It looks as though we will be going to Germany after all. I hoped we could do it on about £50. It does seem a lot when we need it for a home so badly. But then if we wait until we can afford it, we would probably be too old to enjoy it. If we go while there are only two it will be cheaper. Cyril's youngest brother's wife has just had twins, a boy and a girl, they already have two a girl and a boy, the girl being about 3 and the other a year younger, he's an officer in the R.A.F. It is a good job he is, the R.A.F. will keep them. I wouldn't mind a family like that. 4 under 3 years old, my, I would have to work a bit quicker than I do and poor you would have to work nights which would probably be a good thing in that case or it might be in 8 in 6 years!!! Next week we will have to be careful or we will have had our holiday.

My darling, I must close it is near my bedtime, goodnight and God bless you I LOVE YOU very very much, I am waiting for next Saturday to see you. 4 ½ days I hope it goes quick.

Love Mrs Johannes Klawitter

28.2.50 TIME 3.15AM

Hello! My darling Isn't it a beautiful day? This weather makes me wish I lived in the country. I have had my window open at the bottom nearly all day.

Please, sweetie, have plenty to eat and look after yourself because you won't feel very lively. I wish I was there to get your meals (eggs with love and bacon and sausage twice a week).

I have put you a nib in. I hope they do not press the letters. Well my love I will close. Be good, and look after yourself

All my love

Jeannie

R 5.3.50   Aschersleben, 12.2.1950

27.2.50

My dear Hans and Jean

Thank God, yesterday we finally received your post after 16 days, and we thank you from the bottom of our hearts. Dear Hans, I am so happy that you have written such a long letter. Your letter is dated 9.2.50. It looks like we are always getting the same weather after you. We are having a really horrible day today, a very strong storm with rain showers, but even this will pass. We had a fortnight of cold weather, up to minus 18⁰C. Who knows, perhaps winter has been and gone? At home we used to have quite different winters, which I like much better because the wet climate does not agree with us at all. My nettle fever has been better now for about eight days and I know what did it: shock. I put both bottles of medication together side by side, the menthol spirit was for application to my skin only and the other medication in the bottle was to be taken. As I was in a rush the other day, I drank the menthol spirit by mistake. You can imagine how shocked I was. I kept spitting and spitting and was very frightened. Since then I have been feeling much better. Well, every cloud has a silver lining. On the other hand, I seem to have a lot of bad luck these days. On Saturday a week ago we had a lot of slush in our yard. As I went to close the chicken coop I felt my legs being pulled away and crashed down onto my knee with my chest landing on the wooden board. I can tell you it was very, very painful. I immediately made some warm compresses and put them on my injuries. I am now finding walking difficult, in spite of only having some pale bruises. I injured the same knee nine years ago after a bad fall. It took seven months before I was better again. I hope it does not get as bad again this time. Sometimes, one goes through a bad patch.

Tomorrow, the Hairdressers are having their big Fancy Dress Ball. It is meant to be a fine affair. I am supposed to go as well, but I just don't feel like it. However, if I don't go it will upset Horst. Today, on Sunday afternoon, he went to the salon to put the rollers into the hair on the wigs. Tomorrow afternoon he will be combing the hair out. You have no idea how much Horst loves his work and how enthusiastic he is. His Lady boss will be dressed up as 'Queen of the Night'. He even stitched all the sequins on her lace dress. He is so patient. You will see all the photos when you come over. Dear Hans, you are writing about the holiday. We don't mind when you come in June. We just need to have the dates in good time so that Horst can book his holiday at work. We are so looking forward to seeing you again and meeting Jean. It will be an expensive trip for you both. I quite believe that you have to save a lot of money. A lot has changed now compared to a year ago because you can buy food without the ration vouchers now. We would have to pay 40 Marks for the two of us to come and see you. At the moment they are making things difficult again for people who want to go over the border, but we have still got four months till then. This week I bought another half a hundredweight of wheat for 35 Marks. We have spent 100 Marks on the chickens so far already and they are doing very well. The old hen has already laid 14 big, beautiful eggs. I think we might get some eggs from the younger chickens by Easter. It would be nice if we had fresh eggs for you when you are here. Our eggs only cost 1.30 Marks now.

Dear Hans, the reason why you are now so much stronger is, I think, because you are outside such a lot. But you must still be careful and not play around with your health. Jean seems to work very hard as well. I am sure you will remember how hard I used to work, dear Hans, and I always enjoyed it. We are so happy to hear that we shall soon be receiving the wedding photos. We have bought you a nice souvenir and hope you will like it. We shall bring it along when we see you because we cannot put it in the post.

Now, my dear Hans, I would like to finish my letter for today. Stay healthy and write back soon. Give my regards to your mother and to you both, my dears, we are sending our love and kisses, your mum and your brother Horst.

Pickwell,
March 1st 1950.

My sweetest little wife

I thank you so very much for your lovely long letter. When I came in this morning I had a quick glance through the window and there it was. Taking the horse out took only half the time. The nibs have arrived safe.

So my little Jeannie was thirsty when she got home. Never mind about getting fat. Milk is good for you, so a couple of pints more or less won't matter. What I would say if you weighted 12 stone in a few years time? Nothing, nothing at all. You don't have to be ashamed of your husband looking after you so well, do you?

Well, I am feeling fine. It hasn't been all that cold lately. The rain didn't melt me so the cold won't freeze me. One gets used to.

You ought to have brought your boots last weekend. Not only because of the stockings but the cold weather. Look, darling, can't you bring a pair of stockings to mess about in? That would be the safest way, wouldn't' it?

Did it take Mamma 20 minutes from 92 Wharf St to Clyde Street? She must be proper poorly. Poor little Sheila she always seems to be in some kind of trouble.

Well, darling, if you want that material for a summer dress, go and buy it. I've spent some money on my bike so you go and buy it. You'll want a nice summer dress to take along.

Yes, it looks as if we really have to get cracking to make arrangements and get our papers ready for going to Germany. I better find out what I have to do and where I've to write to. You'll want a passport. We'll see what my mother says how much it'll be to live on for a fortnight. So you would like a family like Cyril's younger brother. We'll see what we can do. Perhaps I'll be able to fulfil that wish. Oh! Sweetie, it's only another 2 ½ days to go. I am so terrible lonely. If only you were here. Not because of getting the meals ready but I am missing you so very much. Doris is off this weekend so it looks as if I'll be off the weekend after her. By that time I'll sure need a haircut. I've cut it out a bit last night and it doesn't look too bad now. Still in a fortnight I'll look like an artist.

So you feed me on eggs, love with bacon and sausage. What do you say if it suits me? Can I have some potatoes with it too?

Nothing has happened yet about the bacon I was promised. Though, tonight she asked me what I would prefer. A slice of fry or boiled. Guess what I said. Boiled so I can keep it for tea on Sunday when my wife is here. I know you love a slice of ham. It'll make a lovely tea. It looks as if I have to give the butcher a hint again.

How are things going at home? Everything alright? Yesterday I went watercarting on my own and in the afternoon and all day today cleaning out, as usually.

Can you read my writing today? I can't write the other way with this pen. This is as I used to write at school. The note I got for it wasn't one of the best at all. Doesn't matter now, does it?

Well, my love I'll close for now and say cheeri'o. Be good and look after yourself. I love you more than anything else in the whole wide world.

All my love and kisses
Forever your loving husband
Hans.

92 Wharf St
March 1st 1950

My dearest Hans

How are you my love today? I hope you are feeding yourself properly. I want a strong husband not a weed and strong children, so please eat and have proper meals, until I can feed you.

You poorly darling having to spray DDT at night. I wish I had been walking with you in the moonlight, one day we will go for a walk in the moonlight.

I have not been out this week, I was going to Evington but I thought I had better stay in and wash the floor and clean up in general. I stayed in, but I haven't done anything, I have been lazy. I feel so tired, when I have finished this I will be off to bed. Oh I long for you to be there at the side of me, I lay the other pillow down at the side so I won't feel quite so alone but it is not the same. I will only have to wait until Saturday. I have just drunk my milk, took Mamma some and given Fred some. Fred has a poorly foot, his back leg, left one, has a blister between his toes. I bathed it last night and it seems a lot better. He has settled himself on my knee, he must be uncomfortable but he still stays.

I went to the bank at lunchtime and put £10 in. We now have £54.11.8, it is coming on. I rang Dean & Dawson to find out the rate of exchange in Germany it is 13 marks to the £, less than you thought. I had hoped we could do our holiday on £50. £30 for fares and £20 in food and fun but I had better leave it to you. Don't let us draw all the money we have out of the bank. If we could from this week save £5 a week until week June 10th we could save £75. I know you do everything you can to earn money, I only wish I could do something at night too. Oh my darling I love you so very much. I can't tell you how glad I am I married you. I hope you are glad too.

With all my love I will say goodnight and God bless you and look after you.

Jeannie

R 11.3.50 Aschersleben, 25.2.50
9.3.50

My dear Hans and Jean

Finally, your lovely photos have now arrived. We were so

happy to receive them and thank you from the bottom of our hearts. They are really beautiful. We are now getting to know the whole family. The little girl with her bare legs is very cute, and the two of you look an extremely happily married couple. Please God, long may it continue – we are wishing you our very, very best. Would it not be lovely if young love were to stay like this forever? You have already been married for five months now. How the time flies! We have now 'met' every one in the picture and they all look like one joyous and happy family. I think that we will never personally meet them all because we are separated by too much distance. Do they wear their wedding ring on their left hand over there? And the husband is on the right side of the bride? Well, different cultures, different customs. One can see that you are able to get very good clothes, because everybody is dressed so elegantly. Your mother also looks nice and all the other guests seem to enjoy good health. I like Jean's sister as well. Does she not have any other siblings? Were the photos taken in front of the church?

Horst is creating another hairstyle for the wig. It will be displayed in the window of the salon. When I went through the park yesterday I noticed small green leaves on the shrubs already. It is far too early for that. The starlings have also arrived already, what a pity that we are expecting more snow. I have to say again that we have completely different weather to what we had at home.

The main thing is that everything will be alright with our trip in June. At the moment, they are making things quite difficult again, but I hope it will be getting better during the next few months. We are, of course, looking forward to seeing you again very much, and that I will be able to take my lovely daughter into my arms. I have always wanted a daughter and I regret very much that we are living so far apart.

We received a long letter from Auntie Else yesterday. We had not heard from her for ages. They are always very busy. They like their new house, but Auntie Else says that it can never replace their being back in their homeland. They have to work very hard for their living. Heinz and Günter have applied for a job with the Police because they just cannot make ends meet. There is not enough for eight people.

Have I told you already that Auntie Erna received your letter on her birthday? She was very happy to hear from you and is sending her love. As you know, letter writing is not one of her fortes. Uncle Gustav sent me 30 Marks to buy some chicken fodder. You can imagine how happy I was about that. It will help me a lot. The old hen has already laid 21 eggs and I am hoping that the younger chickens will start producing eggs around Easter. One cannot afford to buy these expensive eggs. I am doing all the washing this week and the nettle fever has returned with a vengeance. It is such agony for me! I am sure it is caused by the awful soap and washing powder we are using. I only hope it does not stay with me as long as the last time!

When you come in June, would you please bring us some pepper? We have used up all ours. Such a pity because the food does not taste half as good.

Dear Jean, it looks like you sent us the photos. Thank you very much. How are you getting on with your language lessons? I expect Hans will have to play the interpreter when you are here. Well, I am sure we will understand each other. Now, my dears, I want to finish my letter for today. The evening has drawn in already.

Stay fit and well. Please give my regards to the mother and all the other lovely people. To you both we are sending all our love and kisses. Your mum, who is always thinking about you, and your brother, brother-in-law Horst.

Hans and Jeans wedding photo

Betty with Shiela, Cyril, Hans, Jean, Uncle Roll, Auntie Gert. Beatrice(Mum)
Susan

R 27/3.50

Aschersleben, 21.2.50 Shrove Tuesday

25/3.50

My dear Hans and Jean

Today I have to get down to answering your lovely letter dated 7.2., which arrived a few days ago. Unfortunately, we have still not received the photos you promised to send us. It is quite unpleasant having to wait from day to day and always to no avail. Well, hopefully they will be with us soon! A few days ago we had some lovely spring weather with 16°C, but today iwe have lots of rain and storms. It's no fun to get soaking wet so often, but the main thing is it does not

result in a cold. Three weeks ago I wrote to Bruno, but I have heard nothing from him, oh well it's his loss! At least I have told him what I think of him. My nettle fever seems to have disappeared again, thank goodness, but I am still plagued by a bad cold. Gosh, your colleague has taken himself a very young wife! I notice that you want to stay in your current job after all. Oh well, you know best, nobody can make up your mind for you. Work brings pleasure but it has to stay within its limits. Don't do too much with your leg. I am on my own tonight. Horst has gone to the Shrove Tuesday street celebrations. The Germans celebrate the end of the carnival season in a big way. Our landlady has also gone there. She is 56 years old and her girlfriend is 64. On Saturdays they go out until three o'clock in the morning and on Sundays they stay out until 1 o'clock in the morning. I much prefer to read my book and then have a reasonably early night. Last Saturday I went with Mrs Lehmann to watch the Grand Costume Ball of the L.V.P. Horst took the young girl who works in the same salon as he does. She is also in the photo which he sent you. She is a very nice girl, this Brigitte. You should have seen how lovely he made her look. They both made quite an entrance and caused a bit of a sensation. Horst does not want to commit himself to a regular girlfriend at the moment. He wants to get on in his career. If he stays fit and well and everything is going according to plan, he wants to do his diploma in Master Hairdressing next year in the autumn. By then, he will have had five years as an Assistant behind him.
I would like to tell you a bit more about the Costume Ball of the hairdressers. It was a very enjoyable evening. Horst had worked extremely hard and created some wonderful hairstyles. The seven best hairstyles should have been judged. Horst had done six. When he entered the ballroom with his six wigs, everyone was stunned. Horstel's former boss was in charge of the evening and I realised right away, what was about to happen. It was not long before all the models were asked to stand in a row, then it was announced that only the

models of the apprentices of Class 3 will be entered into the competition, which meant of course, that Horst did not qualify. His boss was absolutely fuming. The Master Hairdressers could not help but praise and admire the wonderful wigs. His immaculate work was still the talk of the town days afterwards. Therefore, Horst had practically achieved what he set out to, and he also acquired a few more clients. I have been to these Balls twice now because I did not want to disappoint Horst, but I cannot be really happy because my thoughts are always with Papa. If only I knew how he is!! The local Master Hairdressers are now even more envious of Horst than ever before. Last Thursday, the Chief Master Hairdresser came to see Horst in the salon and intended to tell him off. Apparently, he had ruined a lady's hair. Allegedly, her hair broke off after he had given her a perm. Horst's boss asked the Chief Master Hairdresser when this mean behaviour against Horst is coming to an end and told him that they should all be ashamed of themselves. They keep digging and digging and try to incriminate him but cannot really find anything against him. His boss gave the Mayor some examples of how they are trying to undermine him and he said if there is any more of this to contact him immediately. People cannot understand how they can be so envious of a 20 year old lad. On Friday, the Chief Master Hairdresser came back to see Horst again with Master Hairdresser Hörrmann. They just felt they had to do this. Horst's boss told Mr Hörrmann to think back to 1946 how he almost burned one of the clients entire hair off. It nearly cost him his life, had he not taken the initiative to quickly find a wig. Horst was asked to go to the Hörrmann Salon in the evening. The Chief Master Hairdresser and another Master Hairdresser were also supposed to be there. Horst went with his boss's father (who was also a Master of his trade) because he thought it would be good to have a witness. Suddenly, these men had changed beyond recognition. They said to him that he should continue to be enthusiastic in his work and make such excellent progress. They know that he is a superb worker in his field and they hope that he will be working together with them in the future. What do you think of all this? Are they not all big idiots? They obviously ask themselves: 'How on earth can a refugee be so capable and efficient?' This shows you that we, too, have our worries and upsetting moments!

I want to finish my letter, my dear Hans, give my very best wishes to your mother-in-law, and to you both I am sending you all my love and kisses, from your mum and brother Horst.

Aschersleben, 7.3.50

Horst Klarwitter

My dear Hans and Jean

Horst says 'thank you very much for your lovely letter'. He will reply to you personally, but is rather pushed for time at the moment. He was very happy to hear from you again. I received your last letter three weeks ago. I already wrote and thanked you for the photos.

Today we are having a beautiful spring day again and it really looks like winter is behind us. Well, it suits us fine! We are looking forward to the first day of spring in two weeks-time. A few days ago, when I came home from the shops, a young man approached me and asked if I have a son living in England, because he looks so like me. When he was a Prisoner of War he was in the same camp with you, first in America and then in England. He wanted to know if you were already back here. His surname is Müller, but I can't remember whether his first name is Kurt or Herbert. He is not quite as tall as you, in his late twenties. Does this ring a bell? He told me that he lives in Frose, one of our neighbouring towns.

Well, we must look very much alike if this is so.

Horst has been having trouble again with his shortness of breath. I just hope it does not get as serious again as it was the last time! I am really frightened of it. I always managed to make him a very strong cup of coffee, it helps to get him better each time. It stimulates the heart. I used up the last bit of coffee today. Dear Hans, please don't get angry with me but I have to trouble you again with it. Would you, if at all possible, send some coffee to me? I have tried everywhere to get some but with np luckl. I am always feeling quite embarrassed, but the smallest amount would make me very happy. I so want to help Horst. I cannot bear to watch him when he is gasping for air.

I suppose by now you have decided when you will start your journey! We would be so happy if it all came to fruition. Dear Hans, I am sure you will want to work hard every day now, but please do be careful. You know that your health always comes first. When are you going home? You will hardly find time for it. Does Jean come to see you every Sunday? I am curious to see how we are going to communicate with each other. I am sure it will be lots of fun too and, of course, we shall have our own interpreter! I can't wait!! We keep looking at the lovely photos again and again. They are really beautiful and we are so happy to have them.

Our hen has been on strike again for the last four days. It was so lovely when we had an egg from her every other day. She has now laid 24 eggs. We have now got our money back for what we paid for all the chickens, but the cost of the fodder has to be added. Once the young ones start to lay eggs, it will be even better.

Grandma was in hospital for three weeks when she had a gallbladder infection. Werner wants to get engaged in May. He is unemployed at the moment because when it freezes and snows, there is no work for bricklayers. Erna, Frida and Christa don't write very often and when they do, they do nothing but moan about not having any money. Perhaps they are worried that they might have to send us some, but we are quite happy to go without. A pound of margarine costs 1.09 Marks and if we want to buy anything extra, it usually comes to 11 Marks. I have to get extra several times during the month because I cannot send Horst to work with dry bread only. One herring costs 1.20 Marks, a small round cheese costs 2.50 Marks. I wonder if things will ever get better. It is hard to save enough money to buy the necessities. We badly need bed linens but 200 Marks is out of the question.

Now my dears, I want to finish my letter. Give our best wishes to your mother and stay healthy. We are sending you all our love and kisses, your mum who is always thinking of you, your brother and brother-in-law Horst.

Aschersleben, 13.3.50

Horst Klarwitter

My dear Hans and Jean

Thank you very much for your lovely letter dated 23 February, which I want to answer today. I am pleased you like the photos I sent you, they are nice little memories. What are you talking about! A Frau Klawitter! I am not thinking about that yet. We are staying single in this beautiful world. But I wanted to pass on her greetings, although you have not met. When we meet up with you I will introduce her to you via a photo. I dare say she could be the right type for me but once you go out with a girl you can't get rid of her again very easily! As you know, I did not get any prizes for my creations. When we entered the room with our six wigs, we were surrounded by soft murmurs, then the plan of the evening was changed. Only six creations made by the apprentices were judged. Well, I am used to this kind of thing, but in spite of it all, I received many compliments. Yes, dear Hans, as the saying goes 'the more envy, the more luck'. The opposition are out to kill. If all goes well, I shall be participating in the grand hairdressing competition, which takes place in the Kristallpalast in Magdeburg. However I never have sufficient hair decorations. I would love to participate and hope that I will succeed with my application. Dear Hans, calm down, short hair for ladies is also fashionable here now. I am cutting my clients' hair by 7 to 10 cm and I have to say it looks quite dashing. I would like to give Jean a 'German haircut' and hope that everything will be alright for our reunion. I am horrified by the cost of your trip but who knows when we can meet otherwise? The weather is really awful at the moment. We are having strong winds, snow and also rain. People have colds and can't get rid of them and it is very cold in our salon too.

Mum is sitting next to me. She is dozing off every now and then because she is so tired. This is quite catching, my eyes keep dropping too! I will finish my letter now and send you and Jean all my love. Yours Horst and mum.

PS: We are looking forward to a healthy reunion!
Please write back soon.

R   27/3.50

Aschersleben,
13.3.50

25/3.50

My dear Hans and Jean

We have just received your lovely letter dated 5.3.50 and I want to answer it right away. I hope your leg will be better soon and you must take your problem with the knee seriously too. I am sure it gave you an awful pain. The main thing is it will be better soon! But four to five days are hardly enough for it to heal. It does not get better as quickly as it came. Well, the holiday is still on as arranged. That's fine by us. We just hope that everything will run smoothly and we can all celebrate a healthy reunion. Dear Hans, if I were in

your place, I would take the ferry across both ways, especially as it is so much cheaper, even if it takes a little longer.
The trip is expensive enough for you. We would leave home
on 15 June because I want to be there before you arrive.
You can then go with the Express train directly to Braunschweig. Horst could meet you there, and then you can take
the train via Wolfenbüttel direction Schöningen. The place
is called Dettum. It only takes half an hour by train from
Braunschweig to Dettum. Weferlingen is 20 minutes by train
– a very nice walk through the countryside. We have often
said what a pity it is that you are not here with us. We
could have a comfortable home together. As you know, we
have two lovely rooms and everything would be cheaper for
us all. You wanted to know how much you might need for
your two-weeks-stay. Well, dear Hans, this is very difficult
to say because I don't really know what you both expect.
Anyhow, everything is much cheaper there than it was a
year ago. One pound of margarine 1.25 Marks. One pound of
butter 2.50 Marks. Meat 2.50-2.80 Marks. One loaf of bread
weighing four pounds 90 Pfennige. Mrs. Fuchs is not over-
charging us for the room. Outside the town we could live for
a lot less money than in town. I have still got 20 pounds of
wheat flour in West Germany, which I can use for making the
cakes. I shall write to Mrs. Fuchs to get us a hundredweight
of potatoes (4.50 Marks). That will be sufficient for us. I am
sure everything will be alright. We can get the milk from
the farmer. Am I right in thinking that you will have your
Sterling money exchanged into West Marks? Our rate of exchange is a lot worse: we only get 14 West Marks for 100 East
Marks. You can imagine how little we can buy for our money.
We are so lucky that Weferlingen is not far away from the
border, so we don't need a lot of West Marks for the journey.
It will be the harvest time for the pea pods soon and I intend
to go and pick some. I can earn myself a bit of money, because they pay 4 Marks per day. I assume you are not getting
a free passage this year. Horst is already looking forward to

giving his sister-in-law a nice hairstyle. He will show you all the photos of his hairstyles he has created. He has already acquired a few clients in Weferlingen. He has already, dear Hans, got a birthday present for you, but I am not supposed to tell you what it is. He hopes you will like it. I hope the Youth Reunion in Berlin at Whitsun will be a success. Yesterday we suffered some terrible storms here and today it is not much better. The nights are still frosty. Spring Day is here in eight days and Easter is in four weeks. Our hen stopped laying eggs for eight days because it was so cold. Today she gave us her 26th egg. We are going to have one of the photos framed.

I want to finish my letter for today. I have to go into town to the library and get myself another book to read, and I shall take this letter with me to put it in the post. Stay healthy and I hope your leg will be better soon. Give my regards to your mother. We are sending you both lots of love and kisses, from your mum, who is always thinking of you, your brother and brother-in-law Horst.

Pickwell
March 26th 1950

My darling
Oh! Darling it's so empty here now you've gone and I am so lonely. I really wish I could've gone back with you. I was very, very happy these last three weeks. And I hope so were you. It was nice to be able to help you a bit.

When I got back Bonzo was looking so sadly at me. Just as if he was asking me what bus we're going to take.

Darling, you made everything so comfortable. Come back. It'll be awful going to bed tonight with nobody to put my arms around. I'll have to take the cushion.

Well, darling, I'll say goodnight and God bless you always. Be good and sleep tight. All my love and thousand kisses forever your loving husband.

Monday March 27th 1950, 6.30pm

Gerald has come back, he has some kind of trouble with his stomach and goes for xray on Wednesday. Rather fortunate, when I asked Gudger about shutting up, he said, alright we are fixed up for the next fortnight as he gives a hand at it too and the next week it's Gerald. It's better for the leg that way. It hurts a bit, but I think now it's a matter of getting used to. I really have been very careful getting on and off the tractor so everything is alright.

7.45pm

Well, here I am again. Everything cleaned away and tidy. I also enjoyed it. First I boiled potatoes in their coats and then fried them. With some bacon it was really nice. Bonzo finished his anyway. For sweet there were golden plums.

I was lucky at the butchers. He'd saved me a lovely piece of mutton. Price 4/4d. So you can imagine how big it is. All the bills have been paid up to date. Cracked eggs have gone down to 2/6. So that's 2/- less in my budget. Tomorrow I'll have to find out who the coalbill has. After paying that I don't owe anything. My meat is in the oven. Now I could do with some mint sauce. Never mind, it'll do without it too.

Tonight I went round and gave my neighbours ¼ lbs of tea. She didn't want to take it, but when I told her I prefer coffee and could spare it, she took it. Asking me how I found people round here. I at first didn't know what to say. She said she'd tried hard to make friends during the last 6 month, but it is just as if they're pushed off. Her own words 'I loathe these people here.'

I got an invitation to come around any time I feel lonely. What could I say. Anyway I told her I don't have time to get lonely, working or having always something to do.

Well, darling, that's all for today. The second night without you. Oh! It's terrible I am so much longing for Saturday. Let's hope the week goes quick.

Be good and look after yourself. Good night and God bless and keep you safe. I love you more than anything in the whole wide world.

So take all my love and kisses
Forever your loving husband
Hans.

Aschersleben, 26.3.50

My dear Hans and Jean

Thank you very much for your lovely letter dated 9.3.50, which we received the day before yesterday. The healing process of your leg obviously took a lot longer than you thought. These things come on quickly but take much longer to heal. I do hope that everything is alright again now. I am so pleased to hear that you are both very happy together and my inner wish is that it may continue like that forever. I am sure, my son, you know what it means to be in an unhappy marriage. Always bear this in mind. Be kind to your Jean and treat her well. There is nothing in the whole world that is better than a happy and fulfilled marriage. This is what I was blessed with during all the happy years I was able to spend with your Papa. Maybe one day, the time will come when the Lord gives us a chance to spend many more happy years together. I can imagine how surprised Jean was when she came home and saw that all the washing had been done. There are not many thoughtful husbands of this kind about. I would certainly not say 'no' to that.

Dear Hans, it would be absolutely wonderful if we could come and visit you one day, but I don't think it will ever be possible. Where would all the money come from? Our money is not worth much and the currency rate is way below yours. Such an undertaking would be a long way into the future and for now, we are just concentrating on our get-together in June, and hoping that everything will work out according to our plan. Recently they started to give permission to West German citizens to go abroad again. Your clothes are beautiful. We do not have such lovely fabrics here. Horst is toying with the idea of having a new suit made for the summer. I want to go to the H.O. tomorrow. They are going to reduce the prices, but they will still not be affordable for people like us. They still charge 2 Marks for an egg, 18 Marks for margarine, 30 Marks for one pound of butter, it's even more expensive than if I were to get it from the Black Market.

The day before yesterday I only bought four Harzer cheeses (the small round ones) for 2.40 Marks each and one pound sugar for 6 Marks. We badly need bed covers but one cover costs over 100 Marks, which is out of the question. They could arrange for a discount for the refugees, who have lost everything. How do they think we can ever get a home together?

Dear Hans, you are not right, people who go on holiday abroad do not get a new passport. We shall be able to manage it again, I am sure. If only the time were here already. Do you still have ration vouchers? In the West, everything is free now.

Last week, Horst was suffering terribly again with shortness of breath. If only it would get better again soon! If I had known that you are not allowed to send coffee, I would never have asked you. Please forgive me. I do not want to become a nuisance and I don't want you to spend your money on us either. I know you have a lot of expenses especially with your big trip coming up. The day after tomorrow is my washday. Do you fancy coming over and helping me?

I don't think that it is possible to do the journey from London to Braunschweig in one day. We shall make sure to come and meet you there. It will shorten your wait. The train to Dettum leaves at 2 pm and you will be pleased when you get there and have a rest. Werner works in the West as a brick layer. We have quite a lot of relatives over there, but when they write to us, they do nothing but moan. I am sure they are worried in case they feel obliged to send us a parcel, but we are quite happy to go without. Our young chicken has laid four eggs this week, one day after another three days running. I am so happy about it. Auntie Lina is sending her best wishes. Bruno has not mentioned anything about me in his letter but he did send his mother a small parcel containing one pound of butter, one pound of coconut fat and some wool. So it did help!

Now, my dears, I want to finish my letter. I hope you will stay well. Lots of love and kisses from your mum and Horst. Best wishes to your mother.

92 Wharf St

March 27th

My dearest,

How has work gone down today? I hope you have settled down alright.

To think I have had four weeks without having to write to you. It takes something getting back into the habit again. I had to look for my pen, I could not find it straight away, it was on the shelf.

Oh, my darling I missed you so much last night. I seemed to be awake ages tossing and turning. I am not at all keen on sleeping on my own. I'm a big baby. I hope our holiday is worth all this being apart. I am really looking forward to it. 11 more weeks to go. 91 days to the 16th June, that works out at 13 weeks. That time I hope will pass away quickly. After that we will have to settle down to do something about our future and darling we will have to try to be careful a little longer yet. I would very much like to be able to stay at home to look after you and a baby but as things are at the moment it would not be very wise. Anyway we have until July to live apart, let's hope it will go quickly.

I arrived home safe. Just in time to listen to Reg Dixon. Fred was upset he had not eaten his toast, I think he must have missed Bonzo. Mamma cut him some meat this lunch. You would have laughed, Mamma went next door for a cup of tea yesterday, left her hat on the table. Fred tried to have a sleep on it.

I went round to Betty's to see how Susan was, her face is still swollen. Betty is taking her to the doctors tomorrow.

I think it is almost certain that we will have Good Friday until Monday, it will make a nice long holiday. I will have to bring my cookery book with me, just in case I get into difficulty I bet I manage to do that alright.

Ena bought that letter with her today. I thought I had better send it in an envelope as it is a bit torn at the top. I thought there was a photograph inside but it looks like a flower. Your brother seems to be a bit of a dandy, it is a good job his brother isn't.

So my darling goodnight God Bless, help and keep you safe I love you right from Leicester round the world and back again.

All my love
Jeannie

Tuesday

I have managed to be out of bed at 7.55 each morning though on Monday Mamma was first downstairs but I lit the fire.

It does not seem to be such a nice day. I have my window open wide just in case the sun comes out. I will be able to sunbathe in a sun suit.

Have you been a good boy and have not lost your temper. Old Gudger may be a bit funny but it would be a funny world if everyone was perfect. No don't let him get you down next time he tries to annoy you don't take any notice. You will find it will annoy him more that way than if you answered him back. So long as you do your work and you are paid for it. When they don't pay you is the time to lose your temper. That is the end of the lecture. One thing more, don't do any heavy lifting on your own. I know you like to show what you can lift, but look what happens that hut fell over on you, and other things so in future <u>YOU ARE NOT TO LIFT ANYTHING HEAVY.</u> I am so glad you won't have to go shutting up.

I have just had to pay a 1/- out for my telephone and I have fetched the coffee 5/8. I will fetch the milk then I will have to parcel it up, a job I am not very keen on.

Well my darling I will say cheeri'O and remember I love you very, very much.

Jean

.

92 Wharf St
March 29th

My dearest darling,

It isn't really time to write but I came without my needle work this morning and I'm bored sitting here on such a beautiful morning. I have been thinking, what I would be doing if I was at home all day and lived in the country. You would have to get your own lunch as I would have come into town to do the shopping. I would have left ready what you could have.

Something terrible has just happen I breathed out and pop went the hook off my bra I feel like a loose woman now.

Arch came yesterday, he has been to London last week, for the week to the Ideal Home Exhibition. I thought after Arch had seen the family picture it would get put away, but unfortunately Mamma forgot to show him. She has never said why she wanted the picture but I guessed she does. We are not having it up if I can help it. I don't like photographs stuck round a room and I know <u>you don't</u>.

Charlie is going to distemper his bedroom. I think they started last night to fetch the paper off. I thought that any moment he would come through the wall. Mamma said they are going to do it pale green. Could you imagine it? Fancy waking up to look at pale green in the morning, the paper we have on our walls is bad enough, I think prefer paper better than distemper or painted walls. Wait until we have a place of our own, I will supervise the decorations and it will look like a place out of a magazine.

I am listening to the play 'To What Red Hell' it was very good. Did you listen? It was lovely and sad, I cried my bluming eyes out. Did you listen to ~~have a go~~ (I am dreaming the bloke on the radio has just said 'have a go' is about to begin) anyway did you listen to the play last night about 'D.P.' that was good and sad. I don't mind having weep on my own but you feel so daft if anyone's there. I am on my own tonight Mamma has gone out with the neighbours. Charlie is still fetching paper off the wall with the help of Enid. She said there were about 10 papers on the wall.

I have been busy tonight, washed the sheet, the counterpane off Mamma's bed, and you will never guess what else. Your grey trousers. The trouble comes when pressing I hope I don't do them sideways. I hope it will not rain, I am leaving them out all night. I have also washed my hair. I feel as if I have a cold coming on. I am sniffy.

I bought some flowers this evening and I got the milk 2/2. All I have to do now is wrap them up. I am going round to look after Sheila and Susan on Friday night, Betty and Cyril are going to a dance. I was going to come home at night, but Betty wants me to stay there, as they may be late.

Well my darling I am still missing you an awful lot. I only have to wait 2 ½ days to see you and I am so much waiting for that moment. Will you have to go shutting up on Saturday and Sunday? Anyway I will find that out later.

Well I have to get cracking to put my hair in curlers and have my milk So all my love darling. I need you so much to look after me. Goodnight God Bless you

for ever
your loving
Wife

<u>Thursday afternoon</u>

Thank you my sweety for your letter. Now let me read it once again and answer it as I go along. Poor Fred did not have a hiding for laying on hat because he did not break the feather, he bent it a bit. Mamma said she would have killed him if he had broken it.

I think we had better have a chicken at Easter, can you think of anything I can bring over that weekend as a treat, but we must not spend too much.

Do you prefer shutting up the whole lot together once every 3 weeks? It will give you a rest in between. I bet you will not have your turn next week. What holiday do you have?

I do still have time to read the papers, I have a routine now. I don't suppose it will last long. After I have made the fire I mash the tea I put the rest of the water out to have a wash, put the kettle back on the gas, the treacle in the porridge, clean my teeth and then have a wash, I am now ready to have my breakfast and read the paper.

Isn't it a beautiful day again? I feel so restless sitting here, I have my needle work to do but I can't settle to it. I will watch

My darling, it is a half anniversary today. Do you regret anything? I don't and I still love you more than anything else in the world.

I have just had a cake given to me. One of the fellows in the transport office is leaving so he brought some cakes, it was just what I needed. I felt hungry.

Freddy returned 3 ½" of Bonzo lead yesterday morning another 12" is still missing.

I have not washed your trousers too well there are one or two marks still on. I will try to press them tonight.

Nancy and I have just been speaking about family names and naming your children after people. I wouldn't want to name ours after your father, Ernst, poor little thing.

I have just had a visitor, GPO engineer the one that was a

POW! in Japan.

Well my dearest darling. I will say cheeri'O. I will be seeing you Saturday.

All my love
and kisses
Jean

Pickwell,
March 29th 1950

My sweetest, little wife,

Thanks so very very much for your lovely long letter. Well, half the week is over, only 2 ½ days to go. I am so much longing for the weekend.

Oh! Work has gone down alright. I've kept going so far, it hurts a bit, but that doesn't matter. It'll be alright soon. It must be the work. Yes! It really was 4 weeks since you wrote last. How the time flies. Believe me I also hope our holiday will be worth this being apart. Otherwise we have wasted a month of happy life together. So you have counted the days till June 16th. It'll pass quickly, I hope. Let's have that holiday first and then we'll see what to do about our future. Alright, let's be careful a bit longer. I think you are right there. Things aren't very encouraging at the moment. Anyway, we'll see how things go on.

Did poor Fred get a thrashing when he tried to sleep on Mamma's hat? Did he bend the feathers?

So it looks as if I can expect you tomorrow week and stay until Monday night. You had better find out how about the bus service on Easter Monday. If you think you'll need the cookery books, well, bring them along. I'll safe some sugar so we can make a cake on Friday night. What about a chicken for Easter? I think we had better take one as the meat won't last that long.

Remember what he said about getting the bedstead in the first week in March 'without fail'? Last night he told me he couldn't get one at the last sale at Melton and the next one is in a month time. So if I could make this one last for another month. I was near to telling him to skip it as it won't be all that long before I leave. But never mind, let him get it.

What do you mean, you could do with a month by the sea to wake you up? Do you think of a month like our honeymoon at Bournemouth? By gum, we didn't sleep much there.

I think I've been a good boy till now. Even followed your advice not to lose my temper with that funny old man. Yesterday I did cleaning out with tractor and trailer and I let the engine run whilst I was doing the job. So this morning he said the tractor had to be stopped every time. I didn't have enough petrol in yesterday to start her up again so I had to keep her going. Anyway I didn't say anything at all, just gave him a real dirty grin and left him standing in the yard. I bet he could have strangled me. He looked like it.

And that makes me really laugh. I have got a clever wife giving me those advices. He won't get me down before that happens I'll break him the new way. I really hate that fellow moaning all the time, but never mind, it isn't for lifetime.

It looks as if I am shutting up next week already. Gerald didn't turn up yesterday and on Monday he looked really ill. He shouldn't have come at all. I can't understand people with that, couldn't-care-less attitude about their health. And don't be surprised, the new arrangement for shutting up is do the whole lot (100 houses) for a week and then have 3 weeks off.

Time for shutting up now is 2 ½ hours overtime.

Have you packed the parcel for my mother? Why aren't you very keen on that job? There's nothing in it.

Bonzo keeps coming to play with me. Up to now he hasn't had a harsh word from me. Let's see how he reacts to that treatment. Funny I do him toast in the morning and at dinnertime but he doesn't touch it till I put some potatoes and gravy on at night.

How are you feeling today my darling?. Do you find time to

read the papers? I wish I could help you, bring tea and porridge up on Sunday morning. I can't even do it here, having to work.

Well, my little sugarplum, I'll finish for now. The next letter will be delivered in person. I'll put a list in about the things you could bring on Saturday. If you can remember anything I have forgotten, bring it.

So be good, darling, and look after yourself. Goodnight, God bless and keep you safe. I love you more than anything else in the world.

All my love and kisses forever your loving
                    husband
                        Hans.

                                J. E. G. Klawitter
                                Home Farm, Pickwell,
                                Melton Mowbray/Leics
                                March 30th 1950

My darling

Hello, my sweetie, here I am again and how are you? Fine, I hope. I am alright too. It is a bit later tonight, 7.30, because I was working till 5.45. But still I have done my odd jobs even had a wash and washed my hair.

I really feel done in and very tired tonight. Starting off with feeding, then watercarting on the chickenfield, collecting in the afternoon and finishing off with watercarting. I am almost ready for bed. Collecting I went with Mrs Montols and I had a laugh when Eileen told her at dinnertime 'if you go with him, he'll get you going' Still we only got back at 4.45 getting lots of eggs. It is hard work now, carrying a bucket with 200 eggs across the field. Never mind, I'll have to get used to it again. There's nothing else to do so I might as well go off to bed. Well, my darling, only 1 ½ days till I see you again. Oh! Jeannie I wish it was tomorrow. And I keep my fingers crossed that time may go quick till next Thursday. Then we'll have another 4 full days to spend together.

Wasn't it a lovely afternoon. My face is red and burns like fire. I wish I could take the shirt off, but it's still too early for that. The wind is still cold.

Well, my one and only, that's all for now. Be good. Goodnight and God bless and keep you safe. I love you from Pickwell round the world and back thousands of times and with it thousands of kisses.

Friday March 31st 1950 8.40pm

Hello, my sweetie, how are you? I feel done in again, but haven't quite finished yet. Thank you so very much for that lovely long letter. I have been reading at least half a dozen times. Yes! You are definitely right in saying that I don't like photos stuck on the wall. Never mind, darling, if we have a home of our own you can please yourself how to paper or paint the walls or what to put on them. I know Charlie was doing the bedroom pale green, he told me about it and asked where I got the distemper from. Though I didn't say anything about the colour as he can please himself. If we do a place it won't like a place out of our magazine but like a palace.

I listened to bits of that funny play, but soon switched it off and went to sleep. No crying. Those things were in the papers hundreds of times.

You're such a sweetie, washing my flannels. Never mind how the pressing turns out it'll be alright for wearing here. Anyway I am sure you'll make a smashing job out of it.

We don't have to go shutting up over the weekend, that is if everything goes well and Gerald turns up again in the morning. It's his turn. He came today and feeling alright tonight he was coming tomorrow. Though I'll have to go for him on Monday as he has to see the doctor again.

I'll see what about about a chicken for Easter. I can't think of a special treat, but let's see tomorrow. I've stocked up alright.

Well, our first half anniversary is gone and I haven't regretted it a single second not even given it a thought. I am perfectly happy and couldn't have a better wife. Ever since I was a small boy I said to myself 'I make good to my wife what my father has done wrong to my mother. She was unhappy, but my wife will always be very happy. I'll see to that and try to do my very best.' And believe me nothing gives me more joy and happiness than seeing you happy and satisfied.

When I fetched the milk tonight I was surprised. The lady was there that lives next to the drive up to the rectory. She said now I would be lucky to get a house. I said what she meant, thinking of the council houses. Oh! She said, there's going to be a big switch over. Mr Bromwich (Doris father) is leaving next month and the house will be empty. She said if I wasn't going to ask for it. I said 'no!' If there's a house vacant and the boss doesn't offer it to me I won't say anything at all. She meant if one doesn't ask one doesn't get anywhere. The funny part is I haven't heard anything about Bromwich leaving. I am sure it's only a bit of gossip. Doris never mentioned anything.

Well, my darling, it's 9.30 and I'll have a wash and be off to bed. Be good till I see you tomorrow. Goodnight and God bless and keep you safe.

> All my love and kisses
> Forever your loving husband Hans

PS Please, get the tea ready for 4.00. We are not shutting up but going to the pictures.

> Love Hans

Aschersleben, 2.4.1950

My dear Hans and Jean,

Today I want to send you heartfelt Sunday greetings. Eleven years ago today, dear Hans, you were confirmed. Do you still think back to that beautiful day? Our dear Papa was still with us then. Those who were recently confirmed were also blessed early today. How quickly the years have disappeared!

We received a letter from you both ten days ago. I haven't been out at all, only to the hen house. Our young hen has laid 8 eggs within 10 days, that's really a great achievement for such a young animal.

I let the hens out an hour later than usual this morning. By then, the old hen had already laid one egg. The others must have ripped the egg down and they had just ate it. That has made me really angry, now I shall have to watch out that it doesn't happen again.

I am alone at home. Horst has gone dancing. I am very pleased for him. During the week we had a letter from Heinz, he is not happy in Schmiedenfelde any more and will see if he can find work elsewhere. Early tomorrow morning I shall have to go back into town again. I want to buy material for a summer suit for Horst. I've already been looking there every few days, but still haven't found the right one yet.

From what Frau Unger wrote to me, I gather that Otto Bendrath has now returned, he also was reported missing. His wife is living with a doctor, with whom she had a relationship while at the military hospital. Who knows what will come of that now?

In nine weeks it'll be the middle of June, ... if only everything goes well !!!

Now my dears, we wish you a really joyous, healthy Easter festival. Best greetings to your mother and our best greetings with kisses from your mum and from your brother Horst.

92 Wharf St
April 3rd 1950

My dearest

I arrived back safe, just in time to hear Frankie Howard, I thought he was very good. We will have to try to listen to the repeat on Saturday if I can get back from Melton in time. I should be able to get back in time if there is a bus just after ten, could you my darling find out for me. As you may have noticed I am using committee paper. I forgot my pad having to come out in a rush this lunchtime. I have had my hair cut and (I think) it doesn't look too bad. The girl that cut it seemed afraid to cut it short at first I had to tell her to cut it a bit shorter.

Helene has brought a guide book of Clacton-on-Sea it looks quite a nice place. It is near to where we catch the boat.

Nancy said today that the Easter holiday for farm workers was Good Friday and Monday. That means the same as Sunday. Has anyone said anything about working all through the holiday.

Charlie has finished his painting and Mamma said it looks quite nice now that he has finished. Aunt Gert looked as though she had been washing the bedroom mats, sheepskin things. I will get busy tonight and wash the sheet and table cloth. Mamma washed the others this morning so I have not much to do.

It is Betty's birthday today 31. I meant to send her a card but forgot all about it.

I have mended my stockings, it took me all morning and a part of this afternoon. I kept doing a bit then leaving it.

I am just making sure about the buses, no buses to Oakham Thursday. I knew there wasn't but you never know there might have been. The last one back on Monday from Oakham 8.0, 8.30 Somerby. I don't know what to wear. I did think of putting my navy dress on, but I don't think it is very suitable for the country I will probably put my country wear on.

Well that's the lot. I will be seeing you on Thursday evening.

        All my love
          Jean

Aschersleben Easter 1950.

My dear Hans and Jean,

Many thanks for your lovely letter of 27.3.1950 which we received recently. I wanted to reply yesterday, but didn't get that far - in the afternoon we were invited to Frau Lehmann's for coffee and in the evening, they came to us. This afternoon we're expected at Ziemanns' and in the evening we want to go to the cinema, after that, the festival will be over again. Yesterday morning I went to church. I thought a great deal about you. Jean will surely be with you and again you will have worked right through the Easter break, which makes me really sad as you will have had nothing of the festival. Horst was also completely exhausted on Saturday evening, he left early at 6 a.m. to go to the salon and came back at half past eight in the evening. He brought his sandwiches back with him, he hadn't even had time to eat them. You can scarcely imagine how busy it was there, ... we would have liked to pull out the till.

His salon manageress gave him 20 Marks at Easter, so it has now been accepted that he earns the 20 Marks a month again that they have been deducting for a few months now. He is the one who brings in all the business, and they still think they can take advantage of him. So we don't seem to move forwards at all, we never have anything left over at the end of the month. Our potatoes will last us only for the next ten days and then I'll have to buy another hundredweight again. As there is such a great potato shortage, they sell privately for 25-30 Marks per hundredweight. And people are prepared to pay 25-30 Marks. Without potatoes - with the best will in the world - we can't exist. Horst desperately wants to get a summer suit made for himself. I've been buying the extras, like wadding at the H.O.– it costs nearly 50 Marks. The Tailor's charges will be something over 100 Marks, plus the cost of the material. Even with my points, I haven't been able to find the right thing. In the H.O. there was something, but for good quality it was still over 68 Marks a meter. There is of course cheaper material, but if you are paying a lot for the tailor, it's important to buy good quality material. After the Easter break I will go and have another look at how much it will be with points.

We are really delighted that Jean is getting hold of coffee for us, I always find it really embarrassing to ask you for it, and if it weren't for Horst's health, I wouldn't ask. In a fortnight there is a big hairdressing competition in Magdeburg, which will be very expensive for him again, I wish so very much for him to have some success, it always motivates him so much. Dear Hans, I can't really advise how much money you should take with you, I don't have any idea how much your costs could be. Work it out to fit your priorities. As for roughly how much food will cost you, I've already written to tell you. Over there, everything is available. It's just good that you don't have our exchange rate (1:7). We'll just have to hope that it all works out for us as we wish. You think it will be abandoned – there you are wrong – it will definitely go ahead.

Now I suppose you'd like to know what you could make Horst happy with, for his birthday. He already has a hair-dryer which he bought for himself last year (for 80 Marks). If you want to, then give him a contribution. He really wants to buy a pair of brown shoes with crepe soles from over there. He's been wanting some for a long time, so that he has comfortable shoes for all the long hours of standing. You would hardly believe how badly his feet hurt in the evenings. That would give him enormous pleasure. They cost around 28-30 Marks over there - there are some really nice shoes. I have no idea what you think about that. We don't want to rob you of the shirt from your back. So, my dear, I must end my letter now, I must prepare lunch. Warm greetings to your mother and much love and kisses from your mum and your brother and brother-in-law Horst to both of you. Looking forward to seeing you - in good health – and really soon.

Home Farm,
Pickwell,
April 11th 1950

My Darling

How are you, my sweetheart? Fine, I hope. Thank you so very very much for lovely Easter, in fact, the best one I've ever spend. You made everything so nice and as soon as I got inside I was comfy. Just sat down and had something to eat. Jeannie I am so much longing for a home of our own. Let's keep our fingers crossed that it'll be very soon. Just the two of us and perhaps little Johnny. It'll be our time and we can do what we like.

I felt awful again last night. At first when I got back from the bus it wasn't so bad, but when I went to bed. Nobody to put his head on my arm and nobody to make love to. So I went to bed at 10.00 and must have fallen asleep just after 11.00 as I heard the clock strike. Funny when I woke up this morning and found myself alone. I was going to turn round to kiss you and – empty. Now I'll have to wait again another 3 ½ days.

Today has passed away quickly. I was watercarting all day. Tomorrow will be a busy day again as Gerald is away. Good thing I am not shutting up tonight. Shower after shower coming down. Gudger asked G today how long it takes to do the shutting up. He told him 2 ½ hours, but Gudger told him he had seen me go at 6.30 and come back at 8.00. If anybody complains that 2 ½ hours is too much they can do it themselves and I have done my last shutting up. Though he hasn't said anything to me yet.

By the way, you have forgotten something. Your foundation cream. Have you got some more at home? Anyway I'll bring it along on Saturday.

Well, my dearest, be good and think of me. I'll be seeing you Saturday.

Oh! Darling, I love you more than anything else in the world. So be good, goodnight and God bless and keep you safe.

All my love and thousand kisses

Forever your loving husband

Hans.

PS I don't know the price of the cockerel yet. We'll settle it Saturday.

Love Hans.

92 Wharf St
April 11th 1950

My dearest darling Hans

Here I am again back in Leicester and feeling very fed up with myself. I have had a really wonderful Easter trying to cook etc. and it wasn't a bit hard for me to do it. I only hope Easter was a bit better for you having to work the whole the time you poor darling. It did give us a chance to be on our own for a while. Those four days went by so fast I wish I had them to come again.

Mamma went to Betty's for dinner on Sunday and to see Mr and Mrs Dale's (Rothley) for tea. Then yesterday she went to Betty's for the day. The bird arrived OK, Mamma said it was very nice.

It is quiet today there is hardly a soul about and there isn'y much at all doing on the board, for two pins I would be asleep.

You know the little glass dish with orange butterflies on. We had as a wedding present from my great aunt at Newcastle. Well on Sunday after Mamma had gone to Betty's Aunt Gert came in to make the fire up. The kitten followed her in and jumped onto the sideboard breaking that dish and knocked Betty's photograph flying fortunately that did not break. The kitten came in this morning but she soon went out when I told her off. I have been meaning to take that little dish away for ages now. But forget it. That should teach me to do it straight away.

WEDNESDAY
Here I am again my darling. Thank you very much for your letter my sweetie. It was at home at lunchtime. Believe me darling I really did enjoy myself.

If Mr Gudger says anything again suggest that he goes round one night when it is raining to make sure how long it really takes to shut the birds up, it would very likely take him 3 ½ hours if not more.

I think I had better have my hair done this weekend that would give it time to settle down before we go away. I wish it was this Friday. But still we will have to wait. Uncle Arthur came this morning to fetch the cigarettes, Aunt Cis was in bed from what I gather she has strained her heart. I know what kind of material I want to have a dress of white spots on either navy or yellow. I saw the style I want in a Harpers, that is a fashion magazine.

Well my dearest I will have to close I cannot think of anything else to tell you I will be seeing you Saturday.

All my love and kisses. I love you more than anything else in the world.

Your ever loving
wife
Jean.

Pickwell,
April 12<u>th</u> 1950

My sweetest, little wife,
How are you today, my darling? My feet are killing me tonight. You know it was my last shutting up, so I thought it would be a good idea to have a nice walk around the whole lot and see how long it really takes. Comfortable walking and on the way looking for rabbits it took exactly 1 ¾ hours.

I left 6.30 and arrived back at 8.15. Never mind, 2 ½ on the time sheet. As long as he pays, alright.

It wasn't too bad here. The old routine. Tomorrow and Friday will be cleaning out I reckon. Perhaps watercarting. Still, it all makes the time go quick. I've just had a look for the 16.6. It is exactly 9 weeks and 2 days. That'll be the great day when we start our trip abroad. I wish it was next week. When I come over on Saturday we'll write the letter to the Home Office. Don't let me forget.

Be good sweetheart and pleasant dreams.

Goodnight and God bless you. I love you more than my own life.

Thursday April 13th 1950 7.20pm

Hello, my darling, how are you today? As fine as the weather was, I hope. I am glad to hear that you really enjoyed yourself in spite of the lot of work you'd to do. Your being here made Easter much better for me. That's why I didn't mind the work so much. Well, Easter is over, but it is only 1 ½ days to go till I see my sugarplum again.

The price for a lb of chicken is still 2/2s so the boss told me. That makes the cockerel 13/-s. You can tell Betty and get the money.

Well, darling, if the little dish has been broken, it's too late now to say anything. It was nice but never mind. I bet that kitten got a good hiding.

Gudger got my timesheet today but didn't say anything. Good for him. I had some answers ready.

I've finished the chicken up tonight and got myself some rice pudding ready just now. I'll have a bit of that as supper. The day has gone alright. I went cleaning out from after lunch till 5.00. No shutting up and, in fact, a rest for the next 3 weeks. Gerald is working the next weekend again as he wants the one off after the next.

Well, darling, how about the gabardine trousers. Do you think I should go on Saturday afternoon to have them measured? We'll see when I come over. Can we afford it?

I think I'd better write to my mother tonight. Haven't written for about 10 days. Plenty of time, it's only 7.45.

Well, my little sweetheart, that seems to be all for now and I'll be getting on with the next letter.

Be good and have plenty to eat in the mornings. I'll get the tea and porridge again this Sunday. Darling, I love you more than anything else in the world.

Goodnight, God bless and keep you safe.

All my love and a thousand kisses

Forever your loving husband

Hans.

Home Farm,
Pickwell,
April 17th 1950

My darling

Here I am again, back in the stables. I got back safe and sound at 8.40, lit the fire and had some Horlicks and biscuits, thinking of you doing about the same. 9.45 saw me in bed.

Don't be miserable or depressed, darling. Do you think I like to leave you? Remember, my sweetie, it's only 8 weeks to go till we have our holidays and when we come back I'll leave here find a place near Leicester and then be with you every night. Believe me nobody can be fed up more with living apart than I am. This is not the type of married life I want to live. As soon as the holidays are over things will be different.

Well, my darling, how are you today? Fine, I hope. When I arrived back last night it was rather late to fetch some milk so I went to the neighbours again. He was there as well and we talked for ½ hour before they let me go again. Anyway I got a pint. She said they had plenty and not bringing it back. Maj. Normann has got a cow now and her husband is milking her. No wonder they've got plenty. I would.

Oh! Something else happened tonight. I was amazed. Fetching the milk, the old lady said, when I left again, 'Didn't I promise you some bacon and you didn't get it?' I said (really surprised as if I also had forgotten all about it) Oh! Yes. Well anyway, it came to she won't forget it again. So let's look forward to it. Believe me I really was surprised. Darling, I thank you for every minute we spent together last weekend. Now I am counting again for the next. Jeannie, I love you more than anything else in the whole wide world.

Be good, my sweetheart, and look after yourself. Goodnight, God bless and keep you safe.

> All my love and thousands of kisses
> Forever your loving husband
> Hans

> 92 Wharf Street
> April 17th

"My dearest"

How are you today? Fine I hope. Aunt Gertie must have been up with the lark this morning, because when I got up at 8.0 she had her washing on the line. She must have got up to make sure Charlie was not late on his first day.

Did you get back to Pickwell safe? Next time we can catch the bus in Belgrave Gate, now we know which way the bus comes. I just thought I would make sure about that so I rang "The Midland Red" and all buses to Grantham and Melton go along Belgrave Rd, and unload where the Somerby bus does, that will be more convenient, especially if I go over to Melton one Wednesday evening it will be handy coming back.

I have inquired what is on the pictures at Melton, "Escape me never" and "Red Canyon". I can't remember seeing either of them. So you can take your pick.

I find now that I have not an envelope to put this in. Only that one I had put a letter into to send to you and you had come home, so I will have to make do with that

I have been inquiring into the measurements of trouser bottoms and so far, I have only asked one person and he had a pair 13", all the way round 26" so it seems. O.k. He does look the spiv type.

I missed you so very much my darling especially when I went to bed. It never seems half as bad when I have been to Pickwell ~~then come~~ to come home and go to bed, as when you have been here then gone back. I feel terribly lonely.

Well my sweetie pie I had better try to fix that envelope so be good I love you very very much

All my love

Jean

_____.

Pickwell,

April 18<u>th</u> 1950

My sweetest, little wife,

Well, darling, I am fine and how are you today? Wasn't it a miserable day. Rain, rain all day. We took it easy, bagging the mash this morning as it was pouring down, so it was 8.15 when we left the yard. I got back 10.05, Gerald at 10.30. Of course we're wet through and so took easy jobs till dinner time. I mashed the stuff for tomorrow (not easy, but dry). This afternoon Gudger and I moved small chicken houses. Still, I was glad when it struck 5 o'clock.

Good thing my trousers will only be 24". So I hope you are satisfied. 24" is alright.

I also missed you when I went to bed. It seems awful being on my own after having had a lovely weekend. It won't be long before we change that. I'll be with Jeannie every night then.

Well, my sweetie-pie I'll finish now. Have some mending to do. My raincoat. So be good. Goodnight and God bless you. I love you so very much. All my love and kisses to you.

<u>Friday, 19.4.50, 6.15 p.m.</u>

 2 ½ days to go. I am feeling fine and hope so do you. Tonight the old lady gave me bacon 3 slices, only fat, but it's nothing to grumble about. It'll make a nice tea or breakfast when

you're here.

Today I received a letter from my mother. The parcel hasn't arrived yet as she hasn't mentioned anything. She and Horst are well and are waiting for June to see us. Otherwise everything is alright.

By the way, have you posted the letter to the H.O? It shouldn't be long before the reply comes. I think they'll have leaflets for holidays in Germany.

Bonzo went outside last night to do his business, after half an hour I got worried. So I went to the gate against the bosses house and whistled. After about 5 minutes he came dashing across from lambing meadow. When I went feeding this morning I found a rabbit stretched out against the corner house and a dead hen. It looked to me as if he has had both. The rabbit definitely because of the teeth marks. I wish I hadn't whistled. He might have brought it back.

Well, my one and only, I'll finish for now and write to my mother. So be good till I see you. Goodnight and God bless and keep you safe. I love you so very, very much. Let me show you Saturday.

> All my love and kisses
>> Forever your loving husband
> Hans.

> 92 Wharf St
> April 18th

"My darling"

Here I am once more, writing the last letter for the week, I shall be seeing you next time 3 ½ days to go.

Oh! If you could see Freddy now, we would both be told off. He has come on my knee and is sleeping. I can't down him off, I'm weak.

I told you Walter (Gladys boyfriend) was a friend of Otto's didn't I? Well, Gladys was telling me this morning, that Walter was passing by where they are living and Miggy called to him and she has invited Walter, Gladys you and I for tea this

Sunday, she is supposed to be coming in to see me tomorrow (Wednesday) I of course will tell we are very sorry we cannot accept as you are working this weekend. They are living in that street opposite to the National Health Offices ~~of~~ on the Humberstone Rd. They have one room. I don't know how she could entertain four in it because the houses in that street are not very big. Probably three on the bed and three under!!! I will tell you more tomorrow my darling goodnight and God Bless you I will be thinking of you before I go to sleep. LOVE

  Jean.

Wednesday

 Miggy has not been in yet so I can't tell you anything yet. I am going to Evington tonight. I have not been for ages, a fortnight before you came home with your knee. That must be 8 weeks ago. I will write a few lines tomorrow when I have heard from you, till then All my love

Thursday

Another day gone, that brings it up to 1 ½ days to Saturday afternoon.

Thank you very much for letter No. 2 I am fine, but bored stiff at the moment, the weather is beautiful again today and I have to sit here until 5.15. I have the window wide open, but the only view I have are chimney pots, not very interesting.

Miggy came yesterday just after 5.0. I thanked her for the invitation and told her we could not go, but she has invited us up whenever we can get, we are to send her a postcard to let her know. They are both working at the John Bull Rubber Co. I went to Evington. Gertrude has a new bedroom suit a very nice one too. Lime oak, it is light brown with a white spot on it. I arrived home just after 10.0. Gertrude went to Coventry to see "Annie get your gun". It is in Leicester this week too. One of the fellows here has been to see it and has also seen the show in London, and he thought it was just as good.

We will see ~~what~~ whether we are going to the pictures or doing anything else. If it is like this I could bring Freddy, then we could take him a walk, we shall be able to go to the pictures the following week when you are home. I will see what parcels I have before deciding

So my darling until Saturday be good I love you very very much Your ever loving wife

Jean

Same address

April 20$\underline{th}$ 1950

"My darling"

Hello, sweetie, here I am again rather late. It's 8.30 already. Oh! I was busy tonight. One of those brainwaves, you know! My bike has had a good rub down and then I painted again. Well, I don't use it at the moment and it has plenty of time to dry properly. Hasn't it been a grand day. As usually I listened to the weather forecast this morning and heard about the nice warm day to come. So when Gudger said watercarting or cleaning out my mind was made up. And I made that watercarting last till 5 o'clock. My arms and face are red. But I am not blushing, in spite of having the "Daily Mirror" in front of me !!!! Do you know what I mean? Have a look at todays front page.

Well, my sweetheart, I'll say goodnight now. God bless you. Oh! Jeannie I love you sooooooo very much, longing to see you again.

Friday, April 21$\underline{st}$ 9.00p.m.

Hello, my sweetheart, here I am again and how are you?

Oh! I am rushed to death tonight. Shopping, some pancakes for my dinner, getting the meat and stock ready, cleaning underneath the stove, washing the floor, now a few lines and afterwards a wash. Well, it won't be later than 10 o'clock.

What a shame I have to work and we can't go to the party. Sill, I can't see how they're going to entertain 4 people in one room. We better go some other time so we can sit on the chairs instead of on the bed. It wouldn't make a change for us.

Wasn't it hot again and my arms are red, but not sore, thank goodness.

Where abouts is the John Bull Rubber Co? Never heard of it before, though you've mentioned it to me.

Why didn't you collar Gertrudes new suite. We could do with it and she's got enough money to buy another one. The house would do for us too.

About the pictures, I'll leave it to you. What do you mean you're going to see what parcels you have before deciding? I can't make it out. Do you mean bringing Fred?

It looks as if tomorrow will be a busy morning again. Gerald isn't coming so I'll have to mix that confounded mash again. That'll take the best part of 2 hours.

Tonight I've recond to see how much money I've got for you. Still, I make it £3. Don't ask how. I really don't know myself. Still I had about 7s left from last week. Perhaps that's why.

I've run out of dog biscuits and poor old Bonzo had to have toast again. I bet he's longing for tomorrow. But not as much as I am. I wish it was 4.00 tomorrow afternoon.

I am just listening to "A.F.N." An Italian singer is on. Not bad, but as I can't understand what he sings, he has to go.

Well, my sugarplum, I'll finish now.

Be good till I see you tomorrow. Goodnight and God bless you always.

I love you so much and am longing for you

      All my love you and kisses

         Forever your loving husband

            Hans.

Aschersleben, 23.04.50

My dear Hans and Jean,

At last, after 3 weeks, we received your lovely letter of 13.4.50, for which we thank you very much. We had already been thinking that you now have lots of work.

Your package has not arrived yet, so it has now been on its way for 3 weeks. We'll hope that it arrives this week. We are full of anticipation. So you both have travel nerves already? Yes, there are only barely seven weeks left, so time is starting to pass very quickly again now. If only it were here already ! Horst is looking forward to it enormously. He is already so excited about meeting his sister-in-law. Yes, dear Hans, I am also looking forward to getting to know my dear daughter, who makes my son so happy ! Yes, the fortnight will fly past quickly again. Your journey will be exhausting as well, but I wish we could travel that way too. It is really too awful, it's never easy, but hopefully everything will work out well. So you didn't get a break at all during the Easter festival? Then you must take it easy during that fortnight. And Jean will probably learn some German in that time. We'll bring Jean's birthday present with us as it would be difficult to send. It's a small gesture that we hope will give her pleasure.

We will probably leave here on the 15th. Will you get there on the 17th? Travelling in 2nd class on such a long journey will be really important for you, as it is so much more pleasant. Tomorrow Horst is going to Magdeburg for the Hairdressing Competition. He is looking forward to it so much: if only he is successful! He is taking part independently and not through the agency of the Hairdressers' Guild. They will be amazed when they see him joining in. Several are going from here and they are already hard at work styling today. But the competition in which Horst is taking part is tomorrow. He'll return at about five o'clock on Tuesday. It should be a really big event, in the Crystal Palace. Well, we'll find out. It'll cost him a pretty penny again.

This week I received a letter from Bruno. He says that I am right and, provided that I have genuinely told him the truth, he will mend his ways and also write more frequently.

He would also like to find a different job. The job he has at present is very hard for him, with his leg, trudging along 'the Acker' behind the horses all day. He sends warm greetings to you both. Aunt Lina and Christel also send their greetings. Bruno sent Aunt Lina a dress for her birthday, which she was very happy about. Edith is expecting a baby. Aunt Elsa should come over but she can't.

Dear Hans, we can get better soap in the H.O, so you don't need to buy any. Now my dears, stay in good health. Send my best greetings to your mother. With warm greetings and kisses for you from your mum, who is always thinking of you, and from your brother and brother-in-law Horst. To an early and healthy reunion. I enclose dad's photo for you, I had to have some made for the the Search Agency.

92 Wharf St
April 24th

My dearest darling.

I thank you for such a lovely weekend, also for being so nice to Freddy though he was a nuisance and had to sleep on the bed. I arrived back safe, Fred slept on my knee the whole of the time. A lady got on at Twyford and sat next to me, she patted Fred you should have heard him, he growled. You couldn't blame him, I shouldn't like anyone to pat me on the head. We were at home just in time to hear Reg Dixon. I had a drink of milk, looked at the papers and then off to bed I went.

I asked Gladys how she got on at Miggy's. she said there was a crowd, two more Jerries with their wives. She said she would come up and tell me all about it but so far I have not seen her. I have corrected my letter to Bernhard, do you mind me corresponding with him or would you rather I stopped. I know you are not very keen on him. If you wished me not to write I could gradually stop.

I have been thinking, I would have liked to have had my photograph for my passport before I have my hair permed. I thought I could go tomorrow night when I leave off. I don't want to look like a fuzzy-wuzzy on my passport, that will cost about 15/-. I shouldn't think you will have to pay anything for whatever you have.

I have something else to buy sometime, half of the buckle of my rain coat has broken. I was putting it on this morning, gave it a good pull and off a little piece shot, it hasn't completely broken I can manage as it is.

Isn't it cold today? I thought my ears would be frozen off going home at lunch time, it has been snowing but the sun is shining at the moment. I don't think it knows what to do. The weather forecast said wet and cold for the next few days I will close now sweetie, I want to pay a visit upstairs. Be good and careful I love you so very very-so very much.

    Your very loving
    Wife
    Mrs Johannes Klawitter.

      Pickwell,
    April 25th 1950

My dearest, darling,

Well, here I am, 9.00p.m. Things are moving fast. After I had spoken to you the boss came and told me I had to see a Mr Thurman at Knossington, for he's the man there to see about council-homes. He asked me how long it would take me to get ready as he wanted to take me over straight away not to lose any time. Well, I was ready in ten minutes so off we went. He spoke to that man first and after that I had a word with him. What the chances are, I don't know yet. The boss said Mr Thurman wasn't sure as he had a man at Knossington, working at his place. Anyway the boss is going to bring me the application form tonight and so I can post it in the morning. You can imagine him talking. Like very clean and decent people, doing him a favour, too and so on. Still, he said if I should be unlucky there he can promise me one here if it is worth waiting for me. Honestly I am still it a bit baffled by all the quick action, but things will go alright. One thing disappointed me very much when I rung you up. Do you know what I mean? You mentioning the orange box. You needn't rub it in, Jeannie. I remember alright we, or rather I, haven't got much. Anyway I'll see you tomorrow night.

Thanks so very much for your letter. You needn't thank me for being nice to Fred. oh I knew if I had chased him off the bed you wouldn't have slept at all. And I don't want my sweetheart to lay awake all night. Here the boss comes. No he's gone again.

After all I think it was good we didn't go to that party. We aren't show pieces, are we? Look, sweetie, even if I am not keen on Bernhard, you please yourself about your correspondence. So just do as you like. How could I tell you not to write to him?

About the photographs, see when you can go and then go. Because we'll fill the form for the H.O. in on Saturday.

Well, my sweetie pie, I'll have some supper now, a glass of Milo and then off to bed. So be good till I see you tomorrow night. Goodnight and God bless you.

  All my love and kisses

   Forever yours

  Hans

Aschersleben, 26.4.1950

My dear Hans and Jean,

I have just collected your lovely parcel. We are so very pleased and thank you from the bottom of our hearts. I had to pick it up from the customs office, no customs duty was payable [as its weight was under 2 Pfund]. The package was completely torn open on one side and it was in a wire-sealed postal container*. It was 2 Pfund and contained 2 cartons of condensed milk. I cannot tell you how happy I am, at least I have help again for Horst.

Horst won another prize again. Yesterday he returned at five o'clock and went straight from the train to the salon. He didn't get home till half past nine in the evening, he was totally exhausted. After all, he'd been on his feet from 4 a.m. on Monday morning until Tuesday evening. He is always very pleased when he wins a prize. He received a voucher for goods worth 60 Marks for his cold perm styling.

I would also like to thank Jean for her efforts with the package. I've bought something lovely for her birthday. Hopefully you will both like it. It was Horstel's wish that I should buy it for her, from the Handels Organisation. He has good taste in this sort of thing and likes things that are beautiful. After all, he only has one sister-in-law. And her young husband is sure to like it as well. I can't reveal what it is! We'll bring it all with us. If everything goes well, then we will start travelling in seven weeks.

This evening we want to go to the cinema with Frau Ziemann, they are showing "The Sinking of the Titanic". It should be a very good film.

Stay in good health! We are looking forward to seeing you again. Again, many thanks and give our greetings to your mother. Your mum and brother Horst send many warm greetings and kisses.

*The packet had been opened by the authorities at the border, to check the contents. It was then officially secured with wire and a wax seal may have been applied.

                        Pickwell,
                April 28<u>th</u> 1950
"My Darling"

How are you my little sweetie? I hope you are at your very best. Well, darling it's Friday night again and thank goodness. Tonight I am really walk on my knees. As usually feeding first thing, then I moved some nightharks. In the afternoon I was supposed to be going cleaning out, but unfortunately I had to put some petrol into the tank and so Mr Gudger caught me just when I was leaving. Well, they're threshing wheat for poultry and at dinnertime 54 Railway bags (18 stone) were ready for us. So what did the poor Jerrie have to do? Carry those 54 bags up to the granary. When I took the first one I never expected to finish the lot. After 20 I got used to it. On No. 30 I thought my back was broken. Still I just managed to finish the load at 4.45. My knees weren't half shaking. If that doesn't show my knee is alright again then nothing else will. But, blimey, I can feel it. Every bone in my body hurts. Never mind. It's only a few hours to go in the morning.

Gudger hasn't said anything yet about the weekend so he's had it. I mentioned the fact that Michel is leaving last Thursday. He said he didn't know what's going to happen. So that's that. There's nothing doing now.

Last night Gerald and I went shooting. We didn't get any besides a half grown. I didn't think it worth wasting a cartridge on it so G. had a bash. His cartridges aren't so expensive.

On coming back the boss gave me the form and told me to fill it in straight away and post it. So I did and posted it, too. Now let's see what the outcome will be. He said he was going to do whatever he could. " Well, I reckon I'll be a-goin' to bed pretty soon" can you tell I'm listening to "Riders of the

Range"?

Be seeing you tomorrow, my sweetheart. Be good till then, Goodnight and God bless you and keep you safe.

I am longing for you and love you so very much.

> All my love and thousands of kisses
>
> Forever your loving husband
>
> Hans.

> Pickwell,
>
> April 30th 1950

"My Darling"

Here I am again, all alone and so terrible lonely. Well, I arrived back safe and sound. A bit of bad luck at Melton. I knew Gerald was leaving Melton at about 8.45 for shutting up. I got off the bus, had a look at the timetables and then thought of it. So I rushed off to town and was about 10 yards from the corner when he passed by. He didn't hear my whistling. That way I could've saved 1/-s and got back earlier. If I hadn't looked at the timetable I would've made it. Still I wasn't in such a hurry to get back to the stables.

Do you listen to "Variety Bandbox"? That fellow doing the Austrian act "Reg Dixon" was quite good, don't you think? Did you understand it?

Well, my sweetheart, my water is boiling so I'll have some supper and after making the bed, off I go.

I love you more than my own life. What should I do without you?

Be good, goodnight and God bless you.

All my love to you

Monday, May 1 st 1950, 7.30p.m.

Well, the first day is over again. Feeding, then creasoting till lunch and collecting in the afternoon. Gerald did the water-carting as he has to put some tractor-practise in for the driving test. Running about again with L-plates.

I've got another guest here. A terrier puppy the sister to the two puppies Gordon has got. When collecting the mother was with it but went off and left it. It started raining and the poor little creature was whining. I didn't want the hens to peck at it so I took it along. Funny, Bonzo doesn't take any notice at all. Ah! He just came and had a smell. I've put it into a basket with a bag in it. Gave it some little bits of meat and it wasn't half hungry. It's a bitch.

My neighbours were here ¼ hour ago. She said he had a telegram to go for an interview to the Warwickshire Master of Hounds, riding second horse. She hopes he'll get it. Well, the end of it was that she wants (when leaving definitely) some cups and saucers, also a half dozen set of fruit dishes and the big fruit dish. Find out, please, how much ½ doz cups and saucers are and also how much the fruit set is (like mine here). Half a dozen. She's going to let me know exactly what she wants when they know about leaving here.

Well, darling, how has work gone down with you? Both my fingers are crossed that we might get the council house. It'll be a decent home for us. That furnishing business really worries me. You know I am not keen on the weekly. But how can we manage best? It isn't only the furniture. Curtains, Indian carpet and so on. That one for £495. I wish we could spend that much on a carpet then we would have enough for the other things, too. Still, it isn't definite yet, so let's wait with the worries till we know.

It won't be long before I am off to bed. Just a slice of Ryvita and cheese.

I'll be dreaming of you all night. Be good, my darling, and take care of yourself, don't work too hard.

I love you so very, very much

All my love and thousands of kisses

Forever and only your

Loving husband

Hans.

92 Wharf St

May 1st 1950

My dearest darling

How are you today? Fine I hope. Did you arrive back at Pickwell safe? I darned your navy and brown socks, and listened to "Variety Bandbox". I must have been messing about most of the time because I didn't get to bed until 11.0. I slept like a top until 8.0.

We have a new girl started today as relief, she seems quite a nice girl, but not has nice as Sonia, she is very good on the board. She has been working at the telephone exchange. Eileen Oakey said one or two people have asked her if I am leaving. I said they won't half be watching me now, to see if I put any weight on. They will be watching for a long time yet. I have started to keep a check on what I spend again. I found the book I used to keep. Then I too will know what I have.

Mr Pickering has just been through, asked how you were and how little John was. I said we're slow, there is no little John yet. I told him that you needed some good advice. I couldn't have said it was more by luck than judgement that there is no little John.

Nancy was saying that Maclean was advertising in the Farmer and Stock Breeder for a poultry man and stockman. I don't know whether it was last week's. Has anyone gone into that house?

Uncle Arthur was here at lunchtime. He is Aunt Cissy's husband. They are going to Germany the week after us. He said it's a pity we were not going at the sametime. I don't know if they are a bit nervous about travelling all that way.

Well my love, it is getting close to my going home time. Pat, that is the new girl's name, has had to go to the duplicating, so I am on my own again. I will close now sending you all my love and kisses. I love you more than anything else in the world now and always

Your wife
Jean

——.

Pickwell,
May 2<u>nd</u> 1950

My sweet, little wife,

Thank you so very much for your letter. I had two this morning. One from my mother with a photo of my stepfather. I'll
show you on Saturday. It hasn't been too bad today. A bit
windy, but warm I went creasoting. Looks as if Gerald has
taken my job over. Never mind, he hasn't done much cleaning out yet, so he can have a taste of it.

So you also started to keep check on the spending. Is it necessary? You don't spend as much as I do.

Bill Pickering hasn't half got a cheek. You should've asked
him what about the little Bill. that would've shook him or
he would've ~~ha~~ given another funny answer, as far as I know
him.

Yes! Mac was advertising for a stockman. I think somebody
has been here to have a look around. Don't know yet if he's
taken him on. No word yet about Knossington.

My neighbours told me today that he's got the job at Warwick and is leaving here week on Monday. They seem both
very pleased. He told me the accommodation is a nice cottage with back and front garden and not like that smelling
drain here on the doorstep

The puppy is getting on lovely. Perhaps I've still got it when
you come on Saturday. It follows me about everywhere I go.
Last night when I fetched the milk I was half way up the road
and she followed me all the way. Quite lively.

Wednesday is over and that's all that matters. I dug a big hole
again today and buried the dead hens. Then creosoting and
collecting.

I had a letter from my mother again today. She has got the parcel. It was ripped open on one side, but everything was alright. She told me about a nice birthday present they've got for you, but it's a secret and she won't tell me. They're bringing it along.

Well, my sugarplum, I'll get something to eat and then to bed. Be good and look after yourself. Oh! I love you so very much.

Goodnight and God bless you and keep you safe.

All my love and kisses

Forever your loving husband

Hans.

Pickwell,

May 4th 1950

My sweet, little wife,

How is life treating you? Always busy I bet, what have you been doing with yourself lately. I'll have to wait till tomorrow to get to know all about it. Will there be a letter for me? I hope so anyway.

The farmer fetched the puppy today. I wasn't half mad at Cooper. And this time I told him. It was 12.15 and I was out so Cooper just went in here and fetched it out. So I told him if he doesn't respect the place where I live then I'll lock the door and take the key along. The next time I want anything from him I'll go and open the door without knocking and no matter if anybody is in or not. I asked him how he would like that. And also reminded him of your saying "My home is my castle". When I went out in the afternoon (2.00) he was in the yard, so I let him see it. I banged the door, locked the door and when he looked, put the key in my pocket. What does he think he is? This place isn't a pub where anybody can go in. if I ever see or meet anybody in there I sure knock his brains out. I really was mad. Anyway, he knows now. Still never mind, it won't be for long in any case, even if we get the house or not.

Gerald will be leaving in probably a fortnights time. The boss looked a bit daft when he told him this morning. Still he's going to have the time of his life there at the other place. I'll tell you more on Saturday.

By the way, have you got your passport back? It looks as if it's high time to send my things off. We have to book time, too to get the visas. Perhaps it won't take all that long. I've just had a look. It's exactly 6 weeks tomorrow morning when we start. I wish it was tomorrow. Don't you?

Well, my sweetest, I'll close for today. I love you more than anything else in the world. Sure, quite sure.

Be good, my darling, goodnight and God bless. I love you so very much and will show and prove it to you tomorrow.

All my love and thousands of kisses

Forever your loving

husband

Hans.

Home Farm, Pickwell,
May, 8th 1950

"My Darling"

How are you my sweetie, did you get home safe and sound? I arrived back from shutting up at 9.35 and just when I came into the yard the boss brought the car over. So he started talking again, asking funny questions about the chickens and also asked me if I had heard from the Council. So I said no and I've given up hope. You should've seen his face. Anyway he told me that he has more than supported my application, has had a word with 3 or 4 people who are in charge of the lettings and he knows that I stand a good chance of getting it. I mentioned that the house is empty since last Friday and as I haven't heard anything I had given up hope. He said it doesn't matter if the house is empty, it always takes a week or two to get new tenancy arranged. Well then, pessimist, there we are. Still I am not counting on it before I've got something definite.

This morning I had a lovely row again with Gudger because of not coming over with water on Saturday. I told him a thing or two and he was very polite again at lunchtime. He said he was out all morning, too. My answer was, that I know it doesn't rain in the feeding hut. I was mad, and didn't half let him have it. Silly fool.

From what I've heard up to now, Eileen has had a clash with him this morning too and the result: notice for Friday. I wonder how we're going to get on then with two less. Never mind, I'll do my share of the work and the rest is up to the boss. Gudger asked a lot more questions about overtime. Such as how long it takes shutting up, collecting etc. going on the bike when it is dry. I told him it is wet now and in the other case, I haven't been for the last three weeks. That settled that.

Neighbours want ½ doz porridge plates and ½ doz cups and saucers.

7.00p.m. now I am ready and waiting for shutting up time. I am going to walk round tonight as it is too dirty to bike. The tyres are picking a lot of muck up.

Well, darling, it looks as if we'll just get our holiday money together without drawing any out of the bank. We've got 5 weeks to go, that makes at least £25. Did you say we had enough for the tickets?

Well, my darling, I'll close for now. Be good and look after yourself. Goodnight and God bless and keep you safe.

I love you more than my own life. I've got the best wife anybody in this world could have.

All my love and thousands of kisses

Forever your loving husband

Hans.

92 Wharf St

May 8th 1950

My dearest Hans

Well, Monday has almost gone, that means 4 ½ days to go to Saturday.

Fred has just come to have a sniff at what I am doing and has now settled himself on my knee. I bet he's glad you are not here. I arrived home safe and sound. I looked for you going up the hill, but I couldn't see you. I could not see much of the hill, only along by the hedge at the back of Les's house. I was at the bus stop in plenty of time. The bus was packed. I was lucky I got a seat, but the people that got on at Somerby had to stand. I was in two minds whether to walk round there for a change, it was a good job I didn't. When we got to Borough the conductor rang for another bus, but they (the Midland Red) could not send one. They did not pick anymore up, you should have seen the people's faces when the bus passed by them. There is a bus later from Twyford.

I have been trying on my summer dresses to see if they will do. I can't make up my mind yet whether I need a new one or not I will have to make up my mind soon, if I want it making, to take away with me.

I had a beautiful weekend, I ate all your rations for the rest of the week you have to live off bread and jam. I will try to make it up to you next weekend. Betty found the sausage, she cleaned the shop out so Mamma and her had it between them.

Please darling, when we go to Germany speak German properly you would only make yourself look ridiculous and I am sure it would annoy your mother and brother. I know it would me, so please. Are you ashamed of being a German or something?

Ich leibe seht seht much more than anything else in the world.

<u>Tuesday</u>

I ran into Miggy at lunchtime, she now has a job on a switch-board. Poor old Gudger everybodys on to him. Did I tell you Alice and Bernie are coming on Wednesday evening.

I am going round to Betty's to mind the children. There's a meeting at the school Susan goes to, Cyril is going out, so Betty asked me if I would go.

We have got enough for our tickets £36. And if anything should happen to me before I see you the money is in the gramaphone I put it there last night, would you have thought of looking there.

cheeri'O for now my darling all my love and kisses

Jeannie.

Home Farm, Pickwell,
May, 9<u>th</u> 1950

My sweet, little wife,

Hello, my darling, how are you? Wasn't it a lovely after-noon. The weather forecast for tomorrow gave very warm up to 70°. Today was an easy day for me, just feeding, col-lecting and strawing nest boxes with Gerald from breakfast till lunch. Last night I walked around. It wasn't half coming down. Still I got back at 9.35, just sneaking in here and off to bed without switching the lights on. It looks as if Gudger wants to find out how long it takes. He sees me going out, but I'll see to it so he doesn't see me coming back. Nothing doing under 2 ½ hours. I think the boss will persuade Ger-ald to stay after all. Today he offered him a man's wage with full overtime pay. Now he doesn't know what to do. Eileen is staying on after being offered another 1 ½ an hour. Doris 2 d. Per hour more. Shall I tell him I am leaving. Perhaps I'll get a rise, too. It would suit me alright.

My Leicester Evening Mail should be here any minute now. It came for the first time last night. Now at least I know what's going on over there.

After tonight it'll only be another 3 times shutting up for me. It's still too dirty to go on the bike so I'll be off for a walk again. Everything will be ready so when I come back I can go to bed in the dark.

Well, my darling, I'll close for now. Be good and look after yourself. Goodnight and God bless you always.

To the best wife in the whole wide world and the only woman I love so very much, all my love and kisses

Wednesday, May 10th 1950, 5.25 p.m.

Hello, my sweetheart, A real hard day. Feeding, collecting, shutting up and from breakfast till lunch those big bags again. 46 this time. I can hardly stand up. Anyway it will definitely be my last load. My leg is swelling up in one place at the size of an egg and it hurts. Don't you worry, I shan't see a doctor and go on the sick. Not now before our holidays. A nice little incident occurred last night. When I went shutting up Gudger was in his garden watching me. As soon as I'd passed by he went home. So I guessed he just wanted to know what time I left. Anyway it was 8 p.m. I came back through the back. Just coming up along the crew yards I saw a figure coming into the yard and saw it was him because of his funny walking. He went into the dark place where I keep my bike and watched the yard. As I didn't know if he had seen me already I went on going in here, switched the light on and filled the water kettle so he could see me. I thought, wait, I'll get you. I took my torch and the lock for my bike and walked towards the gateway, suddenly turned towards him where I expected him to stand and switched the torch on right in his face. I said to him "I thought there was somebody sneaking around here" he was trembling, stuttering "Oh! That's where you keep your bike now, is it?" I told him the bike has nothing to do with this. What can one do with a man like that? Jean, if I wasn't married to the best wife and don't want to get into trouble, I sure would've broke his nose. I am not spying after anybody so I don't want anybody to do that to me.

My papers have also come from London. Just a big Certificate of Identity. Not worth 7/6s. After all now I'll have to get the visa to return to the U.K. The form has to be sent there, too. I wonder if we'll get my things settled in time. It's only just over a month to go. I think I'll send the form off straight the way. There's no time to loose.

Well, my darling, I'll say goodnight and God bless. I love you so very much. Be good and take care of yourself

All my love and kisses forever yours

Hans.

P.S.

I'll send the form off tonight.

92 Wharf Street

May. 10th 1950

My dearest darling Hans.

How you today my darling? Fine I hope. Myself - I feel ~~has~~ fit ~~has~~ a fiddle. Hasn't it turned out a beautiful day? I am so glad for your sake while you are shutting up I only wish I could go with you.

I have washed my hair tonight, the perm is still in and I have set it, it does not look too bad. I will have to wait until in the morning for the proper result.

I asked Alice to come this evening but she has not turned up yet and it is now 8.30 I can't remember whether I said I would ring her to make sure she was coming. I am mad I have been wondering all day what we could have for supper now they have not come. Bernie was ~~goingtoo~~ coming too.

I could write anymore last night, Alice came by herself. Bernie had forgotten about coming and had washed her hair. She went at about 10.40.

Old Gudger is a little sneak. How nice catching him red handed I am so glad you did not punch him on the nose. Although he may have deserved it. Fighting doesn't get you anywhere, only a bad name.

It does not look as if we will be able to arrange about the

tickets this Saturday. We could go in and make inquiries to see what we are doing. You will probably have to wait a week before you get your papers back. Where did you have to send for the visa? We still have a month.

Isn't it marvelous, the weather today? I wish I was outside getting my legs brown. This morning I took my stockings off, and sat in the sun. They are still lily white.

I will have to use your envelope, but that is why you left the s off Mrs.

So my dearest I will have to close

    All my love

    Jean.

                        Pickwell,
                        May, 11th 1950

My sweet, little wife,

Just a quick few lines. I was rushed to death. How are you, my sweetie-pie? I myself am feeling fine, just as grand as the day was. Oh! It's just as I like it. After breakfast I changed into my tennis- shoes and went laying nestboxes and collecting. If it hadn't been for that cool wind I would've taken my shirt off. Well, my darling, how is life treating you? When I called for my milk the old lady asked me if I like rhubarb and gave me a few nice and fresh cut stalks. My dinner was ready a bit later, having rhubarb and custard. And also my favourite dish: Fried Potatoes, Egg & Bacon. Even Bonzo had his share and gosh! He liked it too.

I polished my bike a bit tonight. It was dirty from last Sunday night.

By the way my papers have been posted this morning. The boss took it along when he took his daughter to school. Posted at Evington Rd, Le'ster.

Everything else is alright, so far. Only 1 ½ day to go till I see my sweet again.

Well, my darling, I'll say Cheeri'O for now. Be good, till I see you. I love you more than anything else in the world.

Goodnight and God bless.

Friday, 8.00 p.m.

Jeannie, I am mad!! Bonzo has had a very good hiding, but that doesn't bring my weeks meat ration back. That daft butcher left it right under his nose. In front of the wireless. I've told him to put it on the small table. Anyway I'll see him tomorrow dinnertime.

Thanks so very much for your letter, my darling. The envelope looked familiar to me. At first I thought you had left one of your letters here last weekend.

Today it was a rushing about again. Feeding, watercarting the whole lot on my own from 10.00-1.15 got me down. On and off the tractor like a jumping cat. Then after all, Mrs Moulds went collecting and I took it easy. Buried hens and messed about for ¾ hour.

Now in a few minutes shutting up afterwards a wash and then wait for 12.00 tomorrow.

Well, my darling, I'll say cheeri'o. Be good and Goodnight and God bless. I am longing for tomorrow and love you more than anything else in the whole wide world.

> All my love and thousands of kisses
>> Forever your loving
> husband
>> Hans.

Aschersleben, 13.5.1950

My dear Hans and Jean,

Thank you very much for your lovely letter of 2.5.50. We were hoping to receive a few lines from you. I'd already written to you on 26.4.50 to say that we had received the package.

Horst has had another bad week. It is unbearable to watch when his breathing difficulties start. What will come of it? It worries me so much. The day before yesterday he went for another examination. The doctor always says the only thing that will help is a change of air. We've had eight awful days of rain here, and the damp air even makes breathing hard for me, although I am not so susceptible. There are many other people in this area who suffer badly from it. It's probably because this area used to be a marsh. The town is so low-lying that, if you look down at it from the mountain, there is always a haze lying over it. To add to that, there is the Potash mine.

At the moment, Frau Fuchs is here for a fortnight, staying at Frau Lehmann's. She is already looking forward to our visit. On the Sunday and Monday after Whitsun, there will be a big Song Festival there. It's a shame that we won't still be there for it, Horst could have earnt a lot.

Dear Hans, don't get the wrong idea about Horst looking forward to meeting his sister-in-law. You're surely not going to be jealous? Horst is truly not such a Casanova. He's only kidding. If the positions were reversed, wouldn't you be excited about meeting your sister-in-law? 17.6.50 falls on a Saturday, so it will be today, in five weeks. We'll have to go a few days earlier as otherwise it will be a full moon. It makes me sweat just to think about it. Keep your fingers crossed for us! Heinz wants to visit us next week, he wants to go and see Edith!! Well, Edith will be looking forward to seeing the son-and-heir.

I am so thrilled that you are bringing soap with you. The soap you got before was wonderful! Dear Hans, maybe you can bring some black and brown shoe polish with you – the last one was very good and lasted a whole year. And, if possible, a little cinnamon.

Aunt Lina sends you her best wishes. Yesterday she sent us fresh herring and that is truly something ! Christel will be starting work at the hotel on 1st June, she is after all also 22 years old now.

Now my dears, we wish you a very happy and healthy Whitsun. Warm regards to your mother. Greetings and kisses from your mum, who is always thinking of you, and from your brother and brother-in-law Horst. To a happy and healthy reunion.

"My Darling"

Do you know where there's somebody sitting in a stable all alone and very very lonely? Right here. It's just the same. A nice made bed but nobody to sleep in it with me!!

How are you, my darling? Still feeling miserable or depressed? I hope not. I saw you looking for me last night when the bus left, but I couldn't get upstairs quick enough to wave to you. Well, I arrived safe and sound at 8.40, took the cups and saucers round and had a cup of tea there as well. Without sugar as he had packed it away. She took the small porridge plates. I've got the money 12/6. 10 o'clock saw me in bed. Bonzo was a dirty boy. The place wasn't half messed up. About ½ doz lots. So I had something to clean out or rather washed it ~~up~~ out. It must have been the lot of dog biscuits he's had. I didn't hit him. Poor chap would have gone out if he could've done.

Whilst I got my dinner ready I had a brainwave. I saw the butcher and he said to me when I came in "That bl…. Butcher ~~letting~~ leaving the meat for the dog" I just wanted to know if he would have some liver on Wednesday. Anyway he gave me a great big leg of mutton and some rhubarb too. That means I'll have plenty of meat this week. Did you have the wireless one when you came home tonight? There was a play on called "Come to the stolen waters". It was about a German POW in love with a 17 year old girl (prominence). And they send him back to Germany just when it was getting interesting. What a shame.

I have changed Bonzo's bags tonight and thought paper bags would keep the cold from the floor off. So I took 6, put them in an old bag, but it looks as if he doesn't like the noise the paper makes when he lays down.

I've had an easy day, but it was perishing cold. Creosoting on top of the hill from 10.00-5.00 and the cold wind was blowing. My nose was running like a tub.

Well, my dearest, I am figuring out how to make the next weekend as pleasant as possible. It's your first birthday when you'll wake up and me beside you. I love you so much, my darling. If there only was a way of showing you instead of just telling you. Let us get a place of our own first and I'll make everything as comfy for you as ever I can. You deserve it. The best wife in the whole wide world. You can't imagine how much I love you.

Well, my sweetheart, it's 9.00 and I'll have an early night. Be good and look after yourself. Good night and God bless you and keep you safe.

> All my love and thousands of kisses
> > Forever yours if you want me for that long
> Your husband
> > Hans.

> 92 Wharf Street
> May 15th 1950.

"My dearest"

Here I am again, I have just been to the park to take Freddy a walk. I only intended to take him around the car park. We only walked as far as the river, it was too cold to stay long.

How is my darling today? Oh I have missed you so very much last night, 4 ½ days to go then I will be seeing you again. I love you so much.

Everything has been very much the same as usual today. I was later getting up 8.20, but I made it for 9.5 ~~and~~ I lit the fire and ate my breakfast in that time. I can move sometimes. Fred is sitting on the big stool by me, he would like to get on my knee.

I have been thinking, at Whit I have Friday afternoon and Saturday morning holiday, should I come over Friday afternoon no matter what holiday you have, because in any case you won't have Friday off. I will say goodnight and God Bless you my darling.

Tuesday

Thank you so much my darling for your letter. You were lucky to get some more meat. I have been thinking darling, don't let us have any poultry for lunch on Sunday. We can wait until after our holiday then we will have one, don't you think that is best.

I didn't listen to that play I believe it has been on before. I remember someone tell me, but I have never heard it. You can tell me all about it.

Gladys and Walter saw Otto on Saturday waiting for Miggy to come home. They had an argument about what picture they would go to. So they both went to different pictures and Miggy had the key so Otto could not get in, he was really fed up. He told them they are always arguing. The small plates were the same price as the others 10d

Well my sweetest I will have to do some knitting. I don't seem to be getting on very well with it and I would like you to take it away with you. So for now

    All my love
    Jean
    ____.

                    Pickwell,
                    May, 16th 1950

My sweet, little wife,

How are you today my little sugarplum? Well, I have spent some more money. And thank goodness I took a £ on Sunday. Today I received a form to fill in (from the Foreign Office). It went back straight away today with a 16/-s postal order. Aren't they cheeky? A very polite letter saying further considerations would be given to the matter after receiving the postal order and completed form. Just asking questions about things they've got on the papers I've sent in, and, of course, another signature. Well, that's that. Now I hope it comes back before Saturday so you can "take it from here".

Last night the boss asked me again if I had heard from the Council. I told him I had given up, not expecting the Council to leave the house empty so long. Anyway ~~has~~ he said the house is still empty, 6 applications have come in, 4 have been ruled out. The two left is mine and that fellows we went to see. The chances definitely stand 50/50 if not better for me. So just wait and see. If we get it, heaven help me to decide what to do and where to start. Keep your nerves, Hannes, and let problems come up to you. Then quick decision. We'll see, my sweetie.

There's nothing to do for me tonight. It's too early to get things ready for the weekend. Thursday and Friday I'll be rushed to death again. Is there anything we need for the stuffing? Bring a few cloves, please. Also new potatoes. A 3 lbs young cockerel will be delivered to the door Friday night. I've asked the boss last night and it was a "yes" straight the way. Bring some nice greens to go with it and leave everything else including the cooking and washing up to me. You'll have to enjoy your birthday and just watch me work. No arguing, please. It'll be just <u>your</u> day. Oh! How I would love to look after you every day.

Well, my dearest, I'll close for tonight. Be good and look after yourself till I take over Saturday afternoon. I love you more than my own life, really. Believe me, Jean, I would do anything for you.

Goodnight and God bless you.

<u>Wednesday, 7.00 p.m.</u>

Hello, my precious, how are you? Fine? There was little change in the working routine. Watercartering instead of cleaning out. So Wednesday is gone and that leaves 2 ½ days till my sweet little wife comes again.

Well, darling about whitsun. Gudger asked me this morning

if I would mind working this weekend and Whit as well. Thinking of holiday money I said no I wouldn't mind working, but it would be alright if somebody else does the shutting up. I did it over Easter and would perhaps like to go out at night at Whit. He's going to see what he can do. So you'd better come over on Friday afternoon and have a long weekend till Monday night. It'll be like Easter.

You're disappointing me about poultry for Sunday dinner. Sorry, sweetie, I have ordered it already and in fact , I want you to have a real nice birthday dinner. I've made a menu out last night. It looks alright on paper.

Otherwise everything seems to be alright. Eileen is leaving after all. A little incident yesterday dinnertime got her temper up again. It was 2 minutes to 1 when she left next door for her lunch. Gudger just came into the yard and told her off. The time for lunch was 1 o'clock and it was 2 minutes to go. So off she went. She said this morning he took her by surprise otherwise she would've asked some questions about his lunchtime.

By the way, best wife in the world, I'll close for tonight. I am longing so much for Saturday. And I love you more than anything in the whole wide world. Be good, goodnight and God bless and keep you safe.

> All my love and kisses
> Forever your loving husband
> Hans.

92 Wharf Street

May 17th 1950

Guten morgen Herr Klawitter Der tag ist fein, und Der Sonne ist Heiss und der wind ist frisch und es geht mir gut.

I have done that without looking at the book, so I don't know if I have made any mistakes. I started to write it in the book last night to see if I can possibly learn a little before I go. When I have finished your pullover I will get down to it properly, but at the moment I am doing a bit of each.

My dearest darling how are you today, I am missing you so very much. I wished today that I had arranged to see you to-night, but it does take rather a lot on bus fares, then having something to eat on top and going to the pictures.

I have found out what is on the pictures in Melton but I don't know anything about them. "Command decision" and "Uncover man" We can see whether or not we go to the pictures on Saturday I don't mind. There is a play on "it always rains on Sunday". I have seen the picture. Did I see it with you? I am not going to bother to listen. I have been here in bed at 9.30 every night. There is not anything to stay up for.

On my way to the office this morning I met Iris, but did not have time to say much as she was on her way to work. She is working at the food office.

I will close now and do a bit more knitting Oh you darling Oh! You sweet one I love you Oh so very very much. Words cannot express it. Goodnight and God bless you my darling

    Your ever loving

    Wife

    Jean

Thank you my sugarplum for your letter, a nice long one. I had quite a few things to tell you but I can't remember. Maybe it will come to me. Betty told Mamma that they wanted £3.10.0 for the mangle wash tub and puncher. I asked my mother what she thought the wash tub and puncher was worth, she thought £1 because Betty wants them, but Betty thought 10/- I think £1.

Have you written to your cousin yet? It is about time you did.

Charlie has the afternoon off and is going to distemper the ceiling in the small room.

I have just had a little dog in here. She would not come to me. It belongs to one of the men.

    All my love ~~my~~

    Jeannie.

Aschersleben, 21.5.50

Mr Hans Klarwitter
Home Farm Pickwell
Melton Mobray
Leicestershire

Great Britain

Dear Hans and Jean,
We are all sending you our loving
greetings from my birthday celebration.

My guests were:
Hanna Weskamp
F. Sievers
Ruth Rilchheit
Hilde Goldmann
Erika Heinzering
Inca Siedenlopf
Resel Rückrop

Also lots of love from your Mum

Dr. Fuchs

Pickwell,
May, 22nd 1950

"My Darling"
How are you, my sweetheart? Wasn't it a grand day. If I see
the man that makes the weather I'll tell him off. Yesterday
on my sweetie's birthday it was pouring with rain. Did you
get home safe and sound? I thought of you when Reg Dixon
came on. By that time you'll have been at home.
Well, my darling, have you enjoyed your birthday? I've tried
my best to make it nice for you and didn't stick to it. I

wanted to do all the jobs myself and after all you poor darling had to do the washing up and get breakfast and tea. And when you had left I could have bashed my nose. You know what the trouble was. Too busy. When I fetched the cake out on Saturday I was really satisfied. You're surprised and your eyes were sparkling. I hope it'll always be like that. Just to see you happy. Oh! I love you so very very much.

The Bonzo problem is settled. I asked Les today and he's going to take him for the fortnight. I told him that the butcher could bring the bones to him and as they always shop at Hill's he can order some dog biscuits every week. I'll pay him when we get back. Thank goodness that's that. Now let's hope my papers come back soon. I am really getting worried. It's only 3 weeks and 4 days to go. We'll have to give them time to get the permits and visas. But perhaps it's a quick do after all. Let's hope for the best.

This morning I wasn't half mad. A nice weeks start. With Gudger again, of course. We two seem to get on well together. When I went feeding in Broad meadow I saw a calf fall flat on it's side and start kicking his legs about. So I left the horse and rushed over. It was having a fit and couldn't breath. The eyes turned right round. Well, I cleaned the nose and opened his mouth slightly and kept moving the legs. It came to again after ½ hour doing that. With having my fingers in his mouth the teeth fetched bits of skin off as he tried to keep them together. Anyway after I had got him round again I went straight back to tell Cooper. He wasn't about so I looked for the boss. Still the funny part was, that on top of the hill I met Gudger. He told me that's a job for the shepherd and not for me to bother about. I didn't half tell Gudger off. On the way I met the boss told him about it. I also mentioned the funny telling me off. At dinnertime he was the politest man on the place. Gosh, I still change that old beggar.

So I'll close now. Be good, my sweetie and please, look after yourself. Only 3 ½ days to go. Goodnight and God bless and keep you safe.

All my love and thousands of kisses
   Forever and as long as you want him
Your loving husband
            Hans.

   92 Wharf Street
   May 22nd 1950.
"My darling"

Thank you so very much for the lovely birthday you gave me. I can't ever remember being made such a fuss of before. I hope I can make you as happy as you make me. I love you so much.

I arrived back in Leicester safe. Mamma was in the neighbours, it was too wet for them to go out. I just called in but did not stay. I had a look at the "Sunday Pie" then off to bed that would be about 10.45. I had not been in bed half an hour when a couple outside started to have a fight, being nosy I had to have a look. He I think was trying to kiss her outside the fish shop. He got her in the doorway, she must have kicked him in the right place because he went down on the floor, but she kept shouting "Go with your prostitutes" when he got off the floor he didn't half give her one. The policeman came then. We do see some excitement in Wharf Street, but it did upset me. I could not get to sleep for ages after that.

I had a parcel this morning from Muriel. It was some Yoya bath salts, when you come over, we can have a bath. I have had another present this afternoon from the girls in pool. I brought some cakes this afternoon 3/-. I have a 1/- to last me all week. I had a birthday card from Sheila and Susan also one from Mamma. I have done quite well for cards.

The invitation to Dora's wedding came this morning 12.0. The register office June 10th. Will you be able to get time off? That is the afternoon we could have done with doing our shopping, but maybe I could do it before. If you cannot get it I would have to come over on the 6.15. Anyway we can settle that at the weekend. I will have to see what I can wear.

I mustn't let the Jerries down must I.

I forgot to tell you yesterday, I wasn't really sure whether or not I was going. Mamma displayed a circus bill in the window and in return had free seats, two, so Betty and I are going tonight. I will tell you about the circus next time I write.

I suppose you were surprised to get a letter so soon, but I wanted my sweetie pie to know how much I enjoyed myself. I want to spend a penny so I will have to close. All my love

> Forever your
> loving wife
> Jean.
>
> ———.

P.S.
Let me know what you want for the weekend

> Home Farm,
> Pickwell,
> May, 23rd 1950

My sweet, little wife,

How are you, my darling? At your best? Well, that's good. I am so glad you really enjoyed your birthday. If you call that being made a fuss of then wait and see how much fuss I can make of you. Wait till we go home on holiday.

Did you finish your cake? I had the last bit today and also finished the other cake off. Was it nice watching the fight? She must have kicked him alright being down on the floor. Did the policeman take them along?

Nice having some presents. What about the one from me. Don't you think you had better go and have a look if you can find some shoes you like. Otherwise you have to wait another fortnight till I come over. Or perhaps I can arrange to work another weekend and then come over on the 10th. That's the one before we go. We'll talk it over on Saturday.

I've made inquiries about the bus service on Friday. There's nothing between 2 and 4 o'clock. The 4.30 goes the long way round and arrives here at 5.05. If you like you can come along when I go shopping. You'll be able to have a proper dinner at home and then we'll have tea together. Fish and chips for me and something else nice for you.

Well, darling, I'll keep my fingers crossed to get the papers tomorrow. Gosh! I am getting nervous about it. Let's hope we'll do it in time. Goodnight and God bless you always. I love you and miss you so very very much

<u>Wednesday, 7.30 p.m.</u>

Hello, my darling, here I am again. After our telephone conversation there's nothing much to say. Wasn't it cold today? I was muckcarting from the chicken field.

How are my trousers looking? I hope they're alright.

Well, my sweetheart, I'll have an early night and turn in after I've had some supper. (Bread and cheese). Be good and look after yourself. It's only 1 ½ day to go. Goodnight and God bless you. Oh! I love you so very very much.

All my love and kisses forever your loving husband Hans.

Shirt Dogbiscuits
Underwear Greens
Pillowslip Tomatoes
Tablecloth Lettuce
Towel Sausages
Socks Soappowder
Trousers Saladcream
Fags Biscuits
<u>P.S</u>.
It's a lot, isn't it. Thank goodness the bus comes to Pickwell. See you Friday. Love Hans.

    92 Wharf Street
    May 24th 1950
"My dearest darling"
Thank you so much my darling for your letter.

I thought I had better write today as I will be there myself on Friday. I have just rung Randall's, their telephone number is Ashfordby 491, and the buses from Melton are 2.0, 4.30. 5.30. 7.0 and 8.0. It would be too much of a rush to make it for the 2.0 so I will be on the 4.30. That will make me 5.0 at Pickwell. I won't be able to have my cherubs dinner ready for him.

I have been polishing my office ~~out~~ and it looks quite nice. Eileen Oaky, one of the girls, brought me some flowers for my birthday and I have left them here, they cheer the place up a bit. I have decided to fetch your trousers tonight, it will give me more time on Friday.

I went to the circus on Monday night and I really enjoyed it. I hadn't seen one for years, in fact I can't remember the last one I saw at all. It only cost me 5 d for the bus fare. It was quite a long show, started at 7.45 and finished at 10.10.

I am in such a mess I have just laddered my stockings and spilt my tea over my nicely polished table. So now I have to mend my stockings. So I will have to say Cheeri'O. Oh! I love you so very very much all the way round the world and back. love and kisses

     Jean.

Friday Afternoon

Since you never gave me time to explain what I have done about our journey I thought I would write at least you won't say "It's no good we won't have the things in time"

To begin with- after you had rung Thursday to let me know your papers were on the way, I thought I had better be up early to meet the postman as he usually knocks then goes, but calls on his way back. That is after 9.0 and too late for me to go to the Coop as they do not open Thursday afternoon. Well I was up at 7.0, but blow me the postman went by so I ran down after him as far as Bow Street. But he hadn't one for me.

It came with the next post, it was too late to go on Thursday so I had to leave it until this morning. I asked permission to go out. I have paid the deposit of £2 for our journey. Now all we want is the permit and visa to Holland. I rang the Dutch office this morning to see what fee they wanted to save time and it was a good job I did, they want to see the permit to enter Germany. You send that with the travel document with 13/9. So I thought I had better ring the Allied Control etc. so he took my address to send the application card on to me, but like a fool I forgot I wouldn't be here tomorrow So I have told Mamma I will ring her in the morning to see if they have arrived then I will have to go over and fetch them on the 10.15 bus to Leicester, you can fill and sign yours. Then I will have to take them to Melton as Somerby closes on Sat afternoon. So you see my darling there isn't a thing to worry about until June 17th then it is too late That's all for now. Any questions

Lots and lots of

love in fact all of it

Jean

.

Saturday	2 ½	collecting
-"-	2	sh. Up
Sunday	2 ½	feeding
	2	Mash
	2 ¾	collecting
	2 ½	sh. Up
Monday	2 ½	feeding

Aschersleben, 24.5.50

My dear Hans and Jean

We received both your letters dated 20 April and 18 May yesterday, for which we thank you from the bottom of our hearts. Would you believe – one of them took 34 days to get here!

582

You say that you don't want to leave your home until the evening. I think this is not very good because if you arrive on the Saturday evening at 7.34 in Braunschweig, the next train to Weferlingen is not going until 11.30, which means you will get to Weferlingen after midnight, which is not a very convenient time. If at all possible, it would be much better if you could get into Braunschweig around mid-day. It is much nicer to arrive during the day and you can then show Jean all the interesting points on the way back. Maybe you can think it over again and let us have your final decision. Please send your letter to me at c/o Mrs. Frida Fuchs:

Weferlingen, 20 b via Wolfenbüttel, near Braunschweig, because we might be on our journey already before the letter gets here.

If everything works according to plan, we intend to start our journey on 12.6, which means that we will be there a few days before you, but who knows if our first attempt will work. We also need to have a little rest and prepare everything for your stay. We shall be leaving, therefore, on Monday fortnight. Mrs. Fuchs left again yesterday. She spent two weeks here with her inter-zone pass. She is looking forward very much to our visit. We get on very well together. She is buying one hundredweight of potatoes for us, I am sure it will be sufficient for our stay, and we have already got the flour to bake some cakes. Heinz is thinking of coming with us. He wants to see Edith. Well, you obviously had quite a feast over Easter with the chicken. It would be something special for me too! You work very hard and you have to eat well. We already had 30°C during the week. Last night we had thunderstorms with pouring rain. You can be well satisfied with your weekly salary. Why did Horst get 20 Marks less? Because the taxes are so high! But now he is getting it back again. Horst thanks you very much for the lovely birthday card. It made him very happy. I made his birthday as nice as I could. You were constantly in our thoughts. I can see that both of you will look very elegant again. Mrs. Fuchs has already taken some of the birthday presents with her and we shall bring the rest. If you have to change in Goslar, then you only have a little bit longer to go to Braunschweig. I am not sure yet whether I will come to Braunschweig. Maybe Horst will come by himself and I shall meet you at the station in Dettum. If we both come, the fare will cost 5.60 West Marks. Converted into our money, it is 35 Marks, almost a week's salary. We have to be careful with our money. If you arrive lunchtime, the wait is not so long.

The air which was created by the thunderstorm has made me feel rather tired, but I do want to go into town and take your letter to the post office.

Give our love to your mother and to you, my dears, we are sending you our innermost love and kisses. Yours mum, brother and brother-in-law Horst.

Pickwell,
May, 30th 1950

"My darling"

Here I am back at the stables. I was so miserable on the bus last night and believe me I didn't want to leave you. It is only 5.15 now and I am going out again as soon as I have had my dinner. Watercarting on the chicken field. It'll be 8.00 when I get back from there and that means having a wash and off again shutting up. At least it means a few hours overtime.

Thank you so very much for a grand weekend. I was so happy and you made everything so nice. I only wish it was a beginning and would last forever starting from right now. But there you are 17 miles apart.

I had a letter from my mother this afternoon. She mentioned our arrival at Brunswick. Leaving at night as we intend to means waiting at Brunswick from 7.34 till 11.30 for the next train to Weferlingen. Still it can't be helped. Horst will probably be coming on his own to meet us, as my mother would like to cut down on expenses. It saves them one railway fare. Though she'll meet us at Weferlingen station. The lady at the place where we are staying has been to see my mother and is gone back and taken a lot of things along already. Horst and my mother will have the first try to cross the border on the 12.6.50. That's almost a week before we go. She just wants to make sure to get there in time for us and have everything ready. I'll have to write to her to the Weferlingen address and tell her we're definitely coming on the 7.34 p.m. if I remember right you've got the times for departure from Brunswick, haven't you? Otherwise we'll have to find out about that, too.

By the way, Horst has put a card from his birthday party in. Even the guests send greetings. I'll bring it out. 8 names, 5 of them girls.

Oh! Jeannie, I love you so very very much. Wait till we have a home. Oh! I'll make you happy. I'll try to do it anyway, and I hope to succeed. You are the sweetest girl in the world and gosh!, the very best wife.

Well, my darling, I'll say goodnight now and God bless you always. Be good and sleep well.

> All my love and thousands of kisses
> > Forever and only your
> loving husband
> > Hans.

92 Wharf St

May 30th

My dearest darling

How are you today? Did you arrive back at Pickwell safe? The bus seemed as if it was ages coming round. I walked quite slowly and had to wait for it so I could wave to you. I met Mamma on the way back on her way to get her beverage.

I felt so fed up when I got back, it was too early to go to bed. So I went round to Betty to fetch the pattern for the baby's coat but they must have been upstairs in the front. I rang the bell but I could not hear it ring.So Fred and I walk home again. I had a good wash and whilst I was doing that Bing Crosby was on, choosing his own records and playing them. Then I listened to Lady's Night for a while. What I heard of it was good. I thought you would be listening. Then I went off to bed at 9.45. I am so lonely and fed up. I shall be glad when we can be together and I want you to have a job you are happy in. We had better have our holiday first then have a look around. Bill Pickering has just been through, he asked how you were.

It's like being at work on a Sunday, when I look into the street there's not a soul about.

The photographs will be ready in a week's time but we can call in on Saturday to see if they are finished.

I put my leave sheet in today 13 ½ days from 12.45 Friday lunchtime. I am sure I will have plenty of time if we leave Leicester in the afternoon. Anyway if we find I won't have enough time I can apply for the other half a day. We shall have to make a list of what we have to do on Saturday – K Coffee, Rommell, strap for case, socks, films, go to the reference library. Can you think of anything else? We can get the milk, boot polish, soap pepper and cinnamon anytime. Are you very disappointed not having a cream shirt until after our holiday. We can get both our birthday presents together then.

Well my darling I will be seeing you in 3 ½ days time so until then be good.

All my love
Jeannie.

PS Don't forget to pay for those eggs.

92 Wharf St
May 31st 1950

My dearest Johannes,

Thank you very much for your lovely long letter, though I was disappointed to find, when I opened it that it was only really half as much because you had sent my Saturday letter back.

Did you listen to 'Window on Western Germany' last night? I did. I suppose you would rather listen to 'Take it from here' It was quite interesting. The value of the mark is 1 /8 ½ . It had people tell what the cost of living is and one man, a tram driver had 250 Marks a month with a family of four to live on. I asked that girl or rather woman how long it took a parcel to get to Germany, she said about four weeks. It is about that since we sent the parcel to your mother so if she is going to get it she would have it by now.

My passport came today. So I have sent your travel things off with a postal order. They have sent me some leaflets back about visas. We need a permit, it gives the address where to send it. I will bring them over on Saturday. I feel quite pleased about having a passport but I don't think it is worth 15/-. There is a piece in the back about people with dual nationality, that means I have one if I am German in German law. I can pick and choose what suits me. I got your books on Monday to have another go at learning German, and I could read your writing so I got my book Heute Abend. I will bring them on Saturday and if you feel like it you can give me a lesson in German.

How is the puppy? Have you got rid of her? Fred was in trouble tonight, I took him to fetch the milk and there was a crowd of dogs and somewhere a bitch. I picked Fred up, brought him across the road, put him down and blow me if he didn't run back across the road in front of a motorcycle. He still wants to go out. Mamma said he was out nearly all morning. I bet he only got a smell too.

Are you thinking of opening a shop at Pickwell. They are 1/3 cup and saucers. 7/6 a ½ doz. The fruit set is 12/6 like your dishes, 8/11 the others, but at the moment we have not a big

dish to the 12/6 set, only the ½ doz dishes. We may be able
to get one.

I don't suppose you have heard anything about the council
house yet I have a feeling somehow that we will not get it. I
am so sorry that I am a pessimist about it. So I have not really
given the furnishing much of a thought of what we shall do.
When I do think about it I wish we were not going away
when I think of what we could buy with money we are going
to spend. If we do get it we shall have to furnish it the best
we can, then get it how we should like when we can afford it.
I definitely do not like to have things on the weekly. This is
probably going to be classed as nagging what I am about to
say and it is only a small thing. Why when you want to have
your photograph taken do you have to have ½ day? I know
it only was 1/6 extra but darling it is those little things like
that, that run away with money so quick. You have only my
word that I don't spend our money on luxury things, believe
me darling there are times when I would love some fruit and
I would like to go to the pictures because I get fed up staying
in but I don't mind going without because it is for something
I want very much, a home, but when you do things like that
it gets me really fed up. I hate having to tell you because I
know it may lead to you not telling me and I would really
hate that. I have really no right to tell you what to do with
the money you earn and I do want you to please yourself, but
I can't see any other way of getting what we want without
saving. When I think I spent 16/1 on a pair of stockings I am a
good one to lecture you.

Fred is wanting to go out but he's had it tonight. Mamma has
just gone out so I am alone again.

You asked i if I was lonely. I am so very lonely, but it is for our
future home, so I can put up with it. You never need worry
about me. I will go where our living is, I am sure I will always
be happy no matter where we go. If we went to Germany I
am sure I would soon pick the language up and I know there
would be people there like the man in the Labour Exchange,

I would understand them and think maybe I would feel the same in their place, the same as I hope you do in the same position.

Oh! Haven't I been writing a lot, I hope that I have not bored you too much. I hope you will fit the words in that I may have missed out.

So my darling I will close. Sending all my love and kisses I am longing to see you on Saturday.

For as long as you want

I am yours

Jean

.

92 Wharf St

June 1st 1950.

My dearest

Thank you so very much for your letter. I was getting worried, I wondered what had happened. It did not arrive until this morning.

Isn't it a beautiful day. I hope it is like this when we have our holiday. Then I will be wishing I had a new dress.

I have not had the passports back yet. Herbert rang yesterday afternoon, he said he sent his police certificate to the permit office as they wanted proof that he was a POW. Let hope they take your word that you were a POW. I went again to the Coop yesterday about the currency and told the fellow what we intended to do 3. ea in Mark etc and wanting another form. He said it would be better to have it on my passport then there would not be any query and that it would be quick as they have to send the passport away to London and you are getting your visa for Holidaylland, it is also easier to change the money back to English money on my passport. The train leaves Brunswick at 10.51 July 1st. We had better make it £21 so we can take £3 in Marks.

Uncle Arthur came yesterday and they have had a letter from Beaty (in Hamburg) saying she is expecting twins, she

is in hospital now and they are not expected until July.
It is only 1 ½ days to go. Then we will have a busy weekend.
Bring everything that you want to take with you that needs
washing. You had better bring a sheet bath if you think they
need it. We will have do everything that needs ironing the
same day.
Betty has just rung up to ask if I was going out tonight. She
wants me to go and look after the kids so she and Cyril can go
to the pictures together.
Well my darling I want to get on with my knitting so be good
love

    All my love
    Jeannie

Same address
June, 1ˢᵗ 1950

My sweet, little wife,
Thank you so very much for your letter which arrived yesterday morning. Last night I wrote to my mother telling her
about the definite time we're arriving and thought of writing to you tonight. Sorry, darling, I can't post this letter as I
haven't got a stamp left. Please forgive me, I'll bring it along
on Saturday.
How are you, my darling? Fine, I hope. Wasn't it a grand day
again. Not for me, though. Cleaning out and it was baking
hot inside the houses. The sweat was running down my face
all the day.
Believe me you're not the only one fed up miserable and
lonely last Monday night. People that saw me on the bus
passing by must've thought by gum that's a miserable beggar.
You're right I listened to 'Ladies Please'. It was quite good.
At the moment Wilfred is on his journey again. Remind me
to tell you something about the house at Knossington. The
boss was on about it again before 7.00 this morning.
Well, my darling, I'll close for now and get myself ready for

shutting up. Once more after tonight. Thank goodness only 1 ½ days to go till I see you again. Goodnight and God bless you.

<u>Friday night 7.30pm</u>

Hello, my darling, how are you? I bet mad with me because no letter arrived for you. I am so sorry sweetie. You'll get this one tomorrow.

This morning a letter came back asking for proof having been an ex POW. Just the same as in Herbert's case. At first I was going to put my certificate in last Sunday, but as they didn't ask for it I left it. So I send it off again straight the way and forwarded the cert and also my discharge papers, just to make sure. It should be in London in the morning. Remember what I said just had to happen. A letter back from the Permit Office. Another few days lost. Never mind and as you said everything will be 'just' in time.

Right, darling, if it more convenient for us to have the traveller cheques on your passport, let's have a go at that as soon as the papers come back. Then the visa for Holland and we'll be ready. What a lot of bother. I hope you find it worth it.

Jeannie, I have made a pig of ~~your~~ myself tonight. 1/- worth of chips, half the tin of meat, 2 eggs and the rest of the bacon. Gosh! I was hungry. No breakfast and only the sandwich at lunchtime. It was too hot to eat more.

If I had had the young chap with me last night he would have got a good hiding. I was so glad no hens were out for the first time since last Sunday. Though, when I came to the last two houses in Lambing Meadow all the lot out and the slides were open. So I went inside I found paraffin tins right in front of the slides. I just gave him a reminder this morning and told him what it is like if he would've to do the shutting up. Anyway it was 11.15 when I got back here. You know yourself what it is like hens out and dark.

I was going to write to Edith tonight but haven't got any paper left. Used two lots for this letter already.

Well, my darling, I'll put some water on to have a wash when

I come back.

Be good my sweetie and look after yourself. Tomorrow I'll do it.

I am so much longing for you and love you more than anything else in the world.

All my love and thousands of kisses

Forever your loving husband

Hans.

Aschersleben, 3.6.50

My dear Hans and Jean

Thank you very much for your lovely letter dated 23.5.50. At the moment, I am suffering from severe hiccups and the saying goes 'hiccups means someone is thinking of you, or talking about you'. I was wondering if you are you thinking of us? We are not worried, but I would like to know if you have all the documents together now which you need for your trip? We very much hope that you get everything before your departure. I do not understand how it can take so long. Perhaps it would have been better had you gone there yourself and picked up all the papers. If all goes well, we shall be together in 14 days. We are setting off on our journey in ten days. How I wish that we were there already! I am going to be very busy next week. There is a big load of washing to be done, and there is so much else to do and organise when you go away for three weeks. Well, I am sure you too have a lot on your plate.

We are having very good weather here and hope it will be equally nice when we are on holiday. Already 18 months have gone since we last saw you. We have not heard from the Streeses for a long time. I wonder if they took offence that we did not go back to them. We would not be able to afford it financially! It will not be as expensive in W. Horst is already looking forward to the milk which they have there. Dear

Hans, I think you will be quite surprised to see that living standards have much improved since the last time you came over. Everything is free *.

Now, my dears, we want to wish you a very happy trip. Look after yourselves and don't get any sea sickness. We are sending you all our love and kisses, your mum, brother and brother-in-law. Best wishes to your mother.

* ie not rationed

> 92 Wharf St,
> June 5th.

My dearest darling,

I had a shock this morning and you will when you read the letter I have enclosed from the Coop. I hope that I have done the right thing. I rang the Coop as soon as it arrived and asked them to try June 16th. That would mean that we would go Thursday June 15th. I did not know what we could do. I thought that would be the best time. Do you think you can have another day off? When you ask explain what has happened. Because it will be nearly three weeks and you can't have all that time without saying why. I thought about ringing Mrs Cooper to give you a message to ring me. You will have to write to your mother again. I am passed worrying now and I have decided to take things as they come and hope for the best.

I have just rung Dora. I wrote this morning before the invitation I was expecting came. I asked Dora ~~what she would like~~ if there was anything she wanted and there wasn't anything she could think of, so I suggested a pair of scales. She hasn't any, so that is what we will get after our holiday. But I will get Muriel's little girl a birthday present. I did not like what you said on Saturday about buying other people presents.

I have written to Muriel since she has been in London and she has always sent me a birthday present and one at Christmas.

I went down there for a week's holiday once and she never charged me anything. When I stay at home it will be different then.

At the moment I am not feeling too hot, I have opened the door and there is a nice breeze blowing through. I have just seen Mr Coy he asked after you.

I took some flowers round to Betty last night and stayed there until 10.0. We had Variety Bandbox on.

I have found out the visa is 13/9 both ways. I hope we have the permits back tomorrow.

I have not found out yet what is on the pictures at Melton. I will find out when Melton come through.

Well my darling I will have to say cheeri'O now, be good.

All my love and kisses

Jeannie

Pickwell,

June 5<u>th</u> 1950

My sweetest, little wife,

Hello, my darling, how are you? Feeling fine, I hope. Wasn't it hot today? I feel as if I have been in an oven for a few hours. Is my face red. Anyway, here I am again, safe and sound. Arrived at 8.35 as usual. Bonzo was alright and no dirt this time. Doris had taken him on the chicken field in the morning so he's even had his walk or rather run.

I've got a smashing job first thing in the morning. The boy has to be trained in feeding as he has to go in my place when I am on holiday. So the boss told me this morning, but let him do the work and driving the horse. He just wants me to go along and see that he gets the hang of it and feeds properly. For the rest of the day I went watercarting. No breeze at all and the sun blazing hot. I've just seen in the 'Evening Mail' it was 92 at 2.00pm. Let's hope it'll be as nice in 11 days time. It suits me alright being warm so I don't have to wear tie and collar. I know you don't like me running about with an open-necked shirt but darling if it is so warm have you tried to walk about in something tied up to the neck and a tie round it as well? It really is awful sweetie. Never mind, my sweetie, what about an open necked summer dress for you?

I've written to Edith and told her that I am bringing the book along, though didn't mention the jacket for the baby. Tonight I just couldn't be bothered to cook potatoes. So I fried two slices of meat, 2 eggs and a slice of bread and that was that. I feel full anyway. I've just done my breakfast for to-morrow. Porridge made with milk and sultanas but I won't heat it up. Cold, just as it is. It's nice. At Wartnaby I had the same as sweet at dinnertime. You try it.

Well darling, I thank you very much for a lovely weekend. The next one here will be the last one before we go away.

I'll close for now. Be good my sweetheart and look after yourself.

Goodnight and God bless and keep you safe. I love you more than anything else in the whole wide world.

All my love and thousands of kisses
Forever your loving husband
Hans.

Pickwell,
June, 6th 1950

My darling

Well, we have had our little conversation and there really isn't much to say. In any case, now I keep my fingers crossed that we'll get seats for Thursday-Friday-travel. Gosh! This isn't half a lot of bother. Never mind, we'll enjoy it ever so much more. (I hope). You're right! It's better to call in for the Dutch visa ourselves. So we can make sure we get it in time. It's the best and only way to do it. You poor darling have been busy again ringing London and arranging things with the co-op. Now I'll be waiting for your next letter to tell me that the papers have come back.

Gordan came over and told me to ring you. It was at 6.15. That would have been a bit late. But still it must have been mind reading.

Well, my sweetiepie, that's all for tonight. Be good. Goodnight and God bless. I love you so very, very much.

Thursday 8.6.50 7.45pm

Hello my darling, how are you? Feeling any better now it's cooler? I certainly do. Still it would've been alright today with the sun shining. Watercarting is quite alright when it is warm. It'll probably be cleaning out tomorrow. So I have kept it down to one day this week. That's not too bad. Next week at this time we'll be on our way from London to Harwich, that is if everything goes well and we get the seats for Friday. My fingers are crossed.

As it was not so hot today I was going to have a proper dinner for a change. So straight away at 5.00 I peeled potatoes and when they're boiling I got meat out and found it hadn't survived the hot weather. So there I was not knowing what to do. Thank goodness the old lady asked me last night if I wanted another cheese. So tonight I asked for it and just had bread and butter to it. It wasn't much, but alright. Bonzo got the potatoes and meat.

It is cool now and that'll mean a good sleep. Be good and look after yourself. Goodnight and God bless and keep you safe.

Friday June 9.6.50 7.00pm

Here I am again, my sweetest and how are you? Fine? I am rather early tonight. It's only just 7.00 and I even had some dinner. Chips, egg and bacon and some vegetables. I tried to ring you to find out if anything had happened or turned up, but the number was engaged twice.

Since this morning when I woke up I had a funny, exciting feeling. So tonight the boss told me it is definite that I've got the house. It'll come in writing tomorrow or Monday at the latest. There we are, now we can start worrying or rather see what we can do. Gosh! I am so pleased if only had a bit more money. It would be nice just to go into a shop and buy the furniture we need. Still it'll turn out alright, I hope. I've just tried again, but 20354 is out of order. So I just must wait till I see you tomorrow. It isn't so very important anyway.

Well, my darling, be good. I love so very, very much. Goodnight and God bless.

Be seeing you tomorrow.

All my love and kisses

Forever yours

Hans.

Melton & Belvoir Rural District Council

L. Hesford

M.R.S.L F.I.SAN.E. 10, High Street

Sanitary Surveyor & Inspector Melton Mowbray

Telephone- Melton Mowbray 343 & 344

Your Ref. 9th June 1950

Our Ref. Housing/W

Dear Sir

The committee at their last meeting gave consideration to the applicants for the vacant council house at Knossington and I am instructed to inform you that they decided to offer you the tenancy of this house.

The keys may be collected from this office tomorrow, Saturday, between the hours of 9am and 12 noon and you may make arrangements to move in immediately.

The maximum rent of this house will be 22/6d per week and I enclose herewith details of the council's Rent Rebate Scheme and if you think you are entitled to a rebated rent you should complete the enclosed application form immediately and return to this office in order that your rent may be assessed correctly.

Your tenancy will commence as from Monday the 12th June 1950 and your first week's rent will be due on the 19th June 1950.

Yours faithfully

L Hesford
Surveyor

Mr. J. Klawitter
Home Farm,
Pickwell,
Melton Mowbray.

Encls:

Larchwood Rise, Knossington, Leicestershire

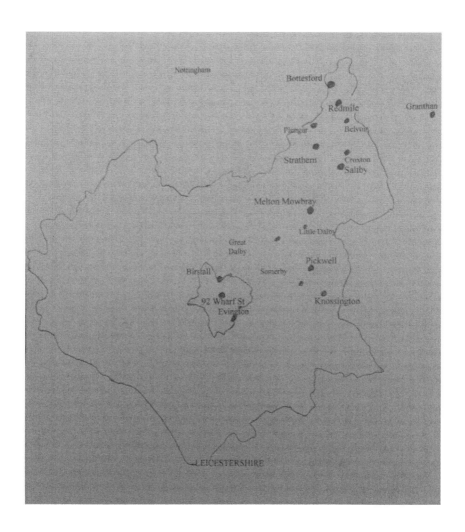

The towns and villages that featured in Hans and Jean's journey.

Aschersleben, Whitsun 1950

My dear Hans and Jean

Today, on the second day of Whitsuntide, I am going to send you a note.

I expect you, dear Hans, are back at work today, and I imagine that Jean is staying with you. Horst went to the Harz

Mountains with two friends yesterday around mid day and they are coming back this evening. He needs to get out sometime. The run up to the Bank Holiday was very exhausting for him at work. He looked dreadful. Well, I would not be able to cope with this unhealthy air in the salon. It's a pity we had such bad weather yesterday. We had lots of rain showers and it was quite cold. It's much better today again and the sun has come out. It was always the same at home. If we had bad weather over Whitsun, you could bet your life that the day after Whitsun, on Sports Marksmen's Festival, we would have the most beautiful weather. Do you still remember this? I replied to your letter last week already. You wrote that you want to leave your home in the evening so that you can show Jean everything. I shall repeat in this letter now what I have already said before. Well, should you arrive in Braunschweig as late as 8 pm, you will find that the connecting train to Dettum departs hours later, and you will not get to Weferlingen before midnight. Would it not be better to arrive in Braunschweig around midday? Maybe you can then arrange to show Jean everything on your return journey? If everything goes according to plan, we shall be leaving home in two weeks today. Keep your fingers crossed! I am sure all will be fine. We are looking forward very much to a smooth trip. I went to church this morning. They consecrated the bells. The six bells, which were taken down during the war, have now come back from Hamburg. It was a lovely service. I am going to the cinema tonight with Mrs Ziemann. They are showing a wonderful film about a circus called 'Tromba'. And that would conclude another Whitsun Holiday. The Youth Gathering in Berlin is taking place at the moment. So far, without any problems, thank goodness.

Three weeks from today, we will be there for your birthday. It will be the first birthday in eight years which we are able to celebrate together. You will have to treat us all! Auntie Erna is sending her best wishes to you both. Auntie Lina and Christel are spending Whitsun at Uncle Erich's.

Now, my dears, I want to close my letter for today! Give my best wishes to your mother and to you both I am sending my innermost love and kisses. Your mum, brother and brother-in-law Horst. Here's to a happy and healthy reunion.
Please write back to my address in Weferlingen:
c/o Mrs F Fuchs 20 b Weferlingenvvia Wolfenbüttel
Near Braunschweig

Hans and Frida Fuchs

Muttti, Hans and Jean

Horst, Mutti and Hans

Aschersleben, Sunday, 2.7.50

My dear Hans and Jean

We arrived here on Friday evening at 11 pm, after a pleasant journey,

We already got to the relatives yesterday morning. Auntie was expecting us. We were so relieved that everything went smoothly with the journey. The only trouble was that I could not walk very well. My leg was badly swollen and I had to see the doctor yesterday. He prescribed me some ointment. Horstel's boss and Mr. Sintopp came to the station to collect us. She already received the letter on Thursday. She was very sorry but fully understands. When Horst is there, she wants to visit him. Everybody is trying to encourage him. I think it is the right thing to do. It is always better to part on a good note than to leave with a bad feeling.

We hope you had a good journey too and got home safely. We have been thinking of you constantly and shall treasure the lovely days which we were able to spend with you. Who knows when we shall see each other again. It was so hard for me to wave you off. I really had to pull myself together. We don't know what the future holds for us. Anyway, we want to thank you from the bottom of our hearts for everything you did to make it possible for us to meet up with you, and we are wishing you lots of happiness in your new home. We hope you will have a comfortable and enjoyable new abode. Dear Hans and Jean, tomorrow you will have to go back to work. Horst went straight back to work on Saturday morning. They were very busy. Now my dears, I am sending you my love and kisses. Your mum. brother and brother-in-law. Mrs Ziemann is sending you her best wishes. She came to see us today.

Were Friedrich and Bonzo very pleased?

Aschersleben, 10.7.50

My dear Hans and Jean

We received your lovely letter dated 3.7.50 and thank you from the bottom of our hearts. We are so happy to know that you got home safely and, once again, your journey went without any problems. Oh yes, we were thinking of you constantly, which must be the reason for your hiccups. Obviously, the same applied to us too. I think by now you might have moved into your new home and we are sending you our love and best wishes for all the happiness in the world. May you spend many happy hours in your new abode. I wrote to you already on 3.7. but I doubt whether it will ever get to you because the address which you gave me when we were in Weferlingen is not the same as the one you have now sent me with your letter. We also had a good journey back and thank you again from the bottom of our hearts for enabling us to spend 14 lovely days with you. We shall remember it for a very long time.

Horstel's boss has been very understanding and she has not caused any problems. He was very pleased about that. He went straight back to work on the Saturday and has been very busy ever since. Tomorrow, God willing, he is setting out on his journey. I just hope everything will be alright. It will be very hard for me, but I am trying not to show it. I think it was the right decision. Horst's friends also persuaded him. Saturday was his last day at work and he is starting his new job on 15.7. He will find it very strange to be alone! But if it helps him to further his career, then I am all for it. I think another family reunion is not going to happen again soon. We are happy to know that Jean liked everything.

Give our best wishes to your mother-in-law and Lotti. Was Friedrich also happy about it all? I am enclosing the photos. Haven't they turned out well? We collected them already on Wednesday.

Lots of love to you both, your mother and Horst.

Aschersleben, 21.7.50

My dear Hans and Jean
Thank God, after two weeks of waiting I have received your

letter. I was so happy to hear from you.

I am sure you have a lot of work to do but now, that most of it is done, it must be well worth it. You can make your life more comfortable now. I take it your mother did not move in with you?

Horst left 11 days ago and has already been at work for 8 days. His boss has been in hospital for 8 days. He has torn his Achilles tendon and had to have an operation immediately. This happened whilst he was swimming in their local outdoor pool. The start of Horst's new job was very hard for him. He still lives in Weferlingen and goes by public transport to work every day. He has not got a room yet as he has no money to move there. He needs to save up some money first. The Agency charges 7.50 Marks for getting him a room, then when he does get one, he has to pay half of the monthly rent and there will be other costs once he has moved in. Rent has to be paid one month in advance. It is not easy. On top of that, he sent me a food parcel because I had to dig deep into our last few savings. I had several expenses to deal with before Horst left. Well, I will just have to do my best to keep my head above water. To run two households will inevitably cost double the money. I know Horst will try his very best to have me come over. I wonder if it will still happen during this year. Who knows! I miss Horst a lot. Now I only have my hair combed every other day, because I can't afford to pay 60 Pfennig (0.60 Marks) every day.

I am happy for you that you like your new home. Everything else will follow little by little. Do you think we will ever have our own home again?

I am now getting two saltwater baths with carbonic acid a week. When I get home after my treatment I feel extremely tired. It is very exhausting. The walk alone there and back takes one hour, which adds to the fatigue. I have a lot of problems with my heart and my legs are still very painful. I would not like to be on my own forever, because I am surrounded by strangers. I am not sure what will happen to my flat now. I do get on well with Mrs Heitfeld. It would be nice to get a note from Jean. After all, she has more time on her hands now! Did you manage to get a bag in the end in Braunschweig?

Dear Hans, I do hope that you have written to Mrs Fuchs! Because I think she really was very nice to all of us and went to a lot of trouble. There are several things I now miss, since Horst has left, especially the milk. He brought quite a lot of items home. I cannot afford 2 Marks for one litre of milk. Oh well, I will just have to do without. I hope, in the meantime, you received my letter dated 10.7.with the photos. On one of them I have a rather ingenious face, but on the other one, dear Jean, well I had to laugh out loud.

I have nearly finished sending all Horsts things to him. The next thing will be the bed cover and sheets. All this is costing a lot of money. I shall pass on your best wishes. Mrs Heitfeld is returning her best wishes. I want to finish my letter for today. Look after yourselves and stay healthy and write back soon.

Lots of love and kisses from your mum, who is always thinking of you.

Aschersleben, 6.8.50

My dear Hans and Jean

Thank you very much for your lovely letter dated 30.7.50. I was very pleased to receive your news. I quite believe you, dear Hans, that you are inundated with work. You have now finally fulfilled your wish and bought a motor bike. If you only take five minutes to get to work, it is hardly worth getting on it.

Horst left almost four weeks ago. Where does the time go! He has now got a room for himself, not in the centre of town, but on an estate on the edge of the town. The bus takes 20 minutes. He had to pay 25 Marks. He wanted to move in last

Thursday. Horst has asked me to stay with him in August. I only hope things will stay calm, otherwise I don't know what will become of us. Let's hope Horst is on the right path in life. He likes his new job and he is also better health wise. It is a very hard new beginning for him. He lived at the Maliges. Mrs Fuchs cooked his food and did his washing. With his travel money he had to really count his pennies to get through the month. He already sent me two food parcels. I think he will send me something this week because my till is empty. It is hard to keep two households going simultaneously. If only I got some help from the Social, then it would not rest so much on Horst's shoulder. I really thought you would have written to Mrs Fuchs by now. I do feel for her. Siegfried is still unemployed. The old man did not give him a job after all. If it carries on like this, then he will never get anywhere.

Dear Hans, if at all possible, can you send me some tea. I would be very happy to have some more. You did tell me that it is not very expensive. I don't suppose you will be able to do anything much in your garden this year in terms of sowing seeds and planting, as we are already in August. It will make a lot of extra work for you. Is Jean not getting bored so alone in the house all day? Do you go home during the lunch hour? If mother is still with you, Jean obviously has some company. How does she like being a housewife? Are you busy with the harvest as well? There will be a lot to do. Horst is sending his best wishes. Now that he has his own home, he will write to you soon. I would not like to be on my own all the time.

Now my dears, I wish you all the best and stay healthy.

Lots of love and kisses from your mum.

Give your mother my love.

All our acquaintances are sending you their best wishes.

Braunschweig/Mascherode, den 17.8.50

My dear Hans and Jean

It is time that I was sending you a few lines today. I have been at Horst's home since Tuesday night. He was so happy to see me. He likes it here and so do I. He has a nice room and his landlord and landlady are very pleasant. They even put a bed into Horst's room for me. Perhaps I will be able to move in with Horst one day, it certainly is what we both want. Horst would not have to pay out so much money if I were there and do everything for him. I came over the border overnight, because it would be impossible to do during the day. Then I had to walk in the dark for another hour. I got to the train station at 11 pm and was very frightened. What else could I do except move on? The salon where Horst works is very busy but he really loves it there. The bus took 20 minutes to get from Braunschweig to here, Mascherode, and it goes every 10 minutes. The houses are surrounded by plenty of gardens, it is a really nice area. Horst lives in a room very close to the market square and his window overlooks a thoroughfare. All the houses have their own garden. There is going to be a children's festival next Saturday and Sunday. I understand there will be a band of 30 musicians and people are already busy erecting the stalls. I think Mrs Fuchs is coming to see us on Sunday. I shall probably be going home again in eight days' time. Horst does not want me to go. He sends his apologies for not having written to you yet. He has very little spare time. He leaves the house at 8.45 and does not get home much before 8 – 8.30 pm. You can imagine how tired he gets. Yesterday it rained all day but today it looks like we are getting a better day. The owner of the flats also owns the food store downstairs. It is very convenient for us. Yesterday I did all the ironing. I dread the return journey and would rather not think about it. On the way here I was not able to take the route through the water, there were too many border guards. It is always a precarious passage.

How are you all getting on? Has your mother moved in yet?

Have you got used to your new home yet? I can imagine that you, dear Hans, are very busy. I would love to hear from you again. Will you write back soon? I don't think the post takes so long from here to you, does it? I want to finish my letter for now. Take care and stay healthy.

We are sending you all our love and kisses, Your mum, brother and brother-in-law Horst

Aschersleben, 3.9.50

My dear Hans and Jean

Many thanks for your lovely letter dated 20.8.50, which was waiting for me when I got home. I had intended to stay at Horst's only for a week, but in the end it stretched to two weeks. He was so happy to see me when I arrived and did not want to let me go back after one week. He is sending his love to you. You must not get upset because he has not written to you. I am witness to how little time he gets apart from his work. Every morning very early he combs the hair of his landlady and her mother. At 8.15 he catches the bus to work and every night he gets home at 8.15. He is then deadbeat! It is always very hot in the salon, because the heating pipes of the town's indoor swimming pool are running through the salon, which brings the temperature up to 30°C. It's an upward struggle for him to keep two households going and I feel very sorry for him. He has still not got his passport. One of the problems is that he did not get a stamp in his GDR passport when he left, because he went to the West illegally. He only fled because of his ill health. He did not commit a crime. Sometimes, the authorities are making our lives very much harder than need be. I cannot go and stay with him until he has his passport, and he is not very happy to be on his own so much. It is very expensive for him to pay people to do his washing and everything else. We wouldn't be able to make much progress. Horst is asking would Jean remember the hairdryer hood she promised to send to him? He says he should be very grateful if she would remember it. Uncle Erich and Auntie Grete want to come and see me on 20.9. I am really looking forward to seeing them. Dear Hans, would you be able to send me some coffee for the occasion? I should be ever so grateful. Horst is taking part in a hairdressing competition today. It sounds like your home already looks very posh. I am very happy for you that you have achieved so much already. You, dear Hans, seem to be extra busy and doing a lot of overtime these days. Now my dears, I want to finish my letter for today. Did you not receive my letter I wrote whilst in Braunschweig?

I am sending you my love and kisses

Your mum

Aschersleben 18.9.50

My dear Hans and Jean

Thank you very much for your lovely letter dated 6.9.50. One can tell that you live in the suburbs now because the stamp on the envelope says 9.9.50. It does take a little longer.

Dear Hans, don't work too hard. Everything has to be kept within reason. I know you want to get on in life but the body must also have enough rest. You can get things for the home little by little. I am sure you have already managed to accumulate quite a bit.

Uncle Erich is staying with me at the moment. He went to Leipzig first and then 'popped in on his way back'. He has a very badly infected thumb with lots of puss in it. The doctor cut it too early. It took six days before all the puss came out. It now looks like it is getting better though. He is going back home on Tuesday or Wednesday. He is sending his very best wishes to you both. I am planning to go to Vorpommern for about a week, that is if nothing else crops up. Auntie Else would love me to come. We have not seen each other for 2½ years, and if I can go and see Horst again, it might not work out.

The world looks very dismal. Who knows, what will happen to us. There is not much to laugh about these days. Horst wishes to be remembered to you. He participated in a hair-dressing competition on 3.9.50 in Braunschweig and won second prize, which was a Wollwinder Diplomat Bag and also 40 Marks in cash. He was thrilled. His boss was also very pleased about it and treated everybody to a drink. At 3.30 the next morning his boss paid for a taxi to take them all home.

Digging up your garden now is not important because it's too late for sowing and planting anyway. You will have to leave it until the spring. You can't do any more work than you already do. You say your mother wants to stay in town after all! Oh well, you can't really blame her. She has lived there for so many years. I can understand that she would find it very hard to leave now. Has Jean got used to living in a vil-lage now or does she feel lonely? I suppose she has enough to do with the cleaning and cooking, and her life has changed completely now, which also needs some adjustment on her part. Have you made quite a nice home for yourself? And you, dear Hans, attended the inauguration ceremony? Were you the Chef? And you, dear Jean, were obviously busy with your domestic duties!

We are enjoying some very nice weather at the moment. I hope it stays like it for a while.

Dear Jean, you promised to write to me one day! When you get the time! I should be very happy to receive a letter from you.

Now my dears, stay healthy and write back soon. The Fuchs family are also sending their best wishes to you. She left on Friday.

I am sending you all my love and kisses, your mum and Uncle

Erich

My dear Hans and Jean

Today I want to thank you from the bottom of my heart for your lovely letter dated 22.9.50. It was awaiting me when I returned home from my travels. I seem to get very little post from you nowadays and I do hope it will get better once you have achieved the majority of your main tasks. All our relatives are sending you their best wishes. They have lots of work there and they wanted me to stay longer, but I had to come back home eventually. After all, this is my home now. Horst is sending his best wishes too. He is always very busy. He is taking it really hard that I cannot come over and stay with him. Unfortunately, it is not possible yet, and very complicated. I was very happy that he made it possible for me to go and see our relatives. It was a very expensive trip but at least we were all able to see each other again. We don't know if this can be done again. Auntie Erna looks really ill. I was so shocked when I saw her. You have been married for one year already! How quickly time flies. I am sending you my belated wishes for a happy life together. We are having lovely weather at the moment. What a pity the weather was so awful during my recent trip. I expect, dear Hans, that you are driving your tractor again today. It means that Jean is alone at home every Sunday. Well, she can pay me a visit. I am still waiting for the letter she promised me!! Is your mother still not living with you? I am sure your house will be lovely and cosy by now?! The paper work is still not alright because of the missing stamp. It costs a lot of money to run two households simultaneously. It would be much better if the two of us could live together. I hope everything works out alright next Sunday. Horst's friend Fritz is staying with Horst at the moment. He was very happy to see him. I must say that Horst is looking after me in the most caring way. He is extremely thrifty with his money. I think I already told you that Horst came second at the last competition? His prize was a Diplomat Bag in light brown Wollwinder leather and 40 Marks in cash. He was really thrilled. There is another competition on 19.11., which the Club has organised.

Dear Hans, I know that this trip must have cost you an awful lot of money, but we don't know when we can see each other again. Maybe not for several years!

Should anything happen, promise me that you will look after Horst if I can't do it. Perhaps everything will change for the better, but nobody knows what life has in store for us and I am constantly worrying about this. To get back to your conjunctivitis, I can tell you that I used to have this a lot as a child. I can only suggest to try and put some cold camomile tea on your eye. It will have a cooling effect. But it will take time or has it already got better?

Now, my dears, be good and stay healthy. I am sending you all my love and kisses, your mum. Best wishes to the mother-in-law.

Aschersleben, 24.10.50

My dear Hans and Jean

It is four weeks ago since I last heard from you and I am slowly beginning to think that you, dear Hans, are forgetting all about your mum! I am very sad about it. I am especially sorry because when one lives alone, one is longing for some news. When one lives that far away from each other, a few lines bring a lot of happiness. I know you don't have much free time on your hands. I expect you have furnished your home nicely by now and are feeling very comfortable in it. It will be particularly lovely when winter comes. Horst has now received his stamp which he badly needed. It confirms that he is allowed to stay in the West, and he is of course very happy about it. If all goes well and I stay healthy, I am planning to go and see him in December and spend Christmas and

New Year with him. He has been begging me to come and stay with him. I have already got all the coal and potatoes in the cellar. It all costs a lot of money. I also have to pay for my health insurance. In the long run, it will not be possible to keep two households going. And Horst needs someone to look after him. If he has to pay for the washing and all other things, it gets far too expensive. He wants to send me some smoked herrings this week. I am looking forward to it already because I love them.

Dear Hans, you must put some warm clothes on when you do your tractor work because I don't want you to get ill. Has your mother moved in with you yet? Or has she not given up her shop yet? Our chickens have gone on strike yet again, they are in the moulting season. How is Jean getting on with her domestic duties?

Uncle Gustav and family, Uncle Erich and family, Auntie Erna and Auntie Lina are sending their best wishes to you. Christel celebrated her engagement two weeks ago. They are also expecting a baby. Erna Schünemann is sending her regards too. She does not live on the island of Juist anymore. Apparently she was offered a very good job and started to work in Wuppertal-Barmen, Schubertstr. 26, Westphalia on 15.10. All our relatives seem to be scattered around the world and I am sitting here all alone.

Dear Hans, the postman has just delivered a letter from you dated 18.10.50, for which I thank you very much. I had to pay 50 Pfennige (0.50 Marks) for extra postage. I think it had the wrong stamp on. Yes, it would be really lovely if Jean could come and see me on a Sunday but unfortunately this is not possible. At least I am happy in the knowledge that you are both well and happy. Yes, Horst was very pleased about his visitor. He is always feeling very lonely. He would love to have me there, but everything takes time and careful planning. I sent him a nice standard lamp and the iron this week. It arrived all in one piece. He needs to buy a cooker now for 150 Marks. Everything is very expensive.

Now my dears, I am sending you all my love and kisses,
Your mum

My Dear Hans and Jean

I was so happy to receive your lovely letter with my birthday wishes and want to thank you from the bottom of my heart for it. I was especially thrilled, dear Jean, with your lovely letter. How come that you can suddenly write in such good German? I was so amazed! And on top of all this your BIG NEWS! I am sending you my heartiest wishes and congratulations. Let us hope that your wish will fulfilled and it is going to be a boy. I am certainly keeping my fingers crossed for you. I can imagine, dear Jean, that you have got your hands full now. Well, you still have a little time to go. And I imagine that the future daddy is now getting anxious to get his garden in order. I can't wait to see if the baby has inherited the snub nose from his daddy.

Dear Hans, I can see from your letter that you have to be very careful with your money now. It would have been better if you had not rented the whole house, now that your mother-in-law is not moving in with you. It seems you now have to work in order to pay the rent, and getting the garden shipshape will also cost a lot of money. Of course, when all is done, it will be beautiful, but it is a lot of extra work for you. How much rent do you have to pay a month?

You want to know how I feel as a future grandmother. Well, I can't really imagine it yet because it does not seem that long to me when you were little. I regret to be so far away from you because I cannot really enjoy it all the way I would like to. Babies are so beautiful and they bring so much happiness into the family. But you must not fixate yourself too much on having a little boy. Little girls are also very sweet. The main thing is, of course, that all will be well. I cannot tell you how much I wanted a little girl!!

He will be a West German then.

Now I want to give you some news too. If all goes well and if I stay healthy, I shall probably go and live with Horst at the end of November. He is waiting for me so much. He gave notice of termination of his room because he still did not have a stove in it and he cannot sit in there any longer without heating. He has rented two rooms with central heating and electric light and pays 50 Marks a month all in. Cooking will be done by gas. It is very expensive but Horst says that the rooms are well furnished and newly renovated. The landlady has lacquered all the floor boards to make everything look nice. To manage two households financially is too expensive in the long run and Horst will at least be looked after by me. Keep your fingers crossed for me. Crossing the border is now almost impossible - much more difficult than it was in the summer. I have already sent lots of parcels.

You are mentioning a Christmas parcel. If you have not got much money then please don't send me anything, just some coffee, for which I would be very grateful because we just cannot afford any here. But don't send anything to this address. Have you written to Horst in the meantime? If not, please do it.

Now my dears, stay healthy and I wish you all the very best. I am sending you all my love and kisses,

Your mum, who is always thinking of you.

Horst is also sending you his very best wishes.

Horstel's new address is:

Horst Klarwitter

c/o M Pöpper

(20b) Braunschweig--Lehndorf

Malstatter Str. 7

Braunschweig- Lehndorf,   3.12.50

My dear Hans and Jean

Today I am so happy to tell you that I have arrived safely and well at Horst's home. I am feeling totally overwhelmed with everything and so happy that I have finally made it. Horst is beaming all over his face. I am looking forward to bringing some order into his life. The weather was just right for my journey. Crossing the border went smoothly even if it did cost me a lot of money. It was money well spent. The main thing is one gets over the border in one piece. Only recently did two women get shot dead and a young man was seriously injured. I left A. at 8 o'clok one morning, had to wait in Osterwieck five hours for my connection and another two hours at Auntie Erna's. By 6 o'clock in the evening, I had managed it. I walked all the way to Vienenburg with an old lady (12 km). Once there, I had to wait a further 1½ hours. At 9 o'clock in the evening, Horst greeted me with a bunch of roses at the Braunschweig Railway Station. We are both so happy and I will make sure that Horst gets well looked after from now on. He is always very busy. He leaves the house at 8 o'clock in the morning and gets home at 9 o'clock in the evenings, totally exhausted. It is also very strenuous to work all day long standing up in this unhealthy, steamy atmosphere.

I will have been here one week tomorrow. The first few days kept me occupied with unpacking the parcels and finding a home for everything. During the last two weeks when I was still at home, I was only able to get four hours sleep a night because I had to pack all the parcels. Opening and sewing up the seams was also very time-consuming . It was a very difficult task. I had to have a good rest after my ordeal. I have already been in town several times and looked at the Christmas displays. They are just amazing, but one needs a sack-full of money. However, I don't mind, one cannot have everything one sees. We were extremely lucky with this flat. We have two lovely, well furnished rooms, very clean and newly renovated. There is a large wardrobe in Horst's room with a matching wide bed. The bed has a silk quilt with quilt covers and a show pillow with pretty lace décor. He also has a wash bowl on a stand, like we used to have at home, a bed-side table and a sewing table. I sleep in the living room on the Chaiselongue. There is also a nice sofa, a large table and a flower stand, which holds leafy plants. We managed to place our radio on the top as well. A nice sideboard is home to our crockery. All our belongings arrived here in good condition. They put some very pretty nets and colourful curtains on the windows. All in all, we have a very cosy and comfortable home. All we want now is for the whole world to calm down and not have to worry about the war anymore, then we can start relaxing and find some peace again.

Uncle Gustav, Erich and family, Auntie Erna and Auntie Lina are all sending their best wishes to you. They are less blessed than we are, which I was able to see for myself. They work so hard physically and still don't have anything to put on their bread. Auntie Erna looks so dreadfully ill. I was extremely shocked to see her like that and very upset for a long time afterwards. When we said our good-byes Auntie Erna asked me if she could have some of my old stockings which I might no longer need. I sorted out several bits of clothing for her and she was very happy. I am so glad grandma did not live to see this!! Uncle Gustav, Auntie Lina and Erich are leading the same sort of dismal life. The taxes are so horrendous that they cannot possibly make any money. They don't even have any milk for themselves, not for the coffee or for the soup. All the milk goes to the government. All the money earnt goes to the village community, then all the taxes and other charges are deducted and whatever is left is so insignificant that one cannot buy the bare minimum. I think you can im-agine somehow what life is like over there. In any event, I feel very sorry for them. We want to try and send them a small parcel for Christmas. We cannot afford much, but even a small amount can bring some happiness to people.

Horst is attending another hairdressing competition today. I hope he is successful. He has already acquired a lot of cli-ents since he has been here and his boss is very happy with him.

How are you getting on my dears? I have written a lot about us. I hope you are fit and well. We are celebrating Christmas Eve in three weeks' time. I pray it will bring us peace on earth. It will be your first Christmas in your own home. Edith, Siegfried and the little one moved to Solingen, where Siegfried found work through one of his war friends.

Their address is:

Jachner

c/o Schmitz

(22 a) Solingen

Vockerter Str. 46/e

Now my dears I want to finish my letter for today. Stay healthy and don't let us wait too long for some news from you. I am sending you all my love and kisses, your mum, who is always thinking of you

*refugees from East to West used to open up seams of clothing to hide valuables.

Braunschweig-Lehndorf, den 16.12.50

My dear Hans and Jean

Thank you very much indeed for your lovely letter dated 1.12.50. We were very happy to hear from you again. In two days' time I shall have been here three weeks already. I have acclimatised myself very well. Horst is not at home a lot. His working hours are so long but he does enjoy his work. When he does come home he is absolutely shattered. I have been in the town eight times already. I am finding my way around Braunschweig very easily now. I went to the City Hall today to get Horst's income tax card, then on to the local Tax Office, then to the Employees' Health Insurance etc. I also managed to get my new Disability Pass. I had to pay 26 Marks retrospectively for 1949 because they did not have that kind of system in East Germany in 1949. They will let me know by 20.12. whether I can join the Local Employees' Health Insurance, because I am unemployed this might not be possible. I will have to be a member of one such organisation because if I did fall ill again, I would not be able to pay for the treatment. I am so pleased that all is well with my residence permit. I also received my passport on 8.12. and this concludes all the formalities for the moment. We shall now have to cut our cloth according to our circumstances and cannot spend too much money. You have to work hard to earn 50 Marks for the rent and it is astounding how quickly the money goes. I am sure you noticed this too when you were here last. Then we have to pay for the gas, my disability stamp, social security etc. Horst needs 10 Marks for the bus every month. I usually walk everywhere. It takes me one hour to get to Horst's work. I don't have to do it but it is a healthy exercise.

I expect you will have finished your work in the garden and maybe you can now rest a little. We have had some quite good weather up to now. And I can imagine that Jean uses every spare minute to sow and knit. Your pram was very expensive. It sounds like you chose one of the best? Your lives will change completely. I hope he will not turn out to be a little glutton like you were as a baby. You kept me on the go every two hours! It is one of your many duties as a father to protect the mother and allow her to rest. These are wise words, aren't they?

In two weeks tomorrow it is Christmas Eve. It is a very difficult time for us because we are thinking of home and how much we are missing everything. And in the New Year, we are asking the same question again: "Where is our Papa and how was he spending Christmas"??? Yesterday, an old lady spoke to me in town. Her son was a POW in Russia and returned home a few months ago. She had not heard from him in all the eight years until he suddenly stood in front of her. This kind of story always gives me fresh hope that our Papa

too will come home one day. Please God!!! I received a letter from Bruno last week. He wrote that he has been ill for two months. Whilst unloading the corn, he fell down the stairs and broke three ribs and his vertebrae. He has asked me not to mention it to Auntie Lina because she is already very anxious and would worry a lot more. He is quite unlucky. They paid him 50 Pfennige (0.50 Marks) per day sick money. How is he expected to support Auntie Lina? What misery!! If Christel becomes pregnant there is no money for a wedding. Auntie Lina is as poor as a church mouse. She will never be able to give her daughter a dowry. Her life is one big sorrow and when you think how well off they were at home! If only there would be peace on earth and the shadows of the war would disappear forever. We do not want to go through these horrific times ever again. Now, my dear children, we wish you and your mother a very happy and blessed Christmas. Enjoy every moment and let Father Christmas bring you lots of lovely presents. The Christmas displays and markets are just fabulous here. You should see it all.
Stay healthy and we are sending you our love and kisses Your mum, brother and brother-in-law

Braunschweig-Lehndorf, 3.1.51

My dear Hans and Jean

We were so happy to receive your two Christmas parcels today. We had to collect them at the Customs Offices and thank you very much from the bottom of our hearts. They took a long time to get here, even though you already posted them on 12.12.50. I was so looking forward to receiving the parcels in time for Christmas and when they did not come you cannot imagine how depressed I was over the Christmas holidays because I thought you had changed your minds and not sent the parcels after all! But we are so happy now that they arrived after all this time. I tried some immediately and it is wonderful. You know how much I love drinking it, and then also the ground coffee in a tin, which is always extra special! We also want to thank you for your lovely Christmas and New Year Greetings. We also want to wish you again lots of happiness and good health for the coming year, and hope that all your wishes will be fulfilled. Next Christmas, God willing, your little heir will be admiring your Christmas tree. We wish you all the best. Just another 2½ months and you are having your baby. Dear Jean, don't worry, it will all pass quickly and the joy and happiness will be greater than anything before. The only regret I have is that we live so far away from you. Dear Hans, don't forget to teach him your mother tongue so that he can understand me when, one day, I will have him in my arms. Because I don't think I shall be able to learn a language. The Christmas holidays are behind us once more. Frau Fuchs wanted to come and see us over Christmas. I was so looking forward to seeing her again and I made everything nice and comfortable in the flat, but we waited in vain. A day after Christmas we received a card from her saying that she is unable to come, because Siegfried did not want her to be away over Christmas. Oh well, when the son speaks, the mother has to obey, otherwise, there would be nobody there when he gets home drunk (which is often the case) and who looks after him and who takes the verbal abuse from him! If he was my son, I would have straightened him out a long time ago! Frida was also a bit miffed because she was waiting for the coffee you promised to send her. If at all possible, please send it to her. I feel quite embarrassed about it and I don't want to let her have mine either!

Father Christmas was busy again this year. He brought me, on behalf of Horst, a very nice, warm dressing gown, a pair of warm slippers, a pretty apron, a leather purse, a lovely pair of shoes and chocolate. I badly needed the shoes as I have been wearing the shoes you gave me every day for the last two years. They are slowly but surely going home now. The pair Horst bought me last year, I would like to keep for Sundays only. He bought the Christmas presents for me from his prize money which was awarded to him at the competition in September. I was very happy about everything. Was your Father Christmas busy as well? Dear Hans, is your work a little less stressful now? And you, dear Jean, are busy getting the baby things together I assume. I would love to help you but then, maybe you would prefer to do it yourself. I was not very well over Christmas. My rheumatism gave me so much pain in my back and shoulders, it took my breath away, literally. How is your mother getting on? Does she also suffer so badly from rheumatism? I wonder what surprises 1951 has in store for us. The world looks rather gloomy. If only we had peace again! We do not want to go through the terrible times we had again. If it came to that again and Horst had to go to war, I would then be all alone in this god forsaken world! What will the future bring us?

I have already been here five weeks now and I have been to the authorities but even here, they will not support me in any way. I am always asked if I have any children and, if yes, they say that my children have to support me. I think this is awful. Do I have to live off Horst for the rest of my life? He has already looked after me for many years!! If only our Papa would come home again. I know Horst likes to support me, but he is getting older and has to start thinking of himself. I feel that I don't want to be responsible.

Now my dears, I want to finish my letter. Auntie Erna, Auntie Lina, Uncle Erich and family and Uncle Gustav and family are sending you their love and they all wish you a very happy New Year.

We are sending our love to you, your mum, your brother Horst and your brother-in-law Horst.

Braunschweig-Lehndorf, 28.1.51

My dear Hans and Jean

I can imagine you have been waiting to hear from me for a while but today I will definitely write to you. First of all, thank you very much for your lovely letter dated 14.1.51. We were so happy to hear from you again. Last week, Horst went on a business trip to Magdeburg, Aschersleben and Halle for five days. He used his inter-zone pass and managed to look up his friends and acquaintances in Aschersleben. He enjoyed the journey and was very happy to have seen everyone again . Whilst he was away, I had a visitor staying with me for three days. Heinzs went to see his parents in Schmiedenfelde and on his return journey he popped in to see me. He liked it here so much that he would have loved to have stayed a few more days but his train ticket would have run out of date, so he had to leave again on a certain day. He also wanted to stay longer and wait for Horst to come home. Heinz is sending his best wishes to you. I read in the newspaper that the meat in your area is quite rationed. I must say that is not a good situation to be in. It means you will have to be very frugal with the amount you are allocated. Our prices have gone up a lot lately. That's all we needed. This week I bought two bed covers for us both, without pillow cases, and paid 34,50 Marks. It takes some time to save this kind of money but we badly needed them. The winter sales are starting here tomorrow but, unfortunately, I will not be able to go. On Thursday we have to pay the rent (50 Marks) plus 6 Marks for the gas. We cannot afford to pay out for other things at the moment.

It is nearly 11 pm and I am not a bit tired. That's because of the coffee we had earlier, which we both enjoyed very much. It is lovely and it stimulates the vital spirits. Füchsel has not come to see us. I would like to know what the matter is with her. I am not aware that I have given her any reason to be upset. It is best not to say anything in these circumstances. They will be coming back all on their own one day.

Now, my dear Jean, how are you? We hope you are well and happy. It looks like your little heir will arrive around Easter.

I think you asked me some time ago whether Horst has a girlfriend yet. Well, he is still footloose and fancy-free and assures me over and over again that he will stay a bachelor forever. I think because he has too many women around him all day long and every day, who tell him horror stories about married life that he loses his enthusiasm about getting married. Well, he is only still a lad. He has plenty of time. We are having some very odd winter weather. So far it rained during the entire month of January. It is really unpleasant, only right for getting the flu. The Housing Office asked me to come and see them about our permanent residence here. We need to get

a certificate for permission to stay. I filled out two forms immediately and am now waiting to see what the outcome will be. The Official was very nice to me. I hope everything will be alright.

I shall pass on your regards to our relatives. Horst went out dancing this evening (Sunday) – his favourite pastime. Oh well, everybody has a hobby.

Dear Hans, if you also have such awful weather as we have, please take care and don't catch a cold, or are you not working outside so much now?

Now, my dears, I want to finish my letter for today. Stay healthy and write back soon. We are sending you our love and kisses, your mum, your brother Horst and your brother-in-law Horst.

Braunschweig-Lehndorf, den 11.2.51

My dear Hans and Jean

Many thanks for your lovely letter dated 3.2.51, which we received yesterday. Today is Sunday and I want to answer it right away. It sounds like you are having more rain than we are having here. We already feel the spring in the air. I hope we don't have to pay for this again later!! It is of course, dear Hans, not very nice if you get soaked through so often. Make sure you don't catch a cold. As you know, there is a lot of flu over there. And be very careful with your leg too because we don't want it to turn into something nasty. You are asking me for some girls' names. That is very difficult for me to do because your names over there are different to ours. How about Monika, Margit, Hannelore, Marlies, Barbara (Bärbel), Gudrun, Christiane, Karin! I am sure you will find the right name. Will you let us know immediately? What a pity you are so far away. I love the little ones and want to cuddle your new baby. How are you, dear Jean. We hope you are well. Most of your waiting time is over now and then you will not be bored anymore!!! I am doing a lot of running around and filling in forms etc. I am currently applying for a pension and have to send all the required documents, witnessed and stamped by a lawyer, because all my paperwork was lost when we had to leave our homeland. I hope I get a positive reply eventually. I must say that the Official got my hopes up. I am sure it will take months before I hear from them. I would be so happy if I got something out of it, if only to make life a bit easier for Horst. Horst received a very good job offer the other day to work in Königstein in the Taunus region, near Frankfurt. It is a most beautiful part of Germany, not far from Rüdesheim on the river Rhine. It would be very good in terms of Horstel's health and also to further develop his career. He laid out his terms and the lady wrote back this week and said that she is accepting them. It would be lovely if he could find suitable accommodation there too. Please keep your fingers crossed. Our landlord and landlady would rather have us stay here, but they said if it helps Horst in furthering his career then it should be done. What do you think about it? After that, I would love to settle down somewhere. It is not easy to keep moving and starting afresh each time. I am anxious to know what the outcome will be. As soon as I know I will write to you, of course.

I want to finish my letter for today. Stay healthy and write back soon. We are sending you our love and kisses, your mum, your brother Horst and your brother-in-law Horst.

Towns and cities of note on Horst's and Mutti's journey

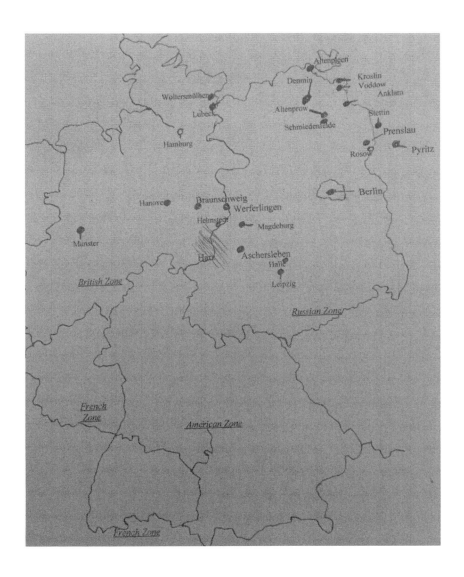

The baby was born 14.3.51 a little girl, Elizabeth Jane. Hans and Jean went on to have 4 more children : Rosamund Ann, Hans Peter Horst, Angela Patricia and Ian James.

Rosamund,(known as Pip) Hans, Angela, Elizabeth, Peter, Jean, Ian.

Horst and Mutti did move to Frankfurt where Horst eventually opened his own Salon and worked there until he retired. The two of them continued to live together, firstly in adjoining flats in Frankfurt then sharing a house in Peterweil, just outside the city. Below is a newspaper article about the refurbishment of the shop

BUSINESS

Horst Klawitter, who has been a master hairdresser at Frankfurt Oeder Weg for 13 years, brought new chic to the Figaro realm. In future the male customers will feel as comfortable with him as in the Tattershall and the women as comfortable as in the salon of Madame Recarnier. Everything that is visible to the eye in the totally renovated and enlarged salon was designed by Master Klawitter himself. Saddle and bridle, whips and stirrups adorn the walls where the men are hairdressed, graceful surroundings in white, gold and flowers opens up where the ladies sit under the hood.
The Pomeranian also has not forgotten the "screen", which

can be set up as a cabin partition, and nor the hot liquid refreshments, coffee and tea bar with milk and lemon, that the ladies can utilise during their hair procedure. Germany's most modern hairdressing salon was created in a flash and in complete silence. The award winning creative decorator wants to encourage his clientele again with prizes and awards and with no price increases to keep them happy.

Pip, Ian, Jean, Horst,Elizabeth, Angela, Mutti and Peter outside Horst's salon c1967.

Should you wish to contact me please do so via email

sendingsundaygreetings@gmail.com

Angela

'In search of home' and 'Sending Sunday greetings' are dedicated with fond memories to

Nana, Uncle Horst and Mum and Dad

Printed in Great Britain
by Amazon